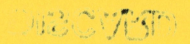

Alice in Murderland

Kaori Yuki

8

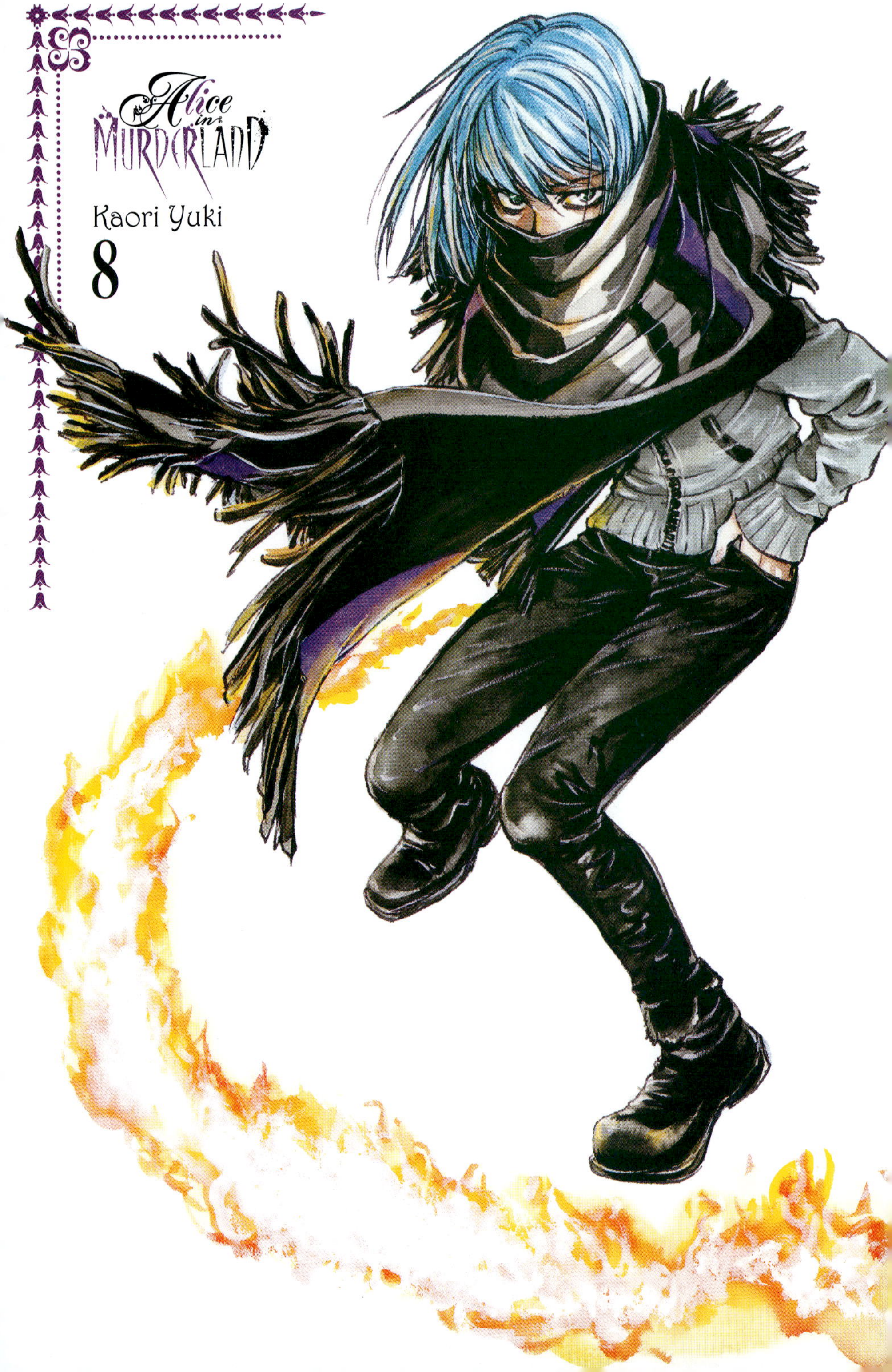

contents

Alice in Murderland

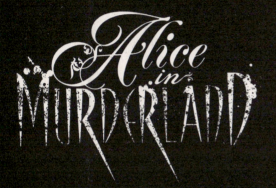

8

Kaori Yuki

Characters & Story

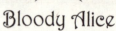

Stella Kuonji
Fourth daughter of the Kuonji family. Was taken in by the Kuonjis, along with eldest brother, Zeno. Loves Zeno.

Bloody Alice
Another personality residing within Stella that appears when she loses all reason.

Tsukito
Grandson of Kokonoe, the chief of the Black Rabbit bodyguards. The true Zeno was a personality inside of Tsukito.

Olga
Head of the Kuonji Group and matriarch of the family.

Kokonoe
Chief of the Black Rabbit bodyguards tasked with protecting the nine siblings.

The Kuonji Siblings

Eldest Son
Zeno
Previously thought to be Stella's beloved brother, but actually impostor who replaced him five years ago.

DEAD!

Second Son
Sid
The culprit behind a wave of local murders. Killed by Stella after her transformation into "Bloody Alice."

Third Son
Sol
Maré's elder twin. Cheerful and uninhibited.

DEAD!

Fourth Son
Maré
Sol's younger twin. He and Stella had an antagonistic relationship, and he died at the end of their showdown.

Fifth Son
Melm
The youngest of the Kuonji siblings. Had been in Claire's care due to his youth.

DEAD!

Eldest Daughter
Ibara
The best fighter among the siblings. She challenged Stella to a one-on-one fight, and Alice crushed her heart, killing her.

Second Daughter
Miser
Reptile otaku. Tricked by Maré into a face-off with Stella, but ultimately brought to her senses by the love of ex-boyfriend Io.

DEAD!

Third Daughter
Claire
Closest to Stella of all the siblings. Was finished off by eldest brother Zeno after her fight with Stella.

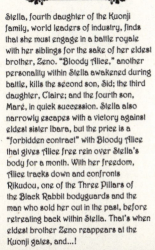

Story

Stella, fourth daughter of the Kuonji family, world leaders of industry, finds that she must engage in a battle royale with her siblings for the sake of her eldest brother, Zeno. "Bloody Alice," another personality within Stella awakened during battle, kills the second son, Sid; the third daughter, Claire; and the fourth son, Maré, in quick succession. Stella also narrowly escapes with a victory against eldest sister Ibara, but the price is a "forbidden contract" with Bloody Alice that gives Alice free rein over Stella's body for a month. With her freedom, Alice tracks down and confronts Rikudou, one of the Three Pillars of the Black Rabbit bodyguards and the man who sold her out in the past, before retreating back within Stella. That's when eldest brother Zeno reappears at the Kuonji gates, and...!

Key Words

Secret of Elysium • A mysterious ability passed down through the Kuonji line that grants the wielder power over life and death, as well as immortality.

Bandersnatch • The true form of the members of the Kuonji family. Attempts to grow the number of people infected with its blood and steals the souls of others for family sustenance.

Murderland Rules • The nine brothers and sisters must kill one another until only one is left standing. The game must be completed within one year, by Zeno's twentieth birthday. The lone survivor will become head of the family, inheriting the Kuonji Group and all its assets.

Black Rabbits • Bodyguards who may be used by the siblings as pawns. There are special methods by which this manipulation can be accomplished.

Alice in Murderland

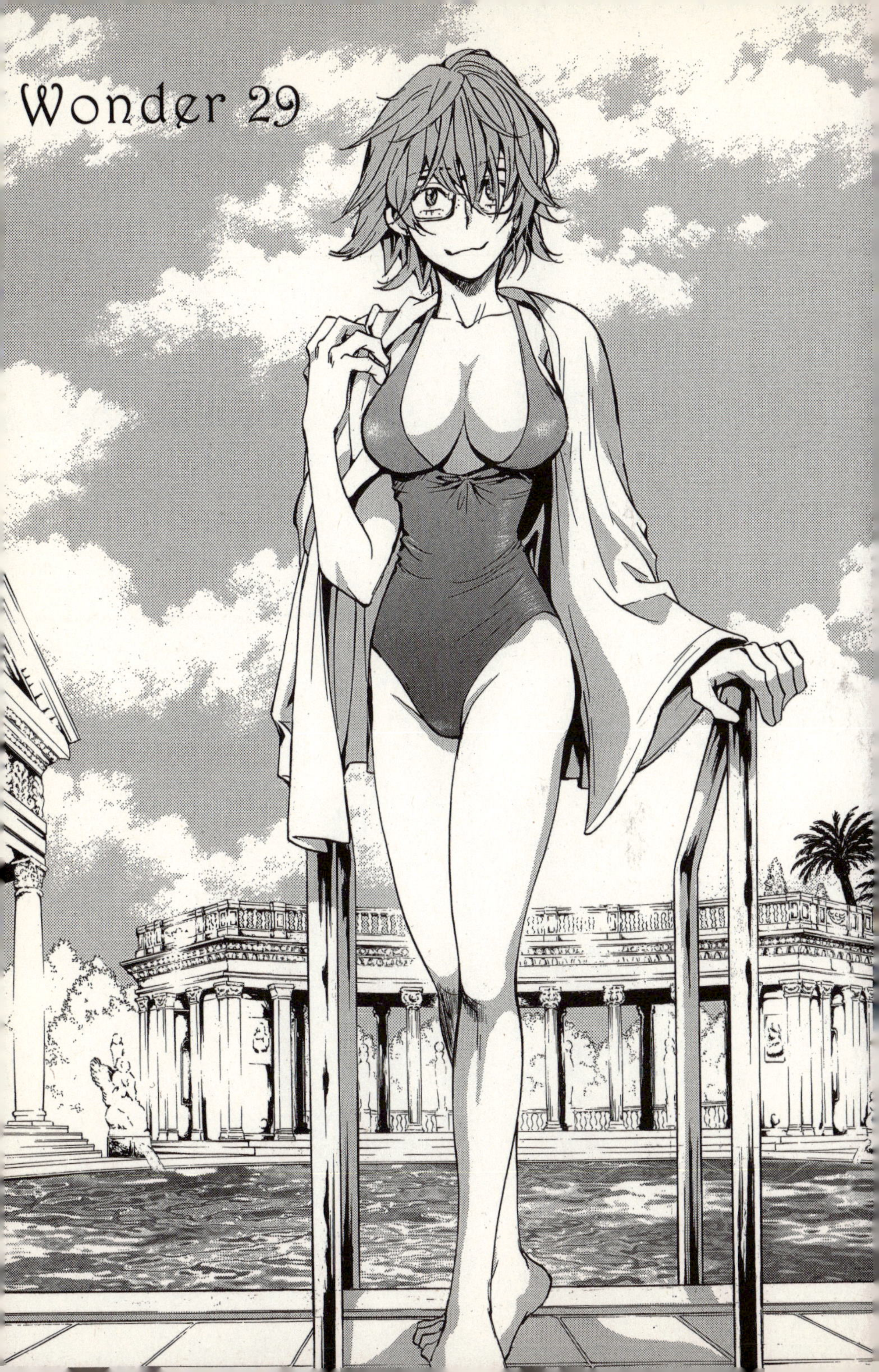
Wonder 29

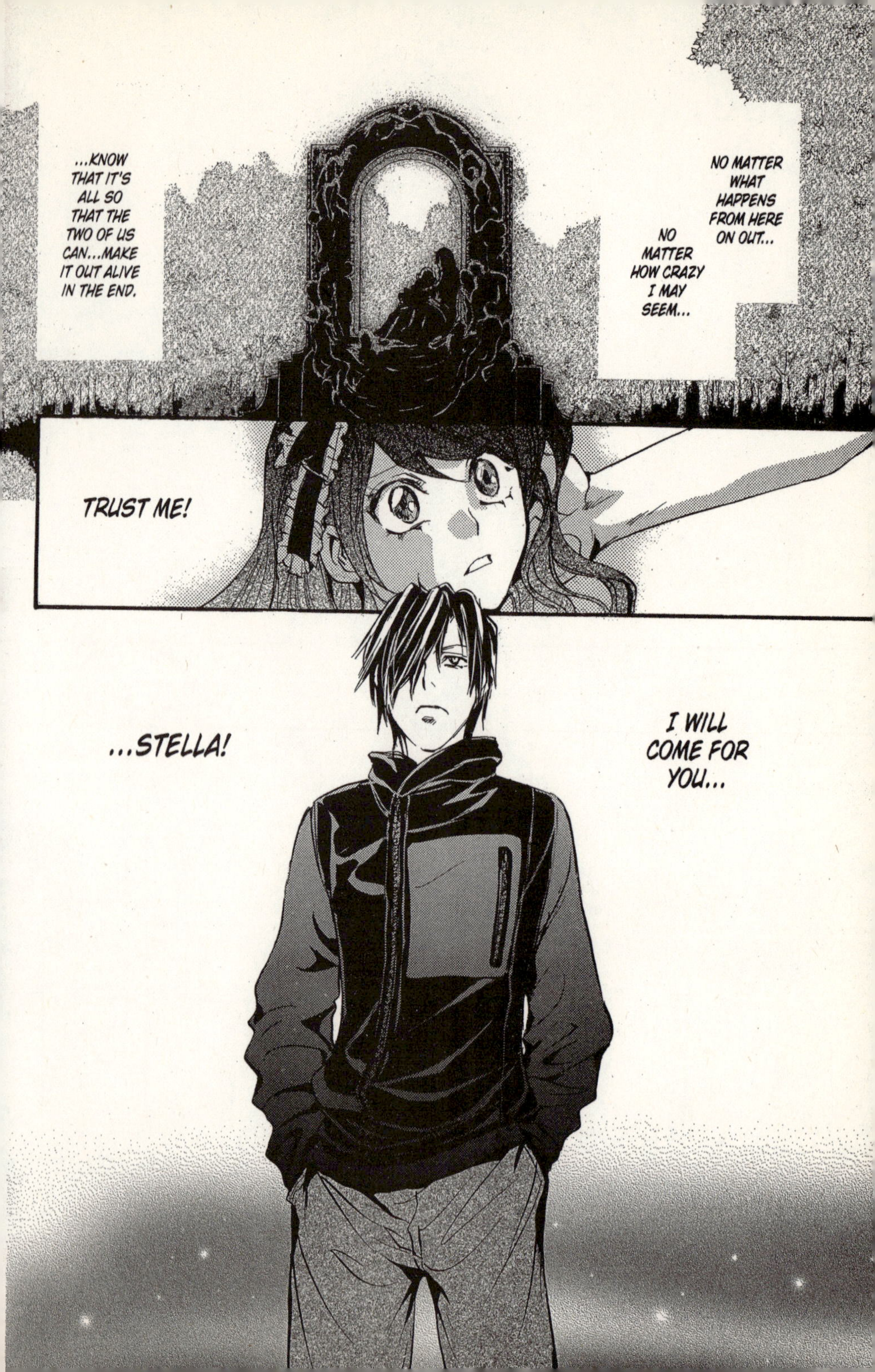
NO MATTER WHAT HAPPENS FROM HERE ON OUT...
NO MATTER HOW CRAZY I MAY SEEM...
...KNOW THAT IT'S ALL SO THAT THE TWO OF US CAN...MAKE IT OUT ALIVE IN THE END.
TRUST ME!
I WILL COME FOR YOU...
...STELLA!

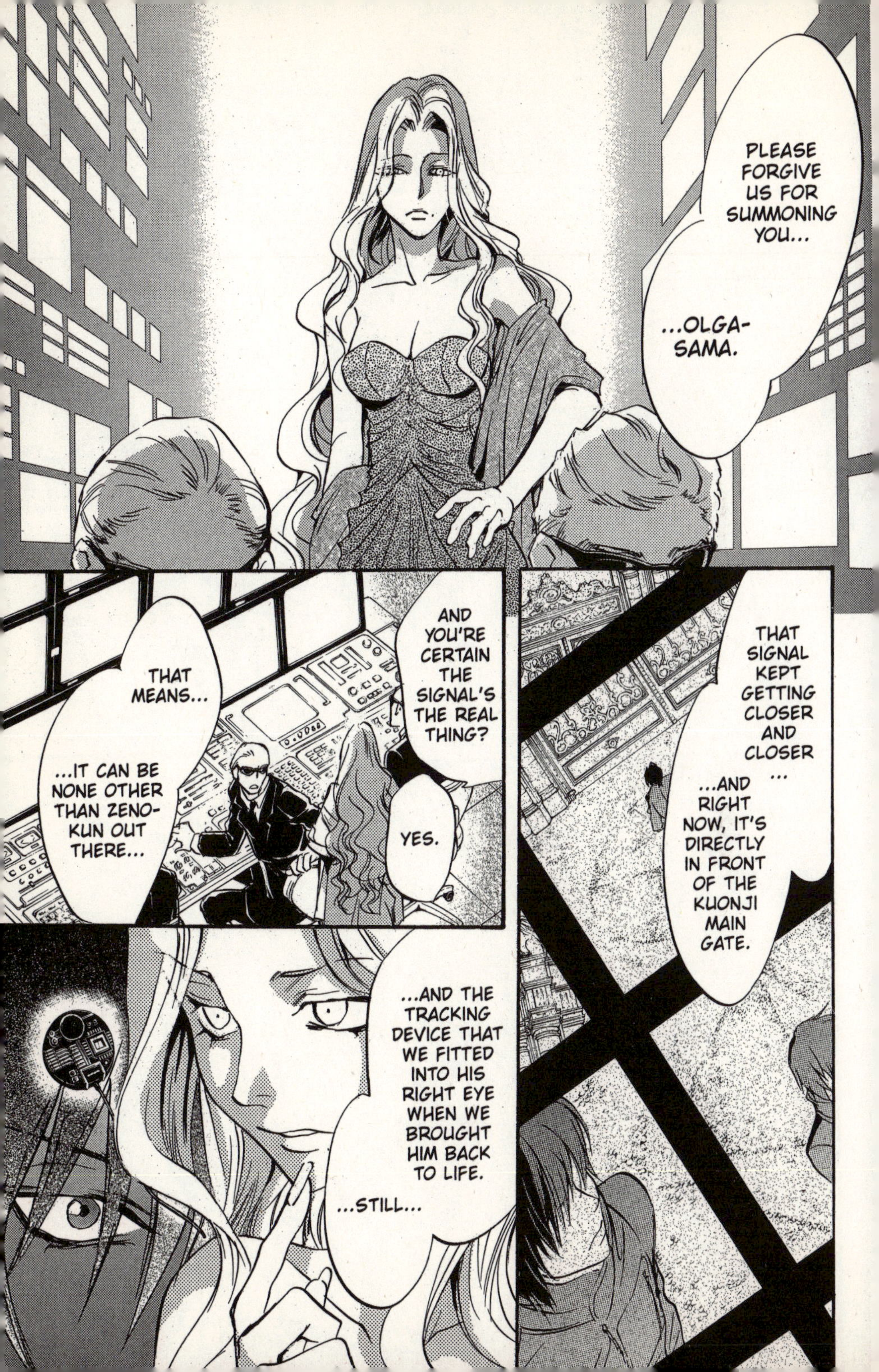
PLEASE FORGIVE US FOR SUMMONING YOU...
...OLGA-SAMA.
THAT SIGNAL KEPT GETTING CLOSER AND CLOSER...
...AND RIGHT NOW, IT'S DIRECTLY IN FRONT OF THE KUONJI MAIN GATE.
AND YOU'RE CERTAIN THE SIGNAL'S THE REAL THING?
YES.
THAT MEANS...
...IT CAN BE NONE OTHER THAN ZENO-KUN OUT THERE...
...AND THE TRACKING DEVICE THAT WE FITTED INTO HIS RIGHT EYE WHEN WE BROUGHT HIM BACK TO LIFE.
...STILL...

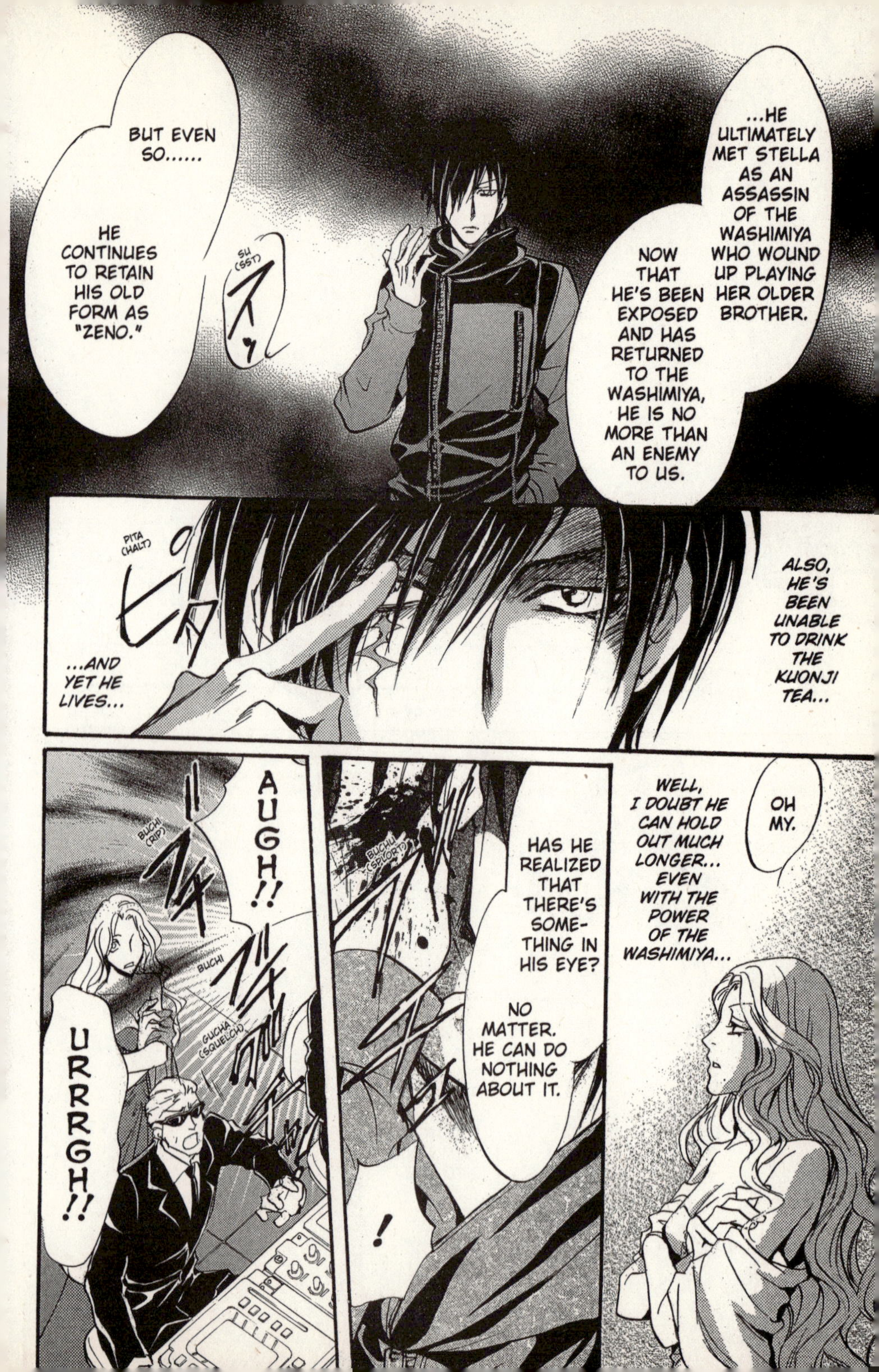
...HE ULTIMATELY MET STELLA AS AN ASSASSIN OF THE WASHIMIYA WHO WOUND UP PLAYING HER OLDER BROTHER.
NOW THAT HE'S BEEN EXPOSED AND HAS RETURNED TO THE WASHIMIYA, HE IS NO MORE THAN AN ENEMY TO US.
SU (SST)
BUT EVEN SO......
HE CONTINUES TO RETAIN HIS OLD FORM AS "ZENO."
ALSO, HE'S BEEN UNABLE TO DRINK THE KUONJI TEA...
PITA (HALT)
...AND YET HE LIVES...
OH MY.
WELL, I DOUBT HE CAN HOLD OUT MUCH LONGER... EVEN WITH THE POWER OF THE WASHIMIYA...
HAS HE REALIZED THAT THERE'S SOME-THING IN HIS EYE?
BUCHU (SPLORT)
NO MATTER. HE CAN DO NOTHING ABOUT IT.
!
AUGH!!
BUCHI (RIP)
BUCHI
GUCHA (SQUELCH)
URRRGH!!

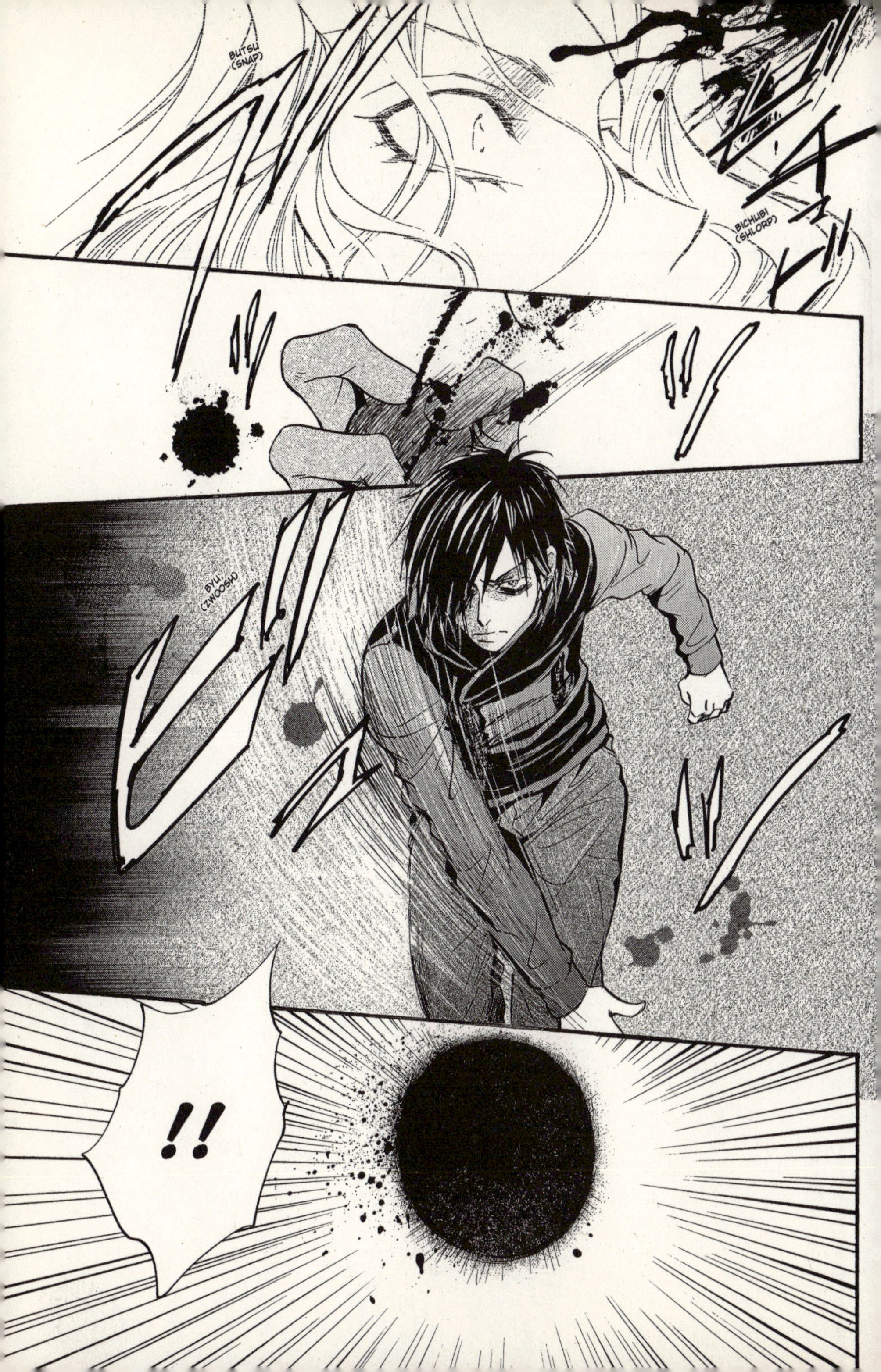
BICHUBI (SHLORP)
BUTSU (SNAP)
BYU (ZWOOSH)
!!

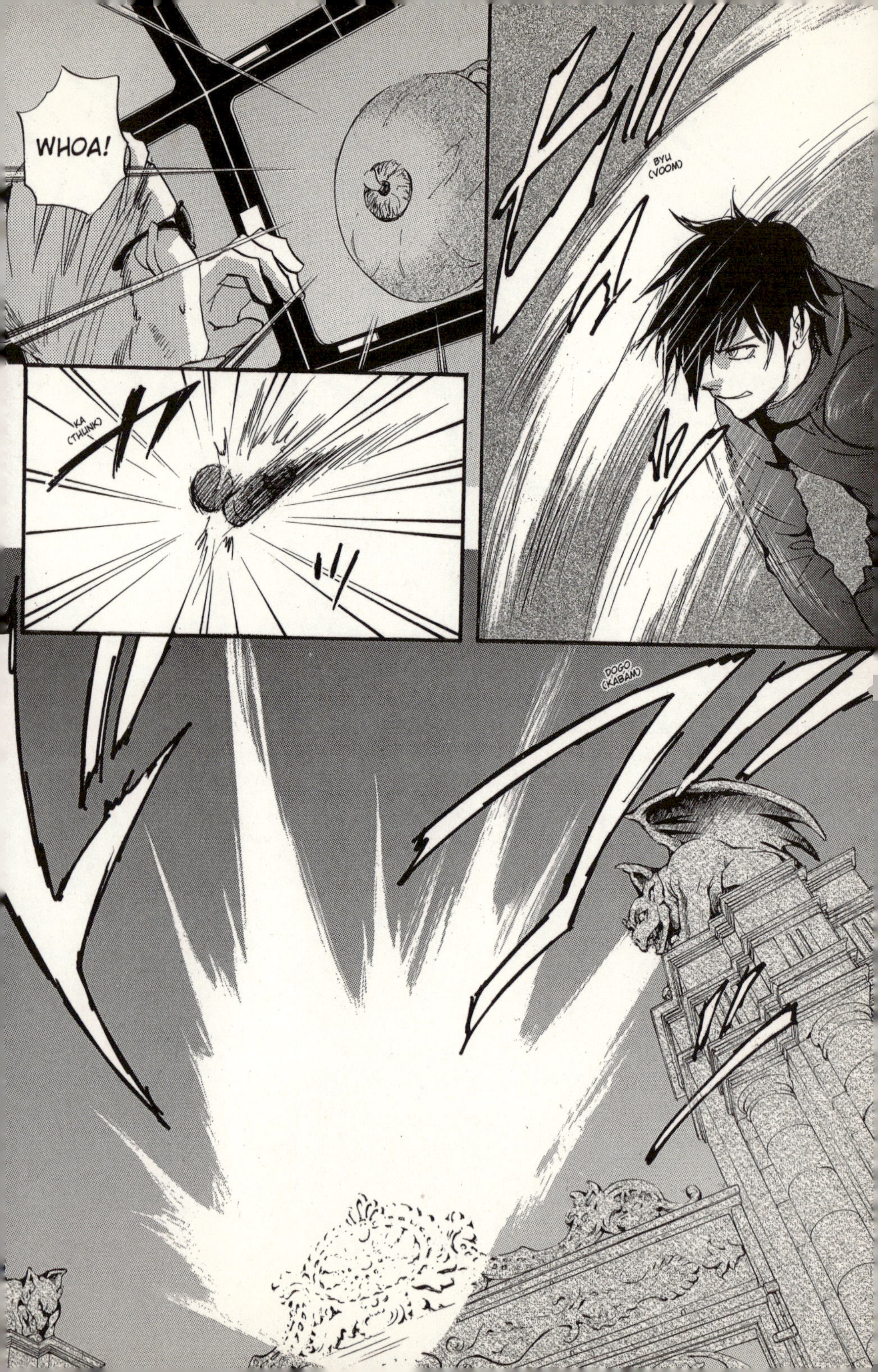
BYU (VOOM)
WHOA!
KA (THUNK)
DOGO (KABAM)

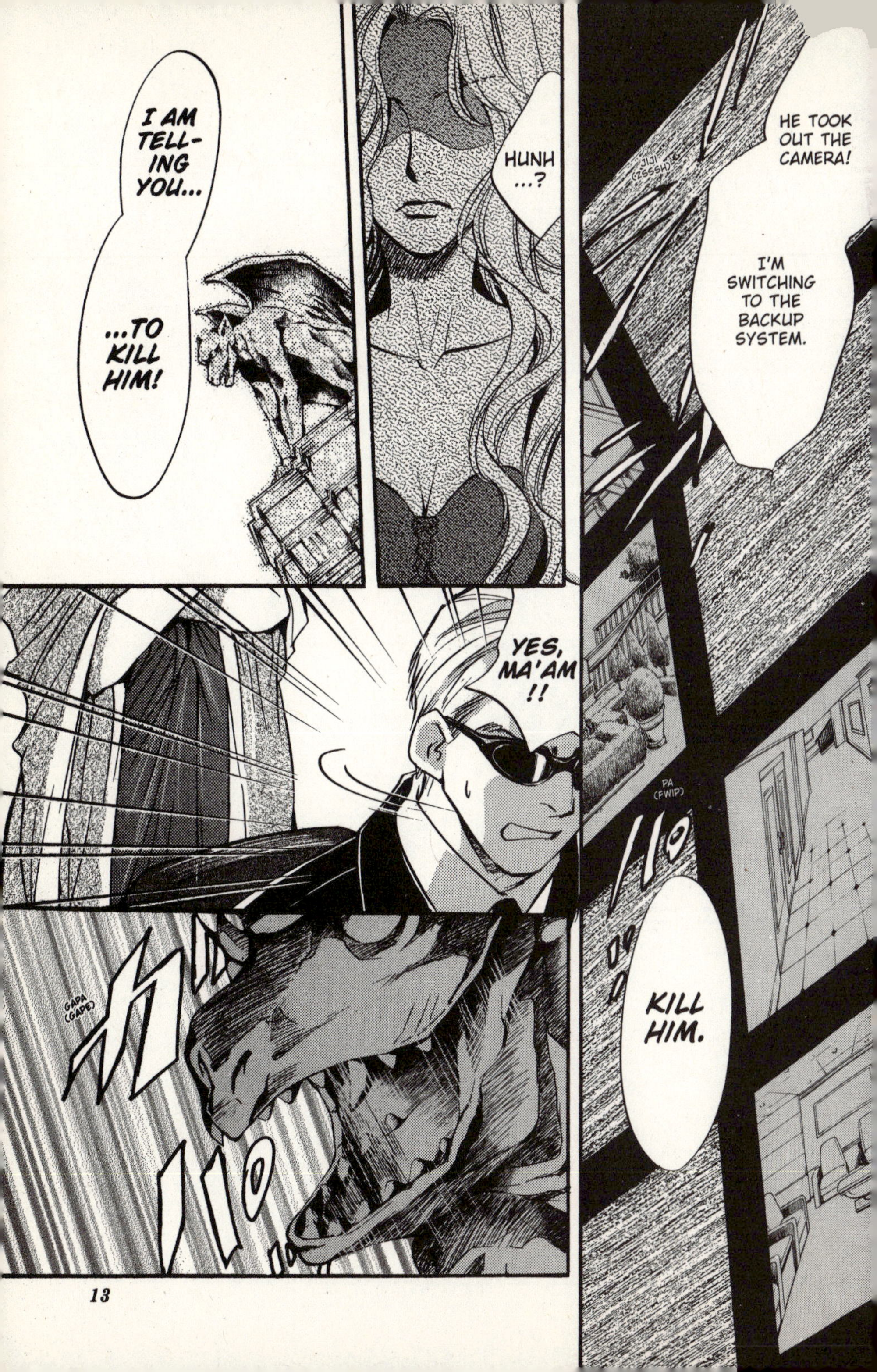
HE TOOK OUT THE CAMERA!
JIJI (ZESSH)
I'M SWITCHING TO THE BACKUP SYSTEM.
PA (FWIP)
KILL HIM.
HUNH ...?
I AM TELL-ING YOU...
...TO KILL HIM!
YES, MA'AM !!
GAPA (GAPE)

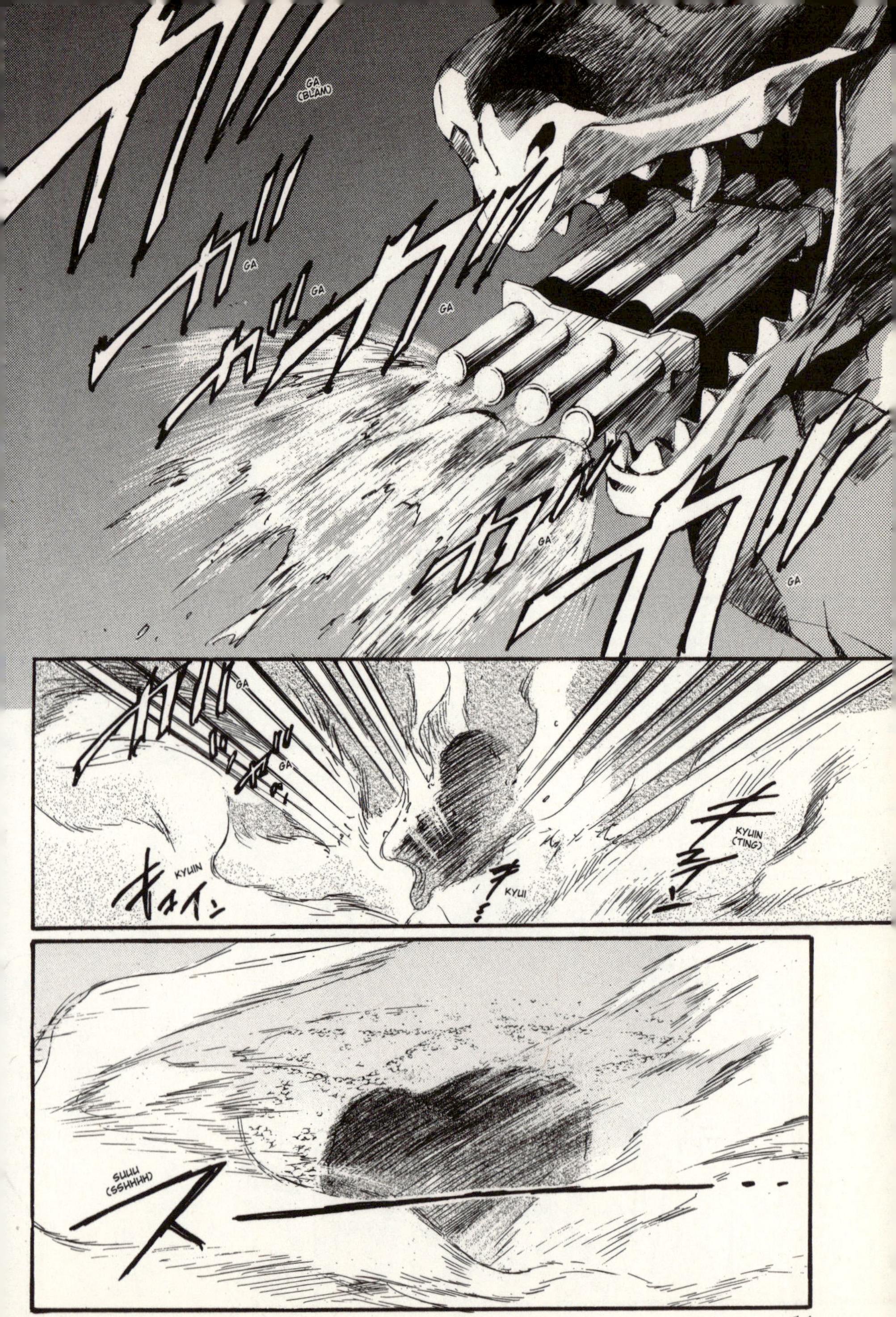
GA (BLAM)
GA
GA
GA
GA
GA
GA
GA
KYUIN (TING)
KYUI
KYUIN
SUUU (SSHHHH)

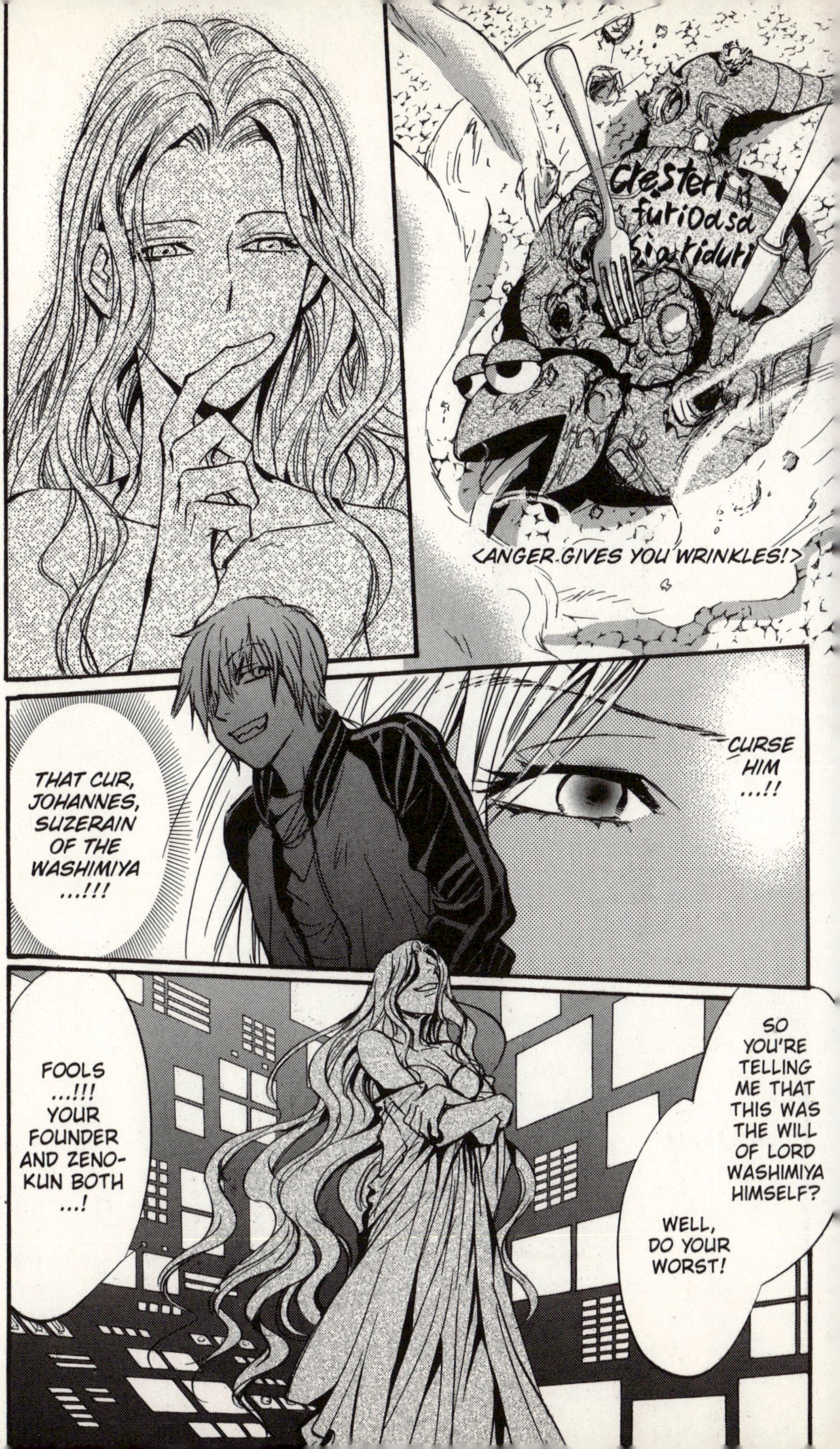
Cresteri furioasa sia kiduti
<ANGER GIVES YOU WRINKLES!>
CURSE HIM ...!!
THAT CUR, JOHANNES, SUZERAIN OF THE WASHIMIYA ...!!!
SO YOU'RE TELLING ME THAT THIS WAS THE WILL OF LORD WASHIMIYA HIMSELF?
WELL, DO YOUR WORST!
FOOLS ...!!! YOUR FOUNDER AND ZENO-KUN BOTH ...!

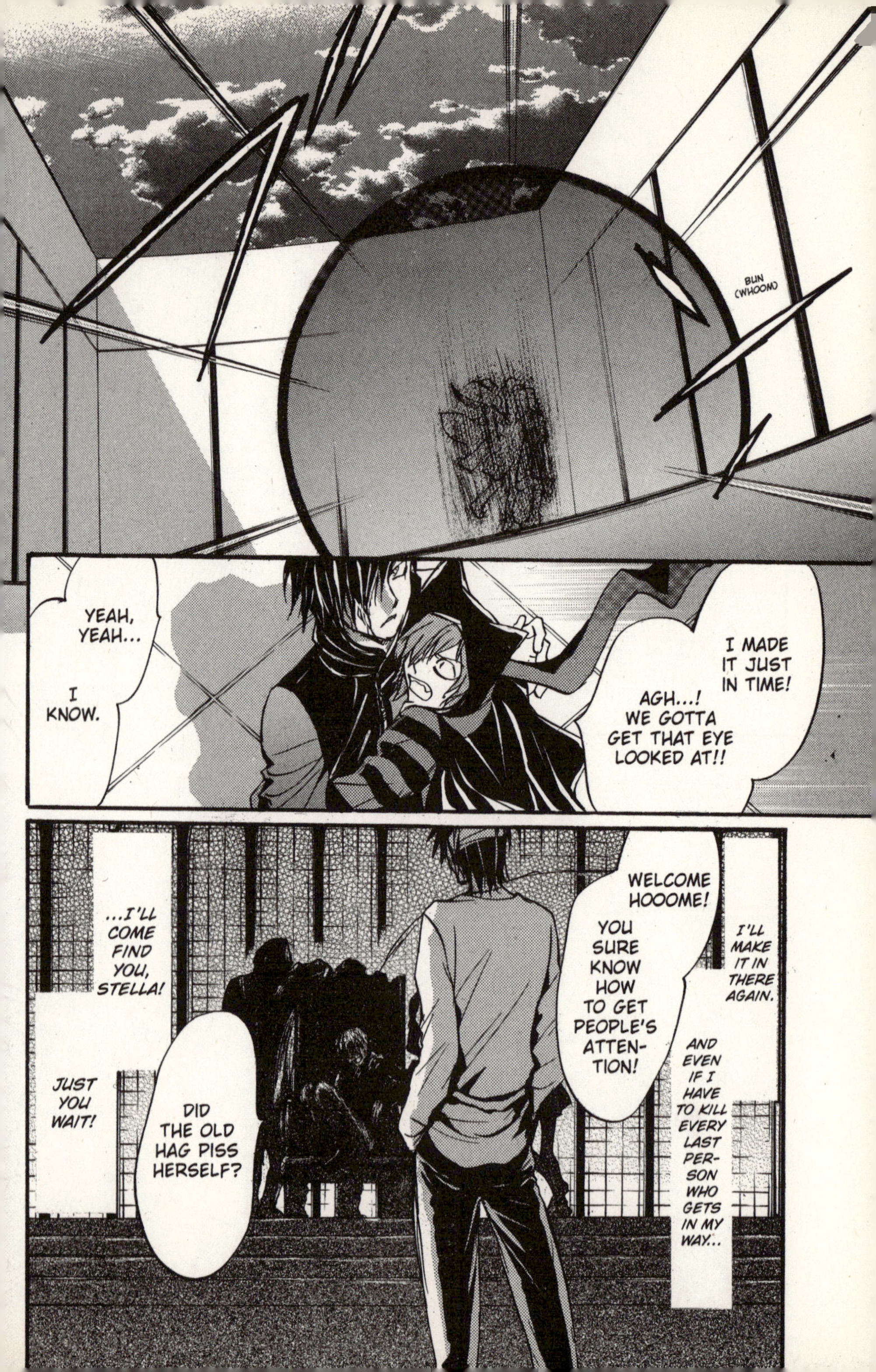
BUN (WHOOM)
I MADE IT JUST IN TIME!
AGH...! WE GOTTA GET THAT EYE LOOKED AT!!
YEAH, YEAH...
I KNOW.
I'LL MAKE IT IN THERE AGAIN.
AND EVEN IF I HAVE TO KILL EVERY LAST PERSON WHO GETS IN MY WAY...
WELCOME HOOOME!
YOU SURE KNOW HOW TO GET PEOPLE'S ATTENTION!
DID THE OLD HAG PISS HERSELF?
...I'LL COME FIND YOU, STELLA!
JUST YOU WAIT!

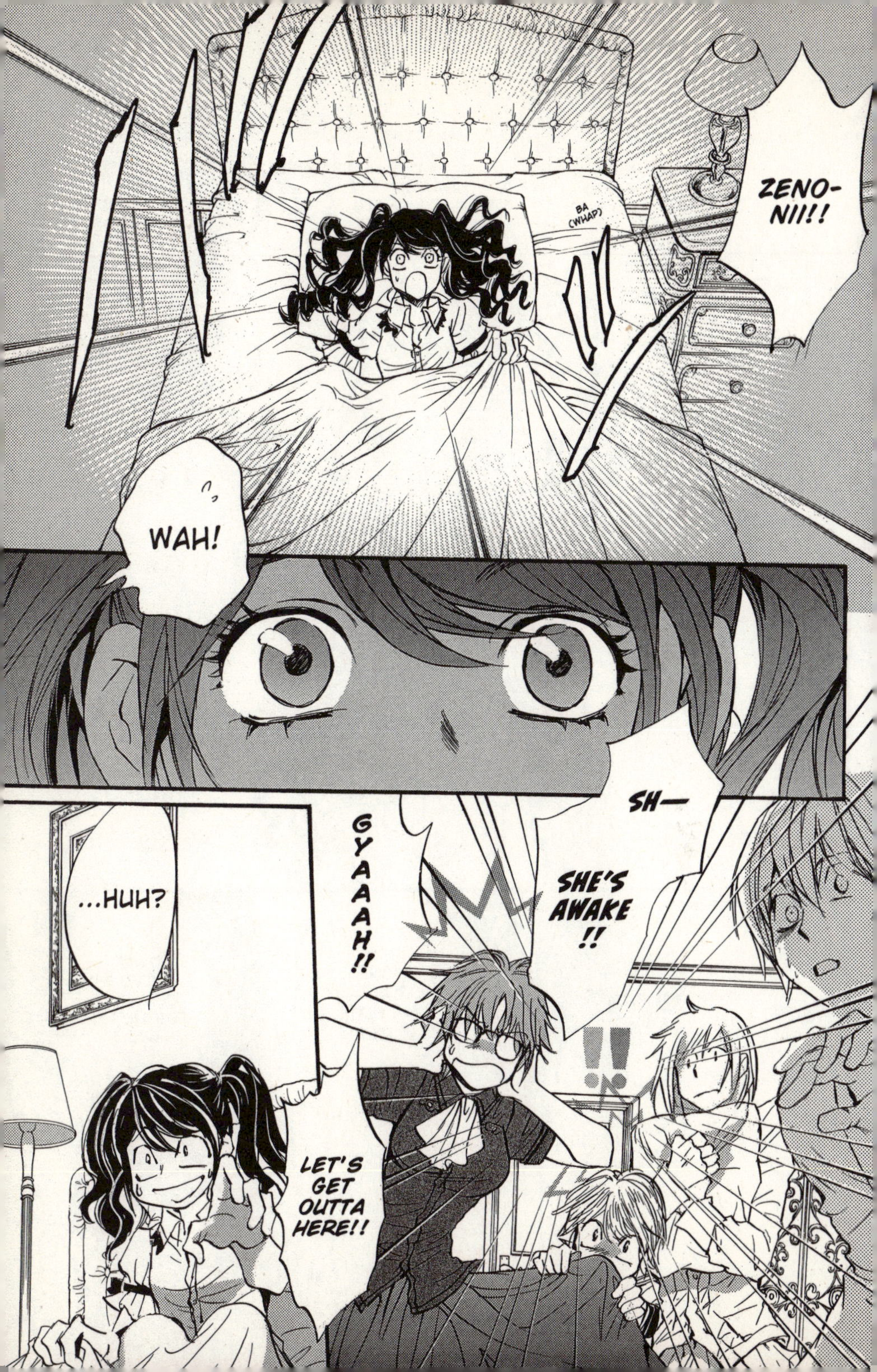
ZENO-NII!!
BA (WHAP)
WAH!
SH—
SHE'S AWAKE!!
GYAAAAH!!
...HUH?
LET'S GET OUTTA HERE!!

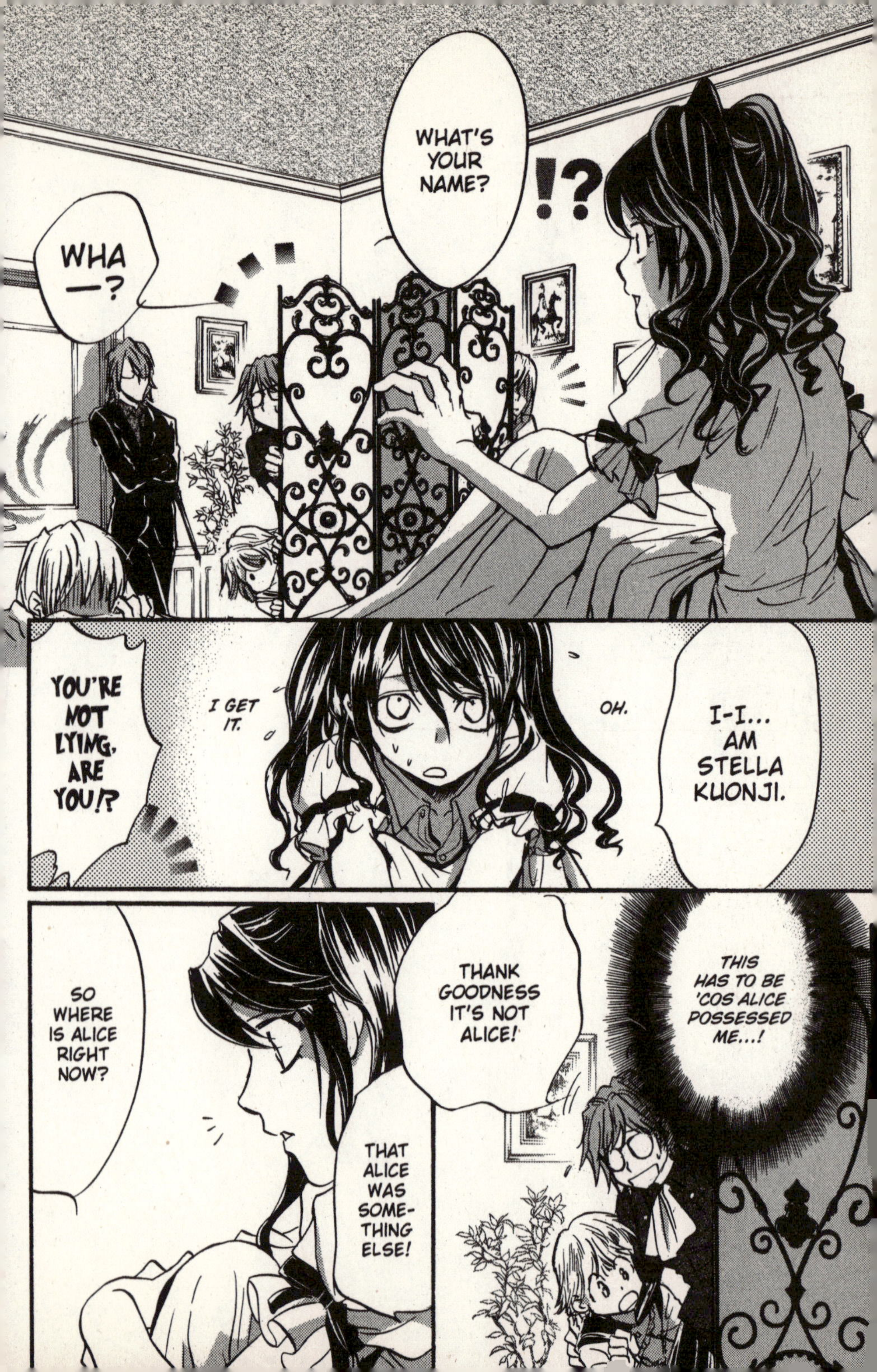
WHAT'S YOUR NAME?
!?
WHA—?
I-I... AM STELLA KUONJI.
OH.
I GET IT.
YOU'RE NOT LYING, ARE YOU!?
THIS HAS TO BE 'COS ALICE POSSESSED ME...!
THANK GOODNESS IT'S NOT ALICE!
THAT ALICE WAS SOMETHING ELSE!
SO WHERE IS ALICE RIGHT NOW?

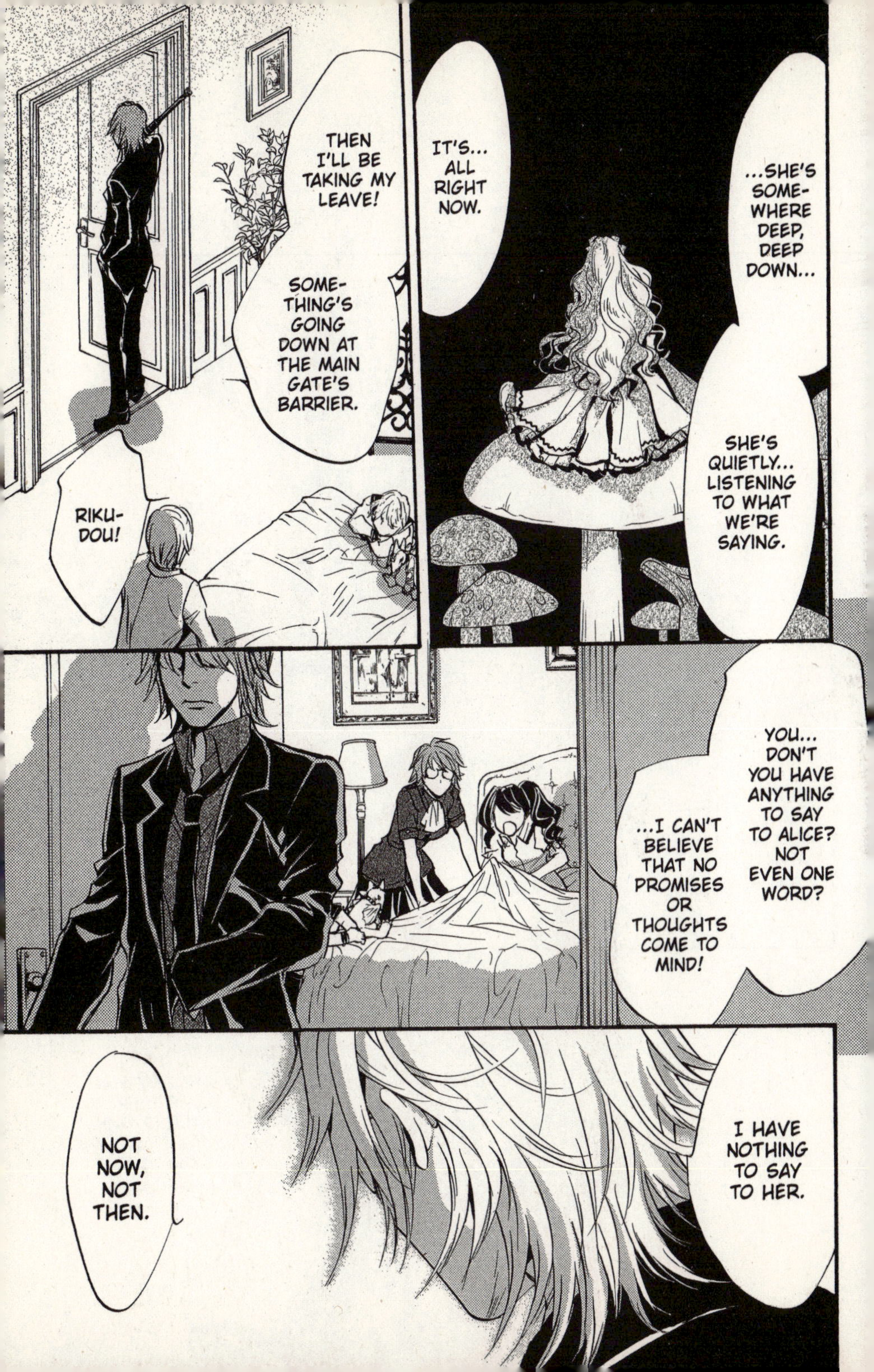
...SHE'S SOME-WHERE DEEP, DEEP DOWN...
IT'S... ALL RIGHT NOW.
SHE'S QUIETLY... LISTENING TO WHAT WE'RE SAYING.
THEN I'LL BE TAKING MY LEAVE!
SOME-THING'S GOING DOWN AT THE MAIN GATE'S BARRIER.
RIKU-DOU!
YOU... DON'T YOU HAVE ANYTHING TO SAY TO ALICE? NOT EVEN ONE WORD?
...I CAN'T BELIEVE THAT NO PROMISES OR THOUGHTS COME TO MIND!
I HAVE NOTHING TO SAY TO HER.
NOT NOW, NOT THEN.

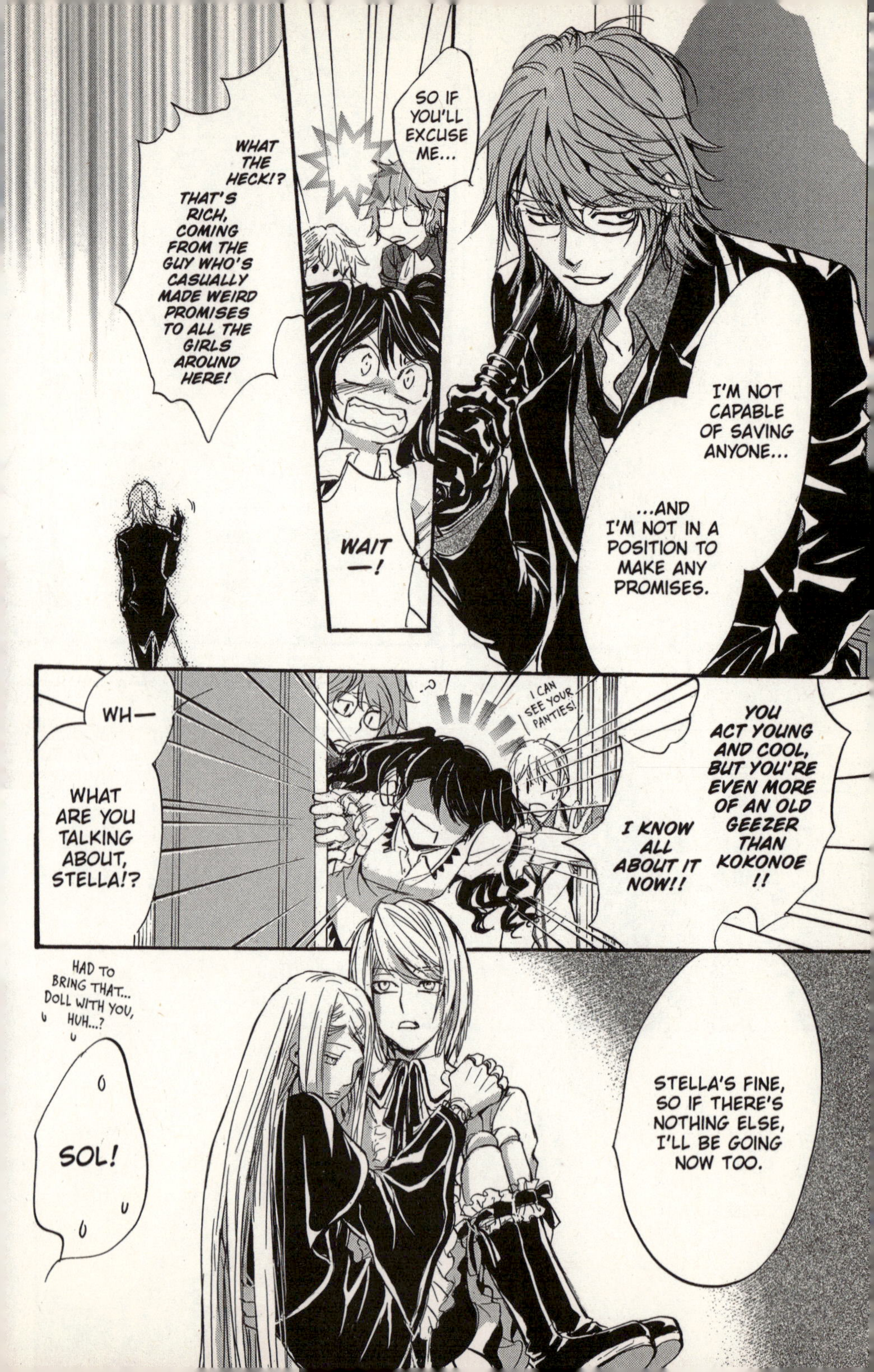
I'M NOT CAPABLE OF SAVING ANYONE...
...AND I'M NOT IN A POSITION TO MAKE ANY PROMISES.
SO IF YOU'LL EXCUSE ME...
WAIT—!
WHAT THE HECK!? THAT'S RICH, COMING FROM THE GUY WHO'S CASUALLY MADE WEIRD PROMISES TO ALL THE GIRLS AROUND HERE!
YOU ACT YOUNG AND COOL, BUT YOU'RE EVEN MORE OF AN OLD GEEZER THAN KOKONOE!!
I KNOW ALL ABOUT IT NOW!!
I CAN SEE YOUR PANTIES!
WH—
WHAT ARE YOU TALKING ABOUT, STELLA!?
STELLA'S FINE, SO IF THERE'S NOTHING ELSE, I'LL BE GOING NOW TOO.
SOL!
HAD TO BRING THAT... DOLL WITH YOU, HUH...?

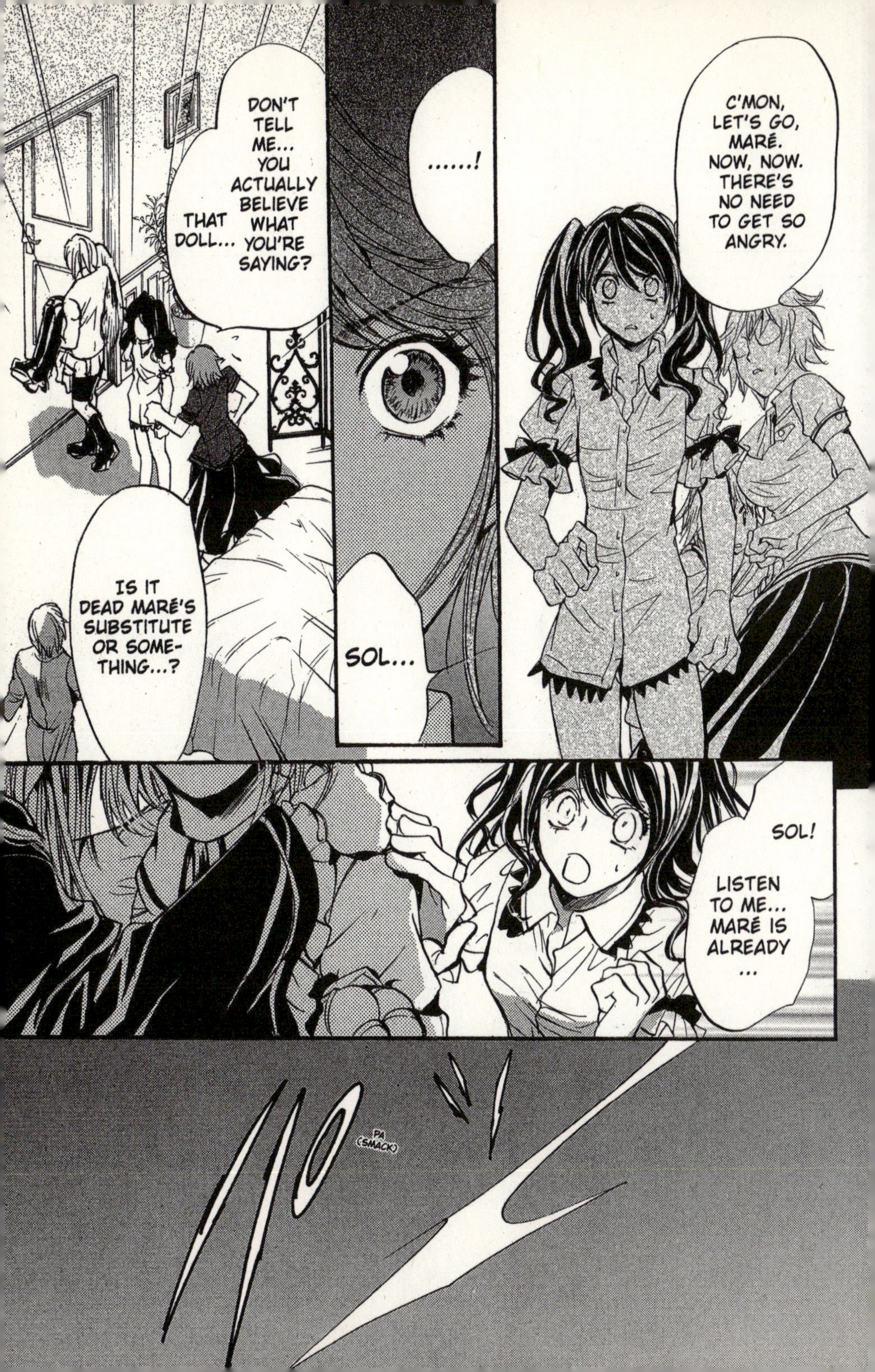
C'MON, LET'S GO, MARÉ. NOW, NOW. THERE'S NO NEED TO GET SO ANGRY.
......!
SOL...
THAT DOLL...
DON'T TELL ME... YOU ACTUALLY BELIEVE WHAT YOU'RE SAYING?
IS IT DEAD MARÉ'S SUBSTITUTE OR SOME-THING...?
SOL!
LISTEN TO ME... MARÉ IS ALREADY ...
PA (SMACK)

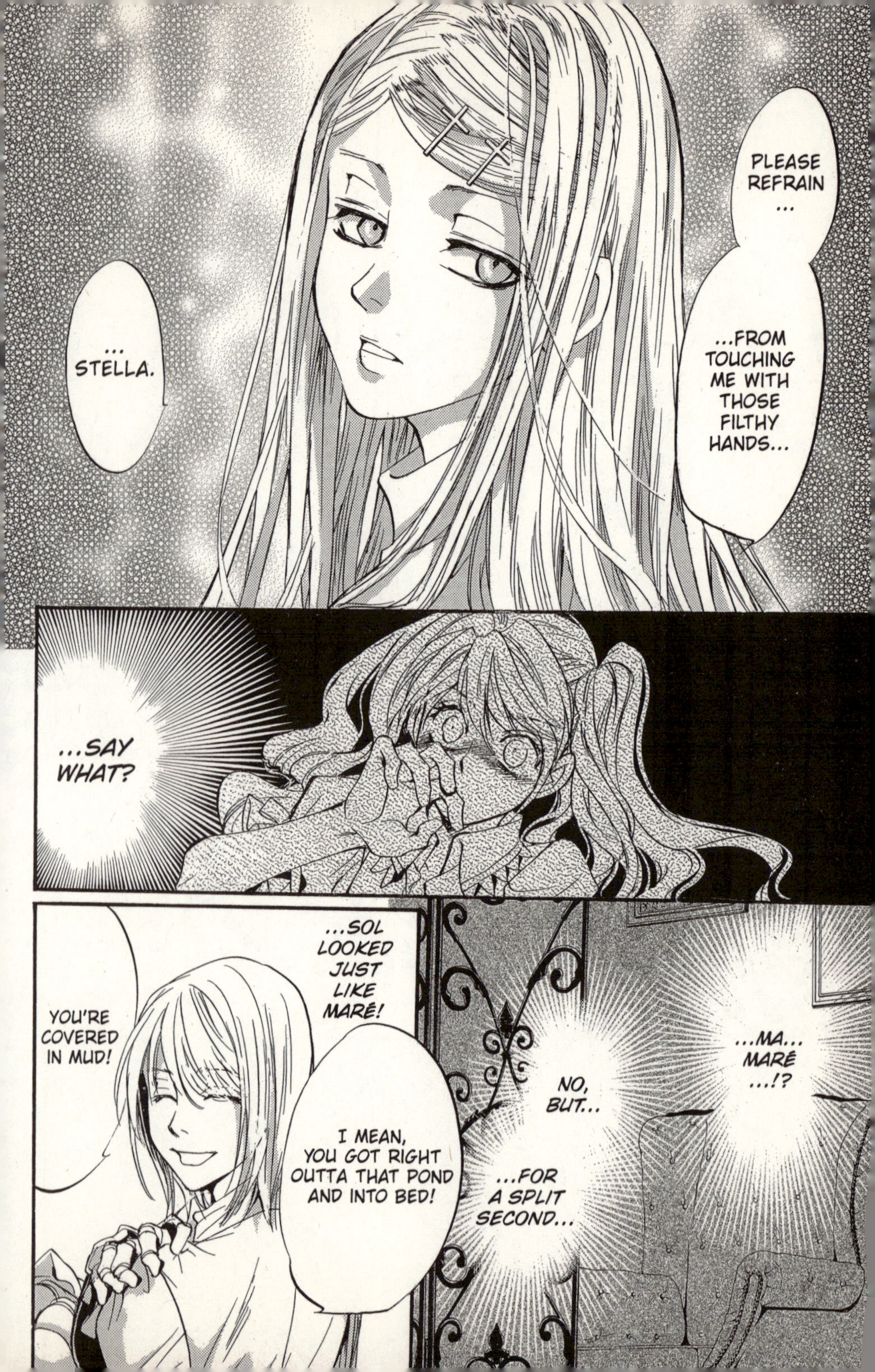
PLEASE REFRAIN ...
...FROM TOUCHING ME WITH THOSE FILTHY HANDS...
... STELLA.
...SAY WHAT?
...MA... MARÉ ...!?
NO, BUT...
...FOR A SPLIT SECOND...
...SOL LOOKED JUST LIKE MARÉ!
YOU'RE COVERED IN MUD!
I MEAN, YOU GOT RIGHT OUTTA THAT POND AND INTO BED!

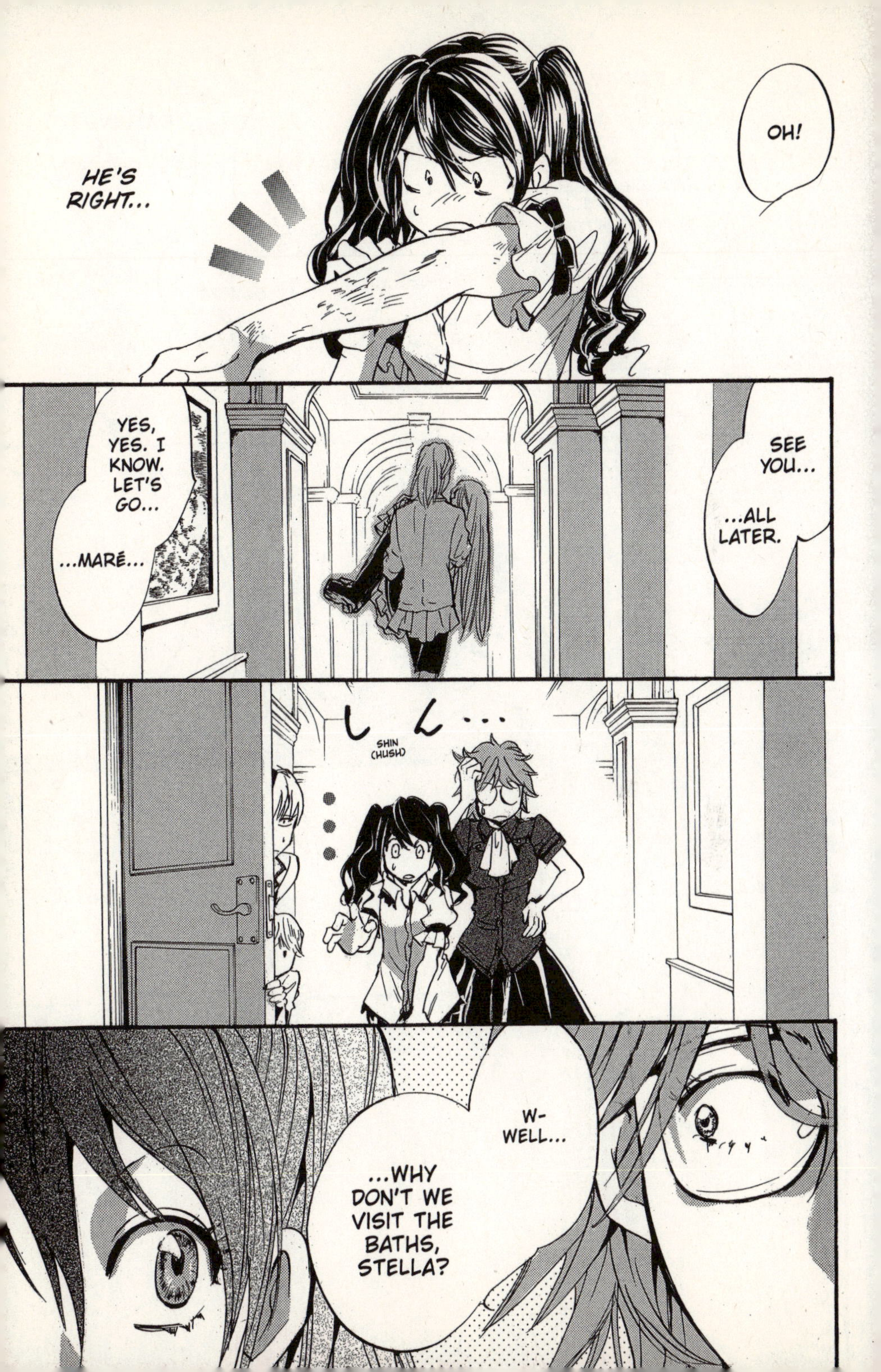
OH!
HE'S RIGHT...
SEE YOU... ...ALL LATER.
YES, YES. I KNOW. LET'S GO...
...MARE...
しん...
SHIN (HUSH)
W-WELL...
...WHY DON'T WE VISIT THE BATHS, STELLA?

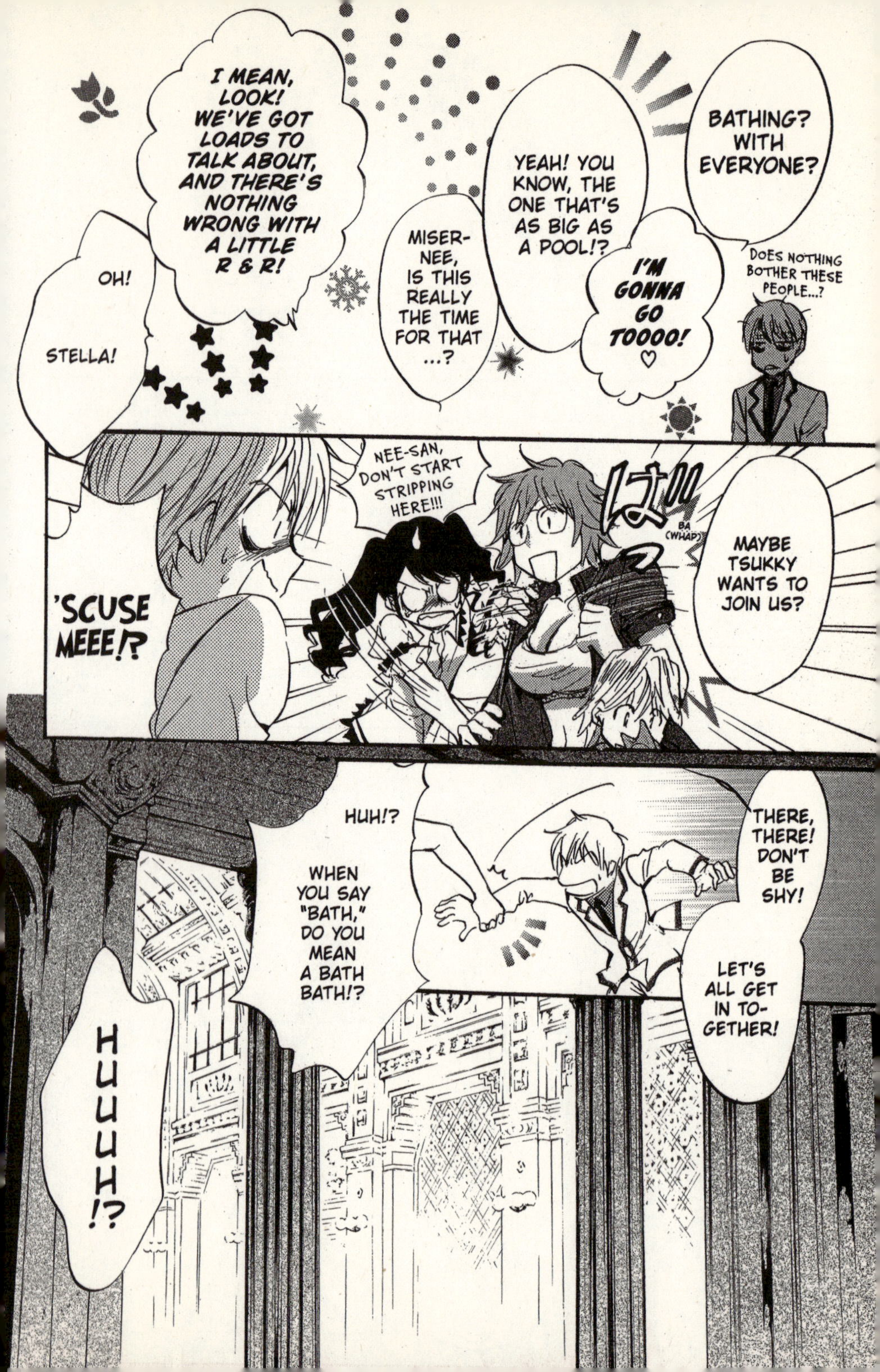
BATHING? WITH EVERYONE?
DOES NOTHING BOTHER THESE PEOPLE...?
YEAH! YOU KNOW, THE ONE THAT'S AS BIG AS A POOL!?
I'M GONNA GO TOOOO! ♡
MISER-NEE, IS THIS REALLY THE TIME FOR THAT ...?
I MEAN, LOOK! WE'VE GOT LOADS TO TALK ABOUT, AND THERE'S NOTHING WRONG WITH A LITTLE R & R!
OH! STELLA!
MAYBE TSUKKY WANTS TO JOIN US?
は
BA (WHAP)
NEE-SAN, DON'T START STRIPPING HERE!!!
'SCUSE MEEE!?
THERE, THERE! DON'T BE SHY!
LET'S ALL GET IN TO-GETHER!
HUH!?
WHEN YOU SAY "BATH," DO YOU MEAN A BATH BATH!?
HUUUH!?

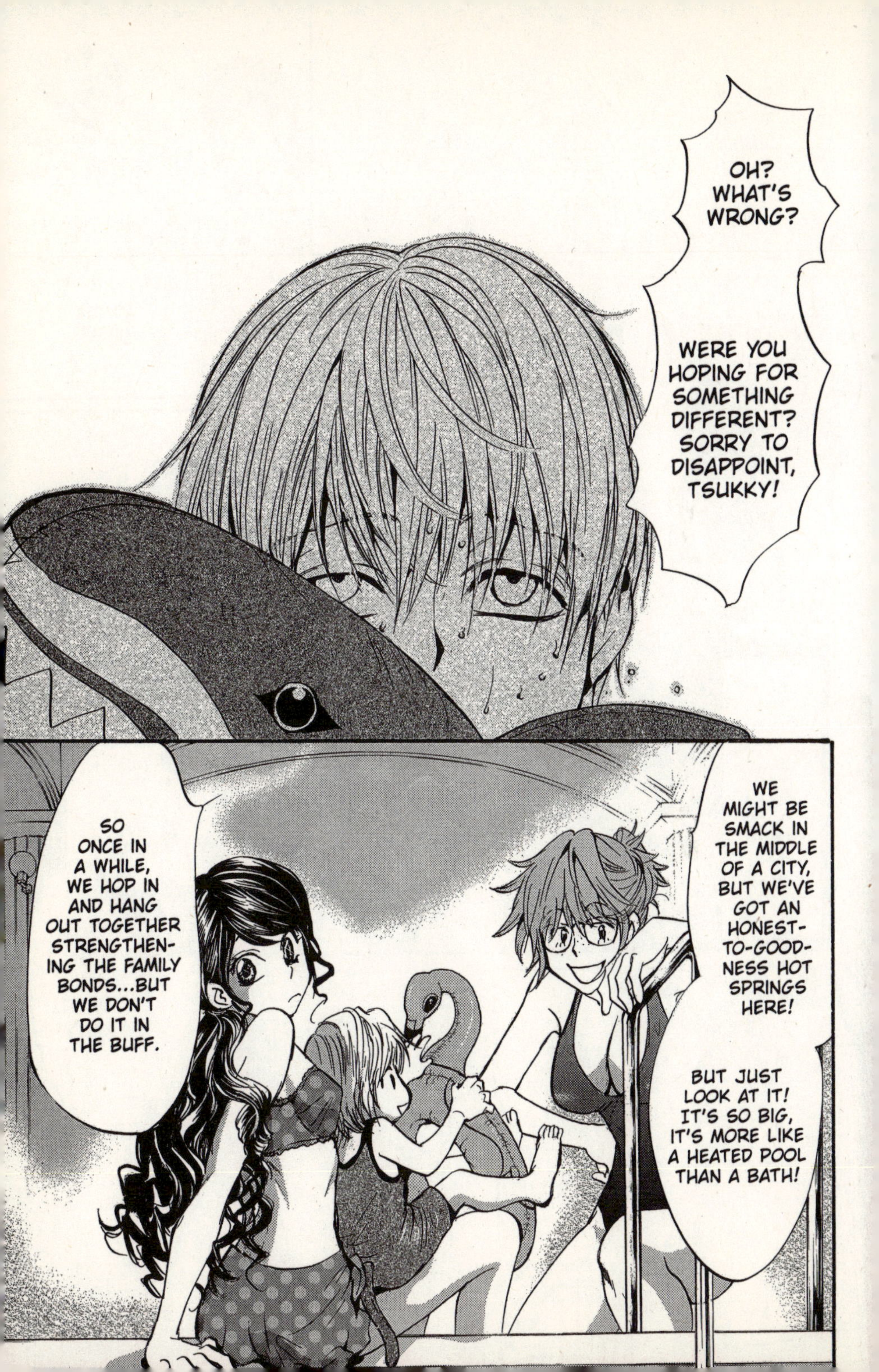
OH? WHAT'S WRONG?
WERE YOU HOPING FOR SOMETHING DIFFERENT? SORRY TO DISAPPOINT, TSUKKY!
WE MIGHT BE SMACK IN THE MIDDLE OF A CITY, BUT WE'VE GOT AN HONEST-TO-GOODNESS HOT SPRINGS HERE!
BUT JUST LOOK AT IT! IT'S SO BIG, IT'S MORE LIKE A HEATED POOL THAN A BATH!
SO ONCE IN A WHILE, WE HOP IN AND HANG OUT TOGETHER STRENGTHENING THE FAMILY BONDS...BUT WE DON'T DO IT IN THE BUFF.

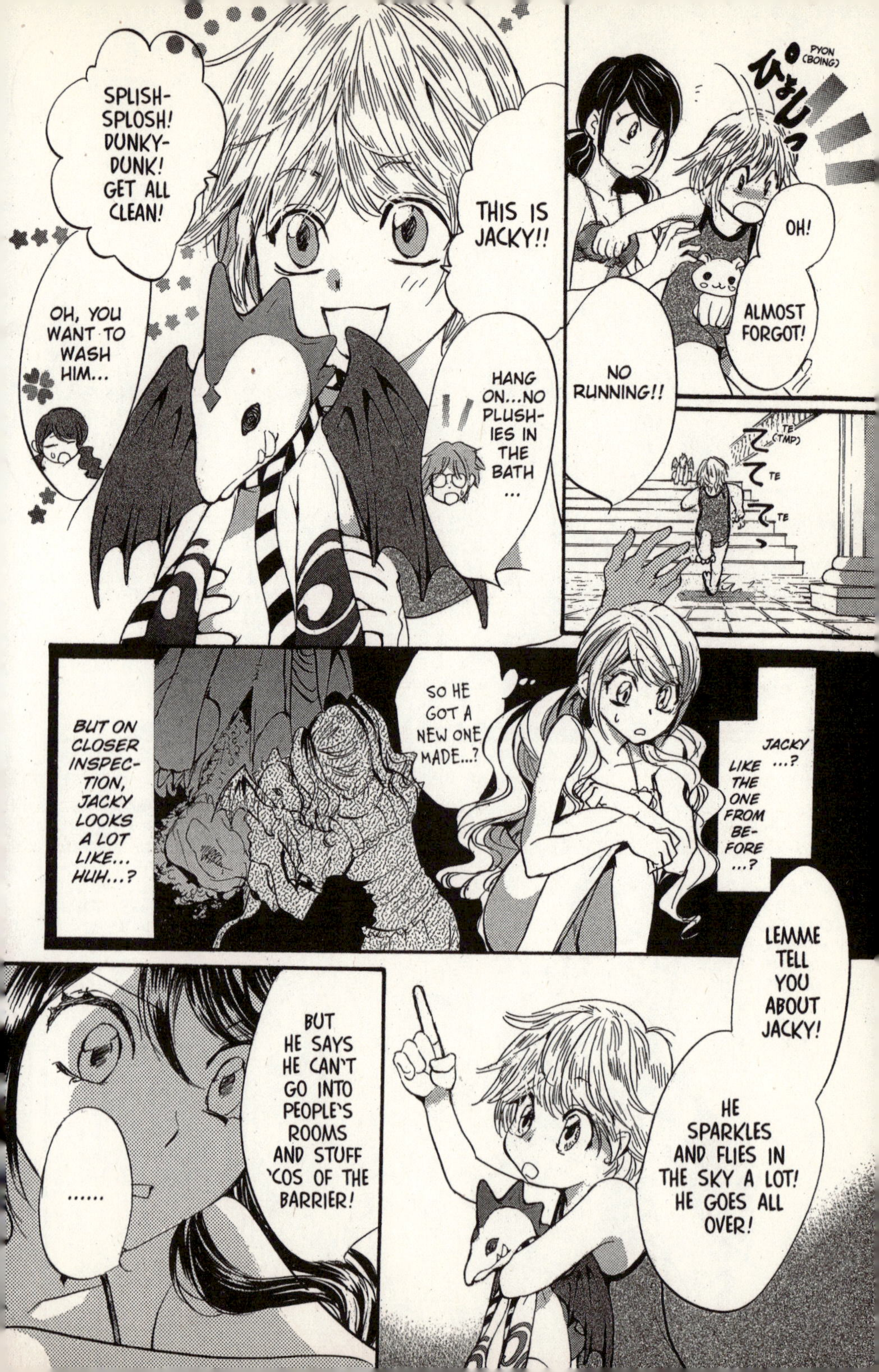
ぴょんっ
PYON (BOING)
OH!
ALMOST FORGOT!
NO RUNNING!!
てててっ
TE (TMP)
TE
TE
THIS IS JACKY!!
SPLISH-SPLOSH! DUNKY-DUNK! GET ALL CLEAN!
HANG ON...NO PLUSHIES IN THE BATH...
OH, YOU WANT TO WASH HIM...
JACKY...? LIKE THE ONE FROM BEFORE...?
SO HE GOT A NEW ONE MADE...?
BUT ON CLOSER INSPECTION, JACKY LOOKS A LOT LIKE... HUH...?
LEMME TELL YOU ABOUT JACKY!
HE SPARKLES AND FLIES IN THE SKY A LOT! HE GOES ALL OVER!
BUT HE SAYS HE CAN'T GO INTO PEOPLE'S ROOMS AND STUFF 'COS OF THE BARRIER!
......

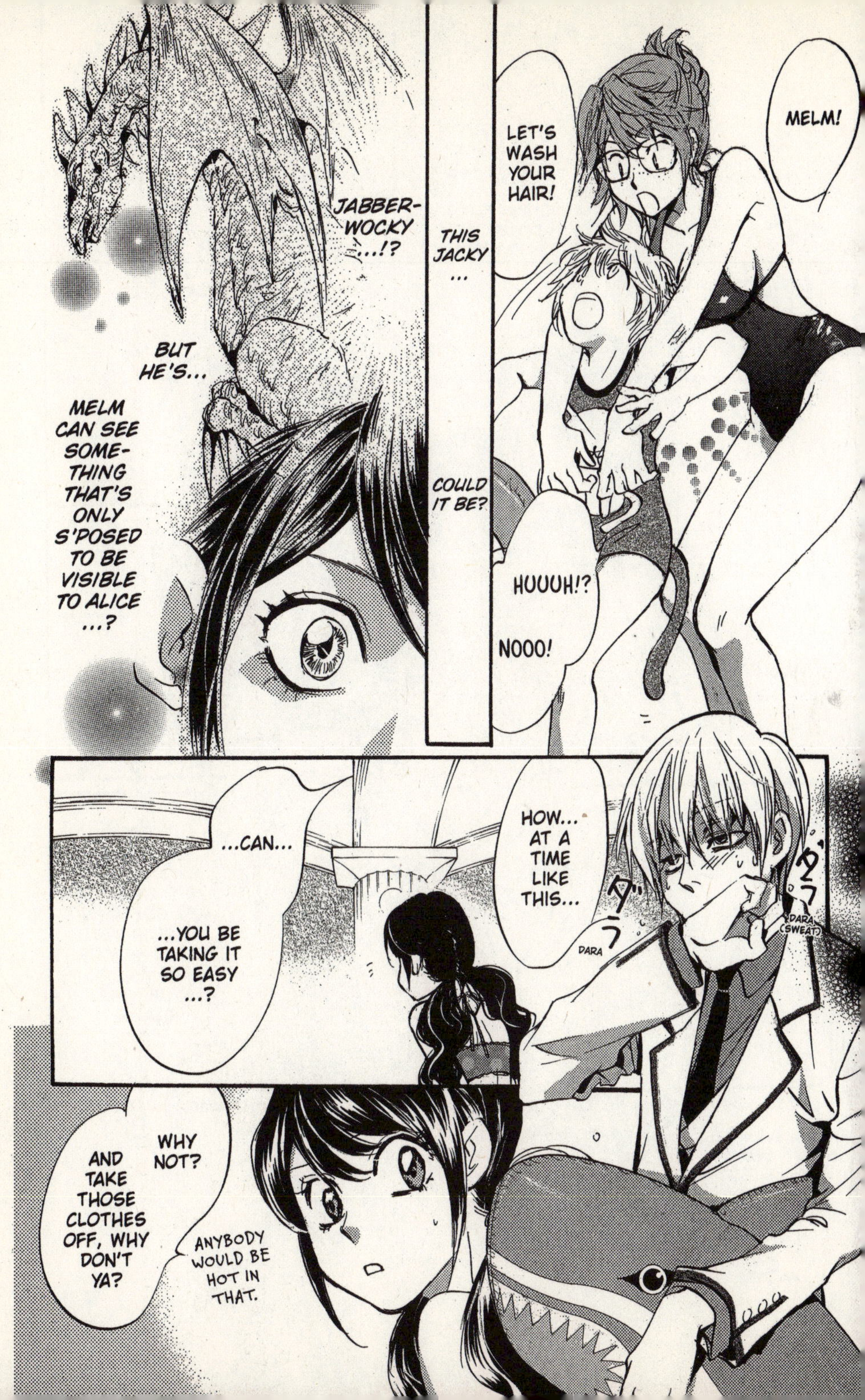
MELM!
LET'S WASH YOUR HAIR!
THIS JACKY...
HUUUH!?
NOOO!
COULD IT BE?
JABBER-WOCKY ...!?
BUT HE'S...
MELM CAN SEE SOME-THING THAT'S ONLY S'POSED TO BE VISIBLE TO ALICE ...?
HOW... AT A TIME LIKE THIS...
ダラ
DARA (SWEAT)
ダラ
DARA
...CAN...
...YOU BE TAKING IT SO EASY ...?
WHY NOT?
AND TAKE THOSE CLOTHES OFF, WHY DON'T YA?
ANYBODY WOULD BE HOT IN THAT.

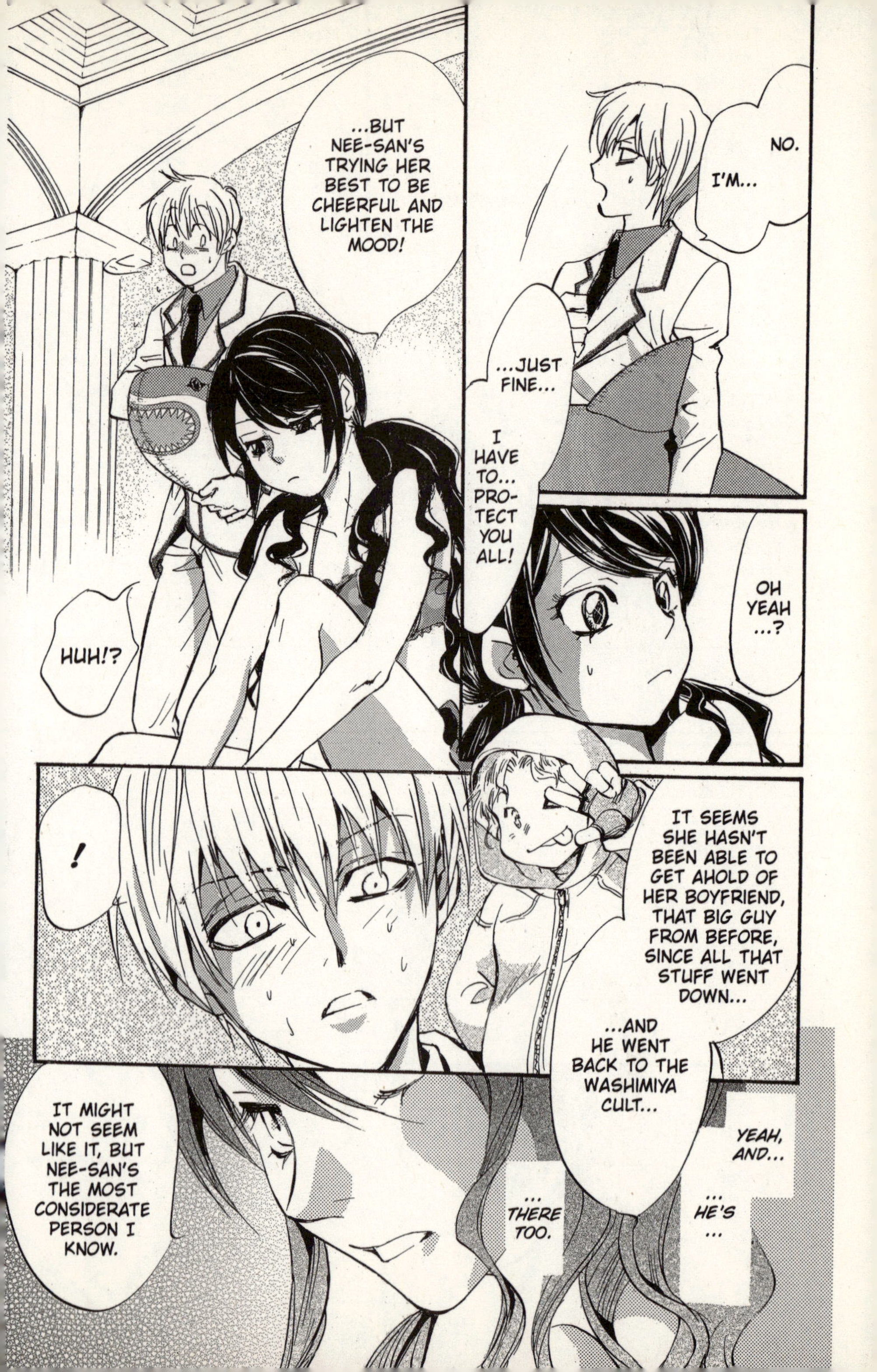
NO.
I'M...
...JUST FINE...
I HAVE TO... PRO-TECT YOU ALL!
OH YEAH ...?
...BUT NEE-SAN'S TRYING HER BEST TO BE CHEERFUL AND LIGHTEN THE MOOD!
HUH!?
IT SEEMS SHE HASN'T BEEN ABLE TO GET AHOLD OF HER BOYFRIEND, THAT BIG GUY FROM BEFORE, SINCE ALL THAT STUFF WENT DOWN...
!
...AND HE WENT BACK TO THE WASHIMIYA CULT...
YEAH, AND...
...HE'S...
...THERE TOO.
IT MIGHT NOT SEEM LIKE IT, BUT NEE-SAN'S THE MOST CONSIDERATE PERSON I KNOW.

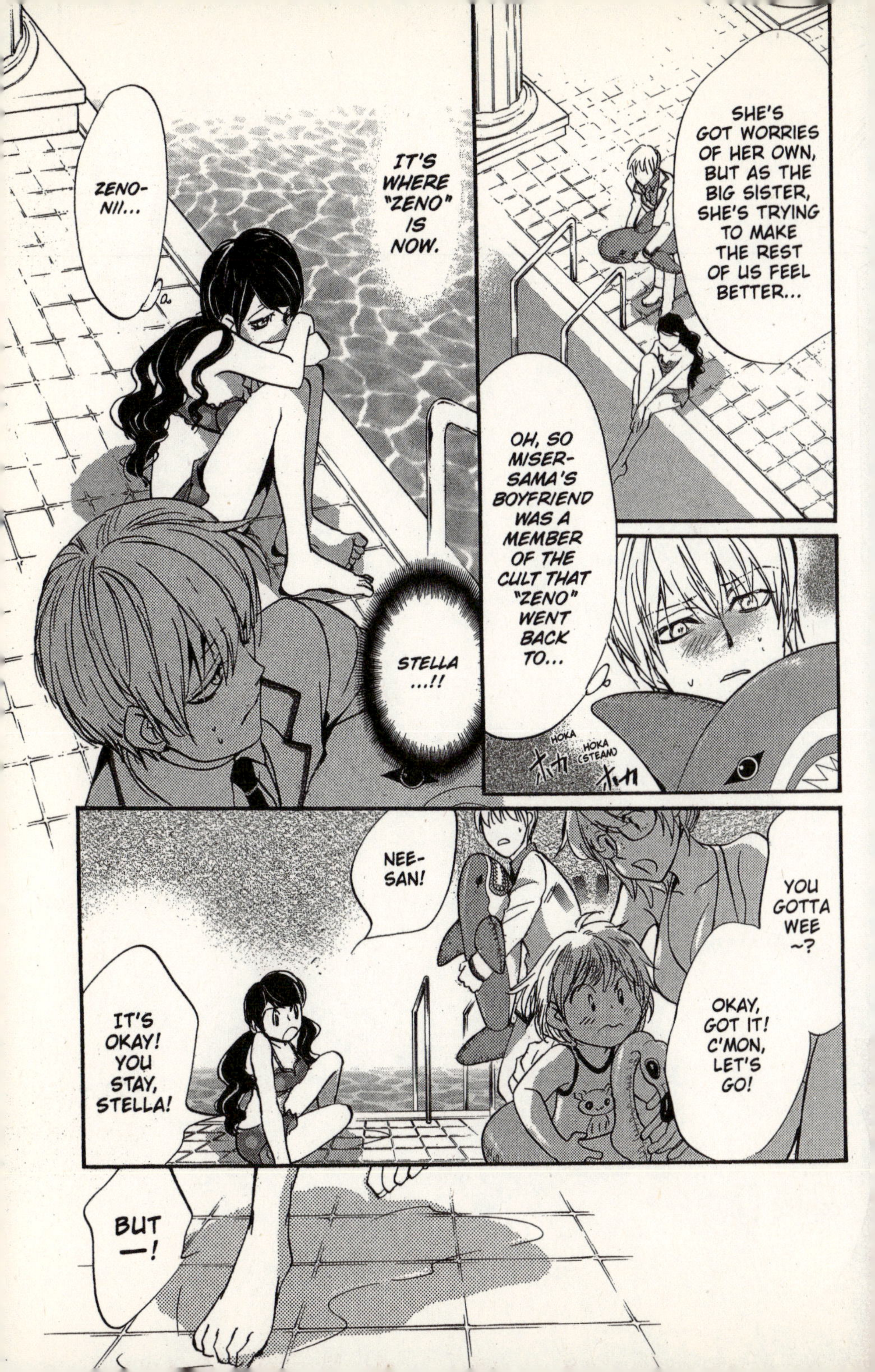
SHE'S GOT WORRIES OF HER OWN, BUT AS THE BIG SISTER, SHE'S TRYING TO MAKE THE REST OF US FEEL BETTER...
OH, SO MISER-SAMA'S BOYFRIEND WAS A MEMBER OF THE CULT THAT "ZENO" WENT BACK TO...
HOKA HOKA (STEAM)
IT'S WHERE "ZENO" IS NOW.
ZENO-NII...
STELLA ...!!
YOU GOTTA WEE ~?
NEE-SAN!
OKAY, GOT IT! C'MON, LET'S GO!
IT'S OKAY! YOU STAY, STELLA!
BUT —!

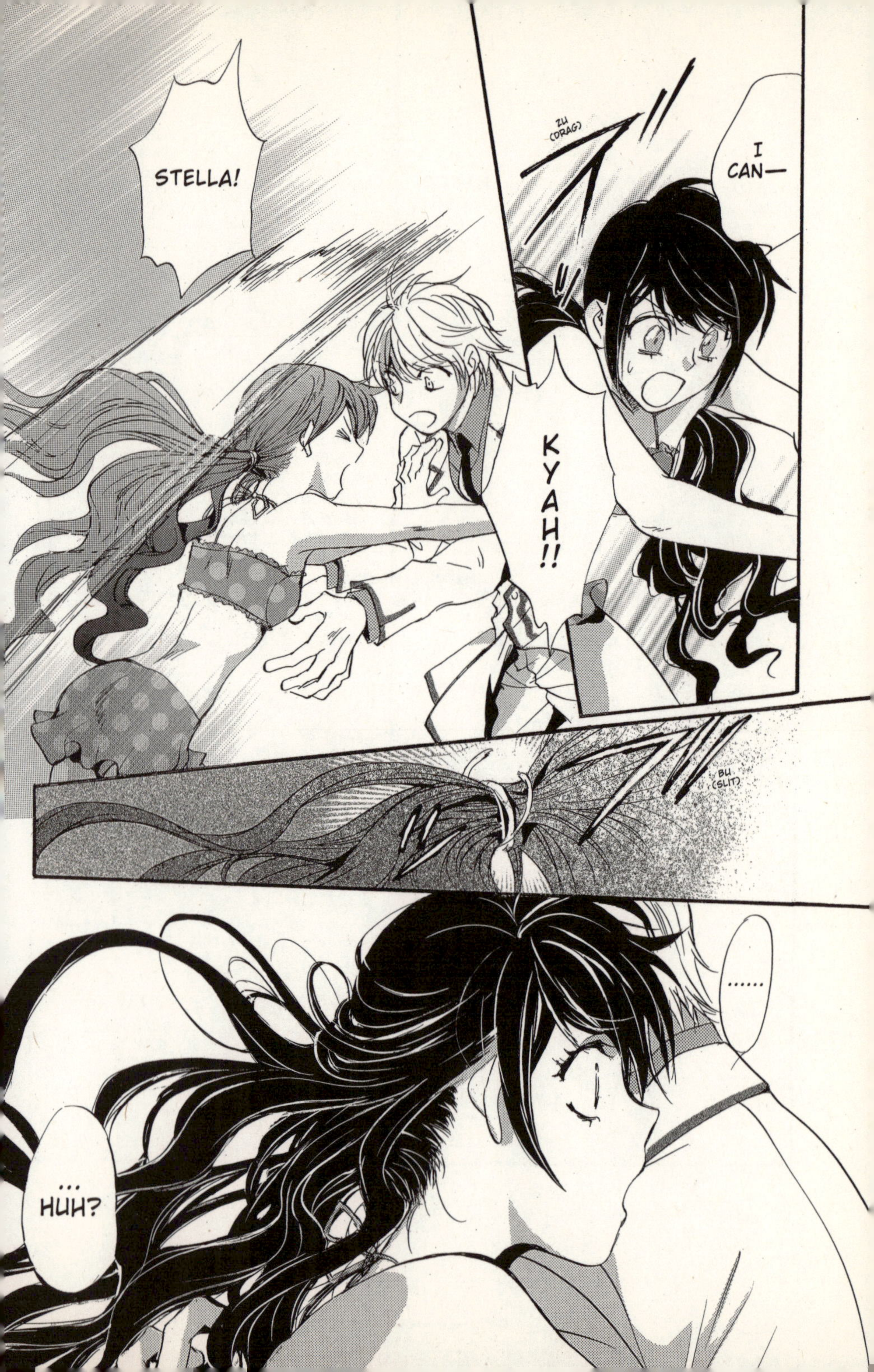
ZU (DRAG)
I CAN—
STELLA!
KYAH!!
BU (SLIT)
......
...HUH?

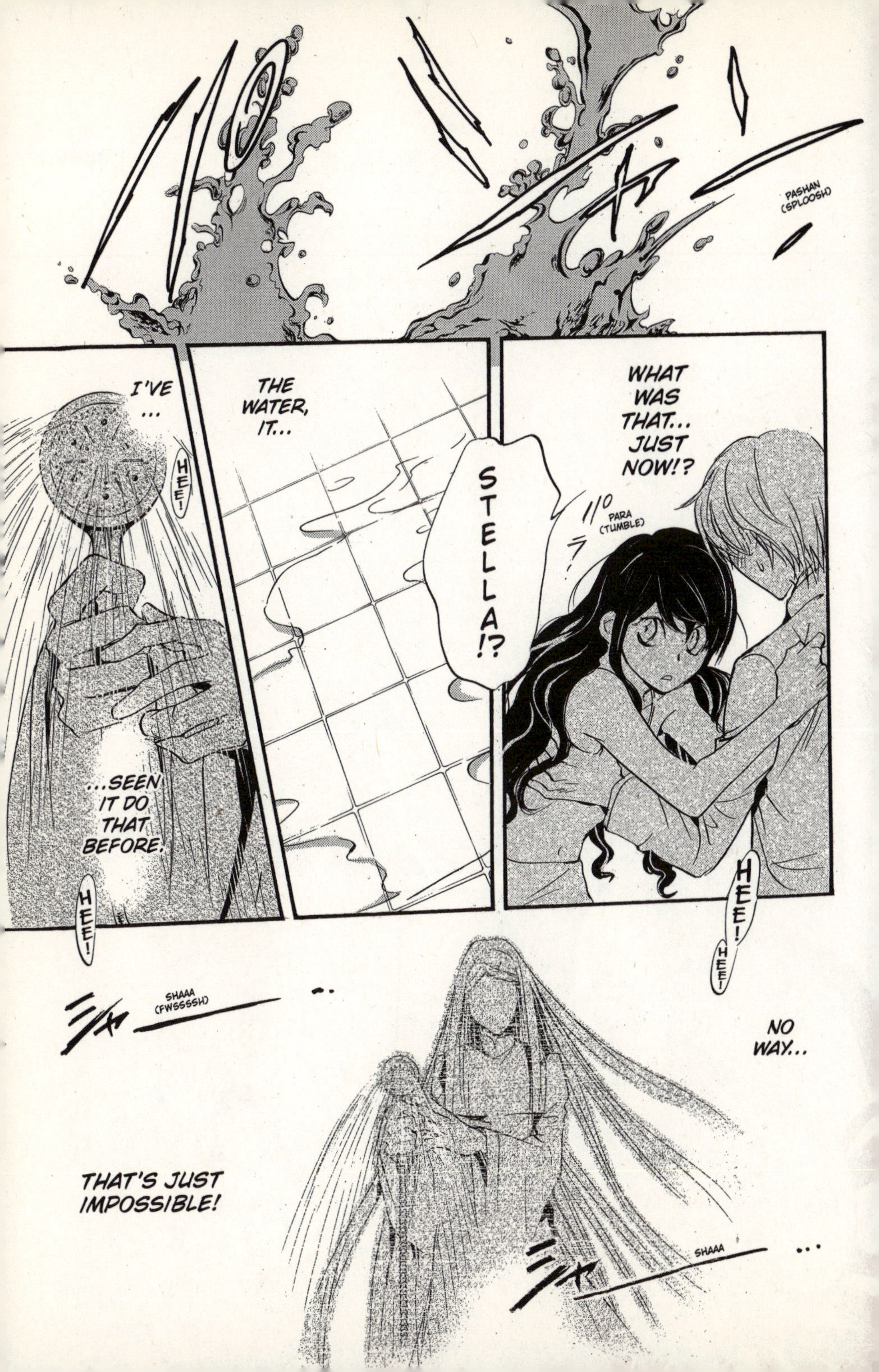
PASHAN (SPLOOSH)
WHAT WAS THAT... JUST NOW!?
STELLA!?
PARA (TUMBLE)
HEE! HEE!
THE WATER, IT...
I'VE ...
HEE!
...SEEN IT DO THAT BEFORE.
HEE!
NO WAY...
SHAAA (FWSSSSH)
THAT'S JUST IMPOSSIBLE!
SHAAA

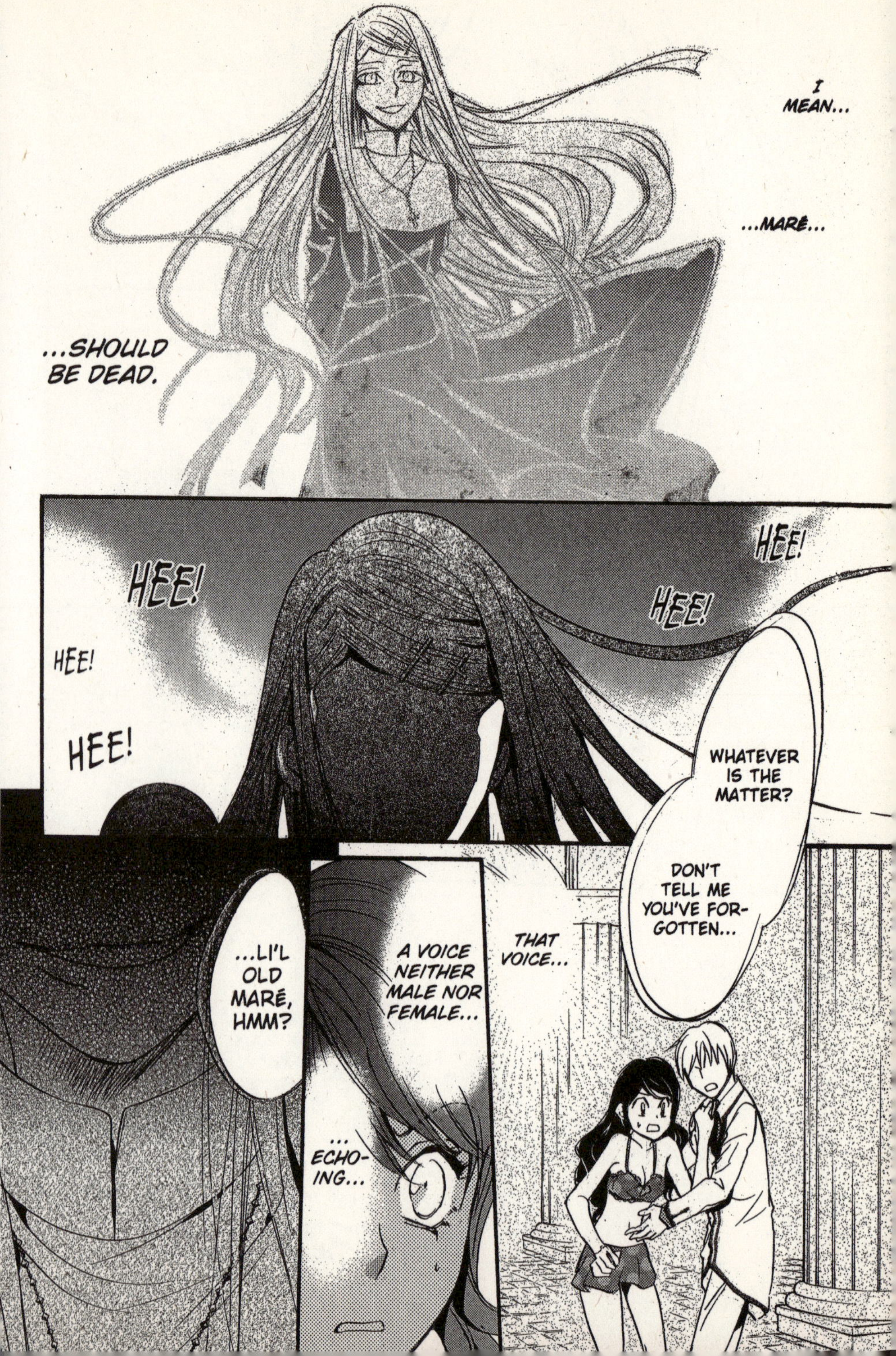
I MEAN...
...MARE...
...SHOULD BE DEAD.
HEE!
HEE!
HEE!
HEE!
HEE!
WHATEVER IS THE MATTER?
DON'T TELL ME YOU'VE FOR-GOTTEN...
THAT VOICE...
A VOICE NEITHER MALE NOR FEMALE...
...ECHO-ING...
...LI'L OLD MARÉ, HMM?

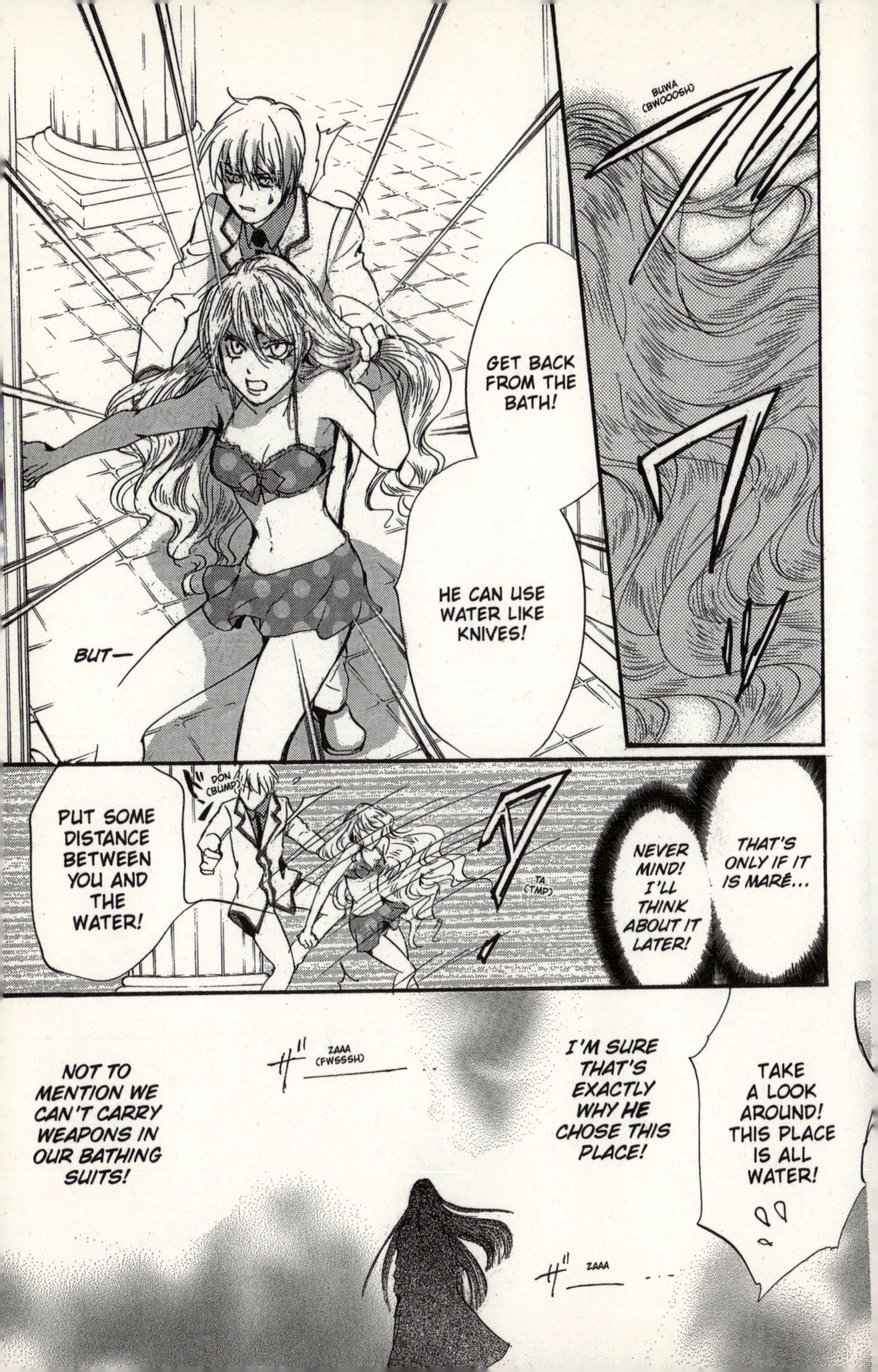
BUWA
(BWOOOSH)
GET BACK FROM THE BATH!
HE CAN USE WATER LIKE KNIVES!
BUT—
THAT'S ONLY IF IT IS MARÉ...
NEVER MIND! I'LL THINK ABOUT IT LATER!
TA
(TMP)
DON
(BUMP)
PUT SOME DISTANCE BETWEEN YOU AND THE WATER!
TAKE A LOOK AROUND! THIS PLACE IS ALL WATER!
I'M SURE THAT'S EXACTLY WHY HE CHOSE THIS PLACE!
ZAAA
(FWSSSH)
NOT TO MENTION WE CAN'T CARRY WEAPONS IN OUR BATHING SUITS!
ZAAA

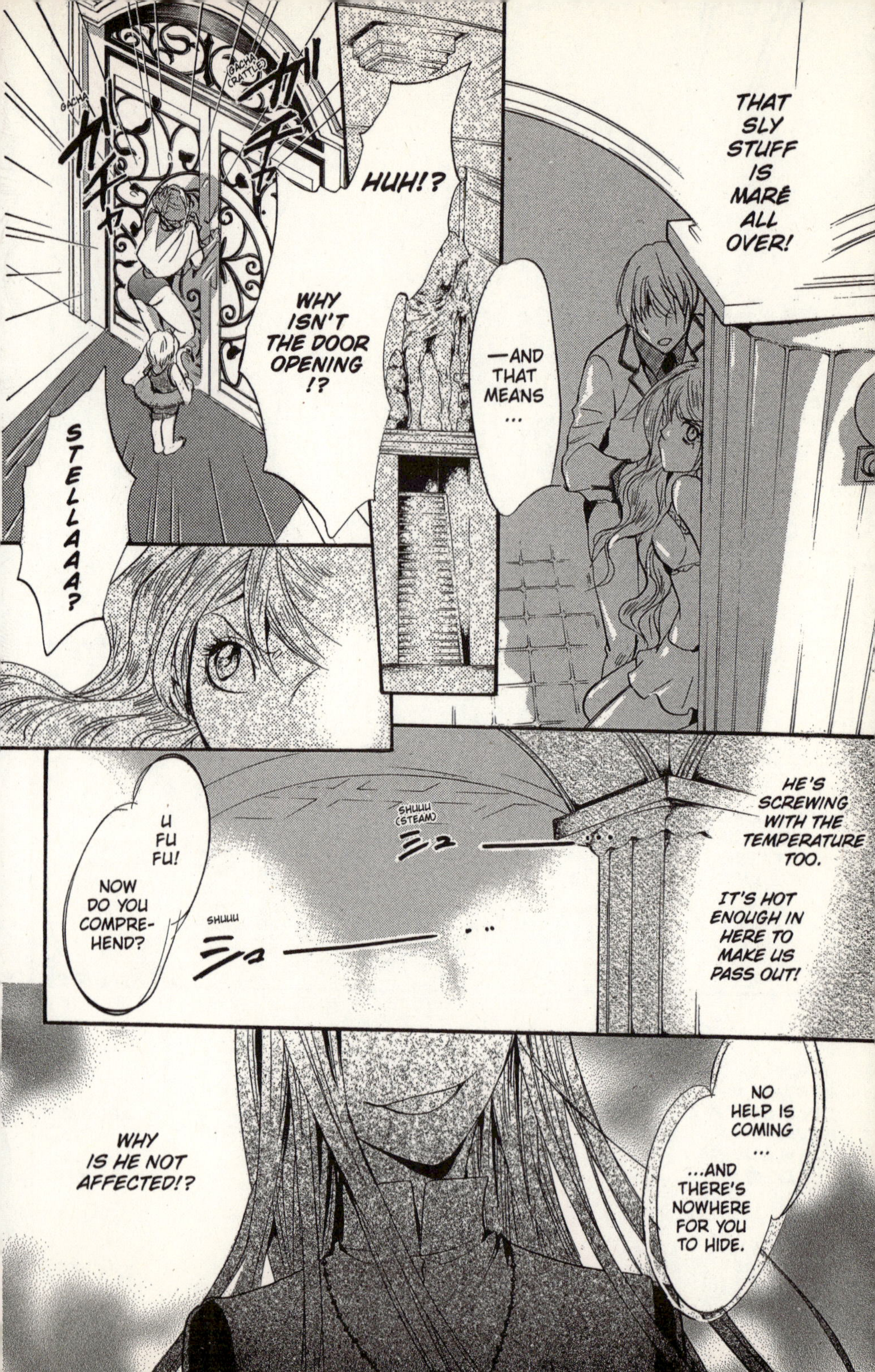
THAT SLY STUFF IS MARÉ ALL OVER!
—AND THAT MEANS...
GACHA (RATTLE)
GACHA
HUH!?
WHY ISN'T THE DOOR OPENING!?
STELLAAAA?
HE'S SCREWING WITH THE TEMPERATURE TOO.
IT'S HOT ENOUGH IN HERE TO MAKE US PASS OUT!
SHUUU (STEAM)
SHUUU
U FU FU!
NOW DO YOU COMPREHEND?
NO HELP IS COMING...
...AND THERE'S NOWHERE FOR YOU TO HIDE.
WHY IS HE NOT AFFECTED!?

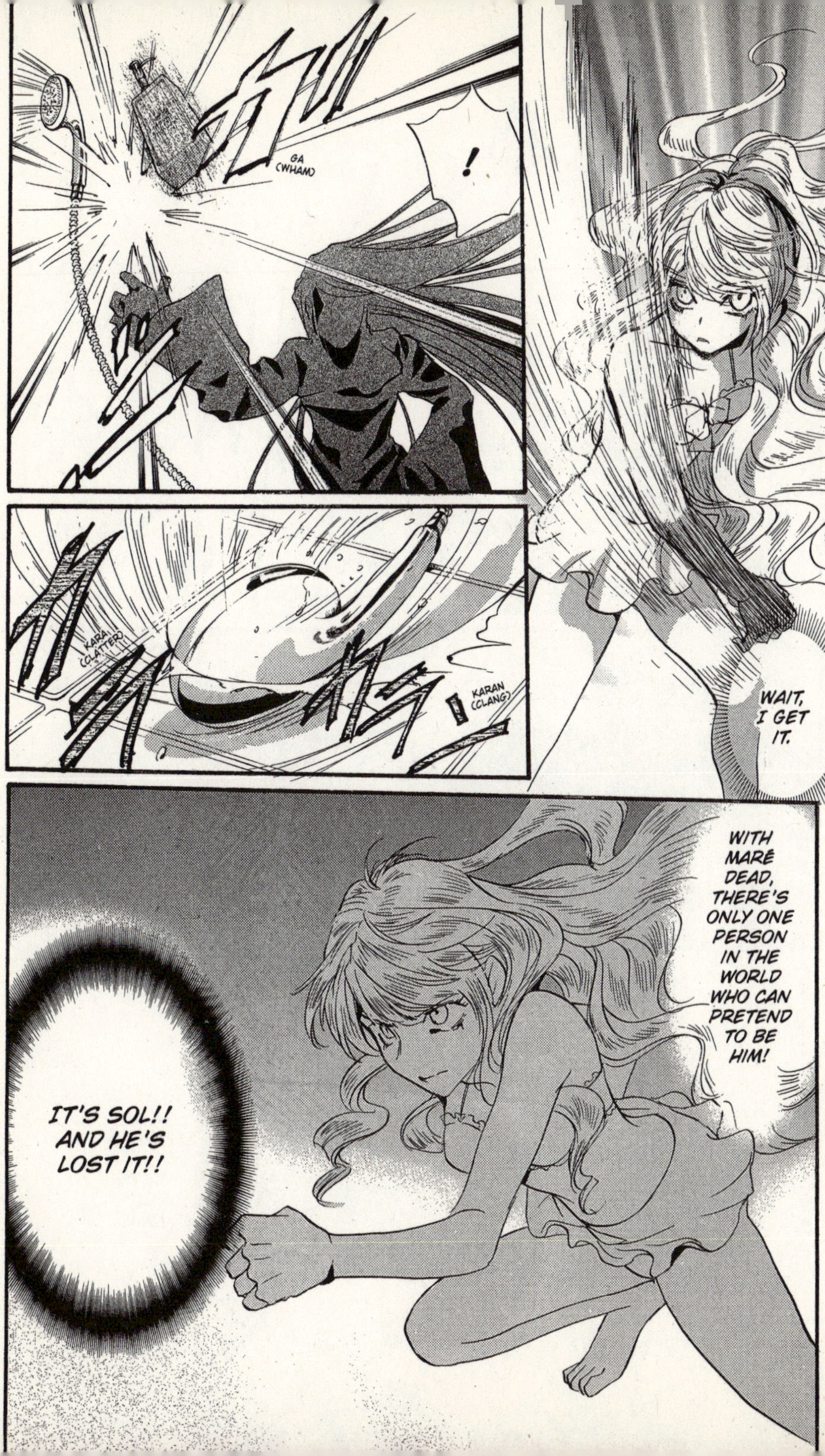
WAIT, I GET IT.
GA (WHAM)
!
KARA (CLATTER)
KARAN (CLANG)
WITH MARE DEAD, THERE'S ONLY ONE PERSON IN THE WORLD WHO CAN PRETEND TO BE HIM!
IT'S SOL!! AND HE'S LOST IT!!

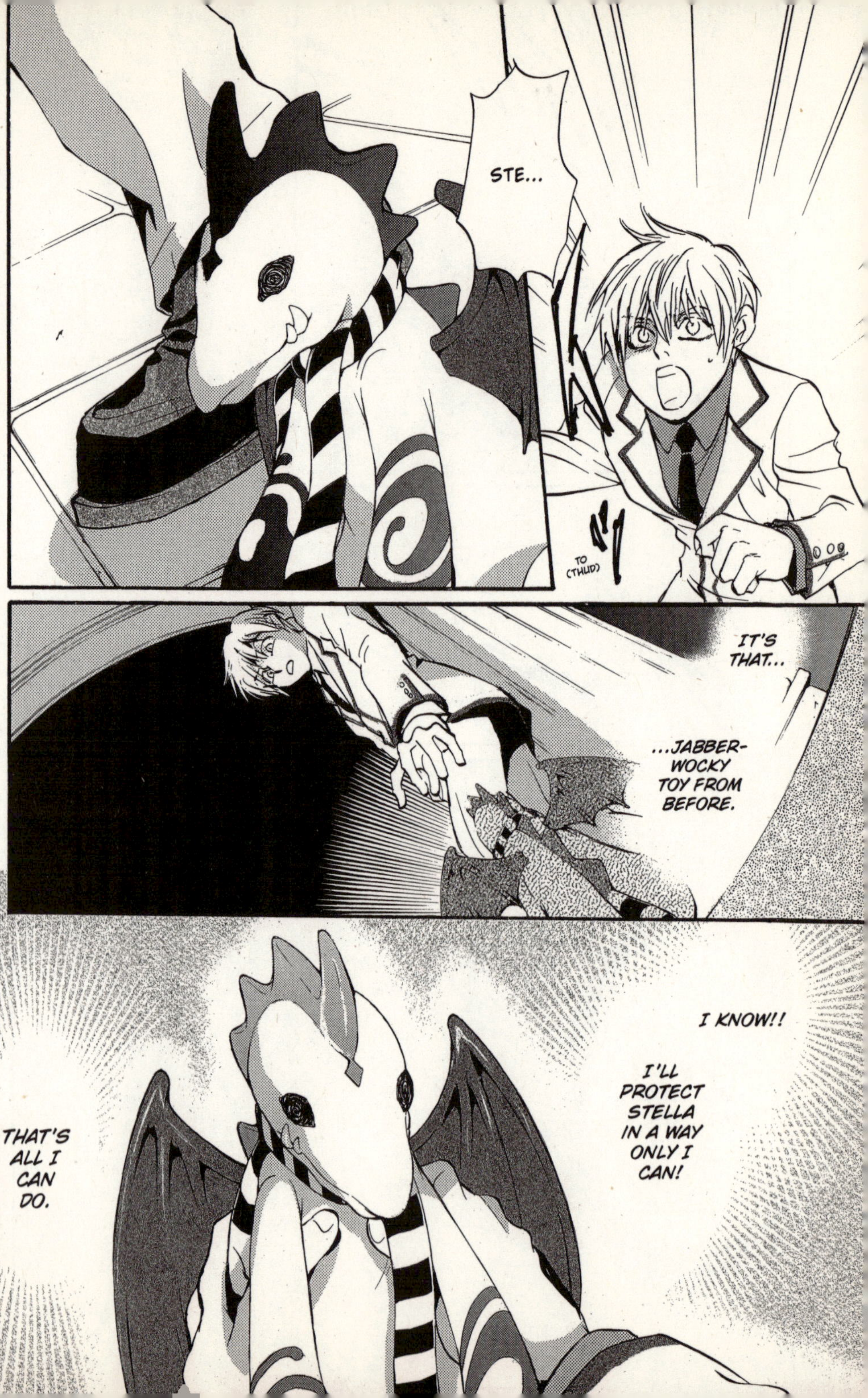
STE...
TO
(THUD)
IT'S THAT...
...JABBER-WOCKY TOY FROM BEFORE.
I KNOW!!
I'LL PROTECT STELLA IN A WAY ONLY I CAN!
THAT'S ALL I CAN DO.

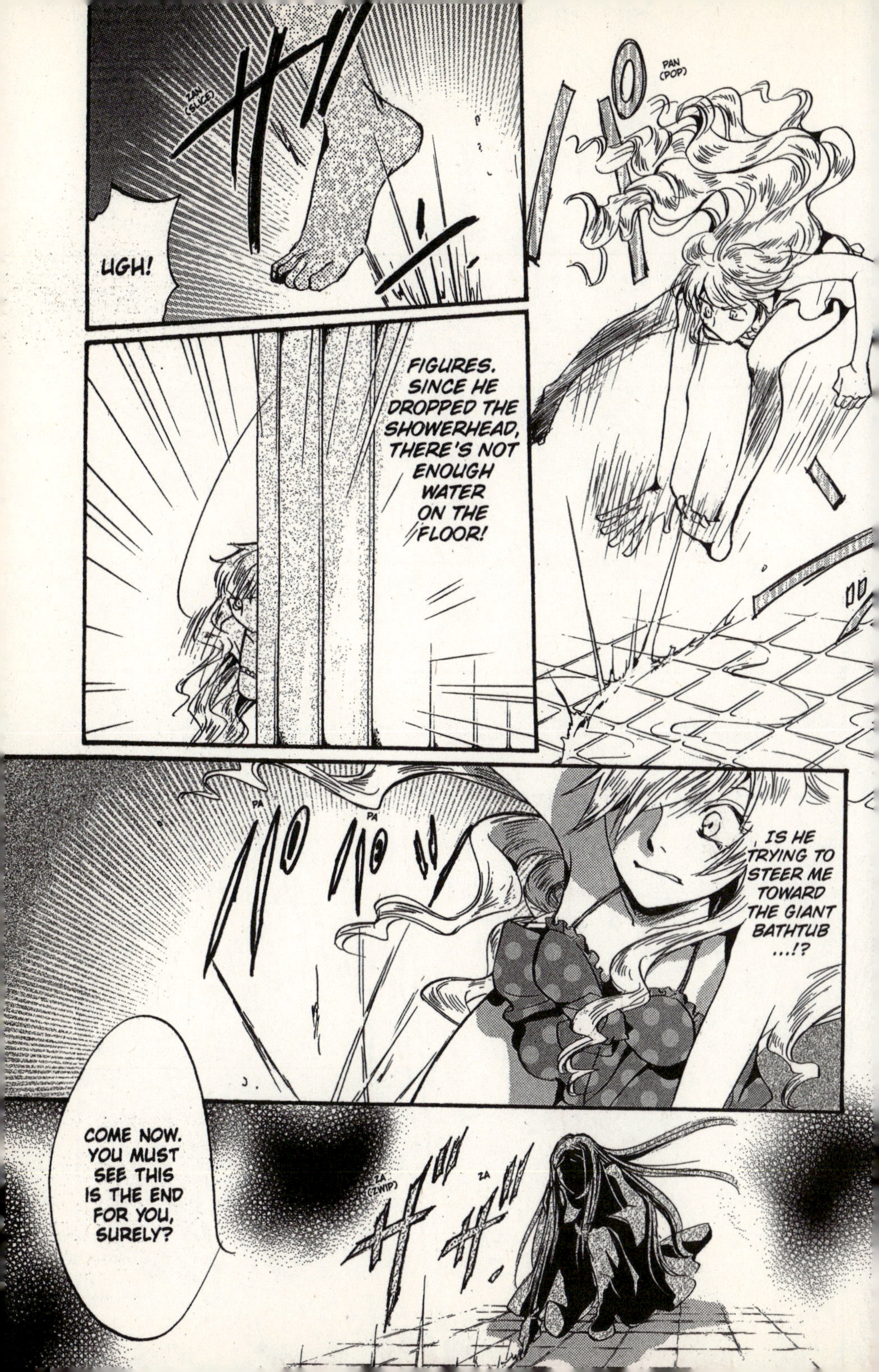
PAN (POP)
ZAN (SLICE)
UGH!
FIGURES. SINCE HE DROPPED THE SHOWERHEAD, THERE'S NOT ENOUGH WATER ON THE FLOOR!
PA
PA
IS HE TRYING TO STEER ME TOWARD THE GIANT BATHTUB ...!?
ZA
ZA (ZWIP)
COME NOW. YOU MUST SEE THIS IS THE END FOR YOU, SURELY?

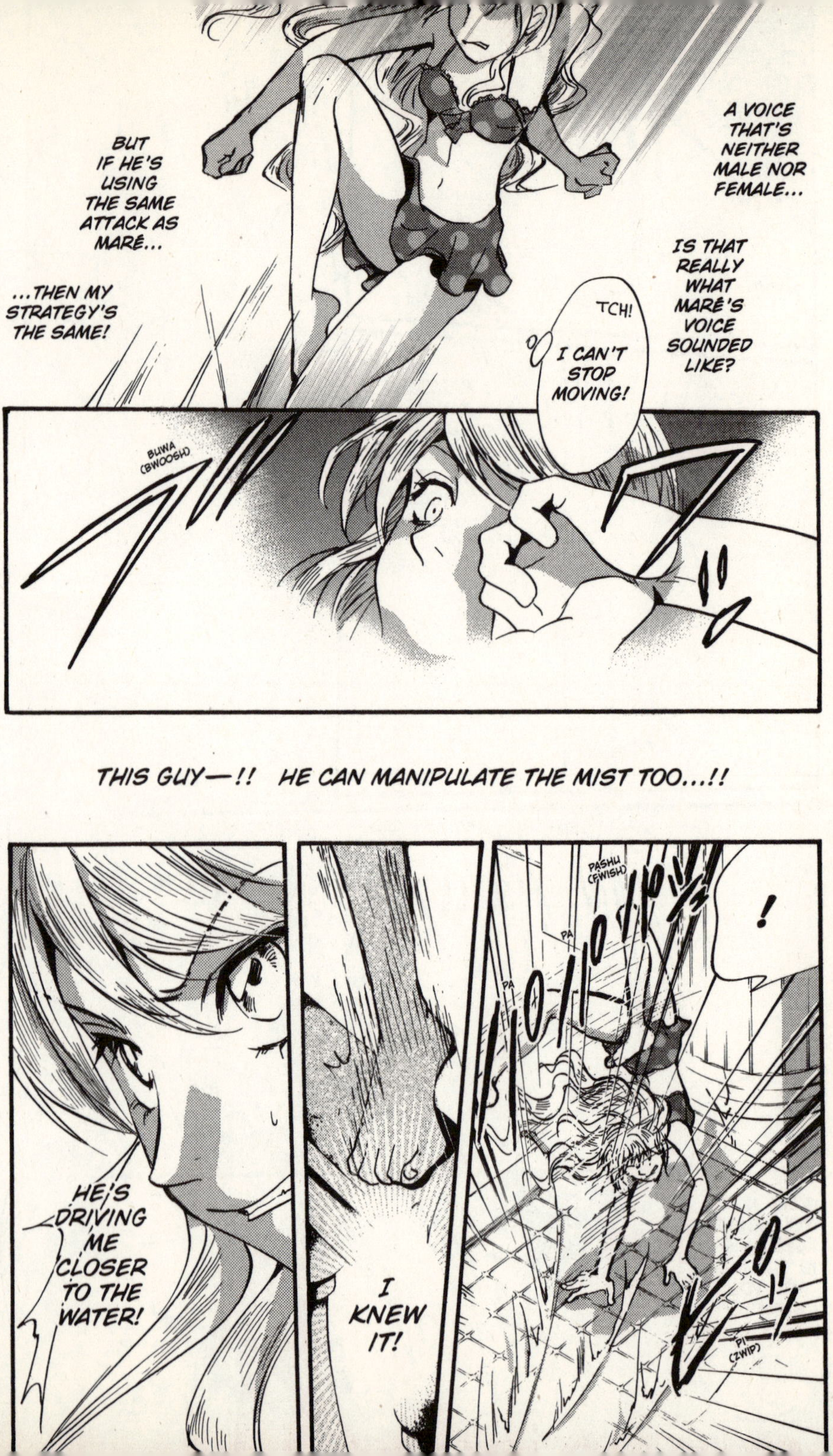
A VOICE THAT'S NEITHER MALE NOR FEMALE...
IS THAT REALLY WHAT MARÉ'S VOICE SOUNDED LIKE?
TCH! I CAN'T STOP MOVING!
BUT IF HE'S USING THE SAME ATTACK AS MARÉ...
...THEN MY STRATEGY'S THE SAME!
BUWA (BWOOSH)
THIS GUY—!! HE CAN MANIPULATE THE MIST TOO...!!
!
PASHU (FWISH)
PA
PA
PI (ZWIP)
I KNEW IT!
HE'S DRIVING ME CLOSER TO THE WATER!

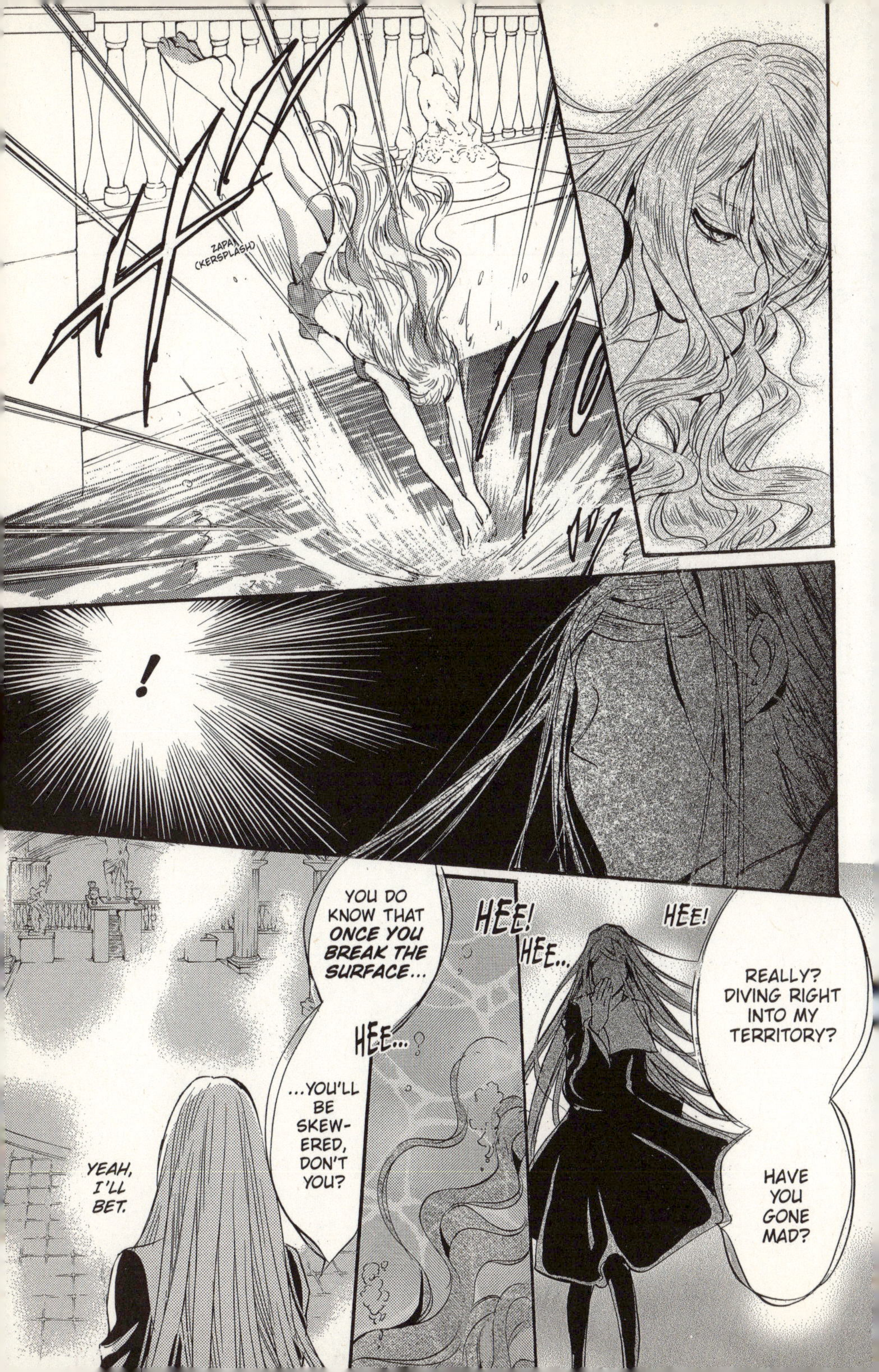
ZAPA (KERSPLASH)
!
HEE!
REALLY? DIVING RIGHT INTO MY TERRITORY?
HAVE YOU GONE MAD?
HEE! HEE...
HEE...
YOU DO KNOW THAT ONCE YOU BREAK THE SURFACE...
...YOU'LL BE SKEWERED, DON'T YOU?
YEAH, I'LL BET.

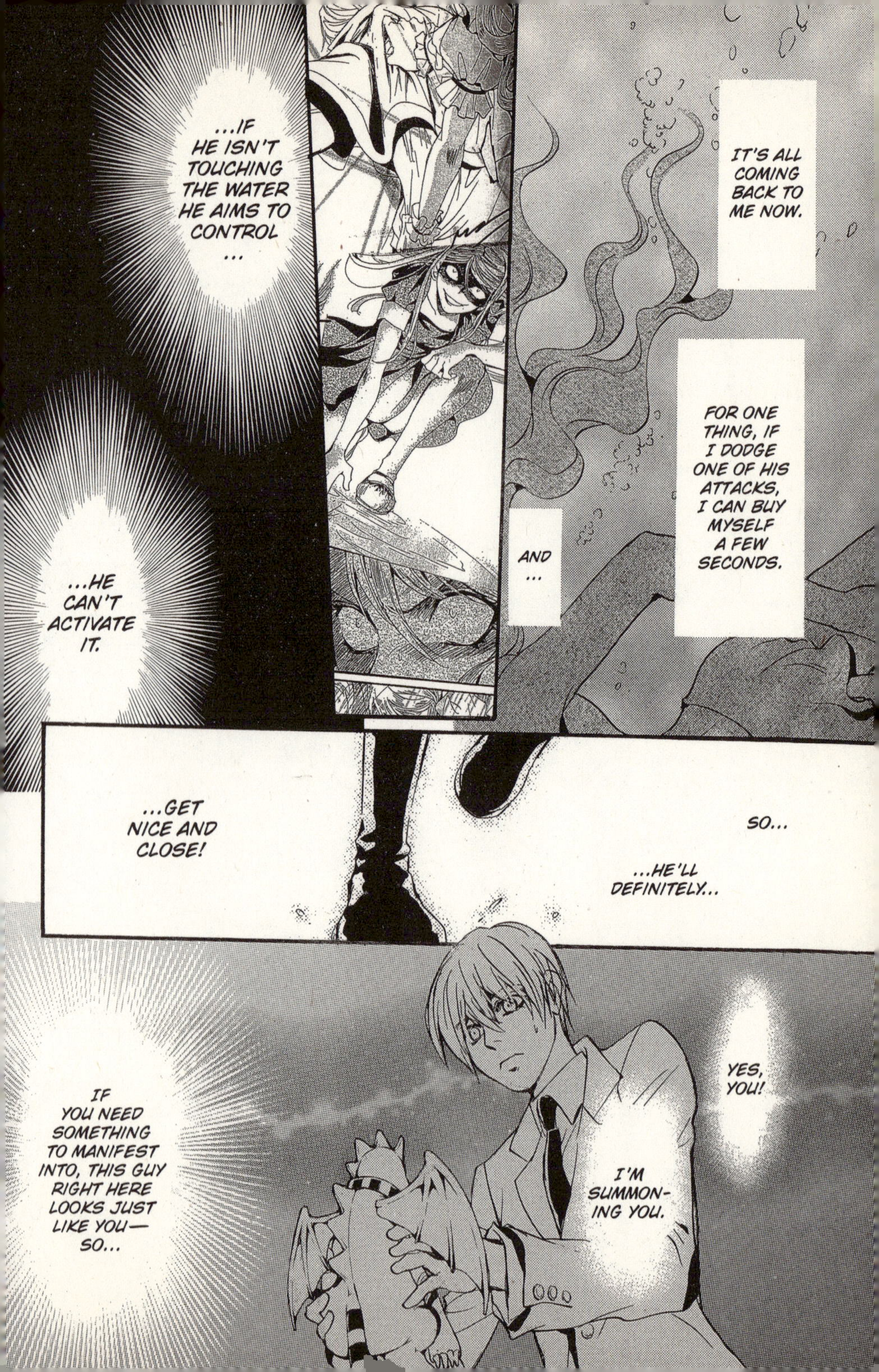
IT'S ALL COMING BACK TO ME NOW.
FOR ONE THING, IF I DODGE ONE OF HIS ATTACKS, I CAN BUY MYSELF A FEW SECONDS.
AND...
...IF HE ISN'T TOUCHING THE WATER HE AIMS TO CONTROL...
...HE CAN'T ACTIVATE IT.
SO...
...HE'LL DEFINITELY...
...GET NICE AND CLOSE!
YES, YOU!
I'M SUMMON-ING YOU.
IF YOU NEED SOMETHING TO MANIFEST INTO, THIS GUY RIGHT HERE LOOKS JUST LIKE YOU—SO...

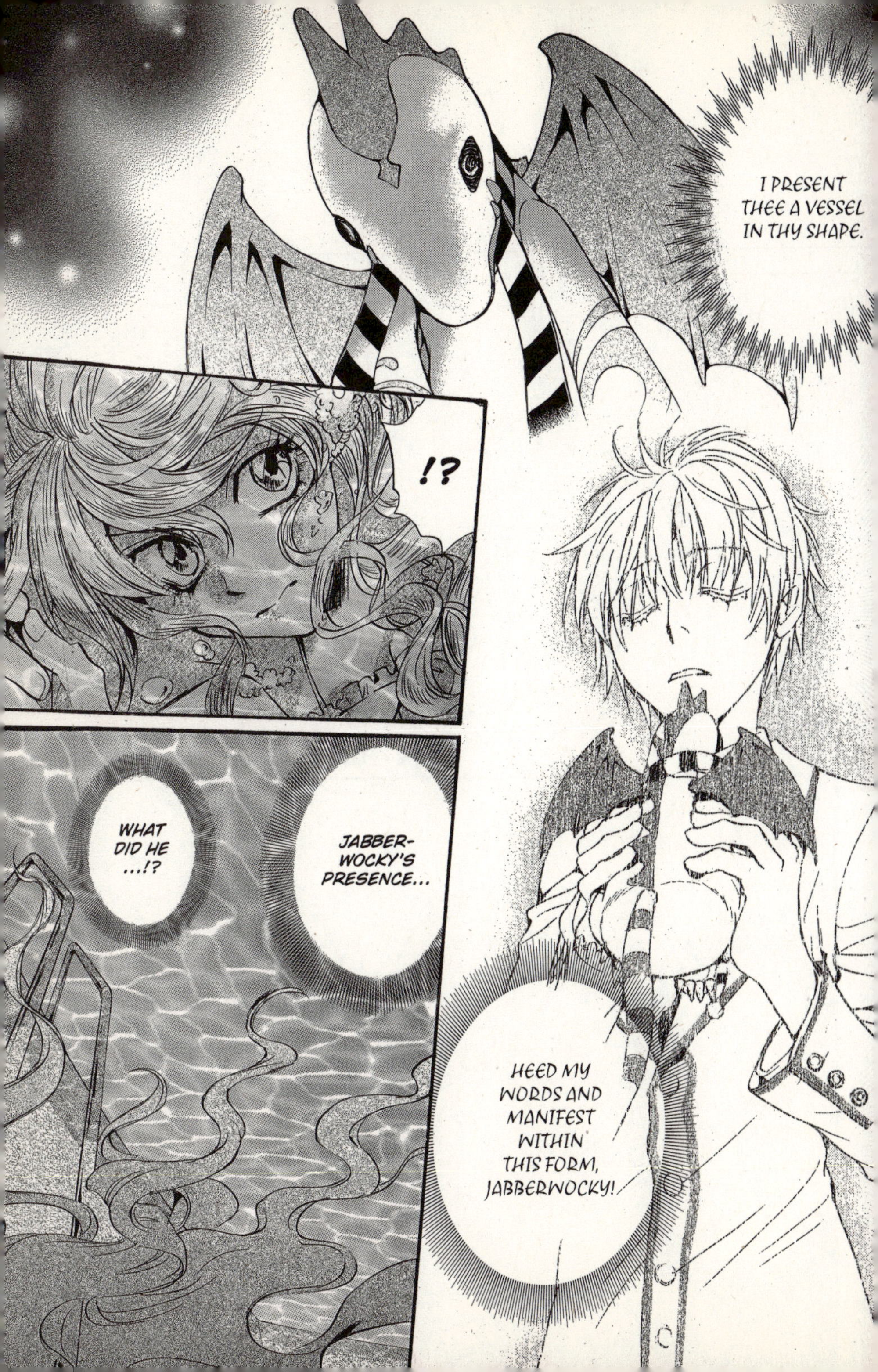
I PRESENT THEE A VESSEL IN THY SHAPE.
HEED MY WORDS AND MANIFEST WITHIN THIS FORM, JABBERWOCKY!
!?
JABBER-WOCKY'S PRESENCE...
WHAT DID HE ...!?

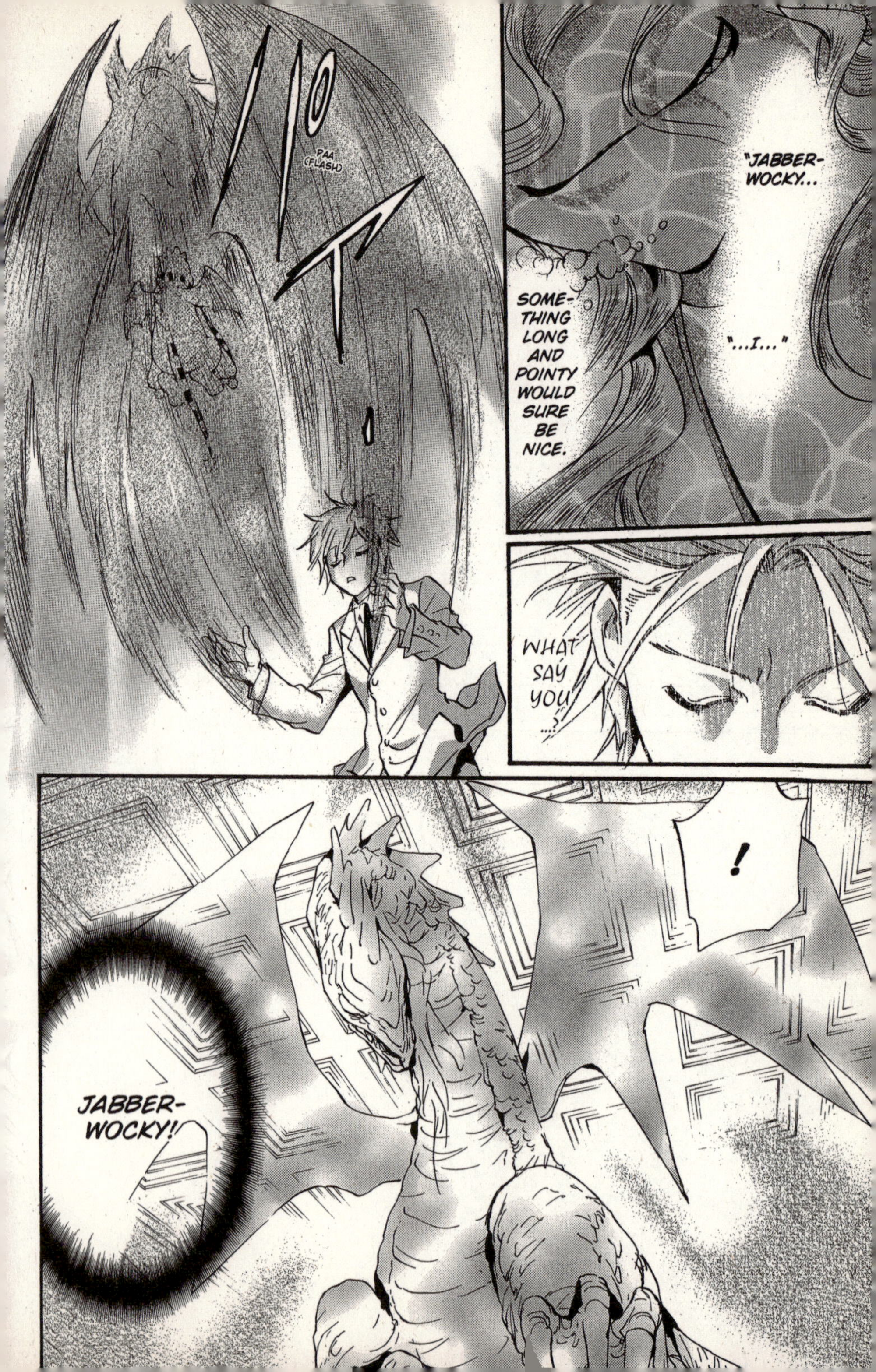
"JABBER-WOCKY...
"...I..."
SOME-THING LONG AND POINTY WOULD SURE BE NICE.
WHAT SAY YOU...?
PAA (FLASH)
!
JABBER-WOCKY!!

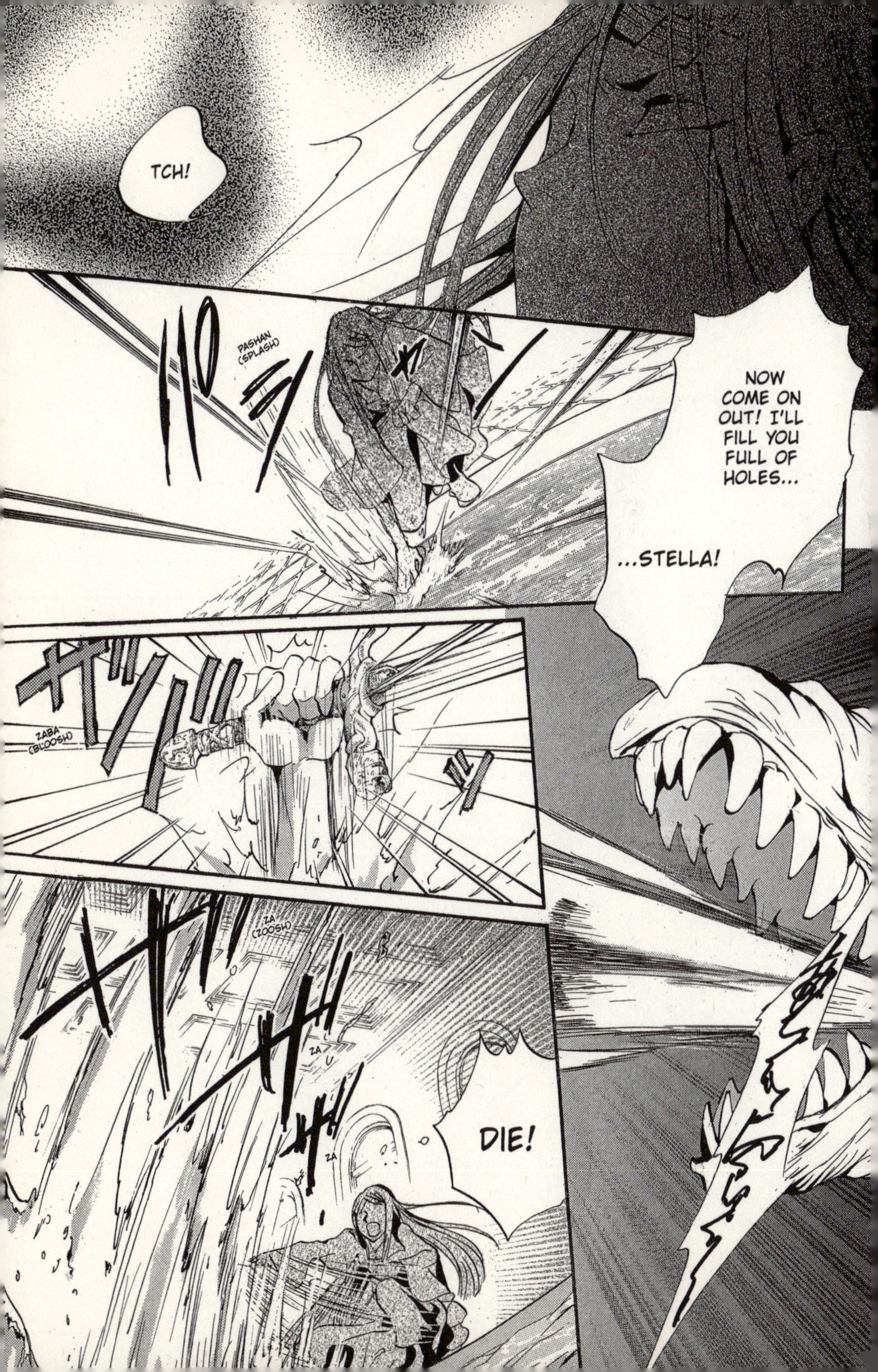
TCH!
NOW COME ON OUT! I'LL FILL YOU FULL OF HOLES...
...STELLA!
PASHAN (SPLASH)
ZABA (BLOOSH)
ZA (ZOOSH)
ZA
DIE!
ZA

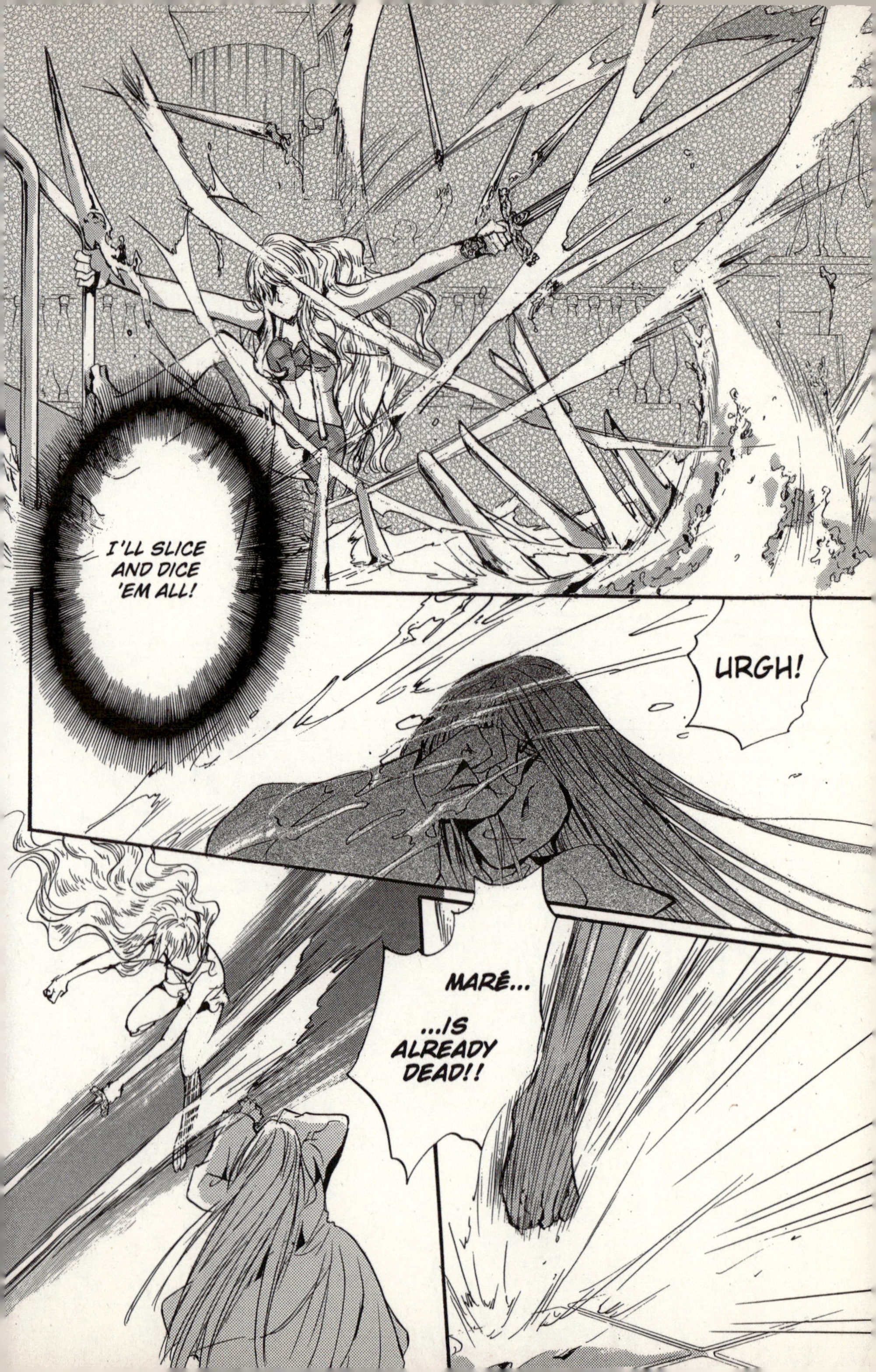
I'LL SLICE AND DICE 'EM ALL!
URGH!
MARÉ...
...IS ALREADY DEAD!!

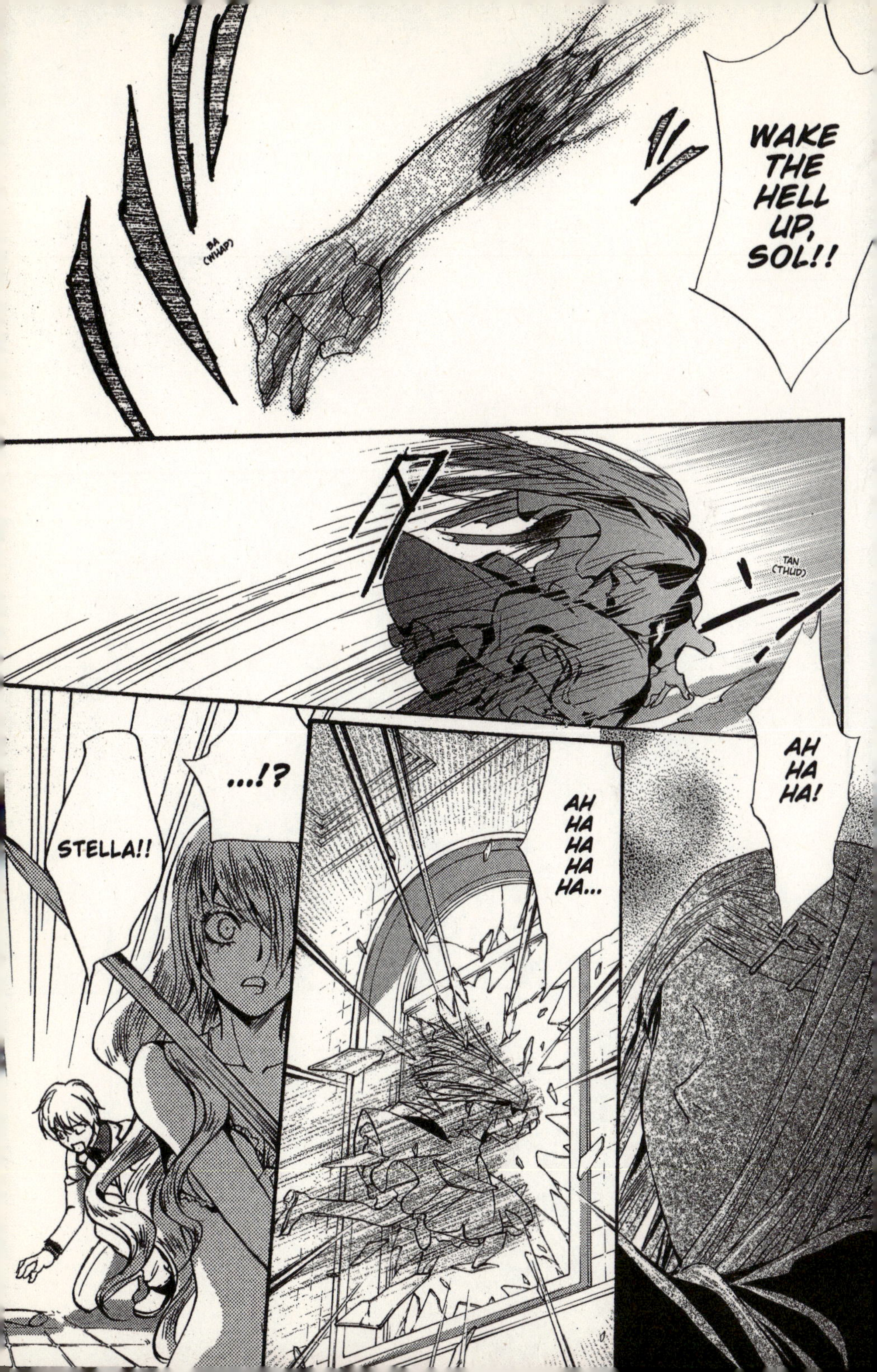
WAKE THE HELL UP, SOL!!
BA (WHAP)
TAN (THUD)
AH HA HA!
AH HA HA HA HA...
...!?
STELLA!!

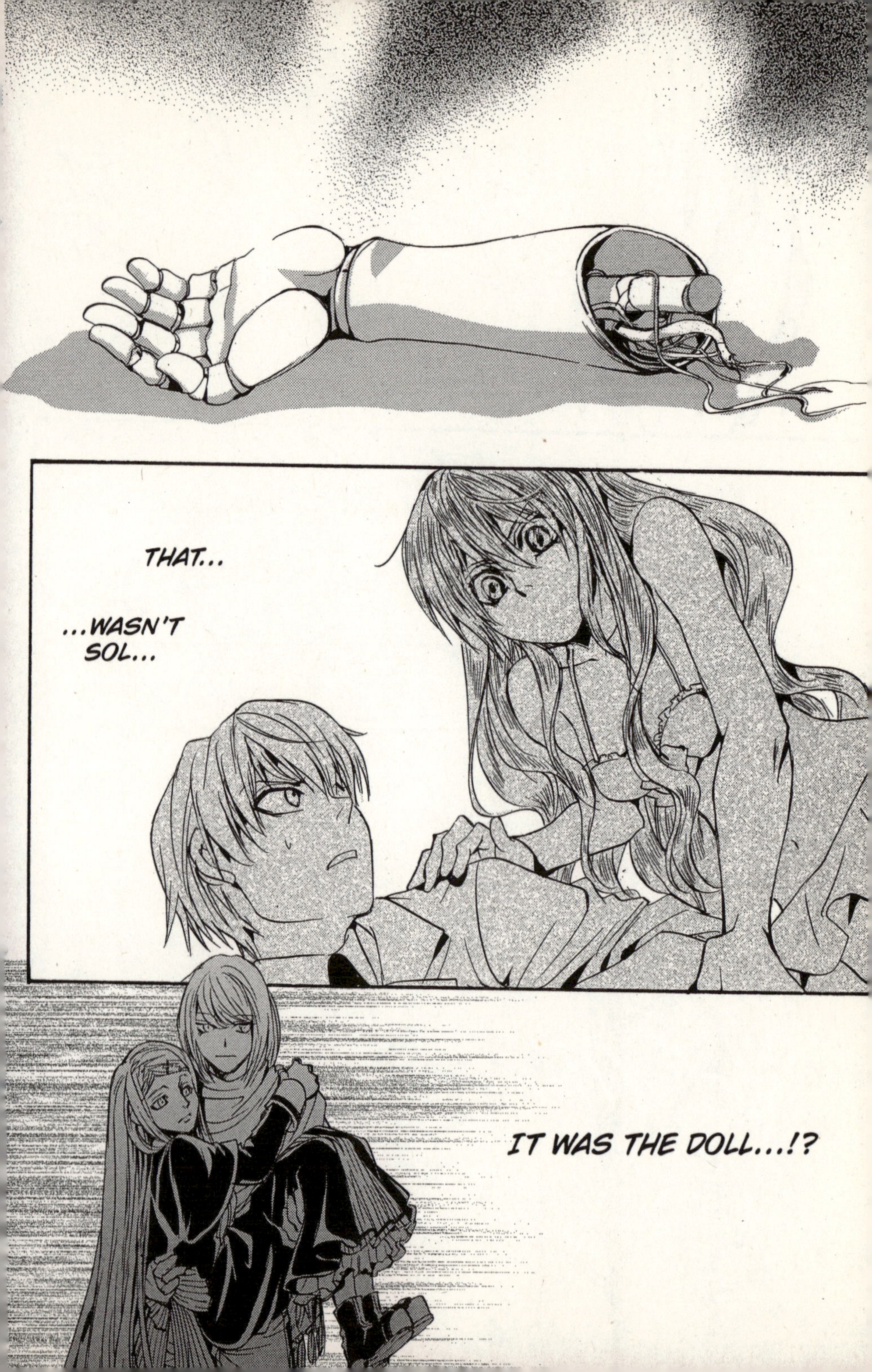
THAT...
...WASN'T SOL...
IT WAS THE DOLL...!?

Alice in MURDERLAND

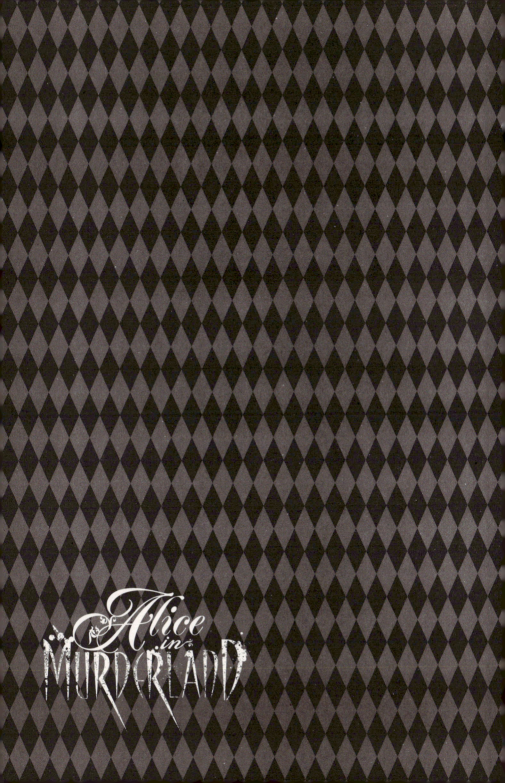

Alice in MURDERLAND

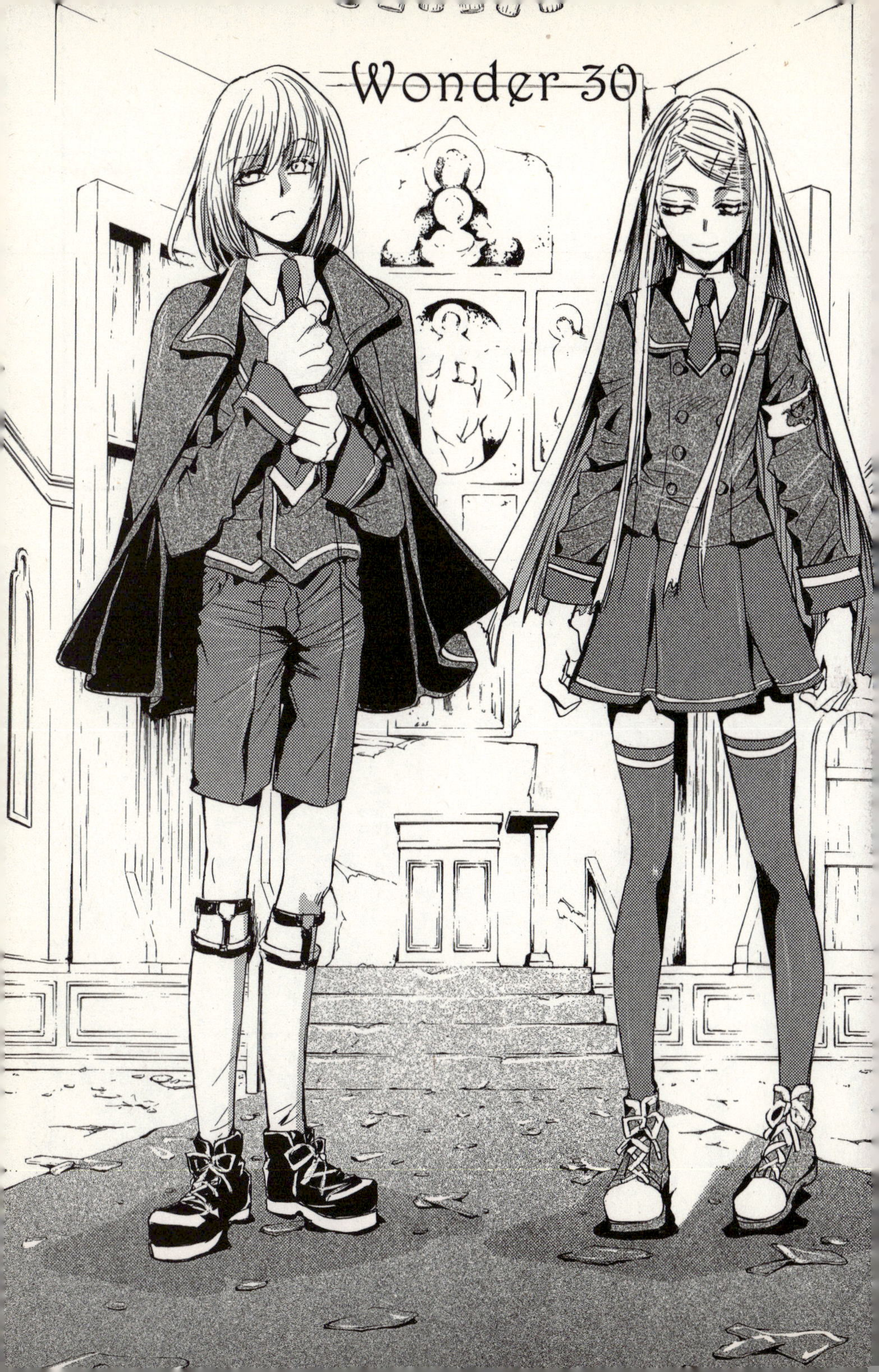
Wonder 30

THIS...

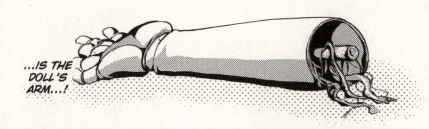

...IS THE DOLL'S ARM...!

SO THAT...

...WAS THE DOLL OF MARÉ ......!?

NO WAY ......!!

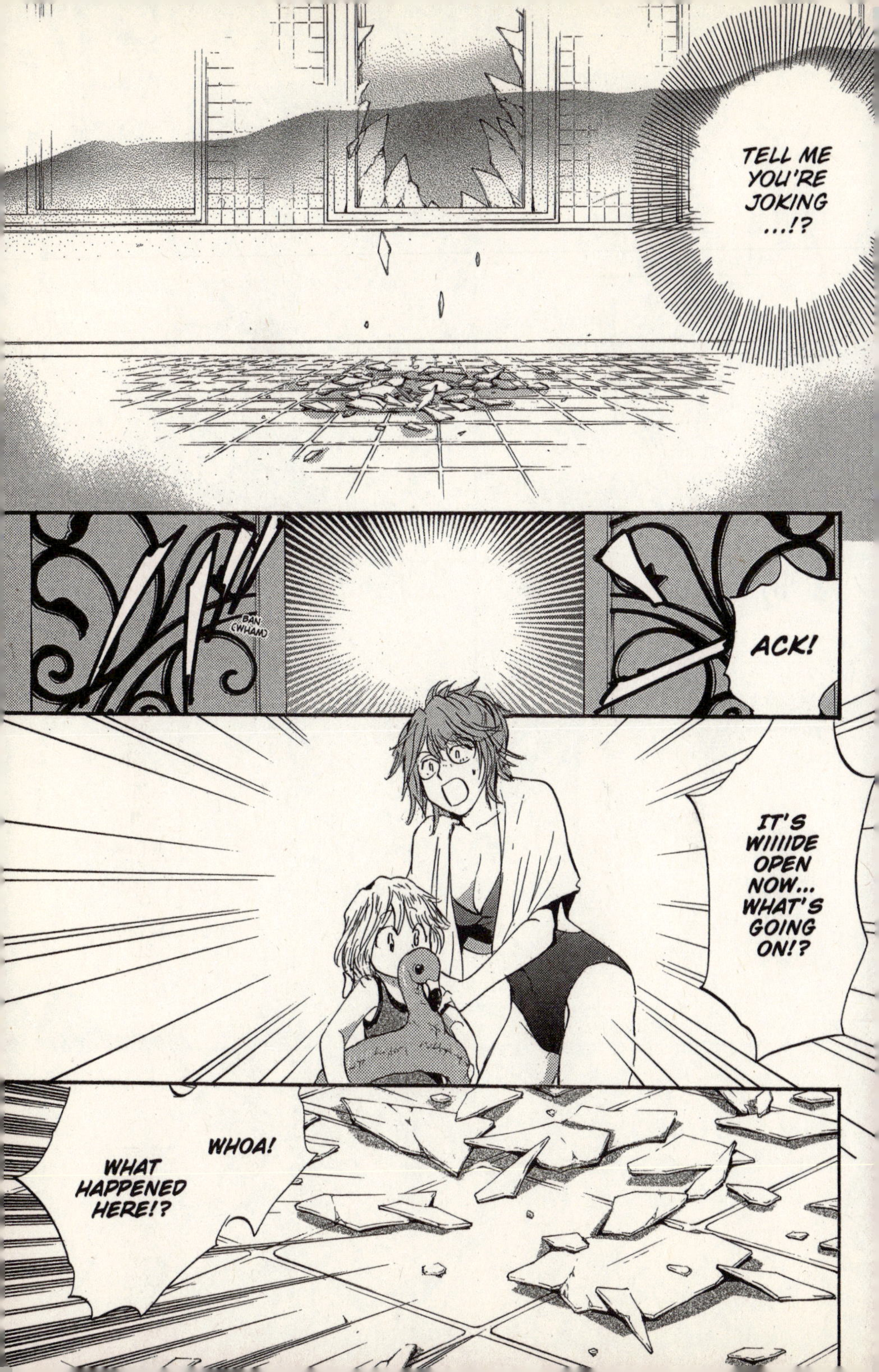
TELL ME YOU'RE JOKING ...!?
ACK!
BAN (WHAM)
IT'S WIIIIDE OPEN NOW... WHAT'S GOING ON!?
WHOA!
WHAT HAPPENED HERE!?

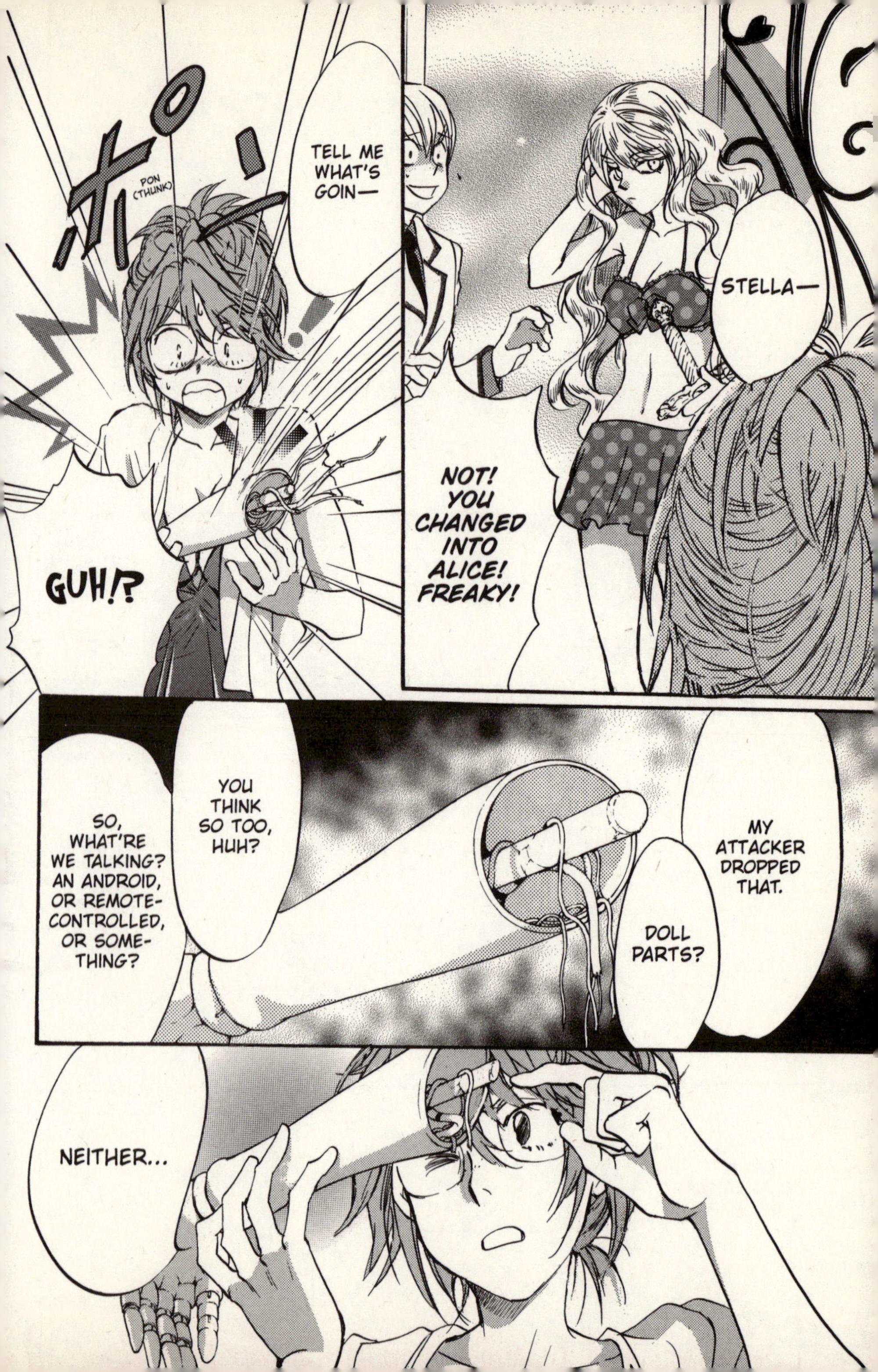
STELLA—
NOT! YOU CHANGED INTO ALICE! FREAKY!
TELL ME WHAT'S GOIN—
PON (THUNK)
GUH!?
MY ATTACKER DROPPED THAT.
DOLL PARTS?
YOU THINK SO TOO, HUH?
SO, WHAT'RE WE TALKING? AN ANDROID, OR REMOTE-CONTROLLED, OR SOME-THING?
NEITHER...

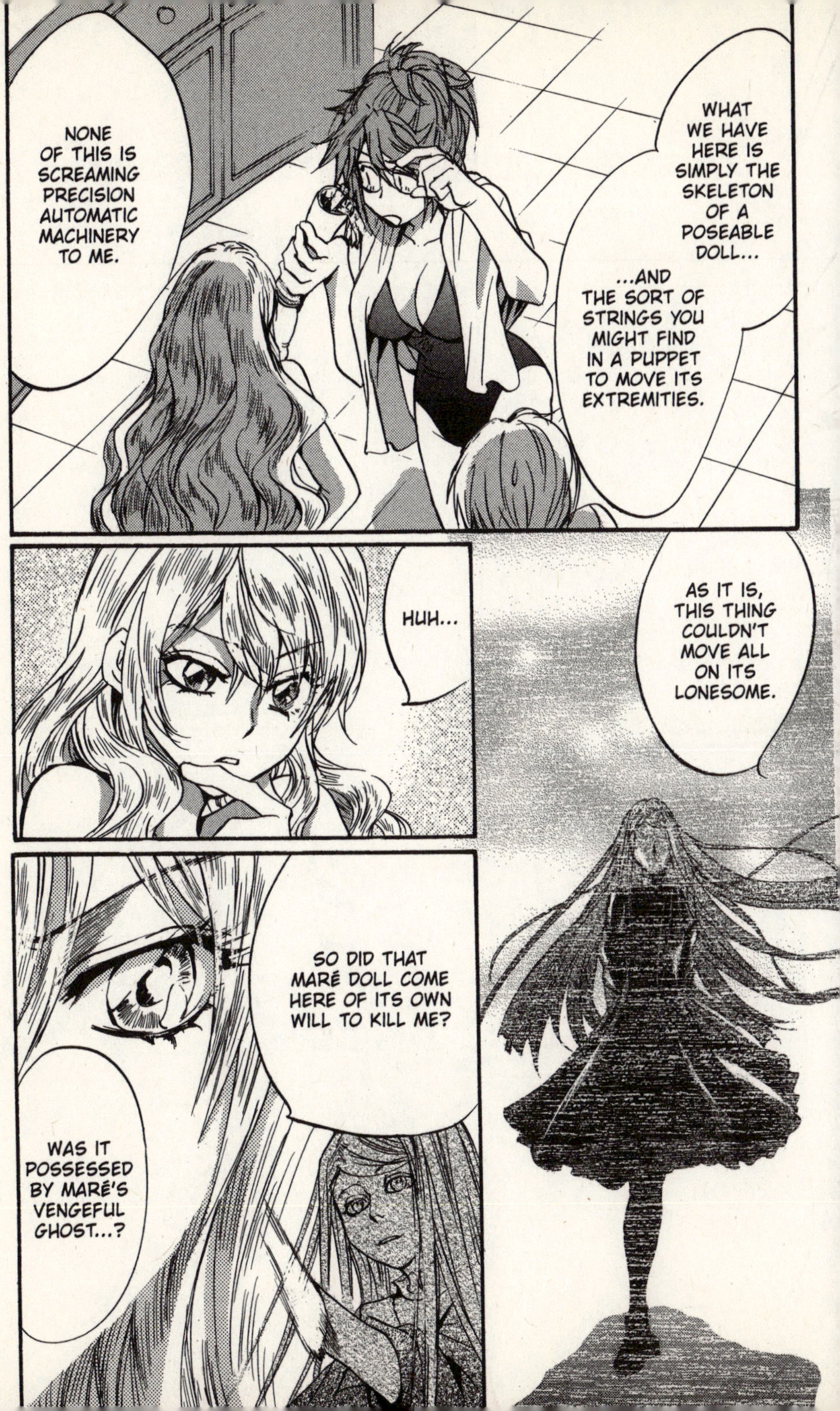
WHAT WE HAVE HERE IS SIMPLY THE SKELETON OF A POSEABLE DOLL...
...AND THE SORT OF STRINGS YOU MIGHT FIND IN A PUPPET TO MOVE ITS EXTREMITIES.
NONE OF THIS IS SCREAMING PRECISION AUTOMATIC MACHINERY TO ME.
AS IT IS, THIS THING COULDN'T MOVE ALL ON ITS LONESOME.
HUH...
SO DID THAT MARÉ DOLL COME HERE OF ITS OWN WILL TO KILL ME?
WAS IT POSSESSED BY MARÉ'S VENGEFUL GHOST...?

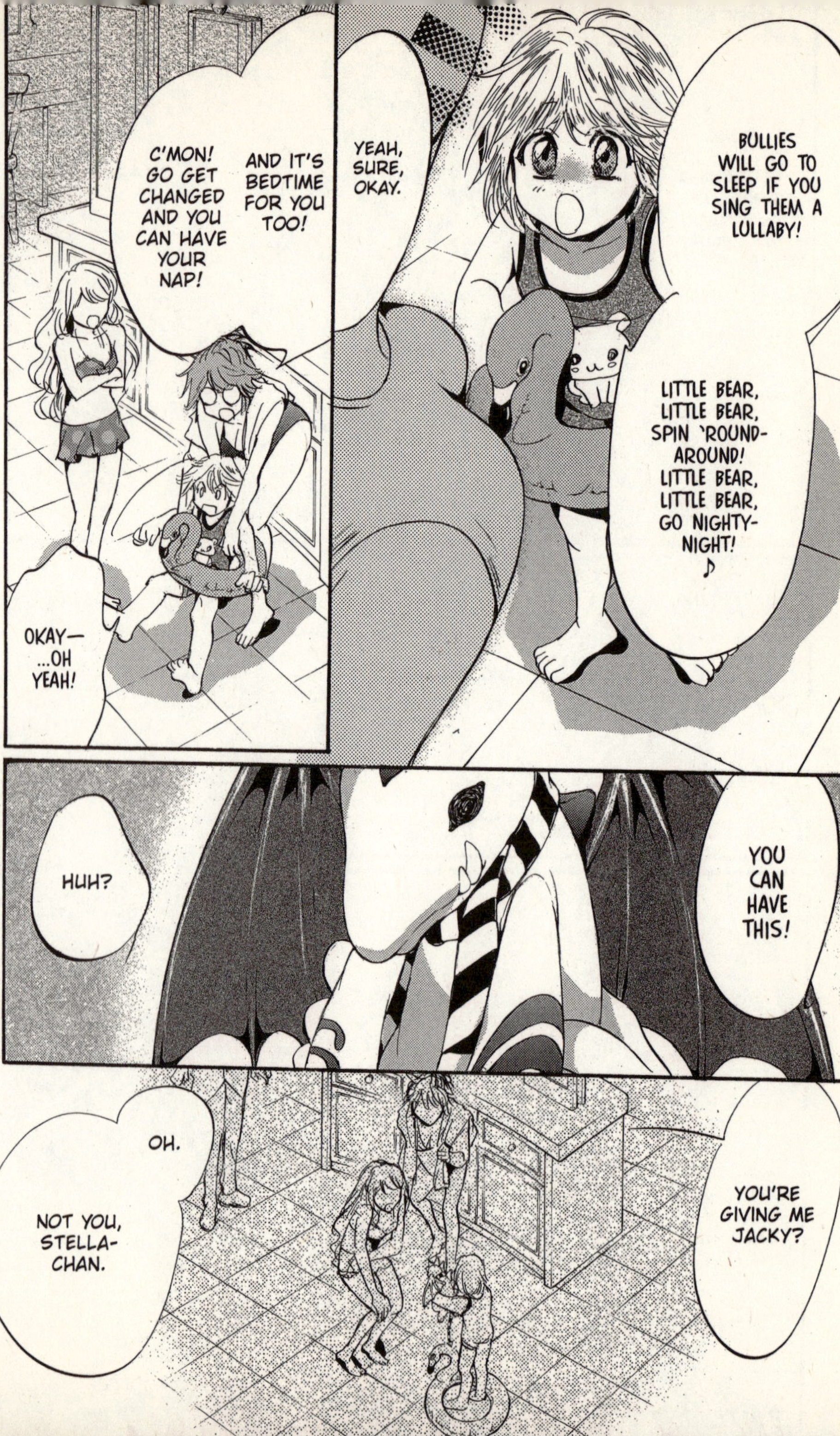
BULLIES WILL GO TO SLEEP IF YOU SING THEM A LULLABY!
YEAH, SURE, OKAY.
LITTLE BEAR, LITTLE BEAR, SPIN 'ROUND-AROUND! LITTLE BEAR, LITTLE BEAR, GO NIGHTY-NIGHT! ♪
C'MON! GO GET CHANGED AND YOU CAN HAVE YOUR NAP!
AND IT'S BEDTIME FOR YOU TOO!
OKAY— ...OH YEAH!
YOU CAN HAVE THIS!
HUH?
YOU'RE GIVING ME JACKY?
OH.
NOT YOU, STELLA-CHAN.

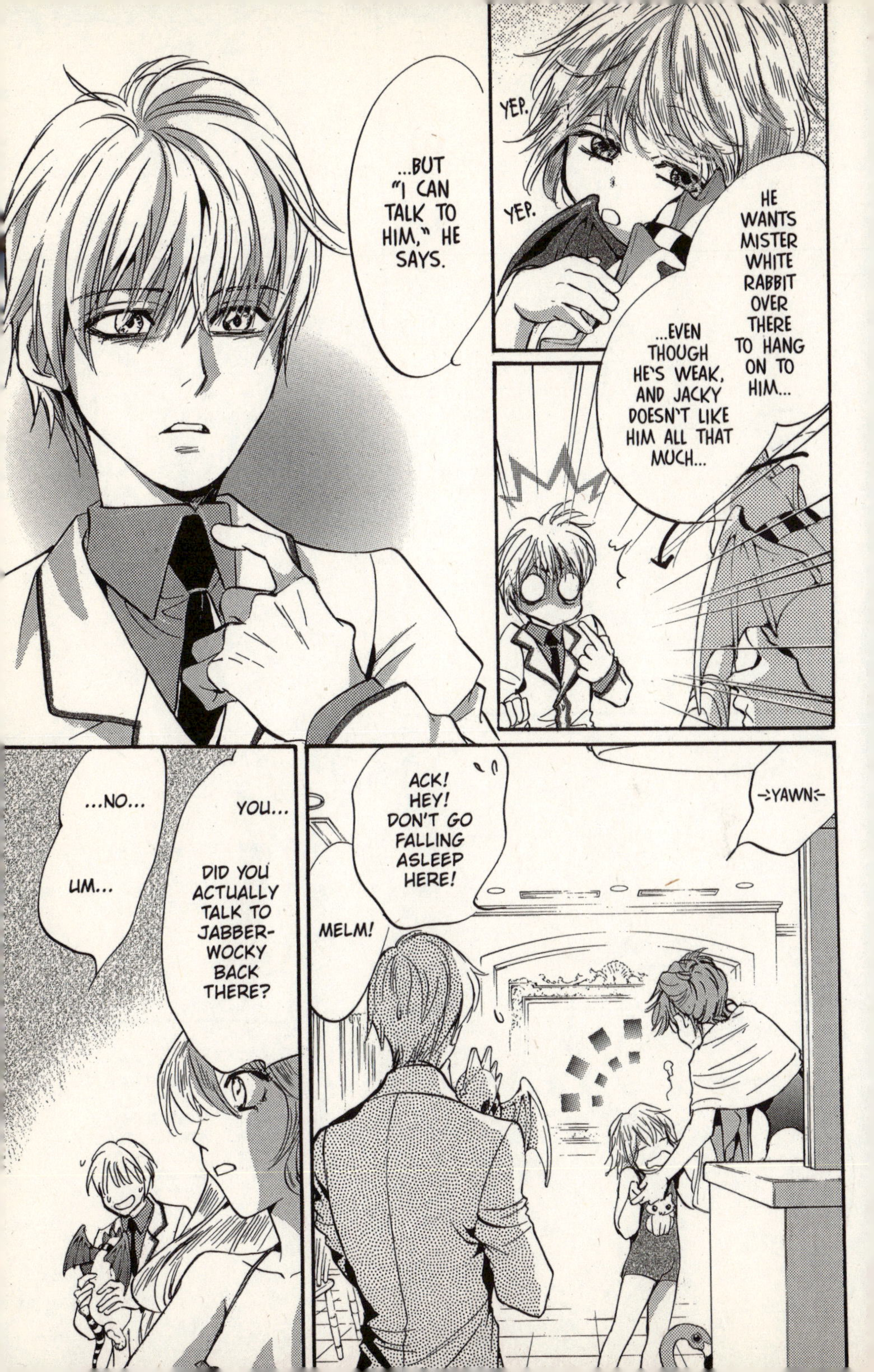
YEP.
YEP.
HE WANTS MISTER WHITE RABBIT OVER THERE TO HANG ON TO HIM...
...EVEN THOUGH HE'S WEAK, AND JACKY DOESN'T LIKE HIM ALL THAT MUCH...
...BUT "I CAN TALK TO HIM," HE SAYS.
≈YAWN≈
ACK! HEY! DON'T GO FALLING ASLEEP HERE!
MELM!
YOU...
DID YOU ACTUALLY TALK TO JABBER-WOCKY BACK THERE?
...NO...
UM...

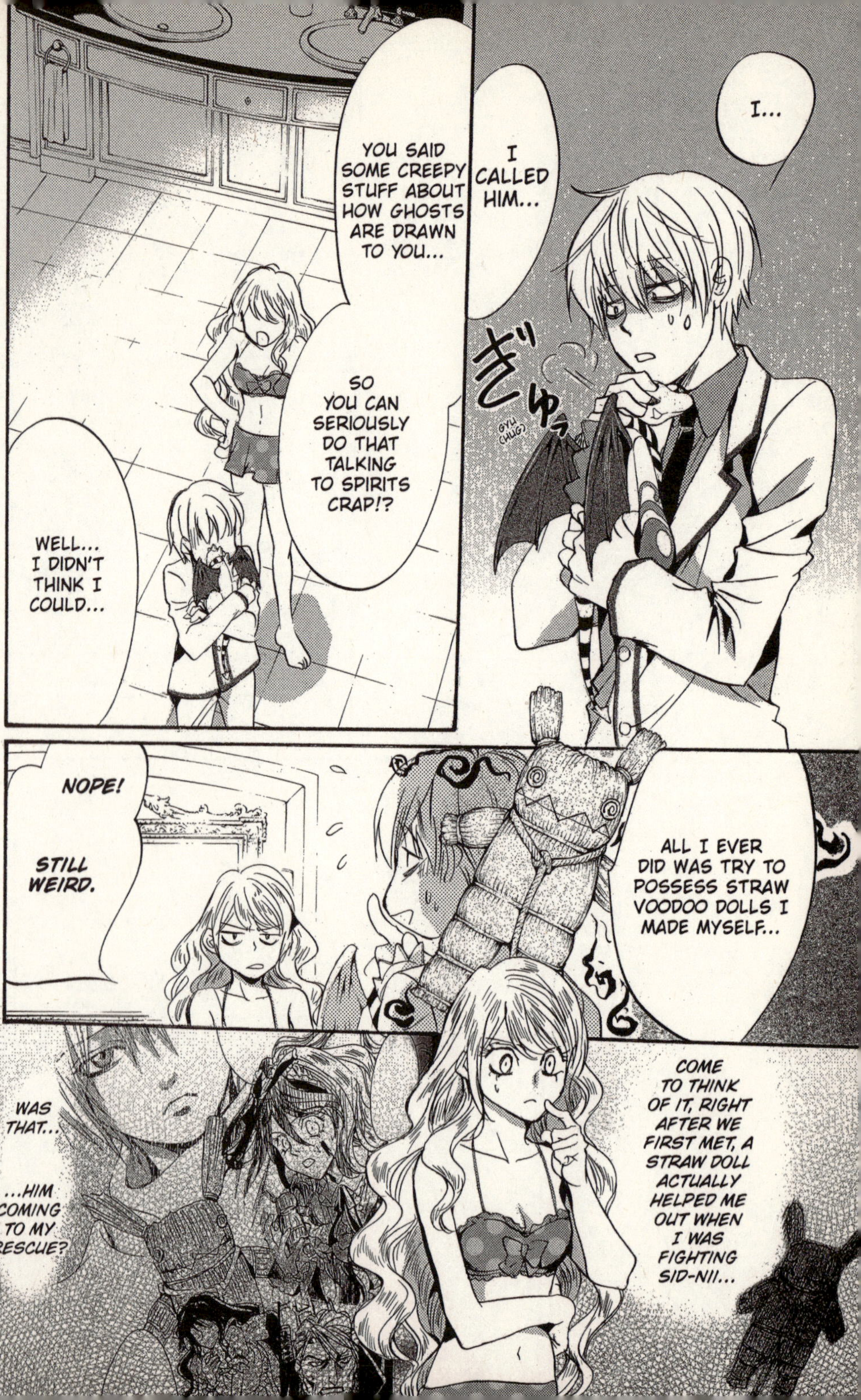
I...
I CALLED HIM...
GYU (HUG)
YOU SAID SOME CREEPY STUFF ABOUT HOW GHOSTS ARE DRAWN TO YOU...
SO YOU CAN SERIOUSLY DO THAT TALKING TO SPIRITS CRAP!?
WELL... I DIDN'T THINK I COULD...
ALL I EVER DID WAS TRY TO POSSESS STRAW VOODOO DOLLS I MADE MYSELF...
NOPE!
STILL WEIRD.
COME TO THINK OF IT, RIGHT AFTER WE FIRST MET, A STRAW DOLL ACTUALLY HELPED ME OUT WHEN I WAS FIGHTING SID-NII...
WAS THAT...
...HIM COMING TO MY RESCUE?

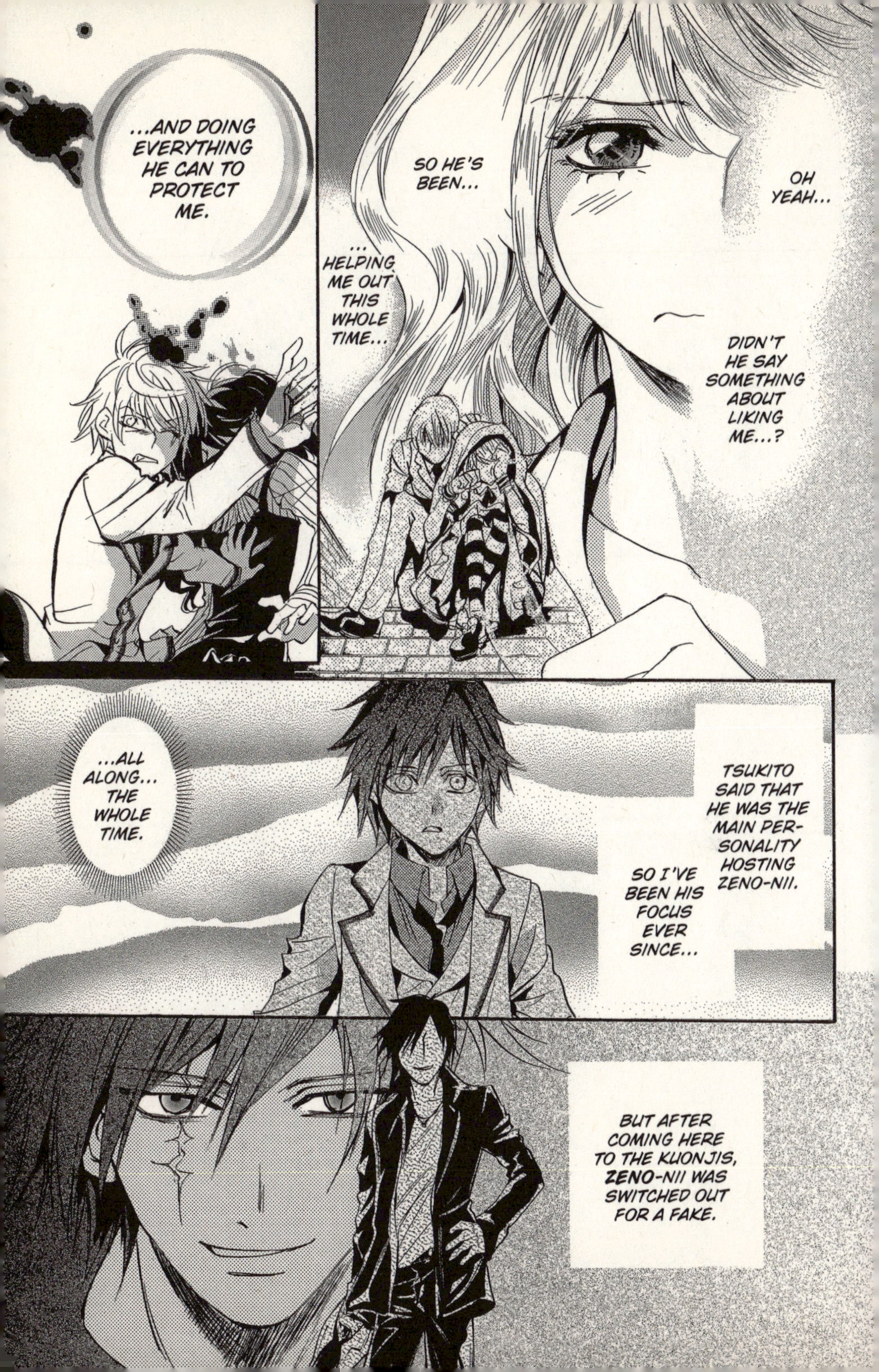
OH YEAH...
DIDN'T HE SAY SOMETHING ABOUT LIKING ME...?
SO HE'S BEEN...
...HELPING ME OUT THIS WHOLE TIME...
...AND DOING EVERYTHING HE CAN TO PROTECT ME.
TSUKITO SAID THAT HE WAS THE MAIN PER-SONALITY HOSTING ZENO-NII.
SO I'VE BEEN HIS FOCUS EVER SINCE...
...ALL ALONG... THE WHOLE TIME.
BUT AFTER COMING HERE TO THE KUONJIS, ZENO-NII WAS SWITCHED OUT FOR A FAKE.

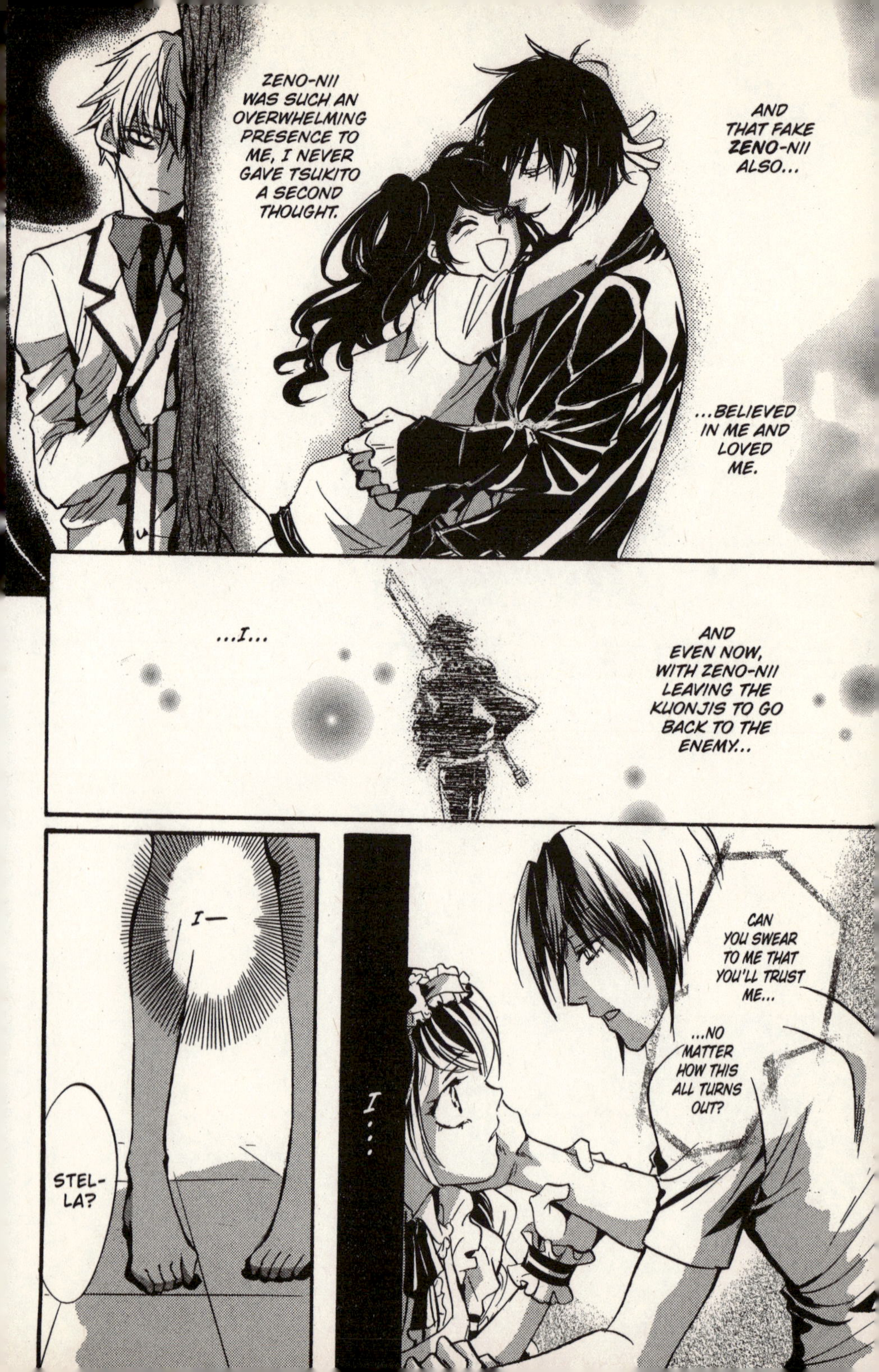
ZENO-NII WAS SUCH AN OVERWHELMING PRESENCE TO ME, I NEVER GAVE TSUKITO A SECOND THOUGHT.
AND THAT FAKE ZENO-NII ALSO...
...BELIEVED IN ME AND LOVED ME.
AND EVEN NOW, WITH ZENO-NII LEAVING THE KUONJIS TO GO BACK TO THE ENEMY...
...I...
CAN YOU SWEAR TO ME THAT YOU'LL TRUST ME...
...NO MATTER HOW THIS ALL TURNS OUT?
I...
I—
STEL-LA?

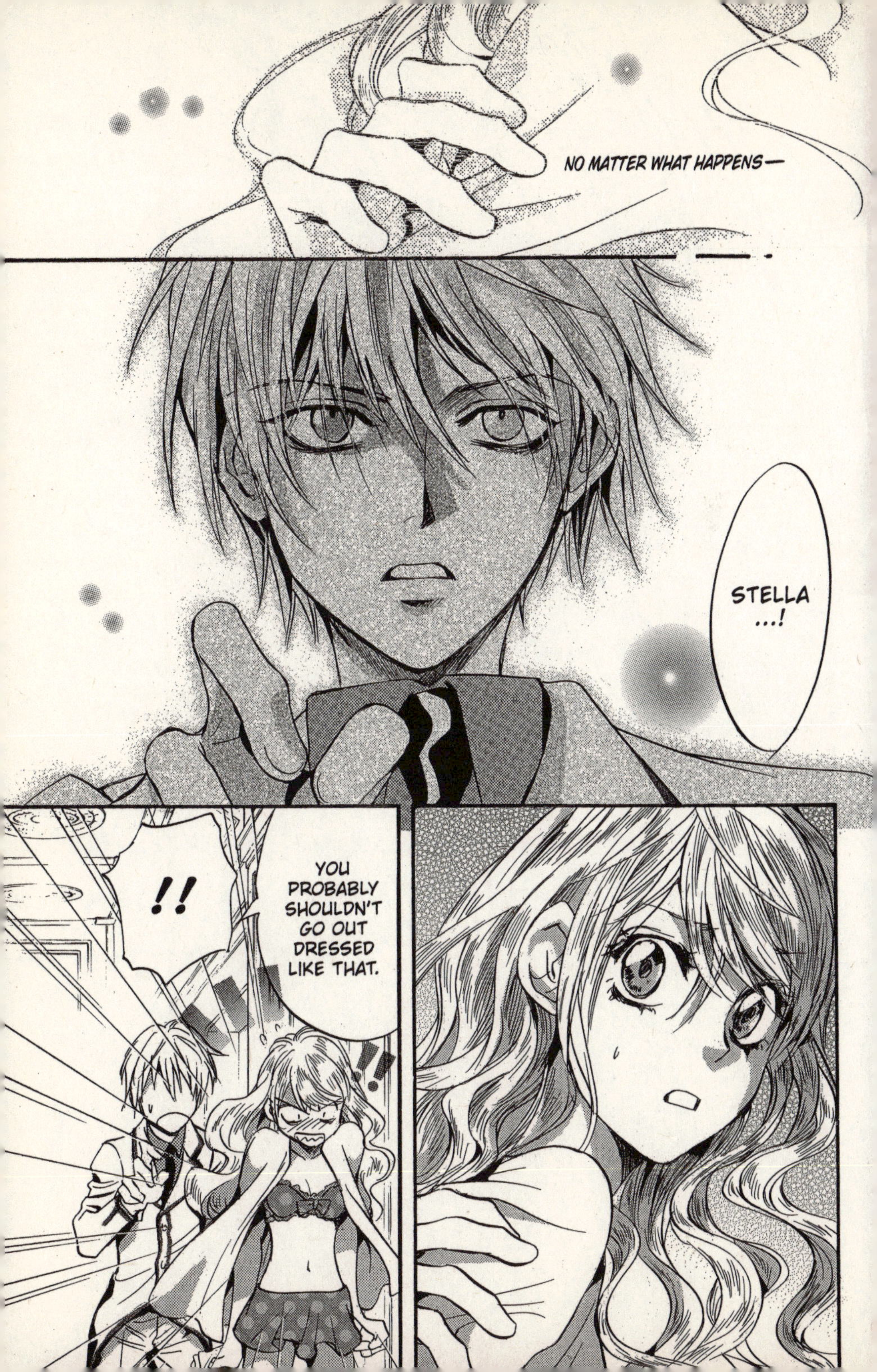
NO MATTER WHAT HAPPENS—
STELLA ...!
YOU PROBABLY SHOULDN'T GO OUT DRESSED LIKE THAT.
!!
!!

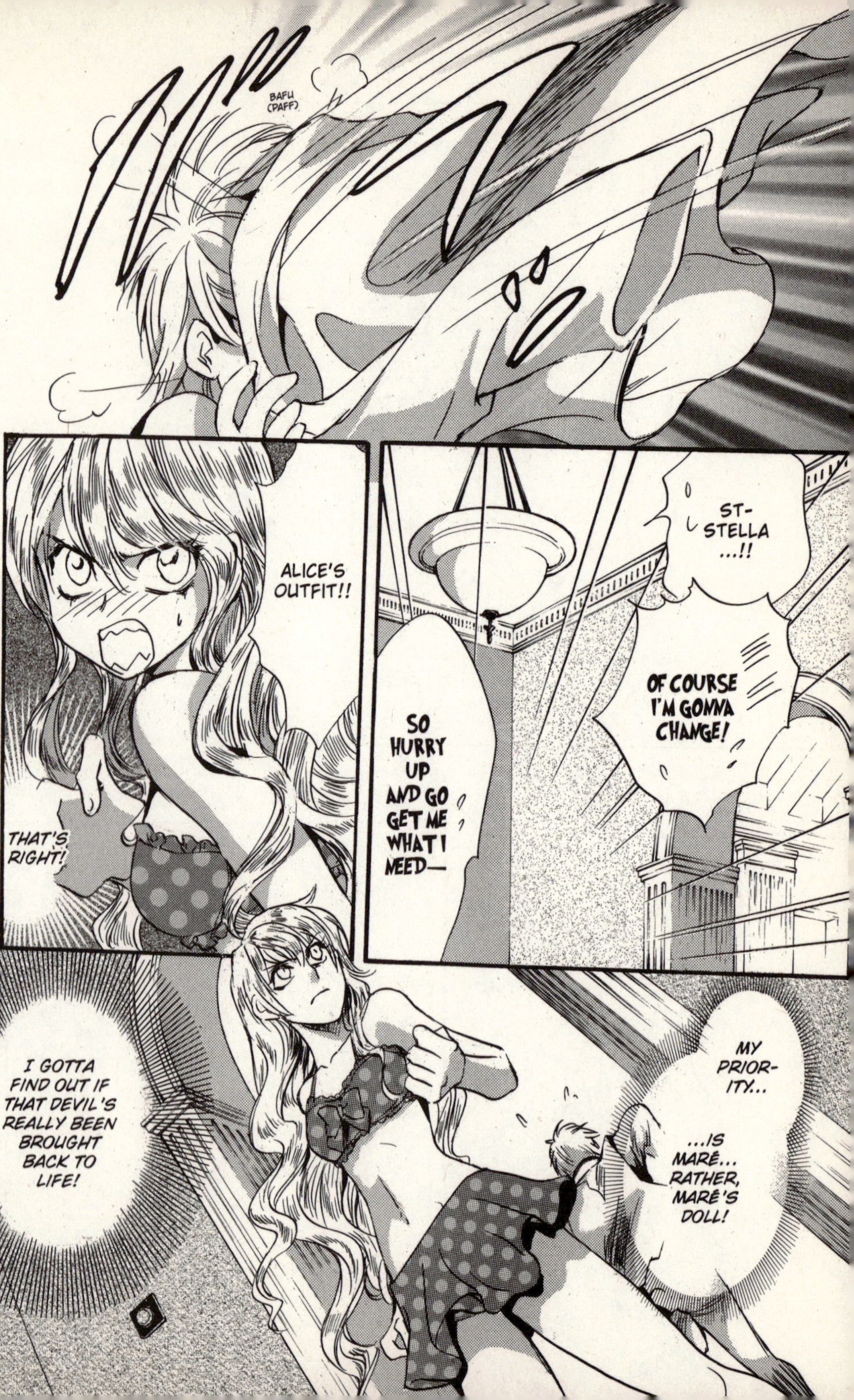
BAFU (PAFF)
ST-STELLA ...!!
OF COURSE I'M GONNA CHANGE!
SO HURRY UP AND GO GET ME WHAT I NEED—
ALICE'S OUTFIT!!
THAT'S RIGHT!
MY PRIOR-ITY...
...IS MARÉ... RATHER, MARÉ'S DOLL!
I GOTTA FIND OUT IF THAT DEVIL'S REALLY BEEN BROUGHT BACK TO LIFE!

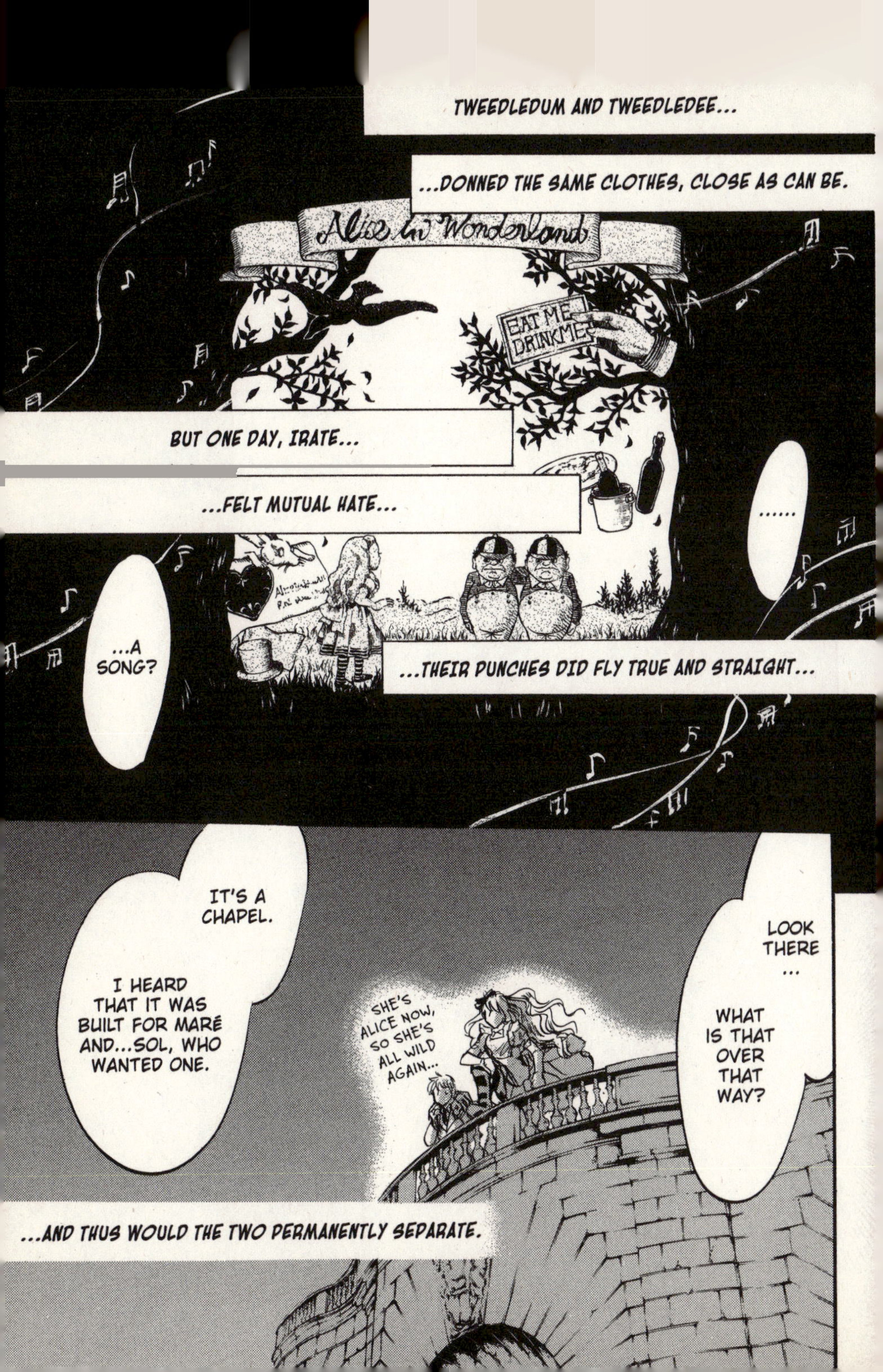
TWEEDLEDUM AND TWEEDLEDEE...
...DONNED THE SAME CLOTHES, CLOSE AS CAN BE.
Alice in Wonderland
EAT ME DRINK ME
BUT ONE DAY, IRATE...
......
...FELT MUTUAL HATE...
...A SONG?
...THEIR PUNCHES DID FLY TRUE AND STRAIGHT...
LOOK THERE...
WHAT IS THAT OVER THAT WAY?
SHE'S ALICE NOW, SO SHE'S ALL WILD AGAIN...
IT'S A CHAPEL.
I HEARD THAT IT WAS BUILT FOR MARÉ AND...SOL, WHO WANTED ONE.
...AND THUS WOULD THE TWO PERMANENTLY SEPARATE.

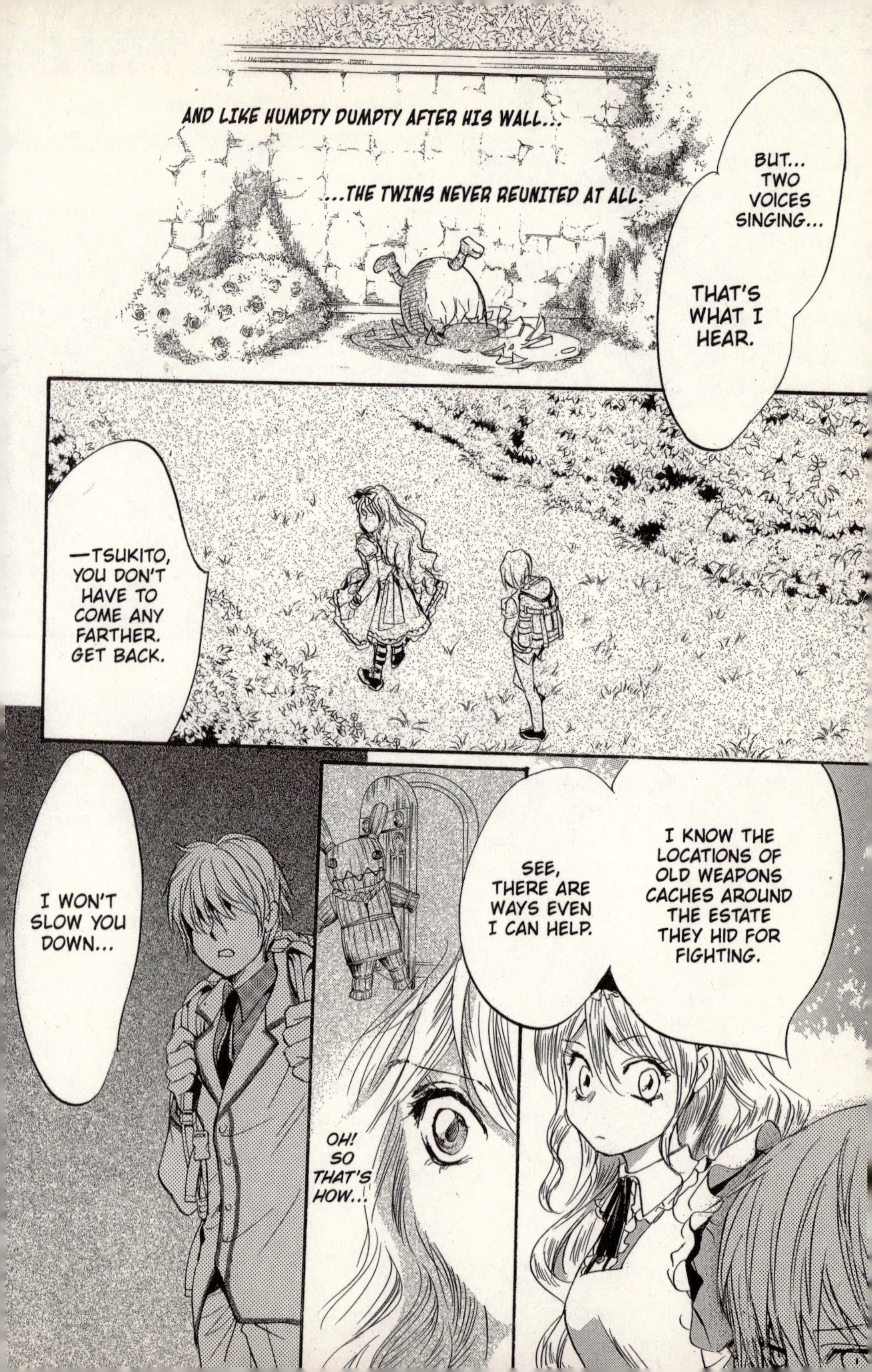
BUT... TWO VOICES SINGING...
THAT'S WHAT I HEAR.
AND LIKE HUMPTY DUMPTY AFTER HIS WALL...
...THE TWINS NEVER REUNITED AT ALL.
—TSUKITO, YOU DON'T HAVE TO COME ANY FARTHER. GET BACK.
I KNOW THE LOCATIONS OF OLD WEAPONS CACHES AROUND THE ESTATE THEY HID FOR FIGHTING.
SEE, THERE ARE WAYS EVEN I CAN HELP.
OH! SO THAT'S HOW...
I WON'T SLOW YOU DOWN...

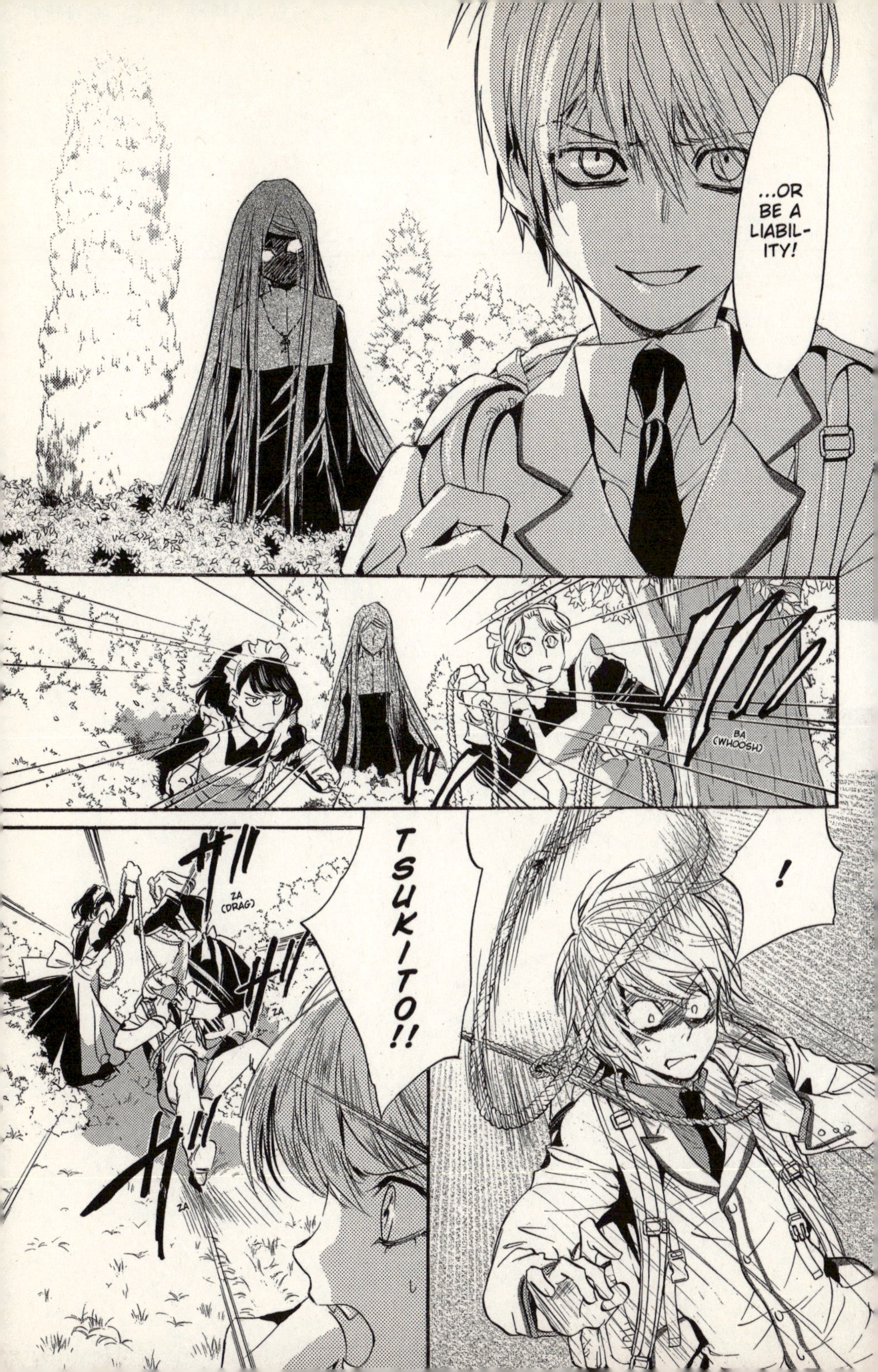
...OR BE A LIABIL-ITY!
BA (WHOOSH)
!
TSUKITO!!
ZA (DRAG)
ZA
ZA

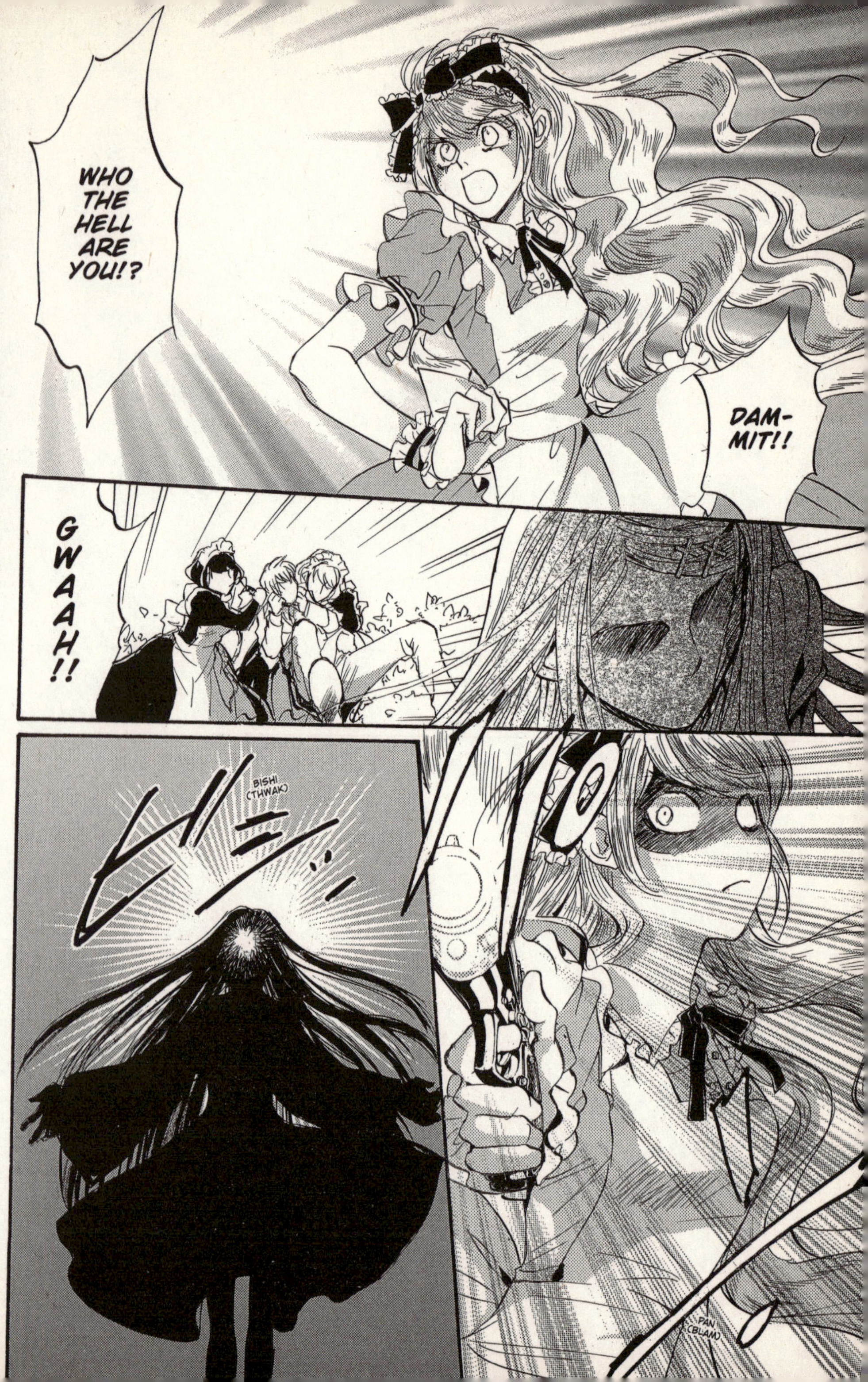
WHO THE HELL ARE YOU!?
DAM-MIT!!
GWAAAH!!
PAN (BLAM)
BISHI (THWAK)

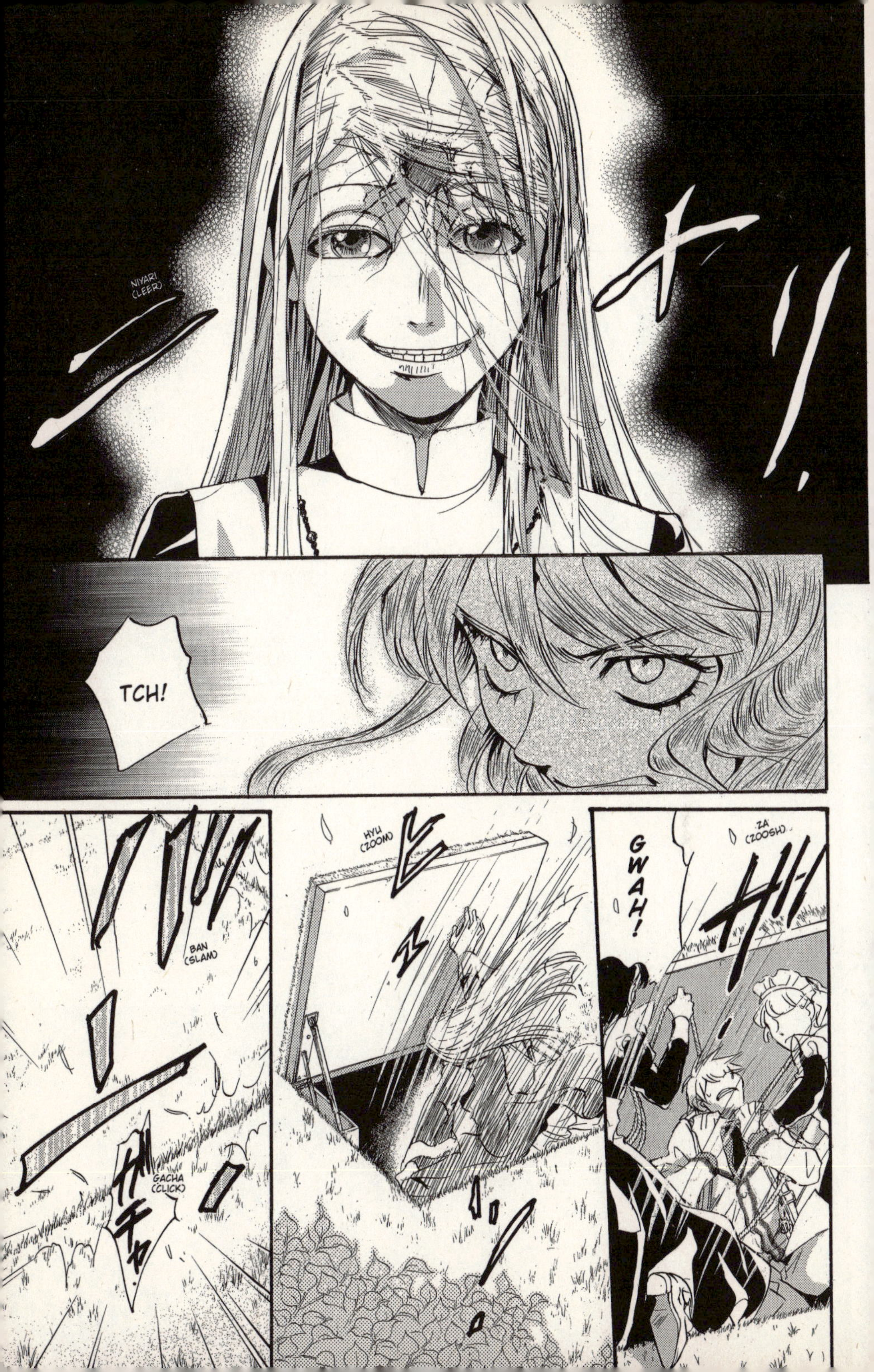
NIYARI (LEER)
TCH!
GWAH!
ZA (ZOOSH)
HYU (ZOOM)
BAN (SLAM)
GACHA (CLICK)

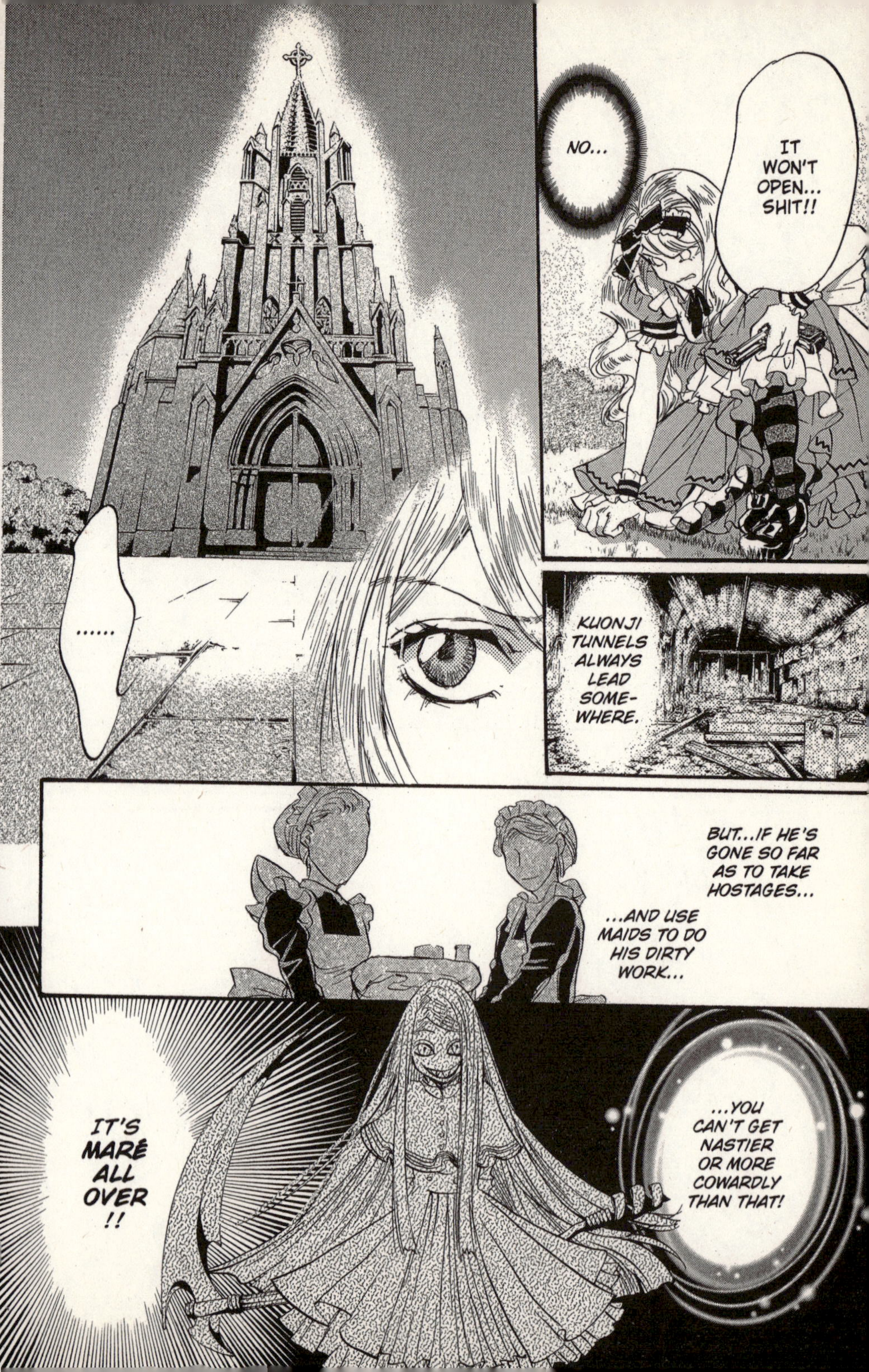
IT WON'T OPEN... SHIT!!
NO...
KUONJI TUNNELS ALWAYS LEAD SOME-WHERE.
......
BUT...IF HE'S GONE SO FAR AS TO TAKE HOSTAGES...
...AND USE MAIDS TO DO HIS DIRTY WORK...
...YOU CAN'T GET NASTIER OR MORE COWARDLY THAN THAT!
IT'S MARE ALL OVER !!

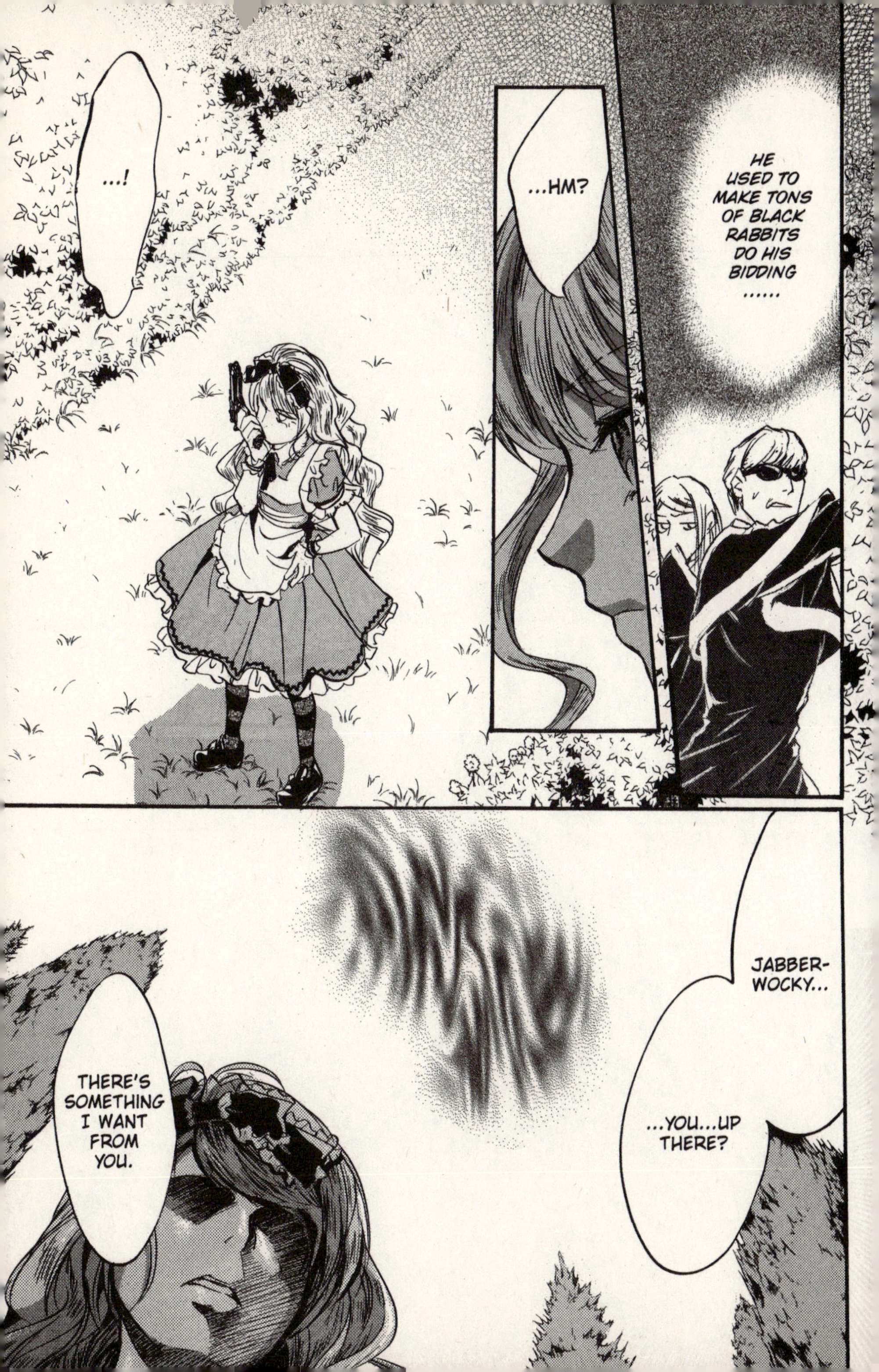
HE USED TO MAKE TONS OF BLACK RABBITS DO HIS BIDDING ......
...HM?
...!
JABBER-WOCKY...
...YOU...UP THERE?
THERE'S SOMETHING I WANT FROM YOU.

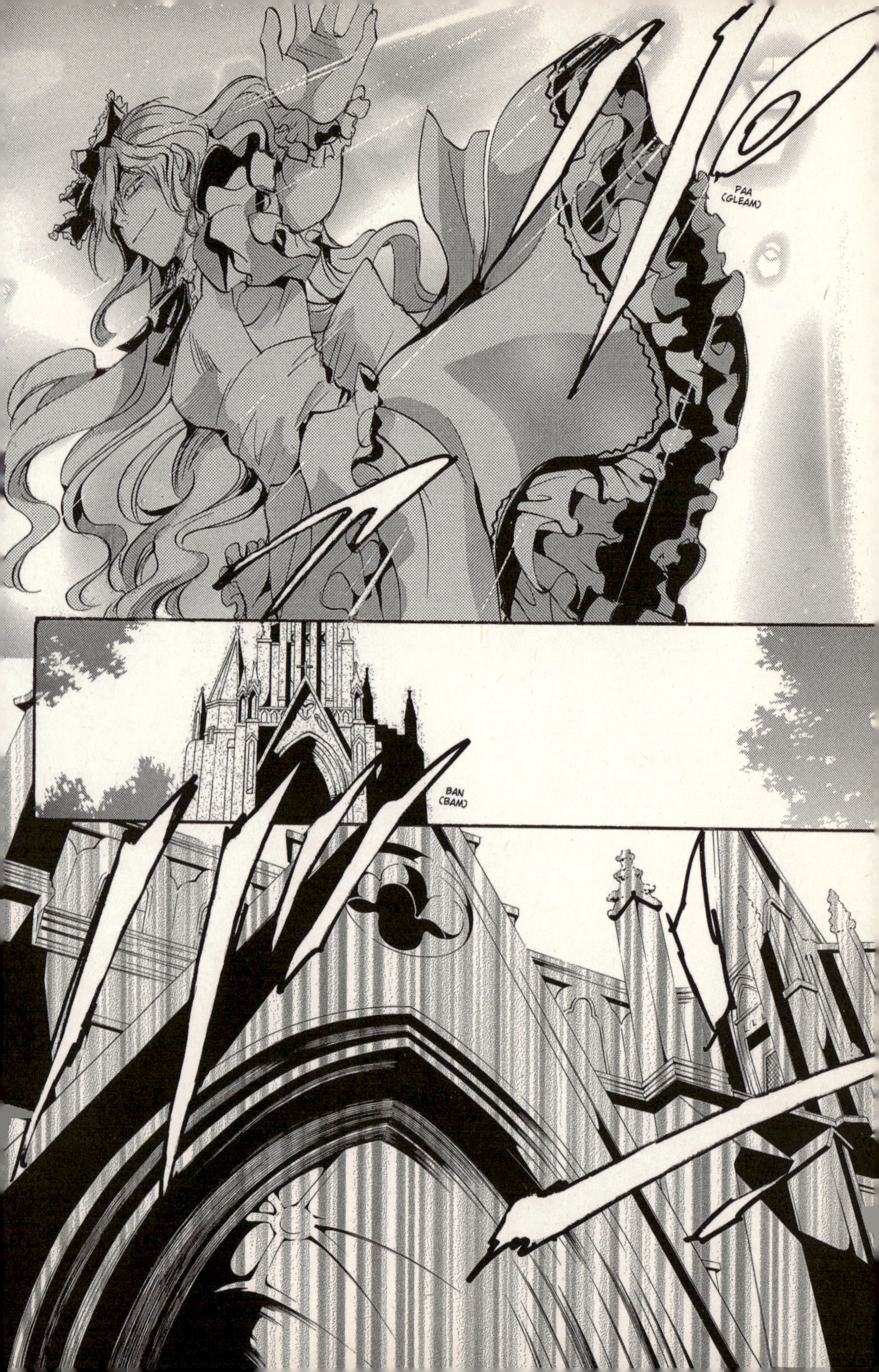
PAA
(GLEAM)
BAN
(BAM)

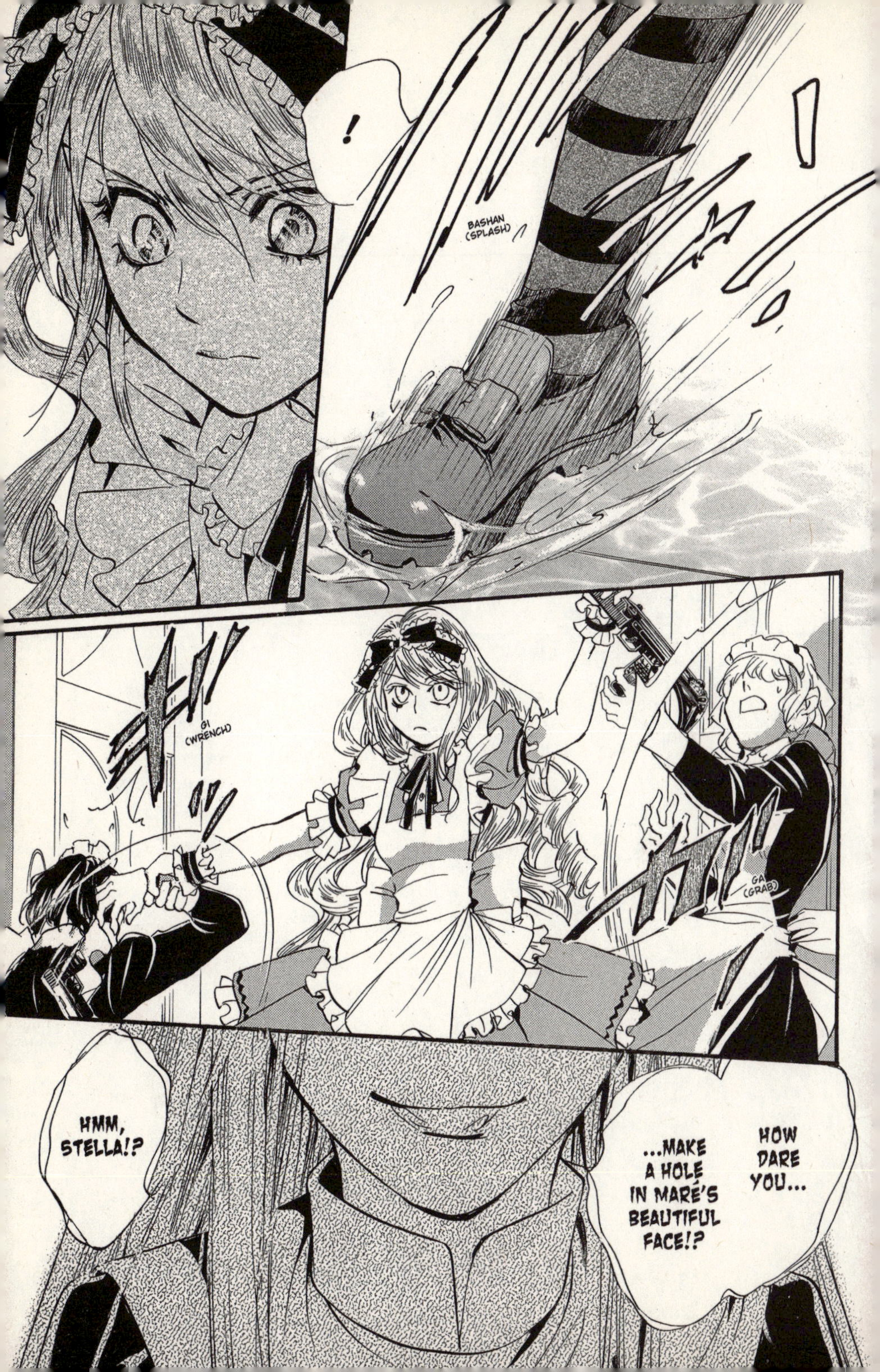
!
BASHAN (SPLASH)
GA (GRAB)
GI (WRENCH)
HOW DARE YOU...
...MAKE A HOLE IN MARÉ'S BEAUTIFUL FACE!?
HMM, STELLA!?

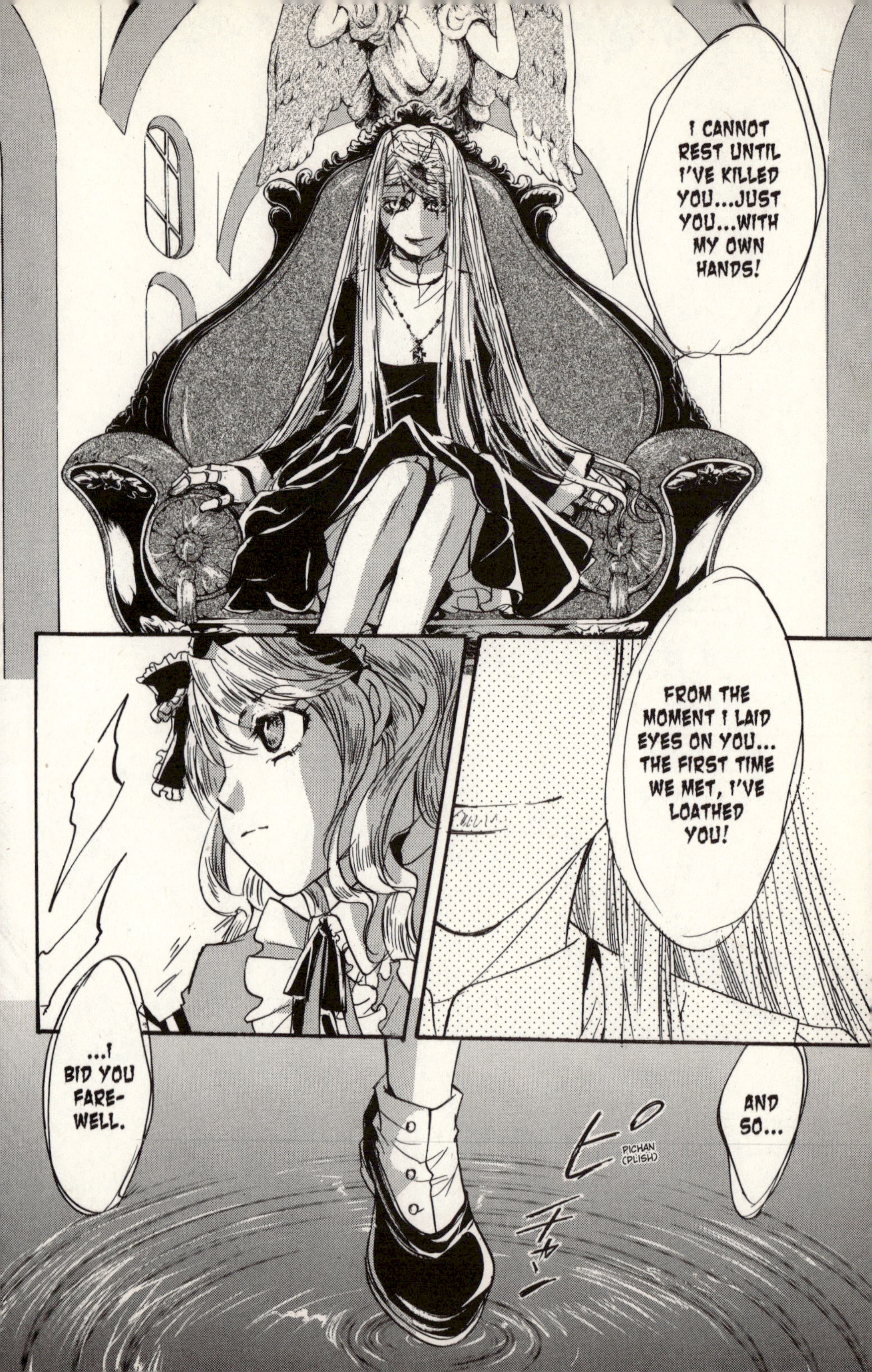
I CANNOT REST UNTIL I'VE KILLED YOU...JUST YOU...WITH MY OWN HANDS!
FROM THE MOMENT I LAID EYES ON YOU... THE FIRST TIME WE MET, I'VE LOATHED YOU!
AND SO...
PICHAN (PLISH)
...I BID YOU FARE-WELL.

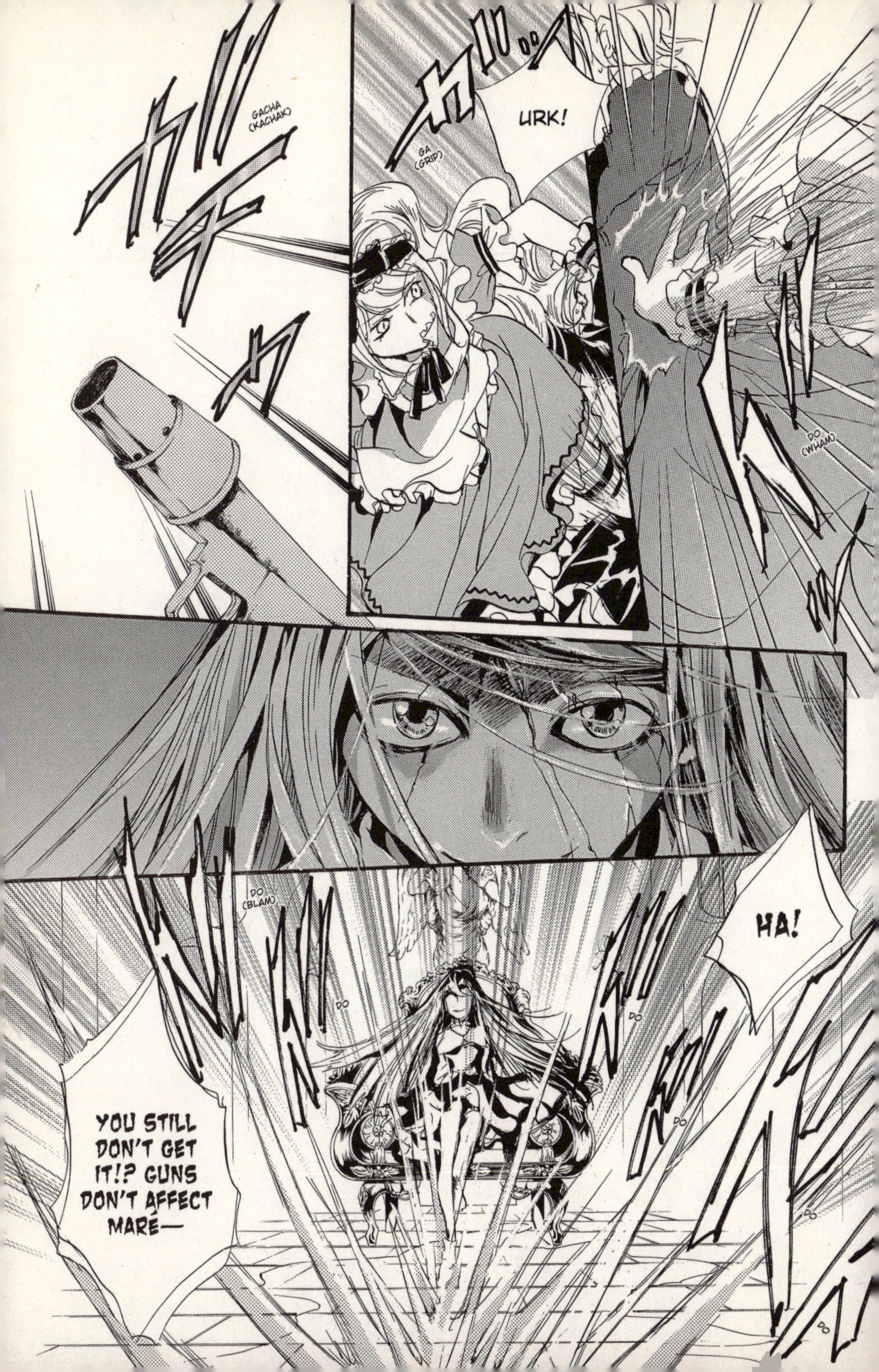
GA (GRIP)
URK!
DO (WHAM)
GACHA (KACHAK)
HA!
DO (BLAM)
DO
DO
DO
DO
DO
YOU STILL DON'T GET IT!? GUNS DON'T AFFECT MARE—

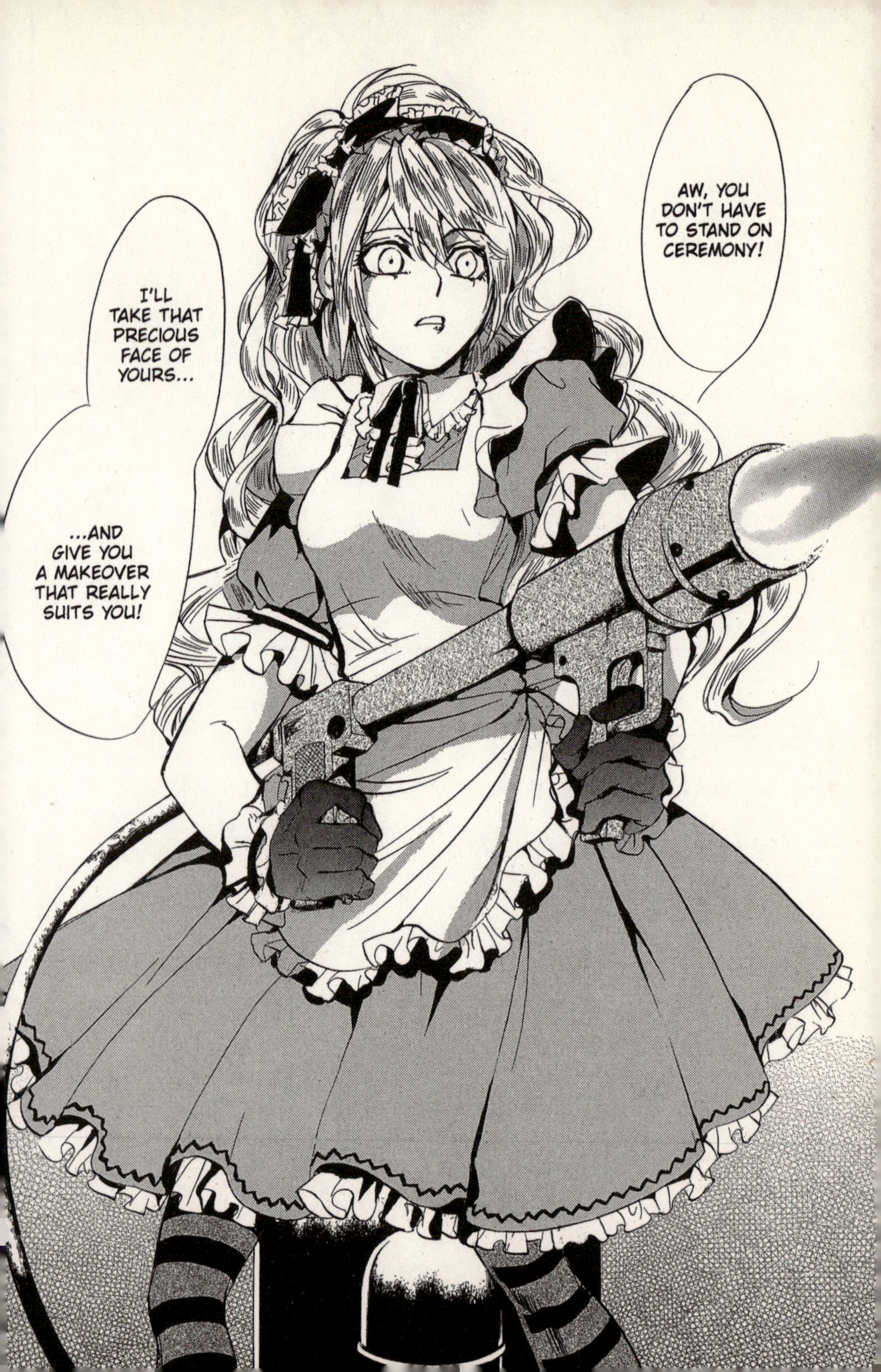
AW, YOU DON'T HAVE TO STAND ON CEREMONY!
I'LL TAKE THAT PRECIOUS FACE OF YOURS...
...AND GIVE YOU A MAKEOVER THAT REALLY SUITS YOU!

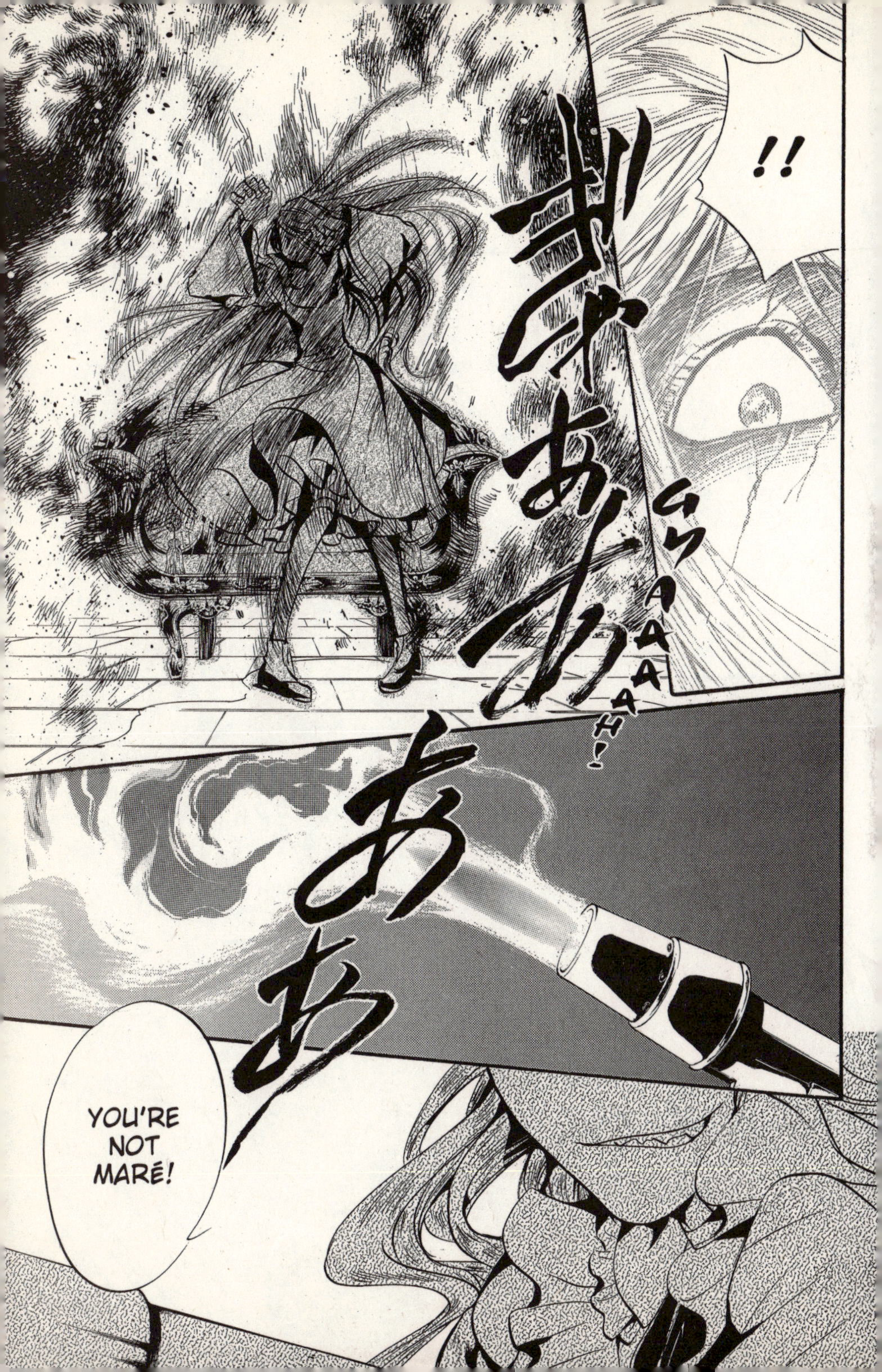

!!
ギャあああああ
GYAAAAAAH!!
YOU'RE NOT MARÉ!

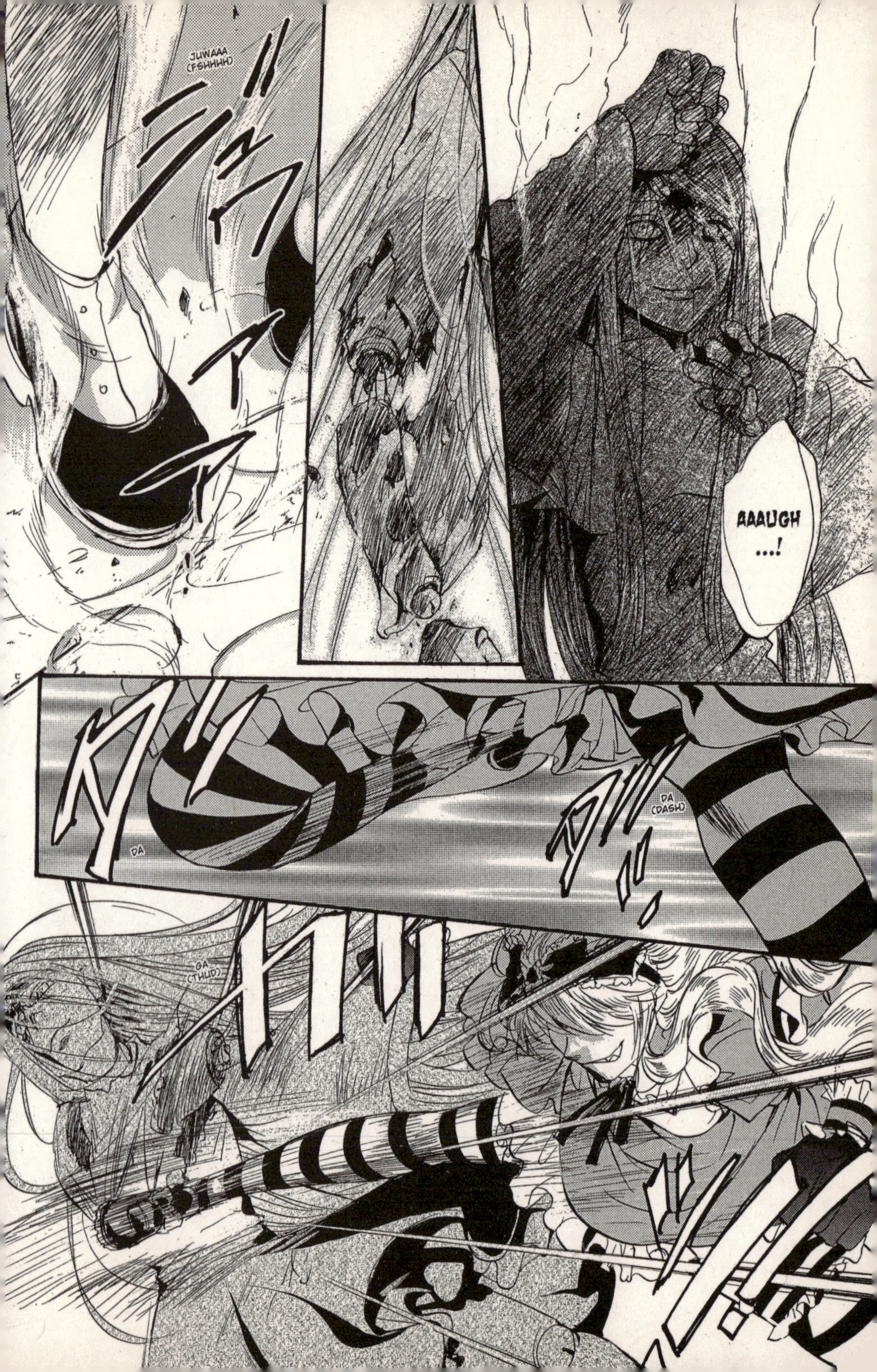
AAAUGH ...!
JUWAAA (FSHHHH)
DA (DASH)
DA
GA (THUD)

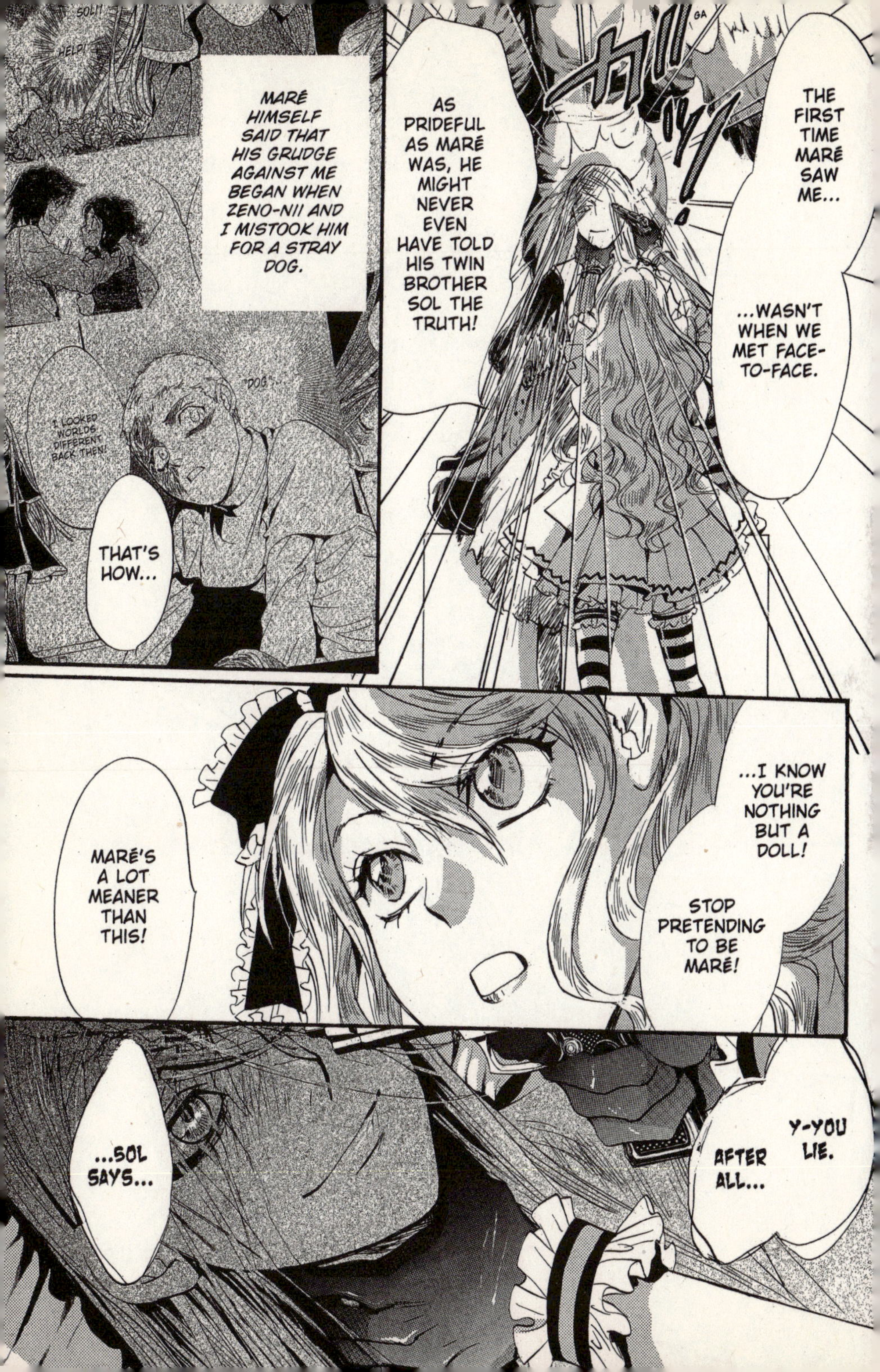
THE FIRST TIME MARÉ SAW ME...
...WASN'T WHEN WE MET FACE-TO-FACE.
GA
AS PRIDEFUL AS MARÉ WAS, HE MIGHT NEVER EVEN HAVE TOLD HIS TWIN BROTHER SOL THE TRUTH!
MARÉ HIMSELF SAID THAT HIS GRUDGE AGAINST ME BEGAN WHEN ZENO-NII AND I MISTOOK HIM FOR A STRAY DOG.
SOL!!
HELP!
"DOG"
I LOOKED WORLDS DIFFERENT BACK THEN!
THAT'S HOW...
...I KNOW YOU'RE NOTHING BUT A DOLL!
STOP PRETENDING TO BE MARÉ!
MARÉ'S A LOT MEANER THAN THIS!
Y-YOU LIE.
AFTER ALL...
...SOL SAYS...

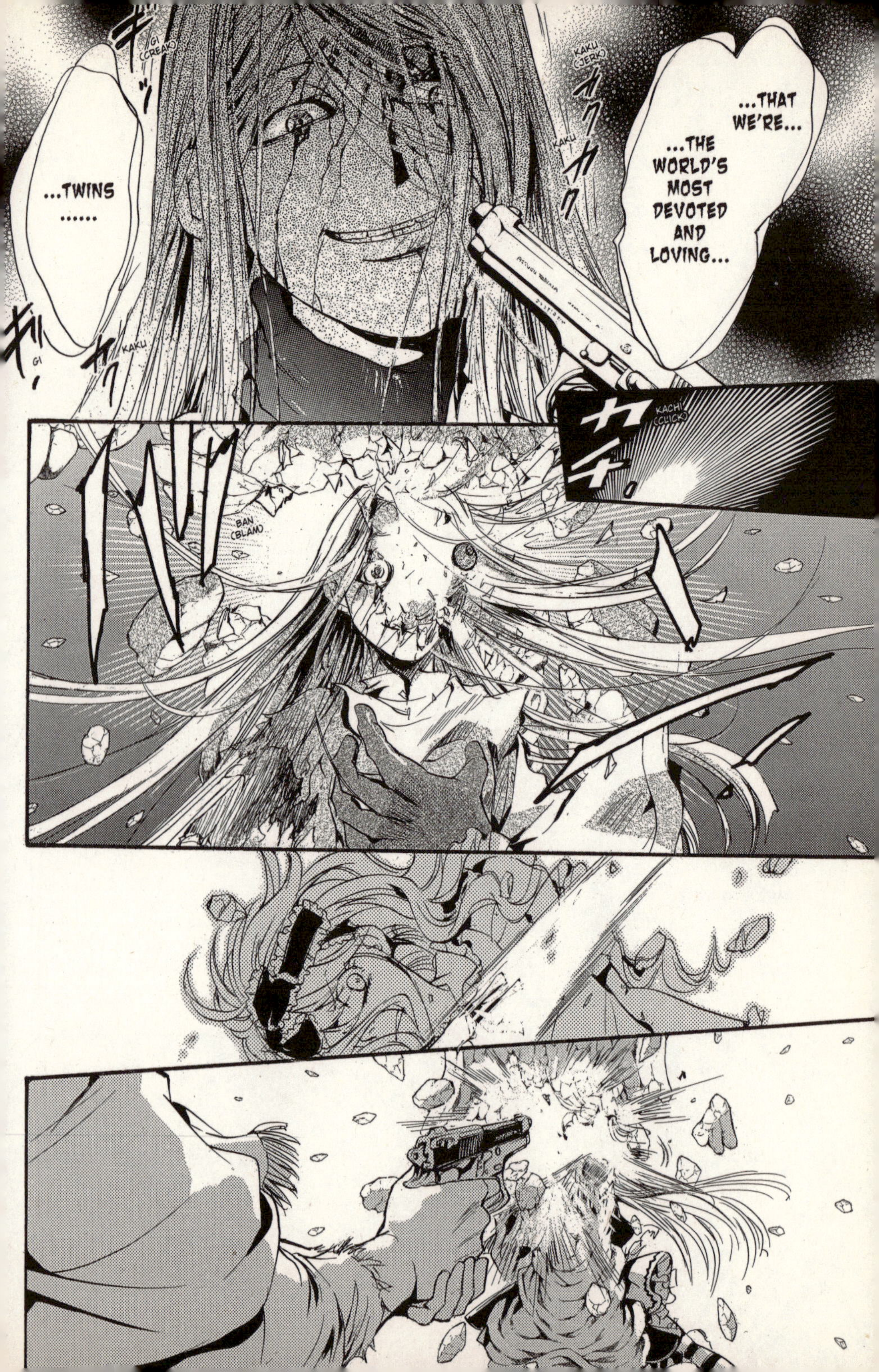

KAKU (JERK)
KAKU
...THAT WE'RE...
...THE WORLD'S MOST DEVOTED AND LOVING...
GI (CREAK)
...TWINS ......
GI
KAKU
KACHI (CLICK)
BAN (BLAM)

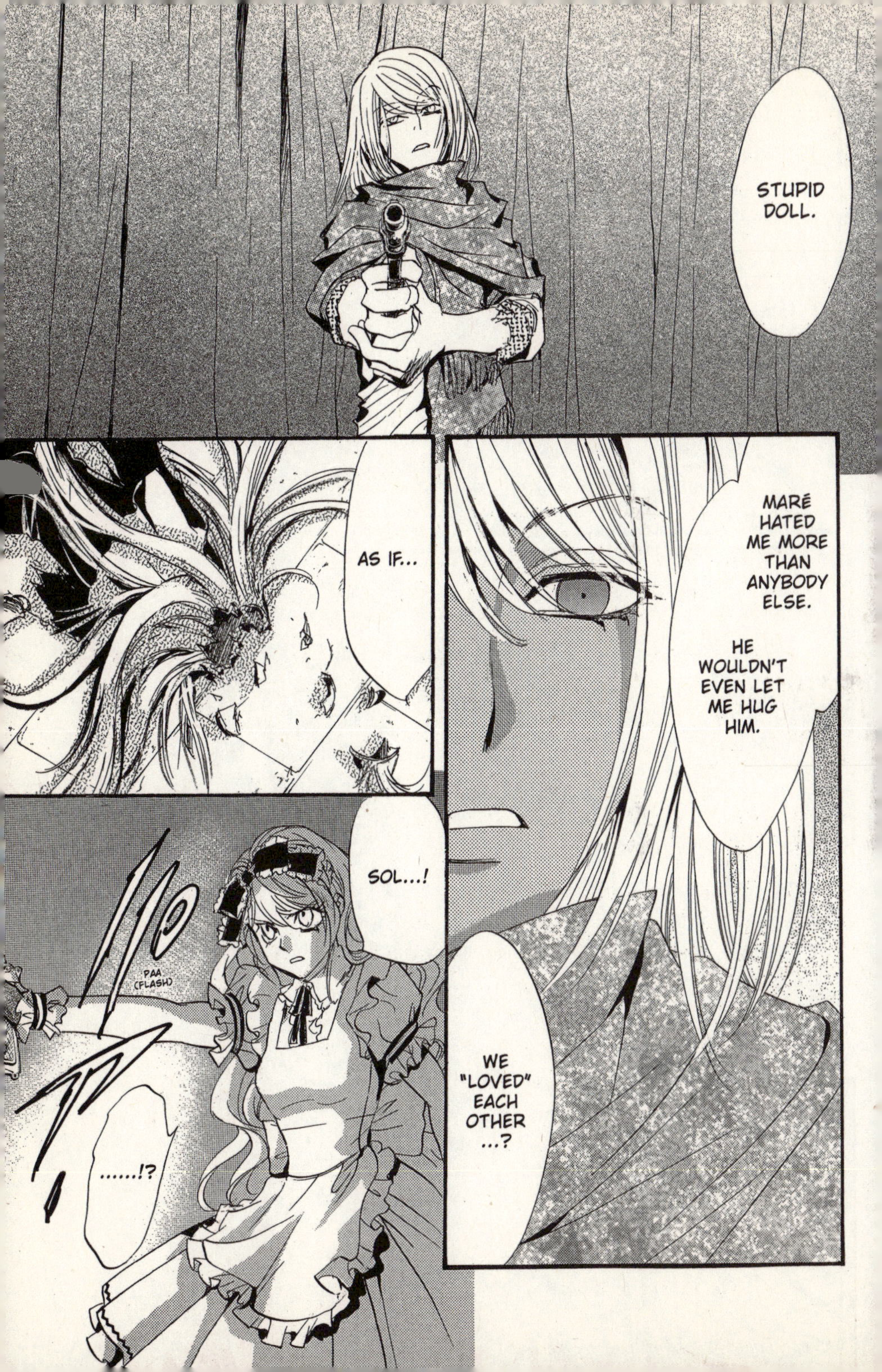
STUPID DOLL.
MARE HATED ME MORE THAN ANYBODY ELSE.
HE WOULDN'T EVEN LET ME HUG HIM.
WE "LOVED" EACH OTHER ...?
AS IF...
SOL...!
PAA (FLASH)
......!?

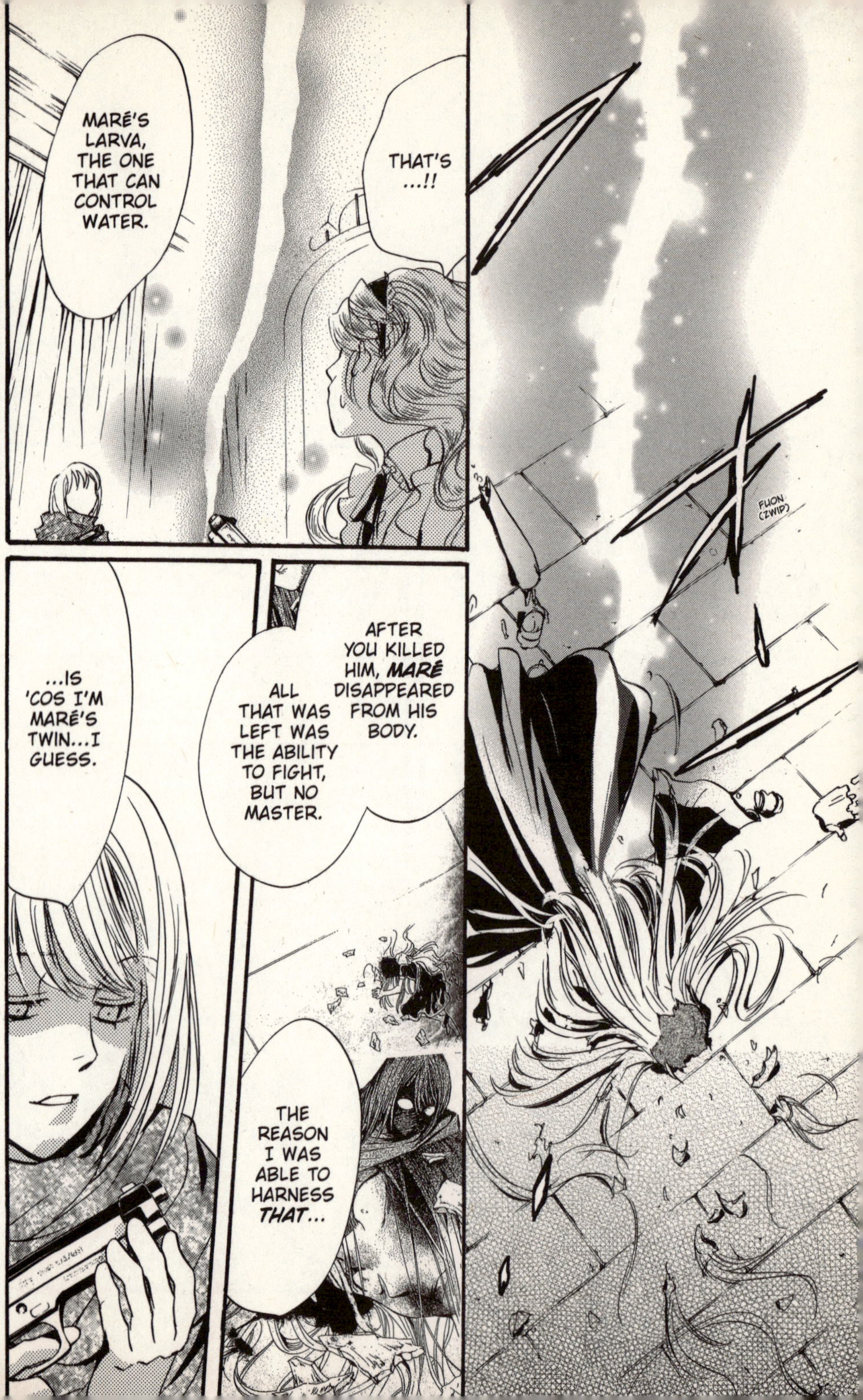
FUON (ZWIP)
THAT'S ...!!
MARÉ'S LARVA, THE ONE THAT CAN CONTROL WATER.
AFTER YOU KILLED HIM, *MARÉ* DISAPPEARED FROM HIS BODY.
ALL THAT WAS LEFT WAS THE ABILITY TO FIGHT, BUT NO MASTER.
THE REASON I WAS ABLE TO HARNESS *THAT*...
...IS 'COS I'M MARÉ'S TWIN...I GUESS.

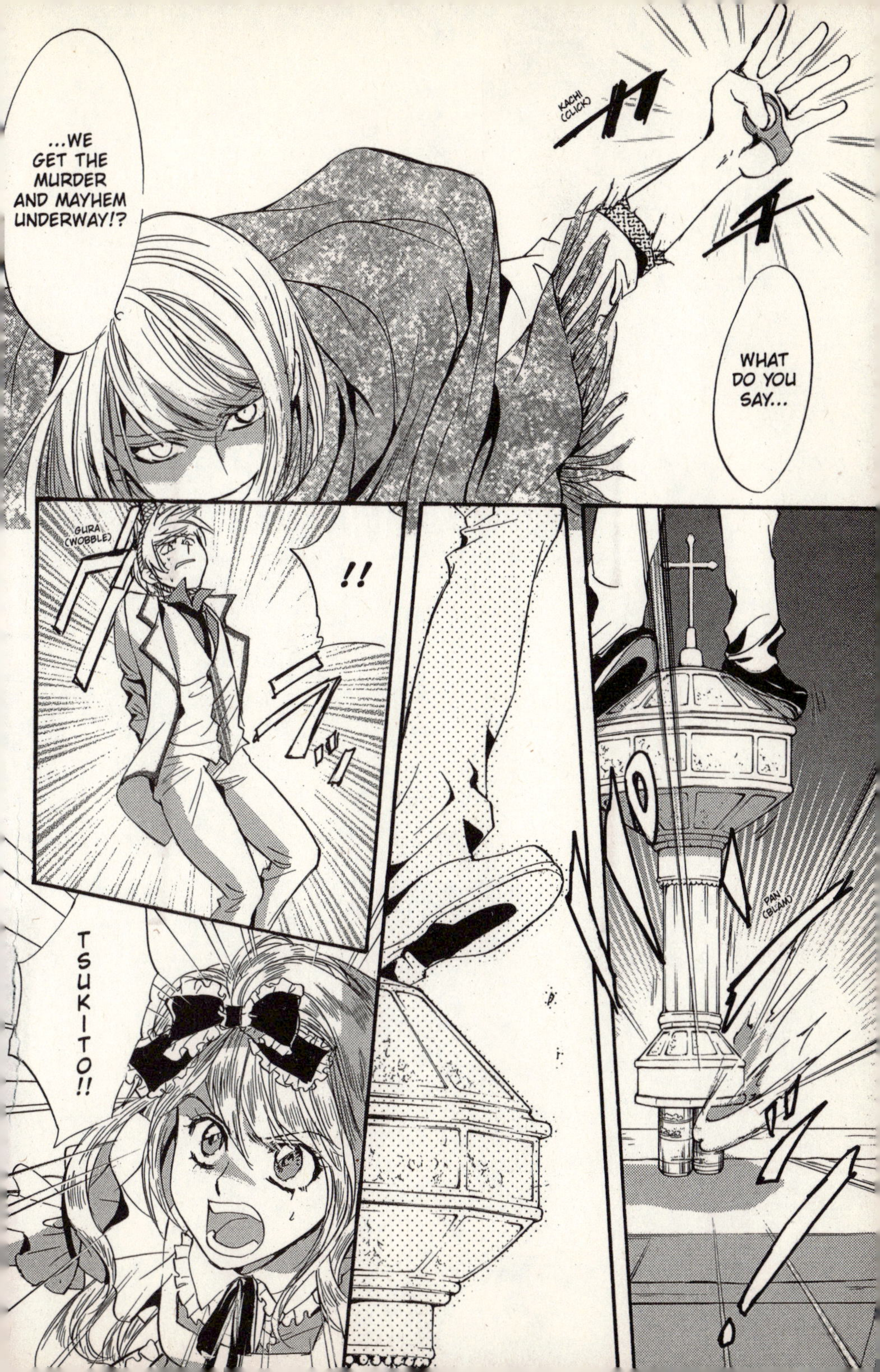
KACHI (CLICK)
WHAT DO YOU SAY...
...WE GET THE MURDER AND MAYHEM UNDERWAY!?
PAN (BLAM)
GURA (WOBBLE)
!!
TSUKITO!!

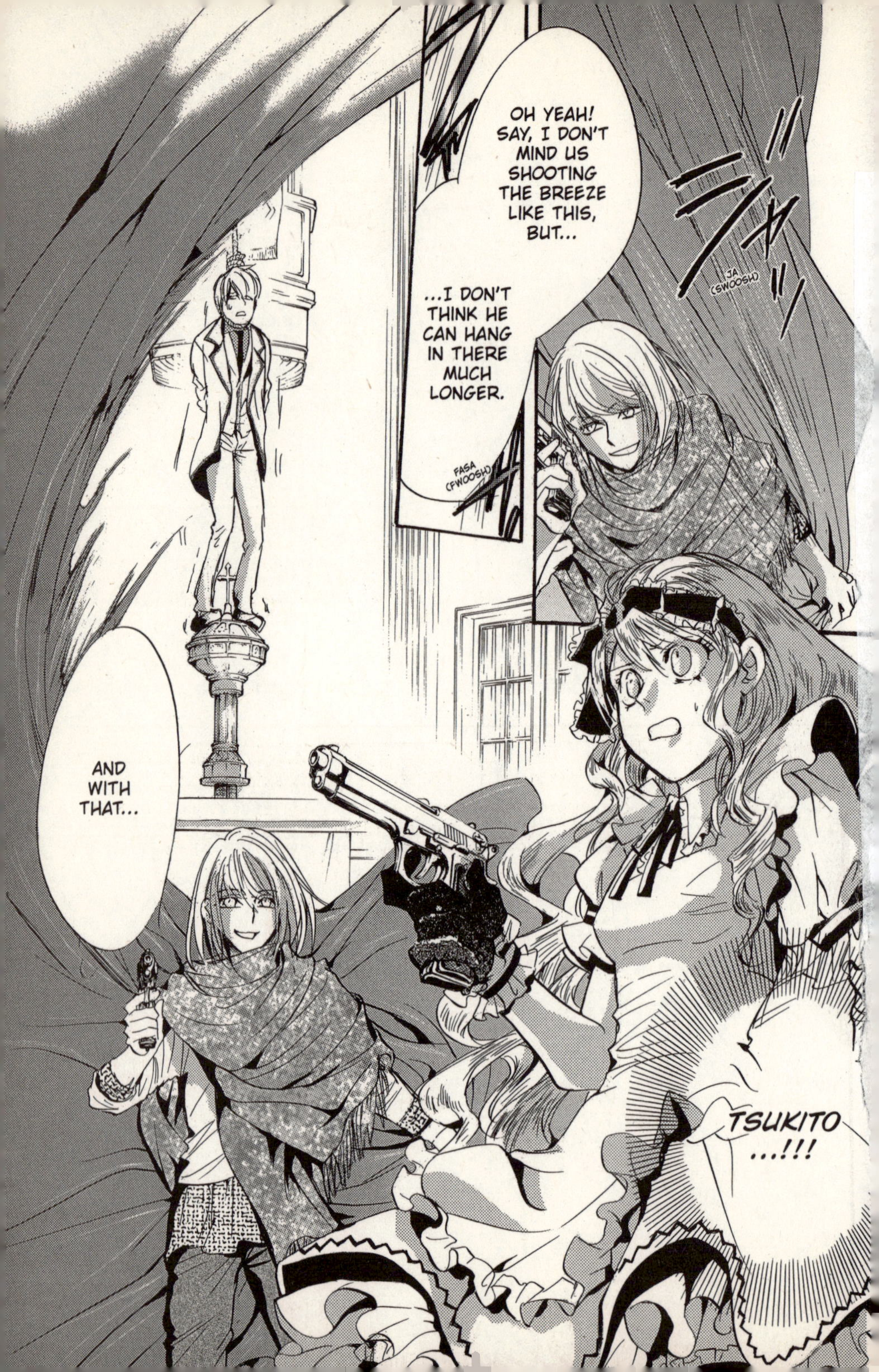
JA (SWOOSH)
OH YEAH! SAY, I DON'T MIND US SHOOTING THE BREEZE LIKE THIS, BUT...
...I DON'T THINK HE CAN HANG IN THERE MUCH LONGER.
FASA (FWOOSH)
AND WITH THAT...
TSUKITO ...!!!

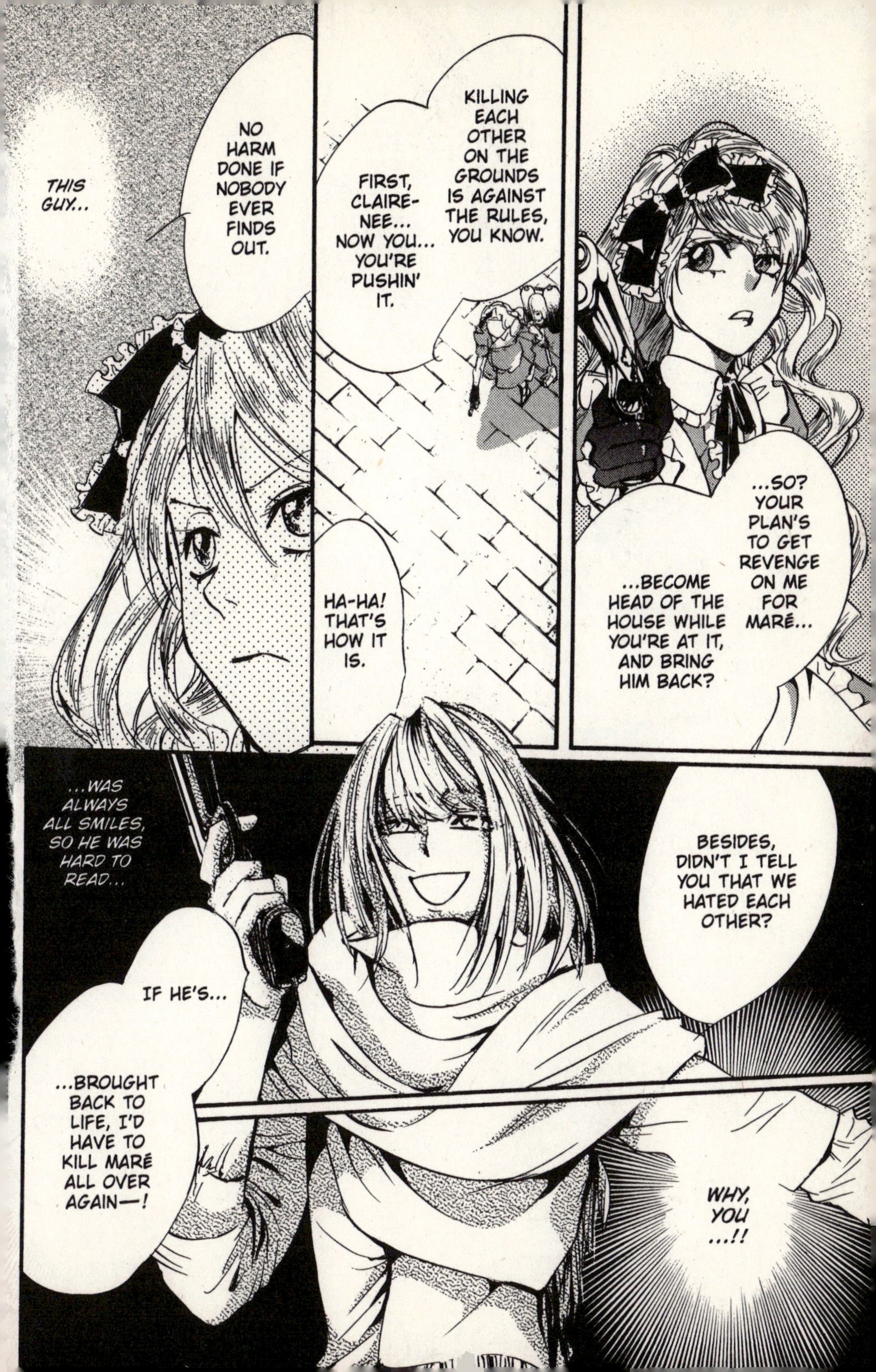
...SO? YOUR PLAN'S TO GET REVENGE ON ME FOR MARÉ...
...BECOME HEAD OF THE HOUSE WHILE YOU'RE AT IT, AND BRING HIM BACK?
KILLING EACH OTHER ON THE GROUNDS IS AGAINST THE RULES, YOU KNOW.
FIRST, CLAIRE-NEE... NOW YOU... YOU'RE PUSHIN' IT.
HA-HA! THAT'S HOW IT IS.
NO HARM DONE IF NOBODY EVER FINDS OUT.
THIS GUY...
BESIDES, DIDN'T I TELL YOU THAT WE HATED EACH OTHER?
...WAS ALWAYS ALL SMILES, SO HE WAS HARD TO READ...
IF HE'S...
...BROUGHT BACK TO LIFE, I'D HAVE TO KILL MARÉ ALL OVER AGAIN—!
WHY, YOU ...!!

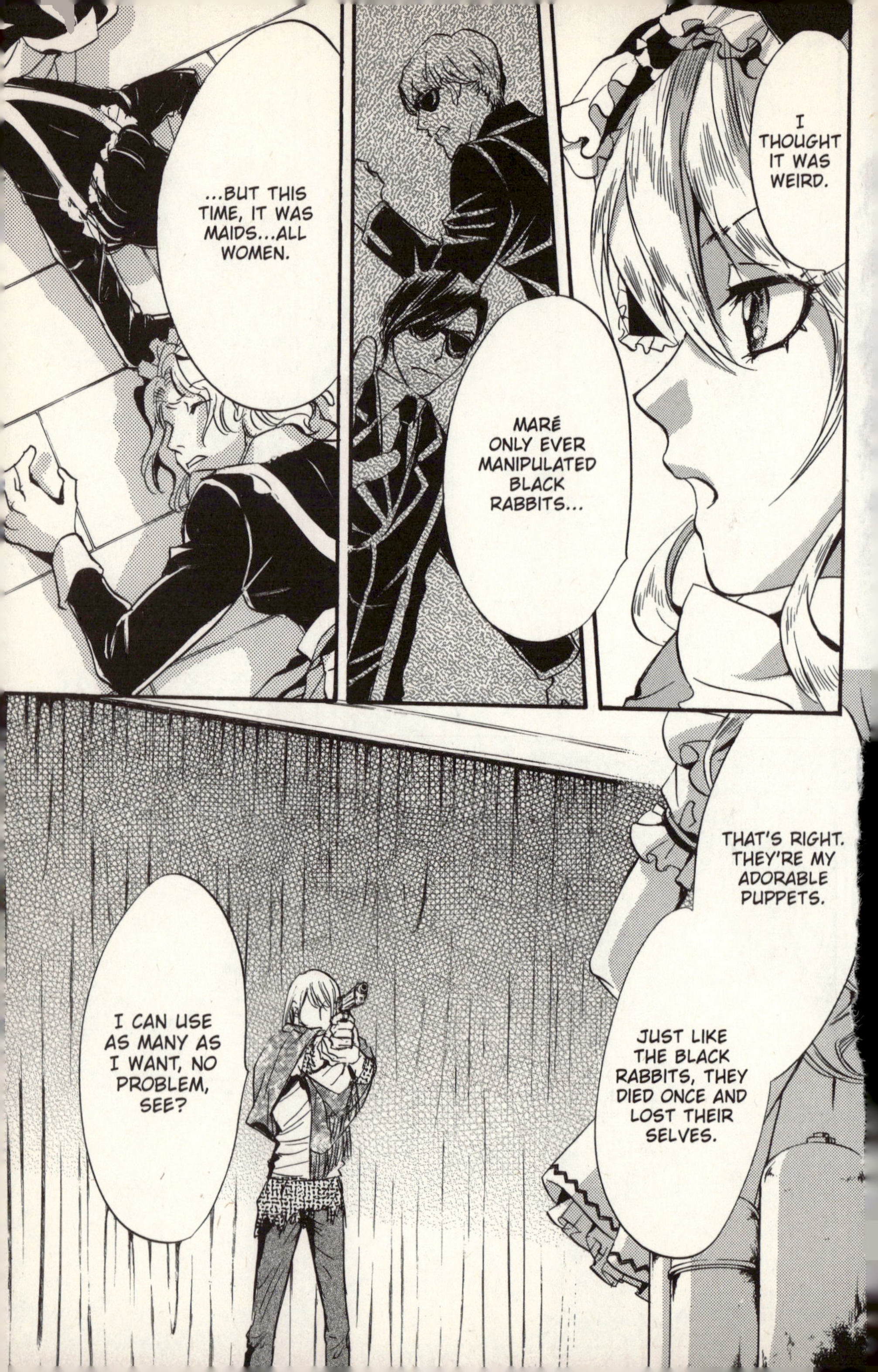
I THOUGHT IT WAS WEIRD.
MARÉ ONLY EVER MANIPULATED BLACK RABBITS...
...BUT THIS TIME, IT WAS MAIDS...ALL WOMEN.
THAT'S RIGHT. THEY'RE MY ADORABLE PUPPETS.
JUST LIKE THE BLACK RABBITS, THEY DIED ONCE AND LOST THEIR SELVES.
I CAN USE AS MANY AS I WANT, NO PROBLEM, SEE?

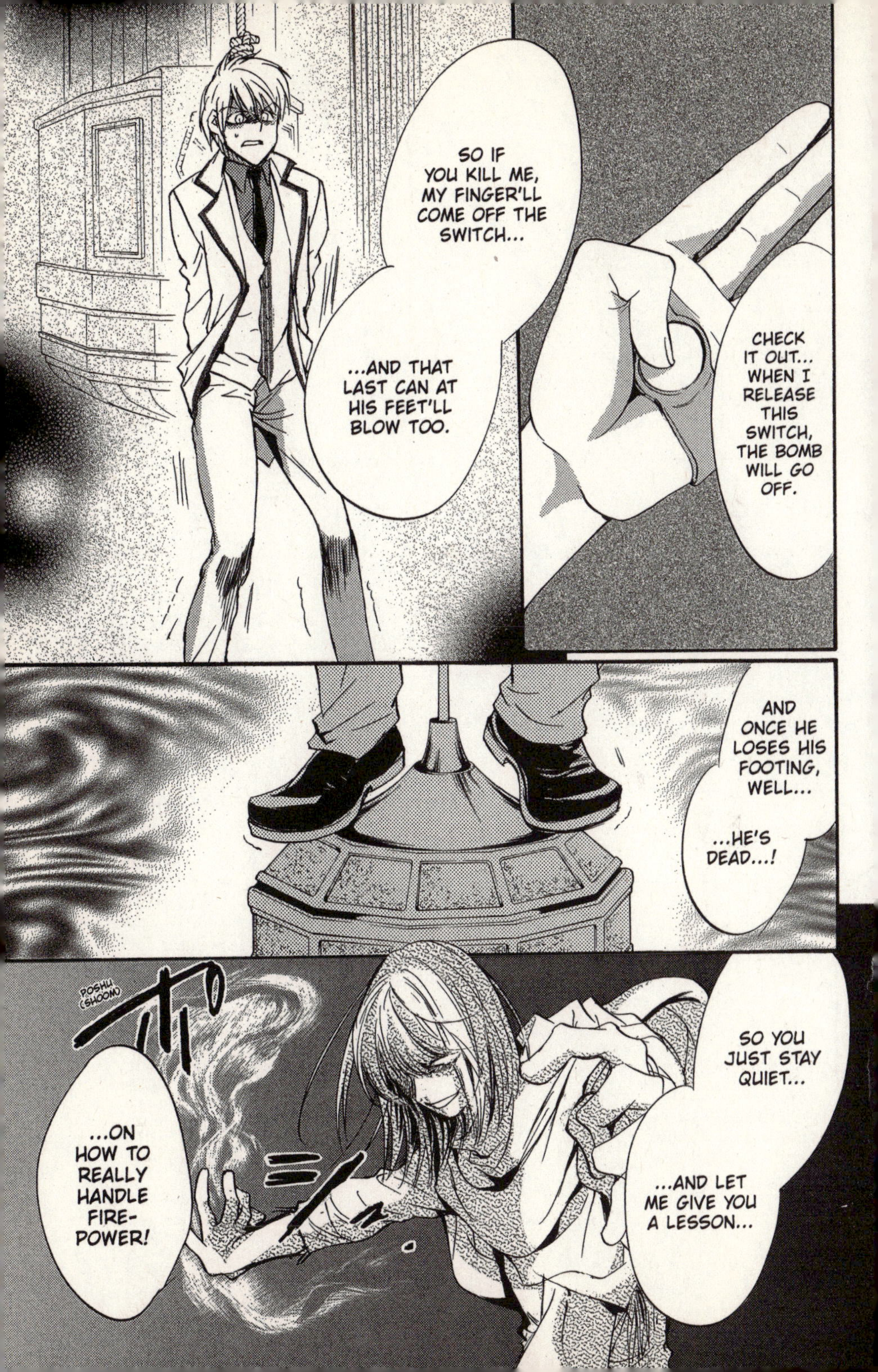
CHECK IT OUT... WHEN I RELEASE THIS SWITCH, THE BOMB WILL GO OFF.
SO IF YOU KILL ME, MY FINGER'LL COME OFF THE SWITCH...
...AND THAT LAST CAN AT HIS FEET'LL BLOW TOO.
AND ONCE HE LOSES HIS FOOTING, WELL...
...HE'S DEAD...!
SO YOU JUST STAY QUIET...
...AND LET ME GIVE YOU A LESSON...
POSHU (SHOOM)
...ON HOW TO REALLY HANDLE FIRE-POWER!

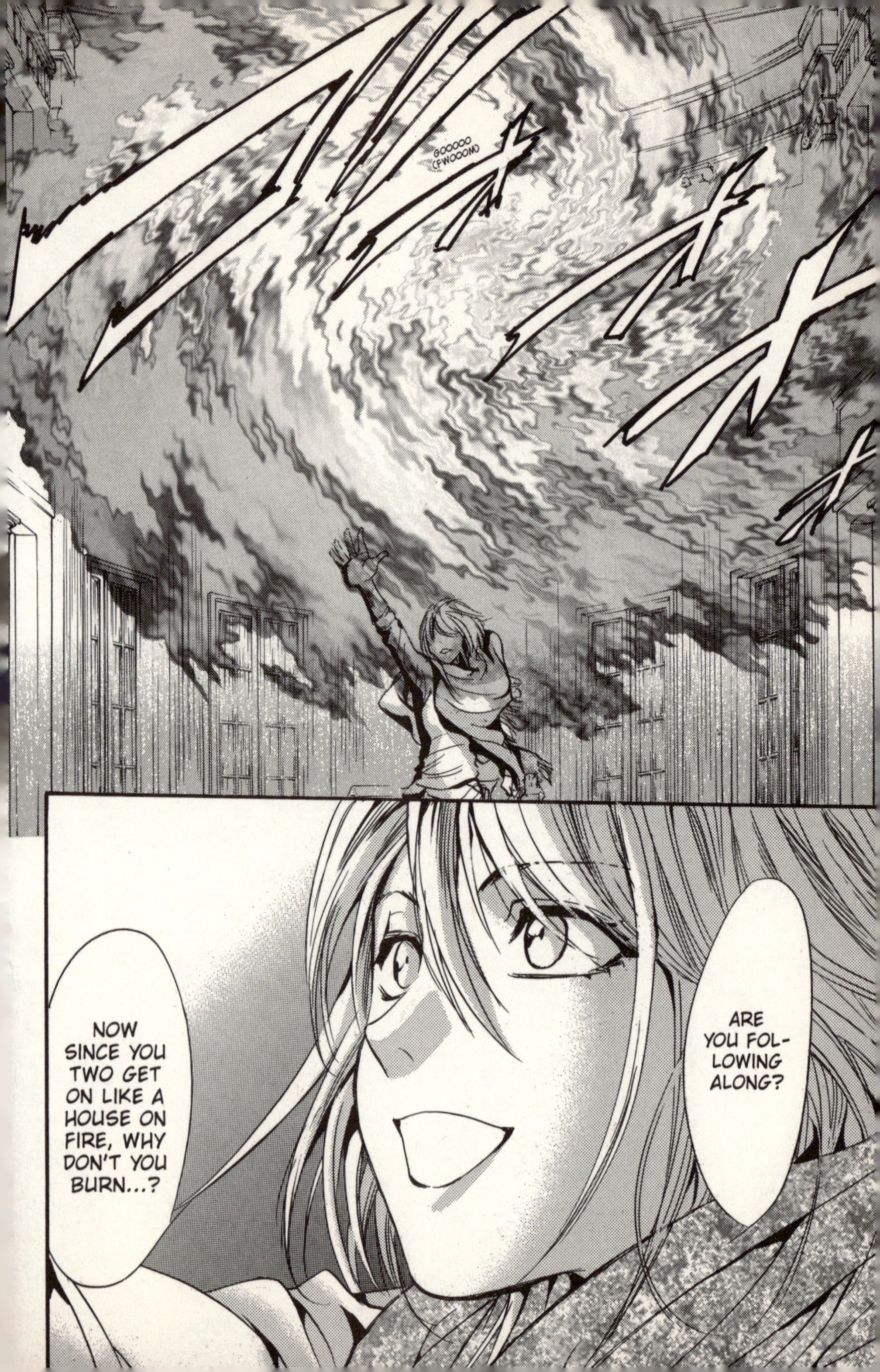
GOOOOO (FWOOOM)
ARE YOU FOL-LOWING ALONG?
NOW SINCE YOU TWO GET ON LIKE A HOUSE ON FIRE, WHY DON'T YOU BURN...?

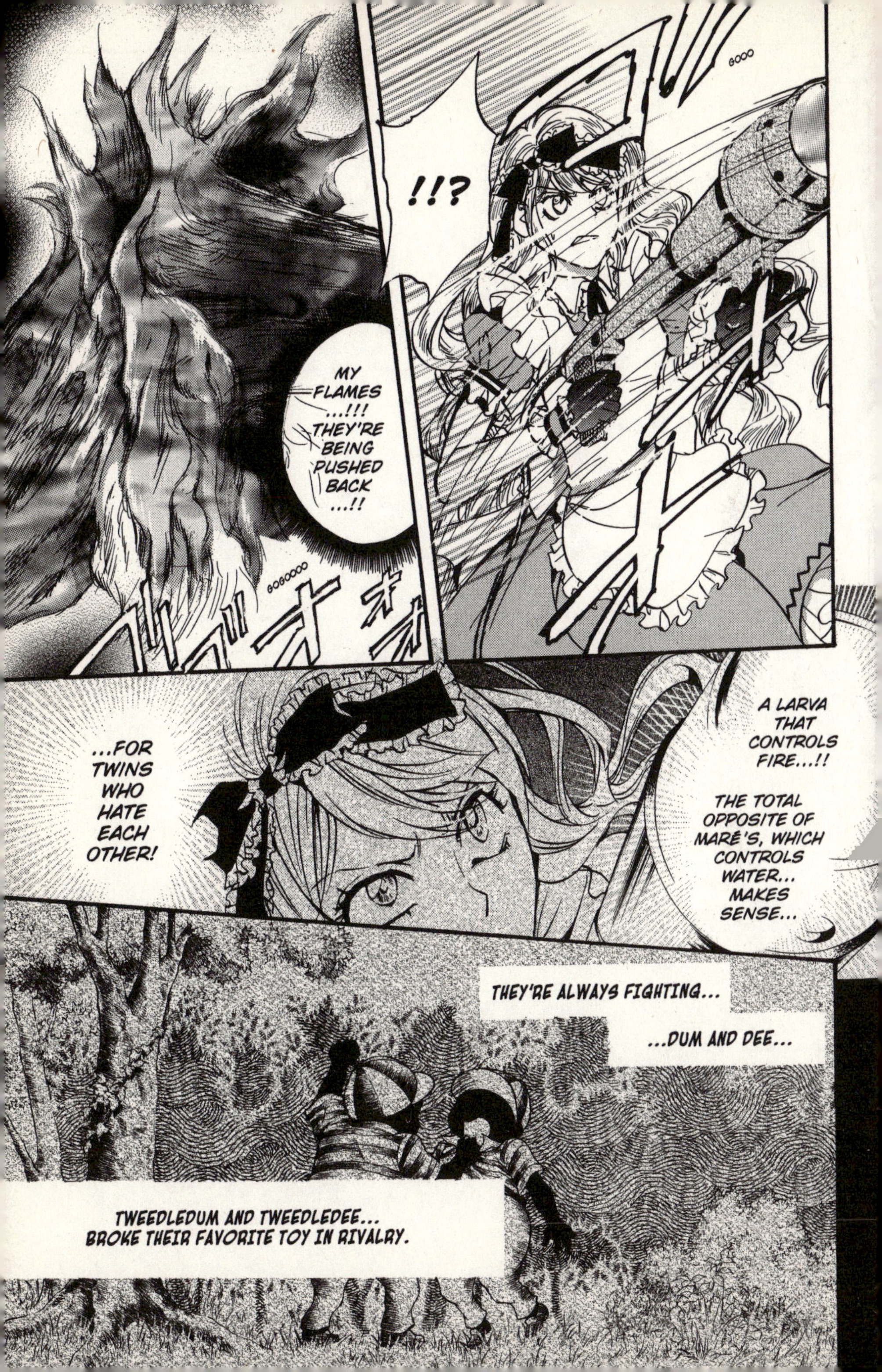
GOOO
!!?
MY FLAMES ...!!! THEY'RE BEING PUSHED BACK ...!!
GOGOOOO
A LARVA THAT CONTROLS FIRE...!!
THE TOTAL OPPOSITE OF MARÉ'S, WHICH CONTROLS WATER... MAKES SENSE...
...FOR TWINS WHO HATE EACH OTHER!
THEY'RE ALWAYS FIGHTING...
...DUM AND DEE...
TWEEDLEDUM AND TWEEDLEDEE... BROKE THEIR FAVORITE TOY IN RIVALRY.

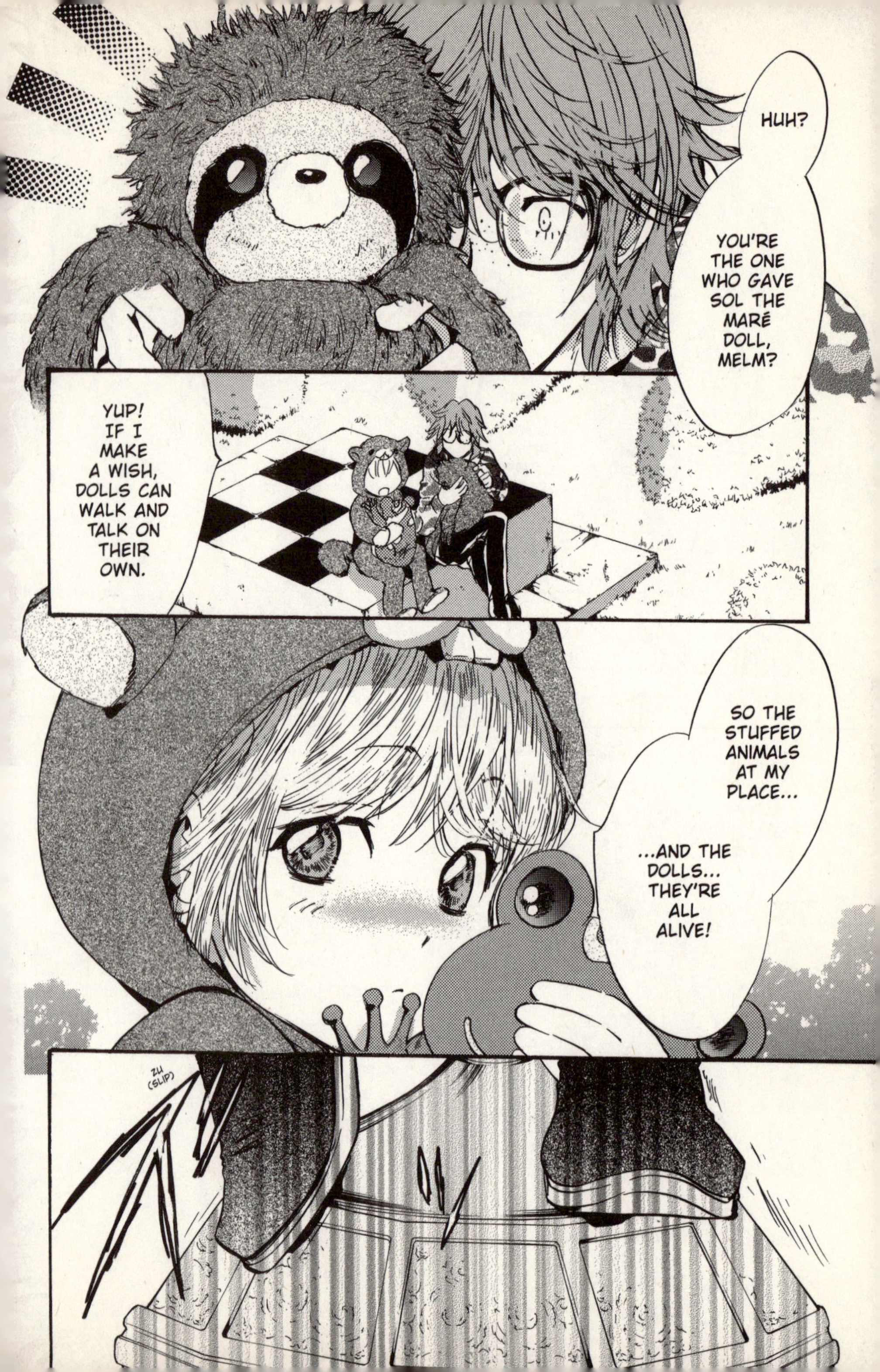
HUH?
YOU'RE THE ONE WHO GAVE SOL THE MARÉ DOLL, MELM?
YUP! IF I MAKE A WISH, DOLLS CAN WALK AND TALK ON THEIR OWN.
SO THE STUFFED ANIMALS AT MY PLACE...
...AND THE DOLLS... THEY'RE ALL ALIVE!
ZU (SLIP)

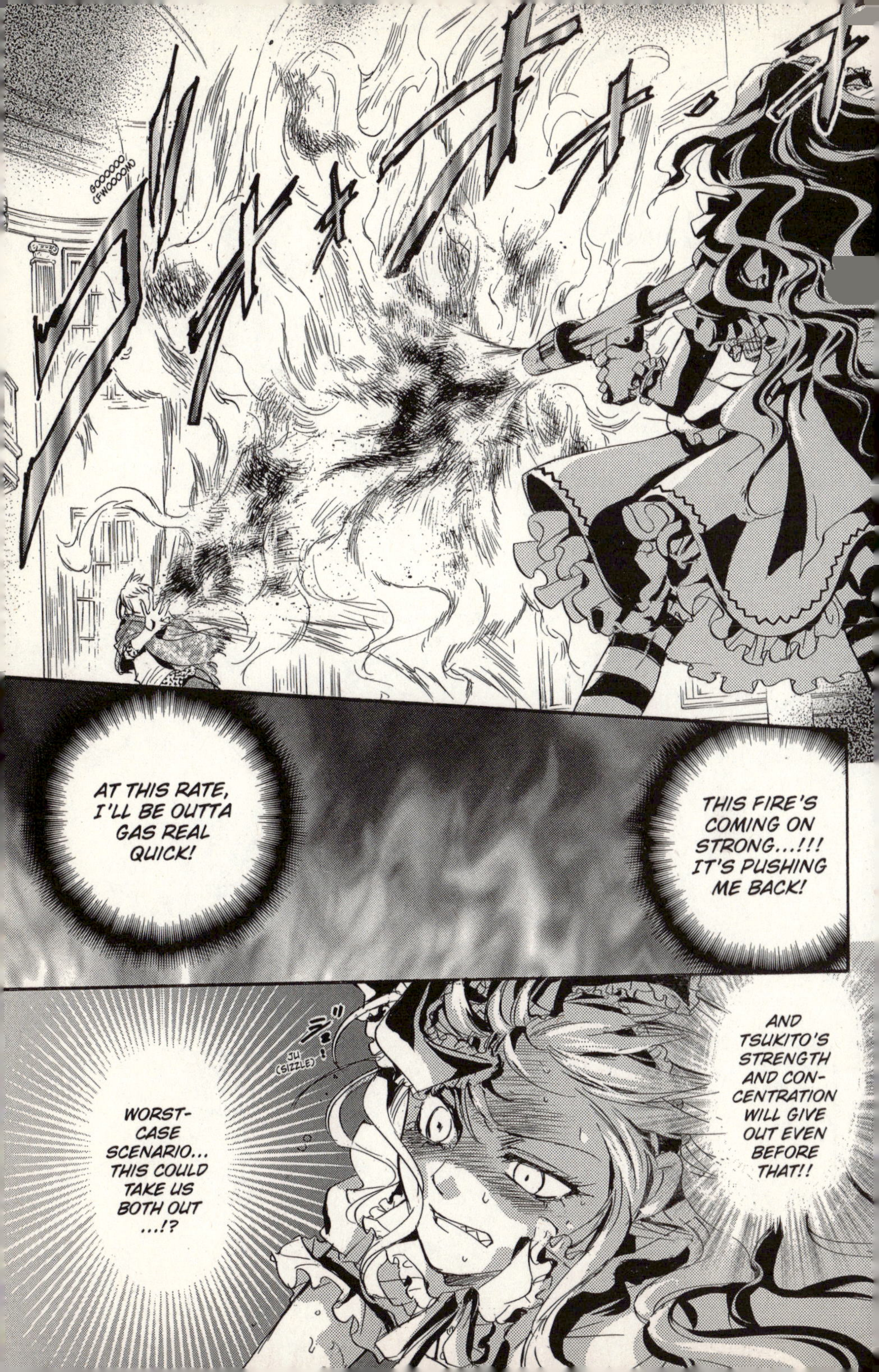
GOOOOOO (FWOOOOM)
THIS FIRE'S COMING ON STRONG...!!! IT'S PUSHING ME BACK!
AT THIS RATE, I'LL BE OUTTA GAS REAL QUICK!
AND TSUKITO'S STRENGTH AND CON-CENTRATION WILL GIVE OUT EVEN BEFORE THAT!!
JU (SIZZLE)
WORST-CASE SCENARIO... THIS COULD TAKE US BOTH OUT ...!?

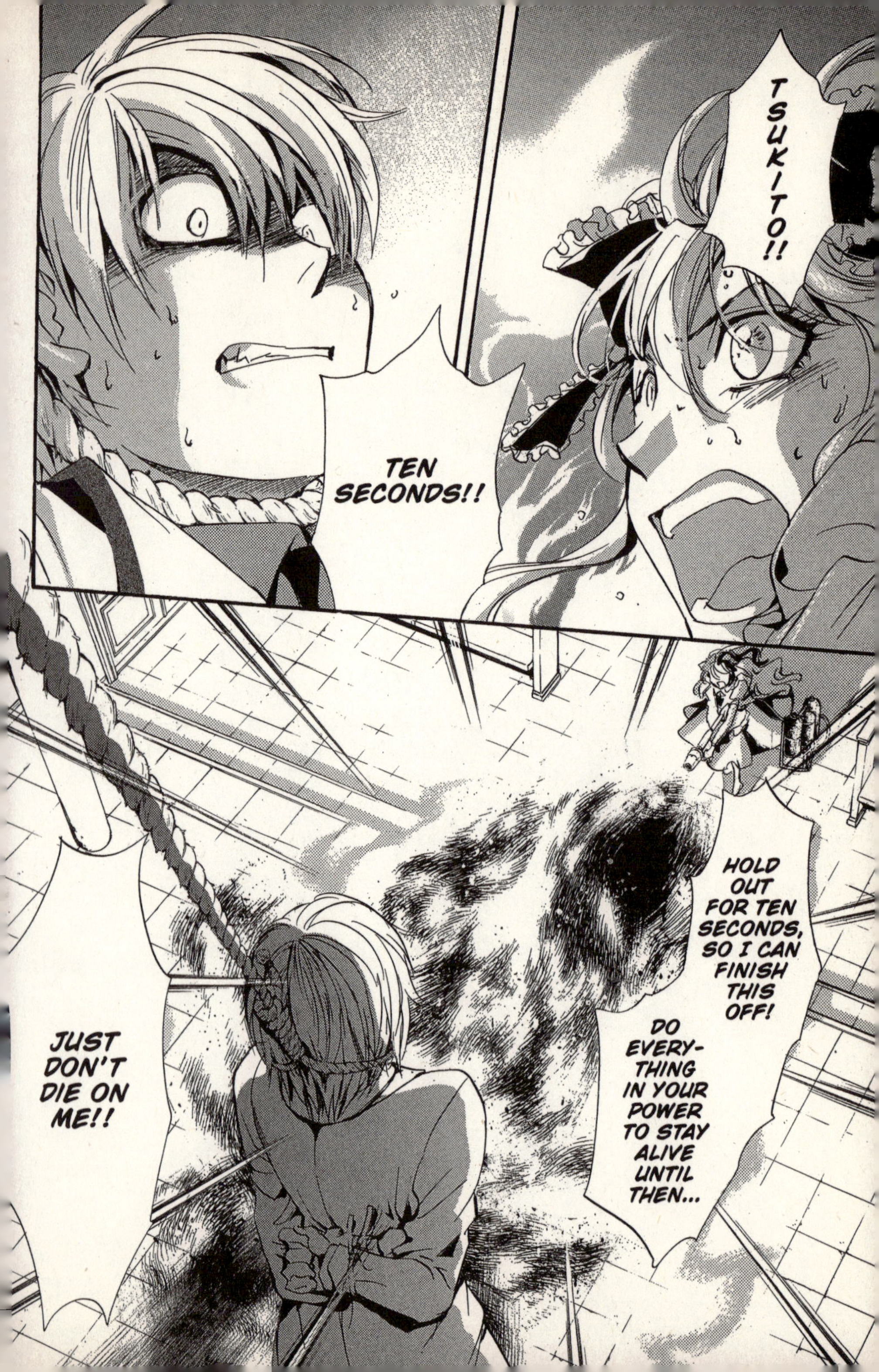
TSUKITO!!
TEN SECONDS!!
HOLD OUT FOR TEN SECONDS, SO I CAN FINISH THIS OFF!
DO EVERYTHING IN YOUR POWER TO STAY ALIVE UNTIL THEN...
JUST DON'T DIE ON ME!!

Alice in MURDERLAND

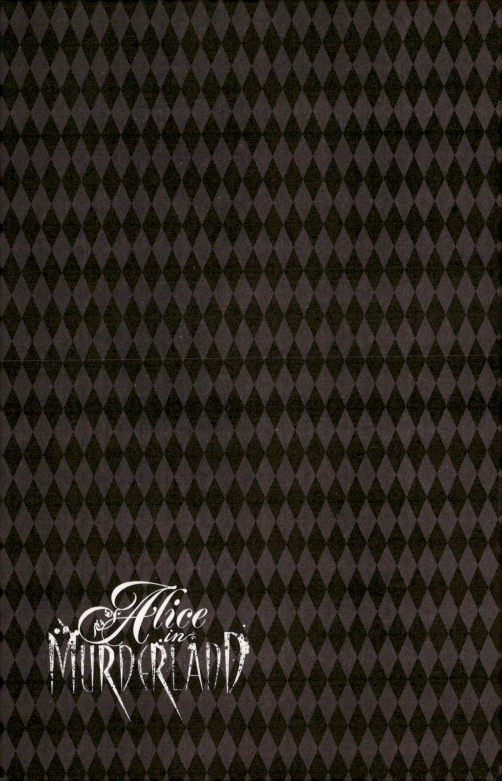

Alice in Murderland

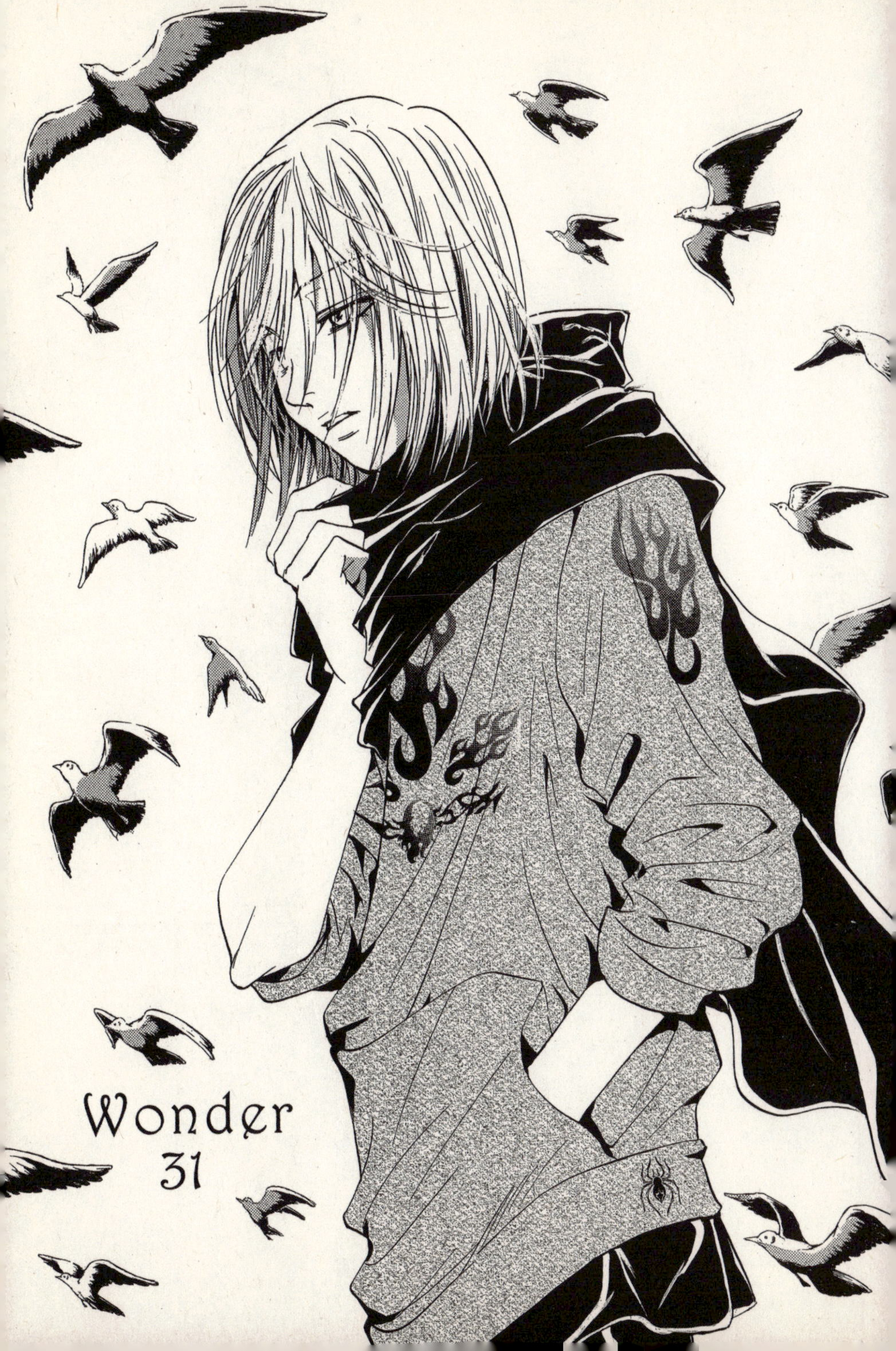
Wonder
31

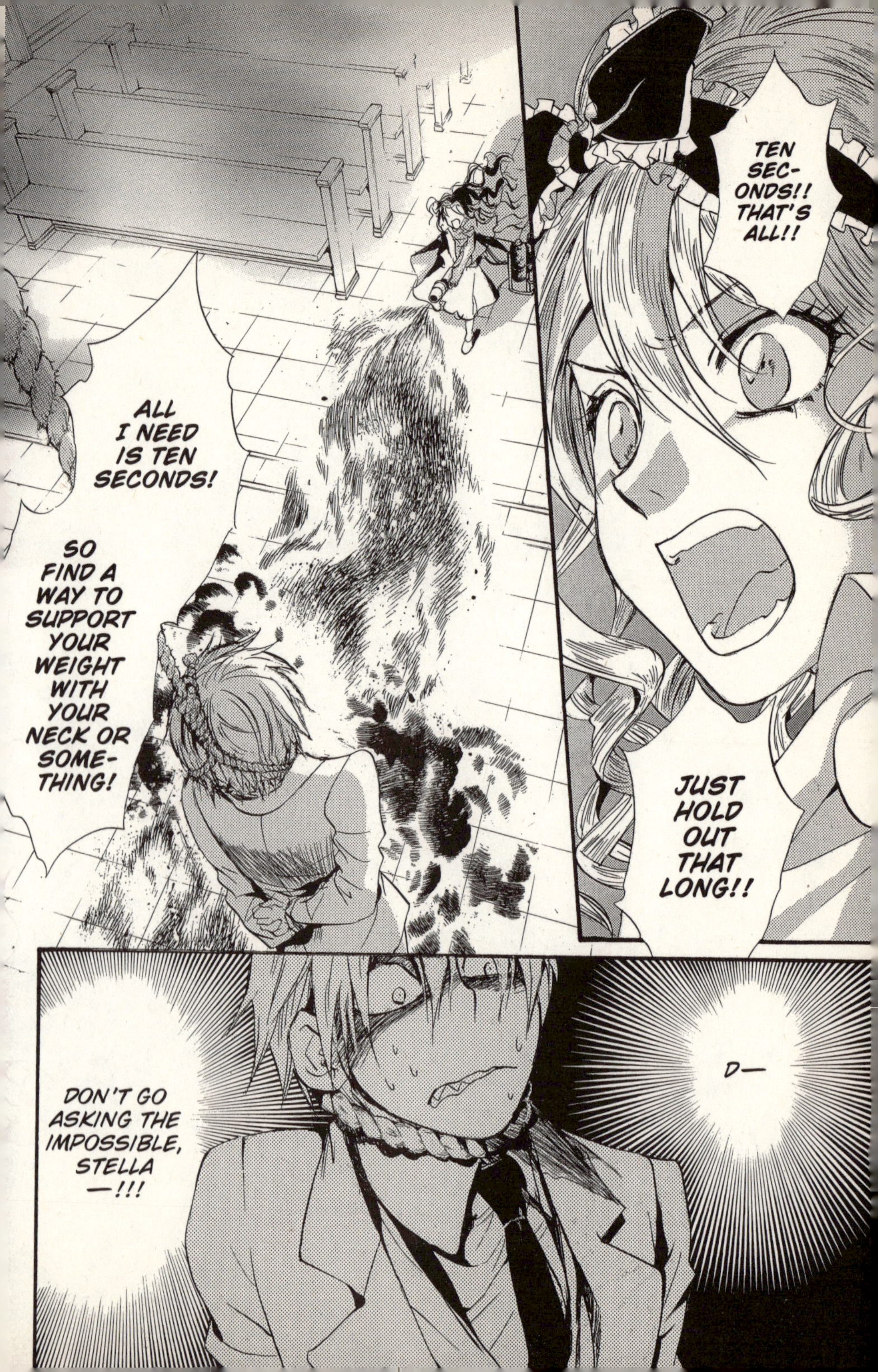
TEN SEC-ONDS!! THAT'S ALL!!
JUST HOLD OUT THAT LONG!!
ALL I NEED IS TEN SECONDS!
SO FIND A WAY TO SUPPORT YOUR WEIGHT WITH YOUR NECK OR SOME-THING!
D—
DON'T GO ASKING THE IMPOSSIBLE, STELLA—!!!

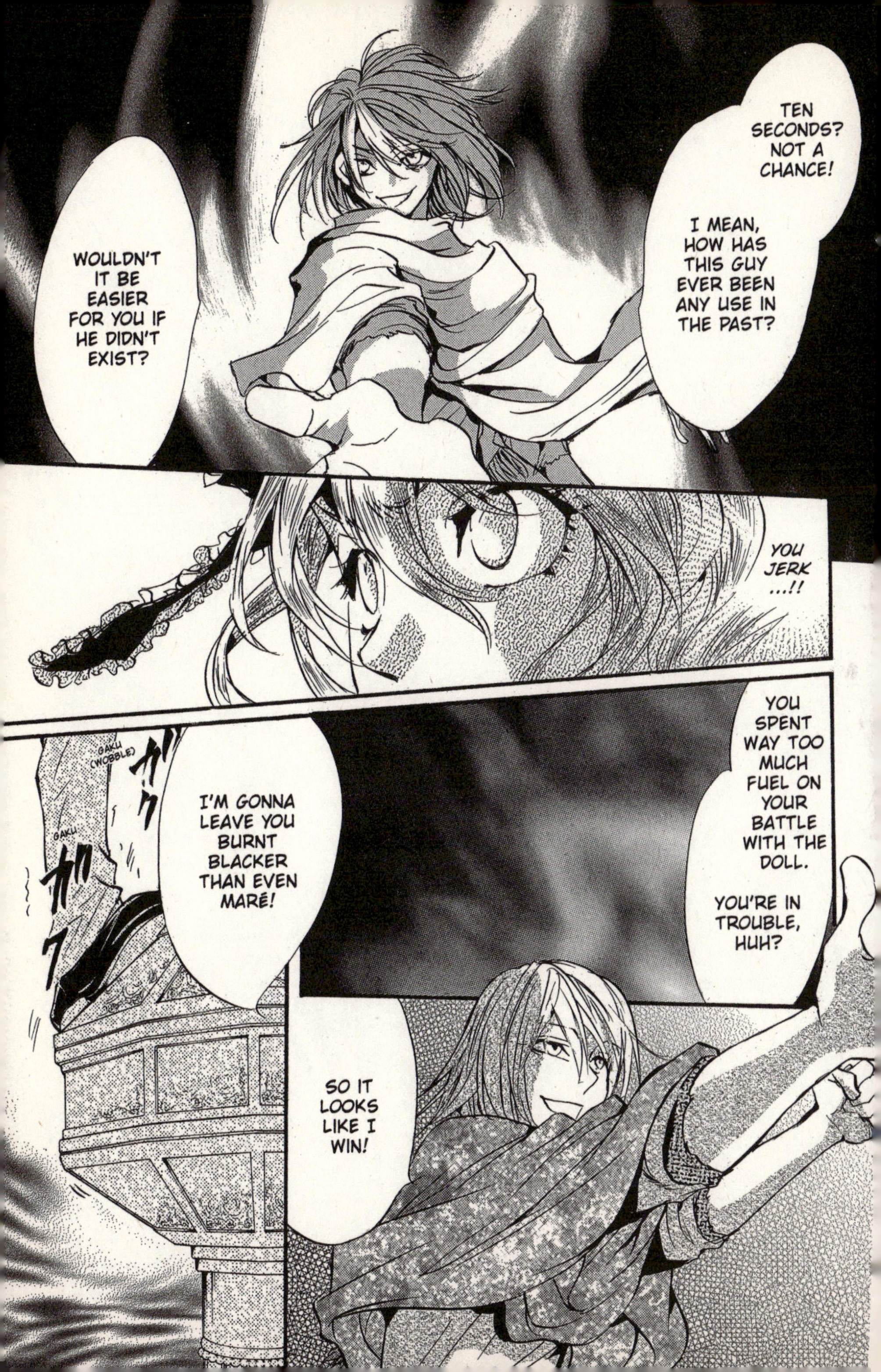
TEN SECONDS? NOT A CHANCE!
I MEAN, HOW HAS THIS GUY EVER BEEN ANY USE IN THE PAST?
WOULDN'T IT BE EASIER FOR YOU IF HE DIDN'T EXIST?
YOU JERK ...!!
YOU SPENT WAY TOO MUCH FUEL ON YOUR BATTLE WITH THE DOLL.
YOU'RE IN TROUBLE, HUH?
SO IT LOOKS LIKE I WIN!
GAKU (WOBBLE)
GAKU
I'M GONNA LEAVE YOU BURNT BLACKER THAN EVEN MARÉ!

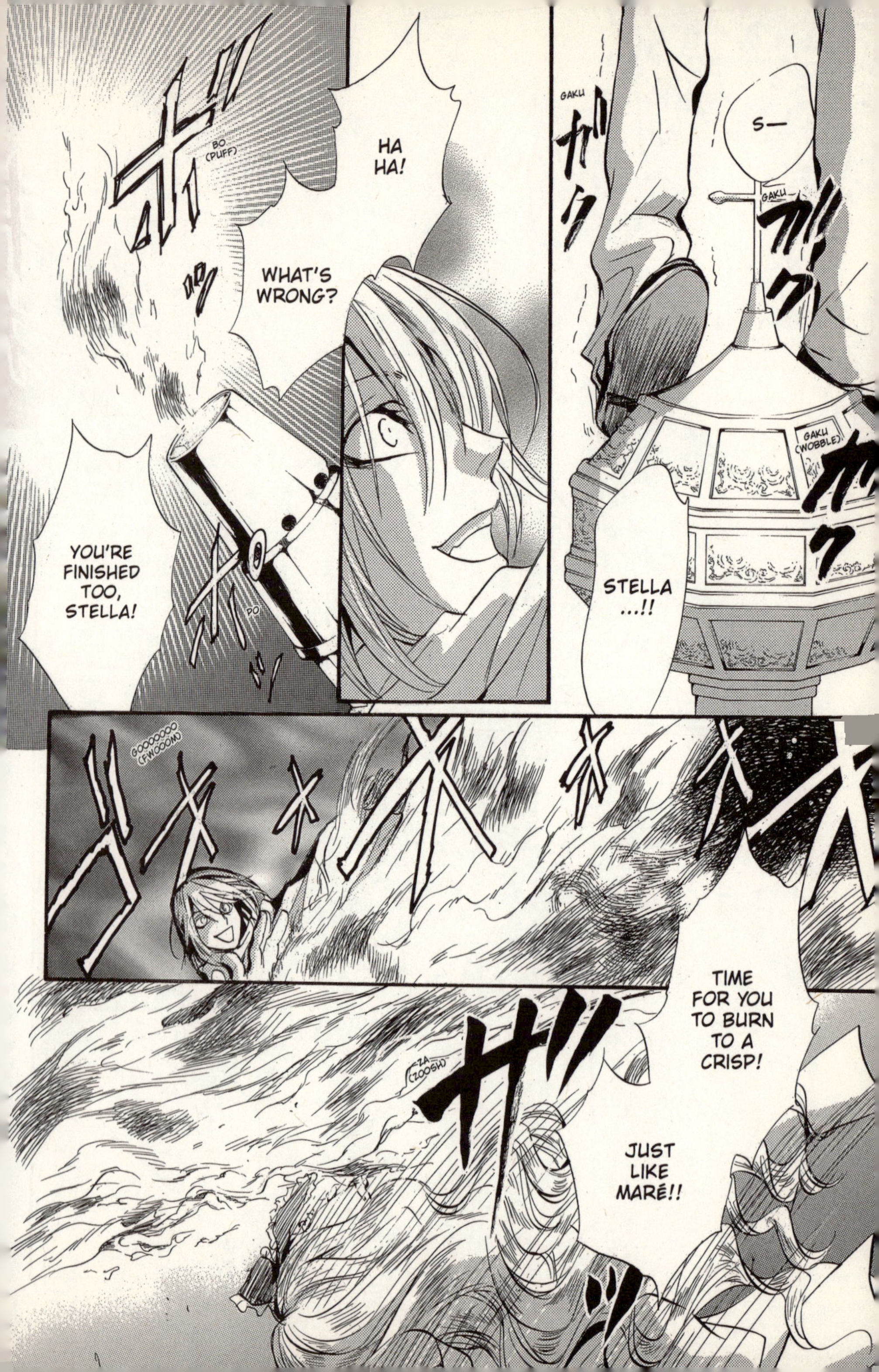

GAKU
S—
GAKU
GAKU (WOBBLE)
STELLA ...!!
HA HA!
WHAT'S WRONG?
BO (PUFF)
YOU'RE FINISHED TOO, STELLA!
DO
GOOOOOOO (FWOOOM)
TIME FOR YOU TO BURN TO A CRISP!
ZA (ZOOSH)
JUST LIKE MARÉ!!

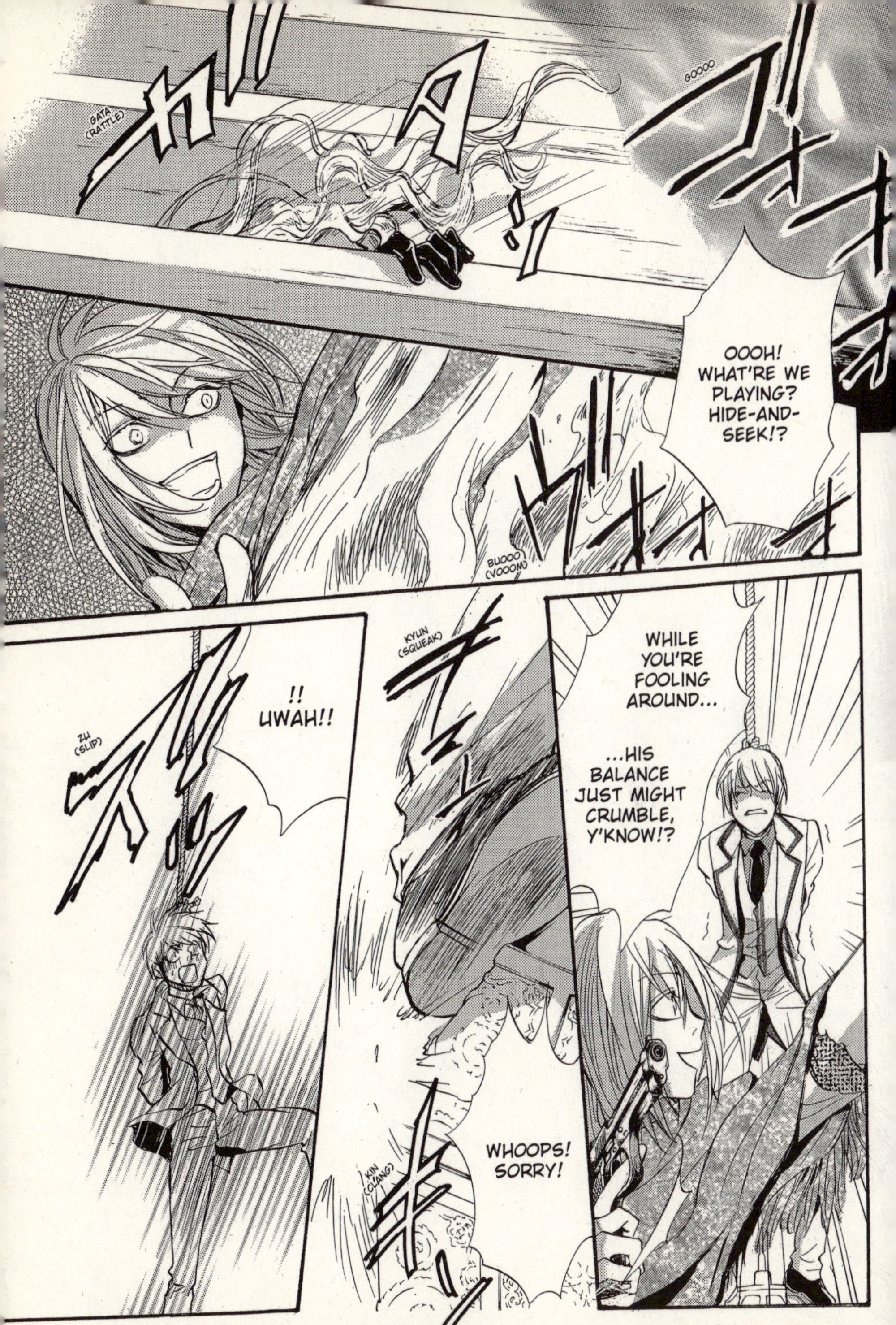
GOOOO
GATA (RATTLE)
OOOH! WHAT'RE WE PLAYING? HIDE-AND-SEEK!?
BUOOO (VOOOM)
WHILE YOU'RE FOOLING AROUND...
...HIS BALANCE JUST MIGHT CRUMBLE, Y'KNOW!?
KYUN (SQUEAK)
WHOOPS! SORRY!
KIN (CLANG)
!! UWAH!!
ZU (SLIP)

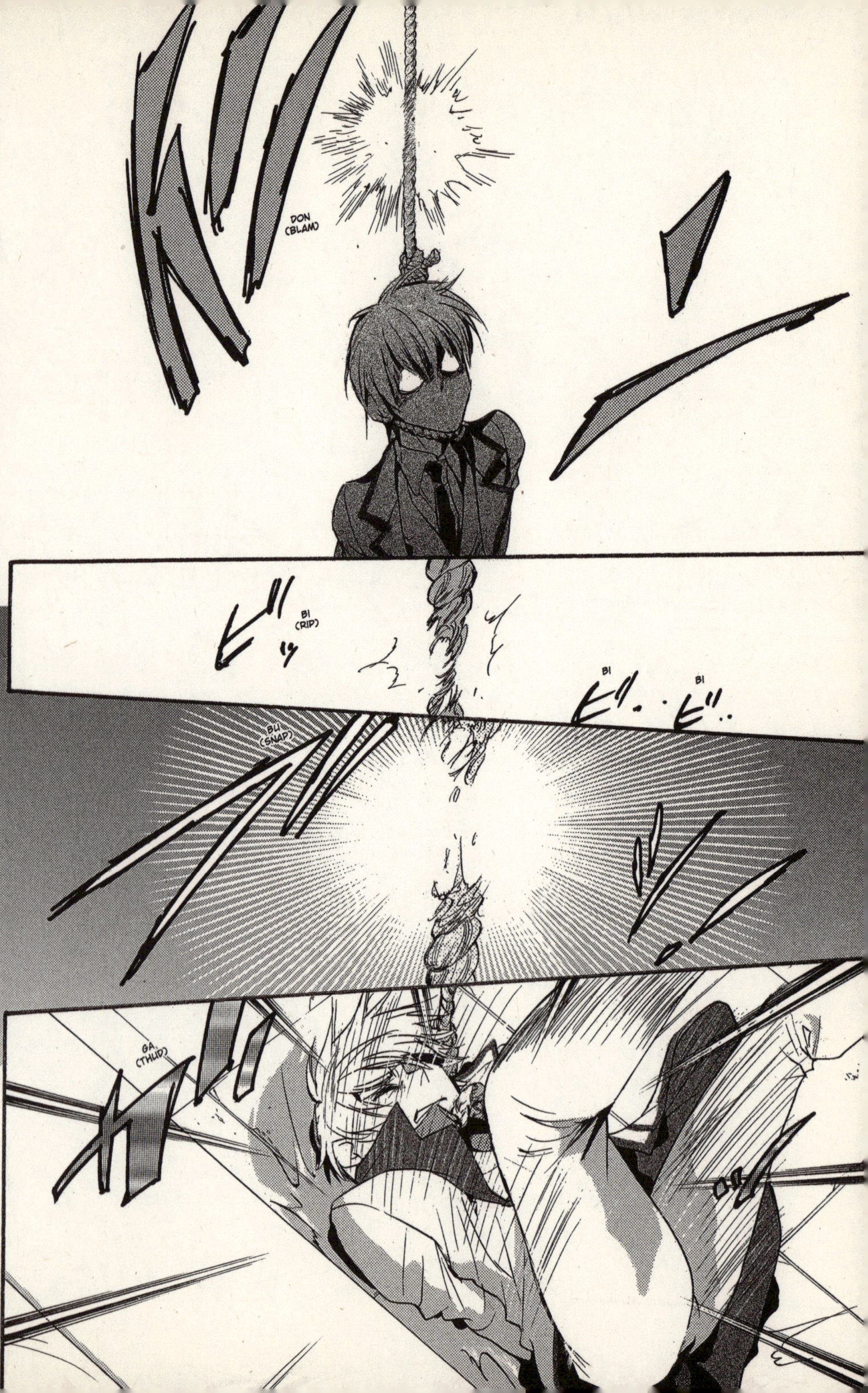
DON (BLAM)
BI
BI
BI (RIP)
BU (SNAP)
GA (THUD)

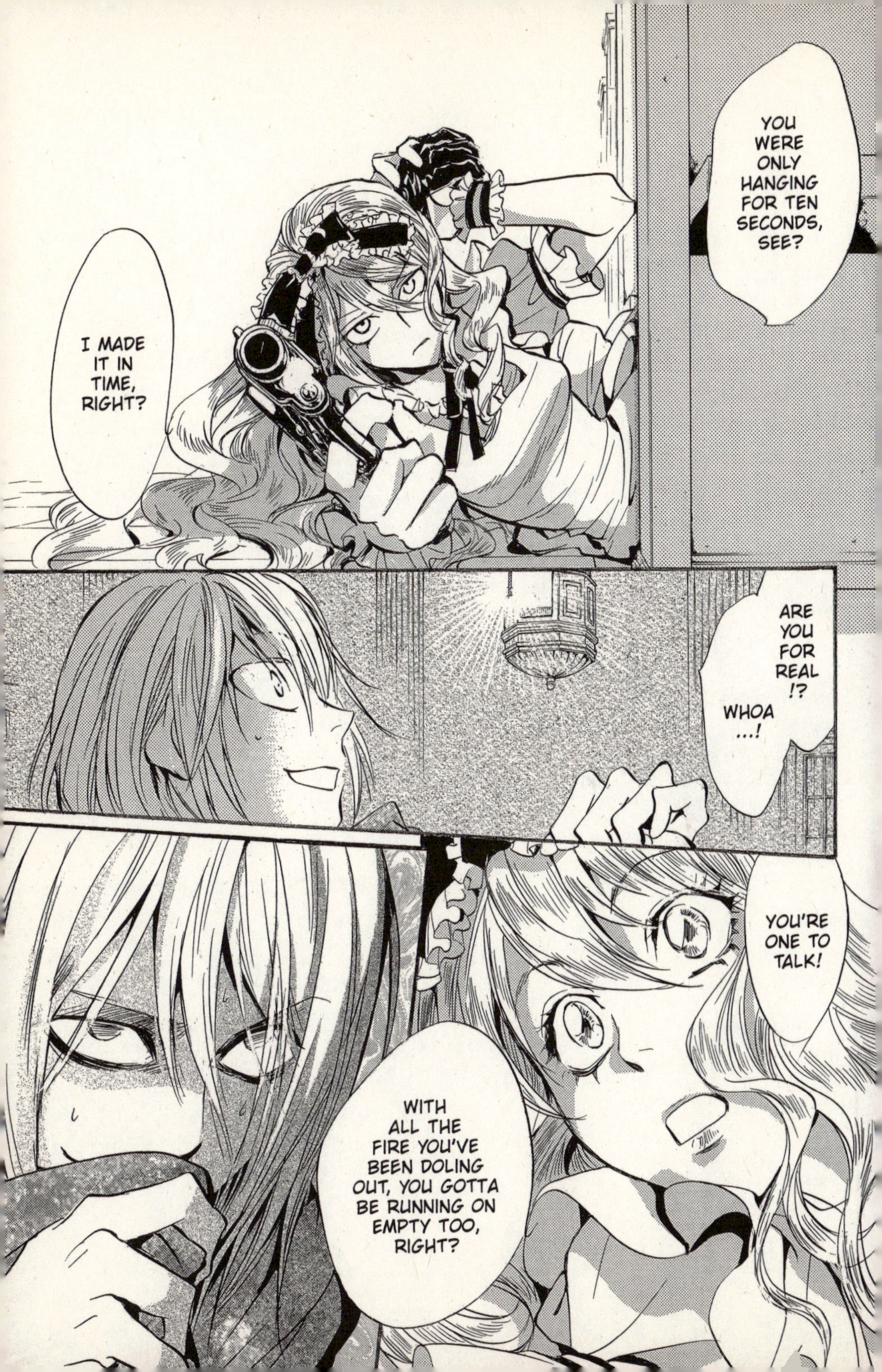
YOU WERE ONLY HANGING FOR TEN SECONDS, SEE?
I MADE IT IN TIME, RIGHT?
ARE YOU FOR REAL!?
WHOA...!
YOU'RE ONE TO TALK!
WITH ALL THE FIRE YOU'VE BEEN DOLING OUT, YOU GOTTA BE RUNNING ON EMPTY TOO, RIGHT?

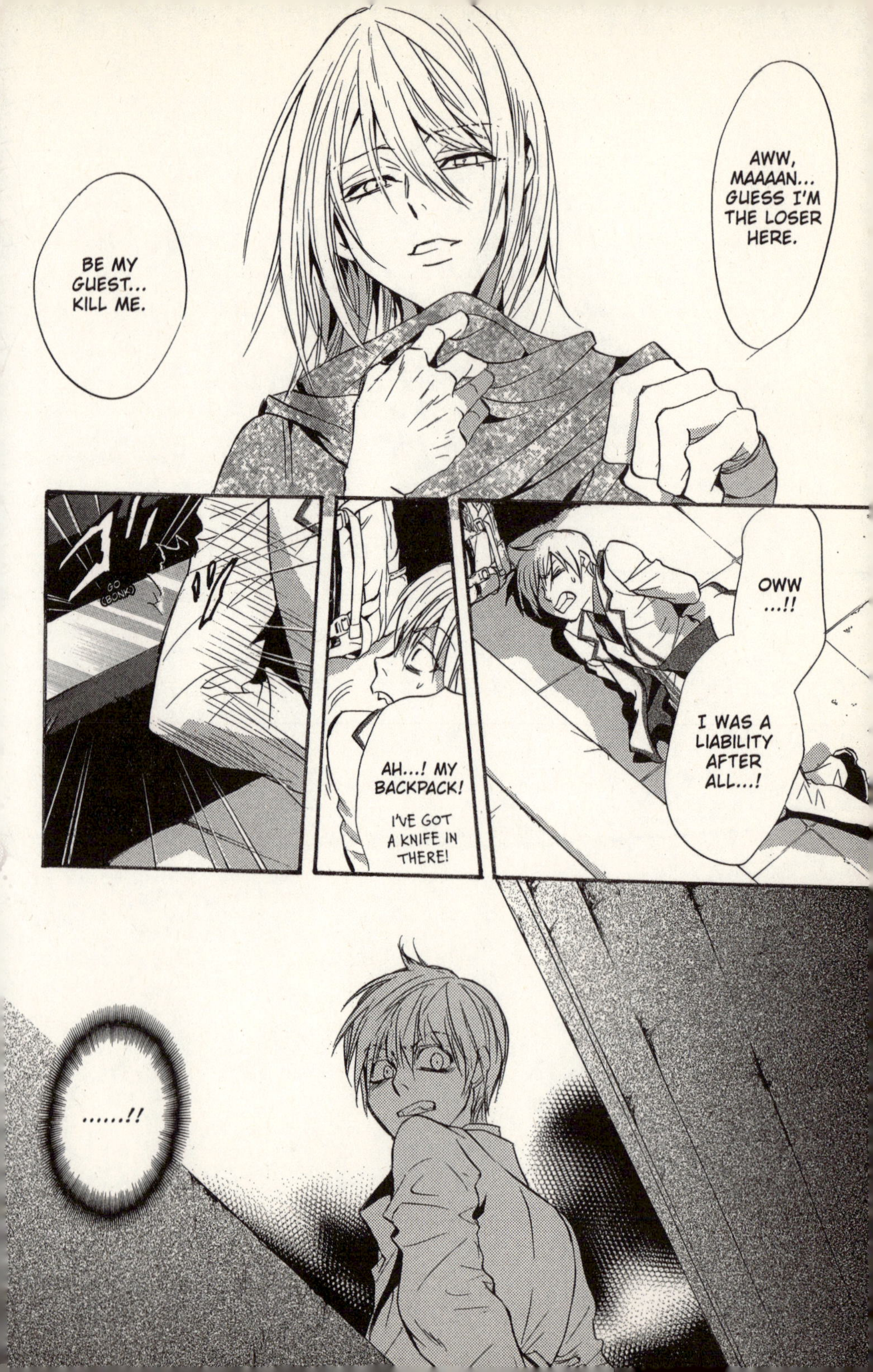
AWW, MAAAAN... GUESS I'M THE LOSER HERE.
BE MY GUEST... KILL ME.
OWW ...!!
I WAS A LIABILITY AFTER ALL...!
AH...! MY BACKPACK!
I'VE GOT A KNIFE IN THERE!
GO (BONK)
......!!

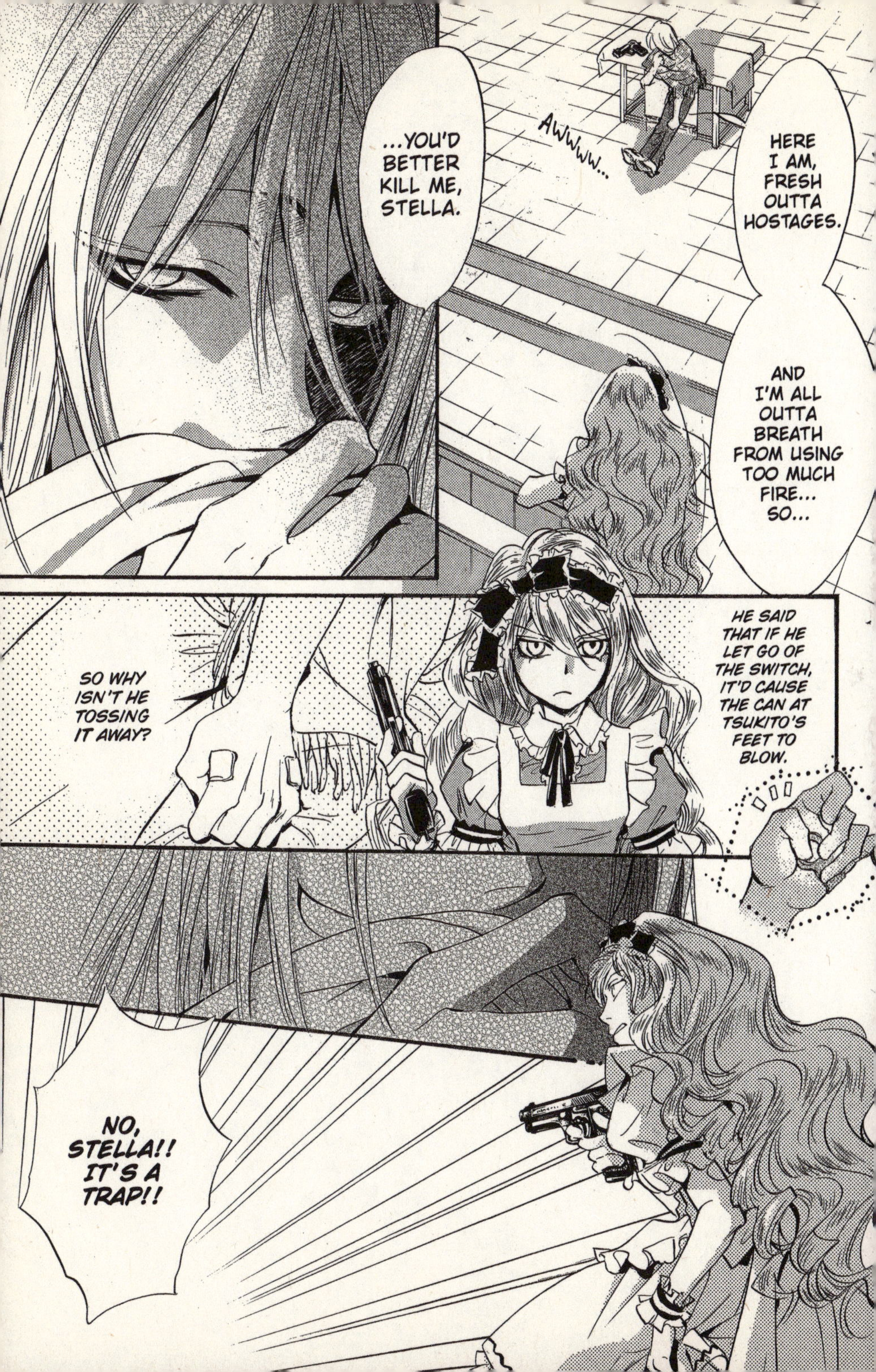
HERE I AM, FRESH OUTTA HOSTAGES.
AWWWW...
AND I'M ALL OUTTA BREATH FROM USING TOO MUCH FIRE... SO...
...YOU'D BETTER KILL ME, STELLA.
HE SAID THAT IF HE LET GO OF THE SWITCH, IT'D CAUSE THE CAN AT TSUKITO'S FEET TO BLOW.
SO WHY ISN'T HE TOSSING IT AWAY?
NO, STELLA!! IT'S A TRAP!!

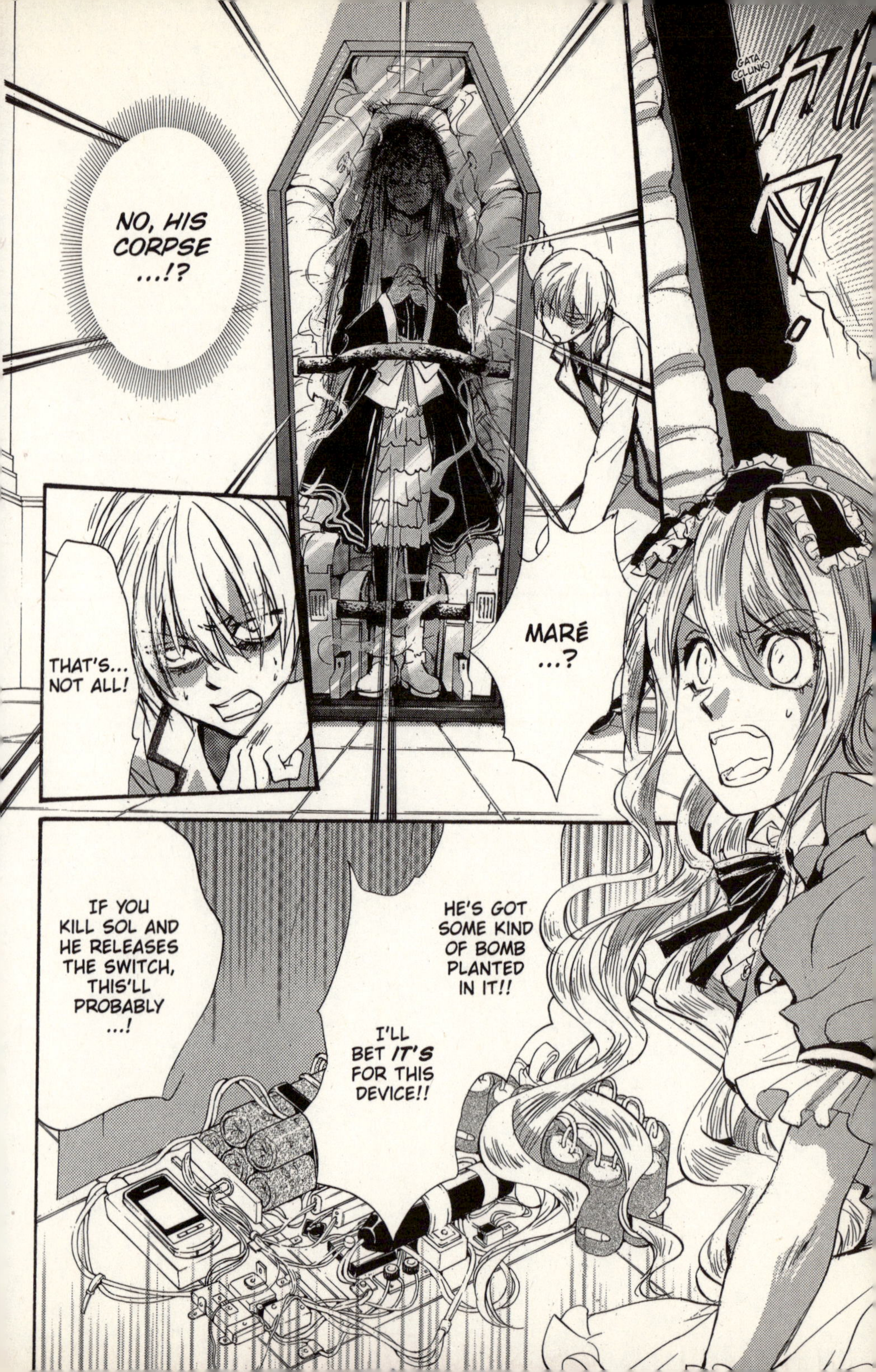
GATA (CLUNK)
MARÉ ...?
NO, HIS CORPSE ...!?
THAT'S... NOT ALL!
HE'S GOT SOME KIND OF BOMB PLANTED IN IT!!
I'LL BET *IT'S* FOR THIS DEVICE!!
IF YOU KILL SOL AND HE RELEASES THE SWITCH, THIS'LL PROBABLY ...!

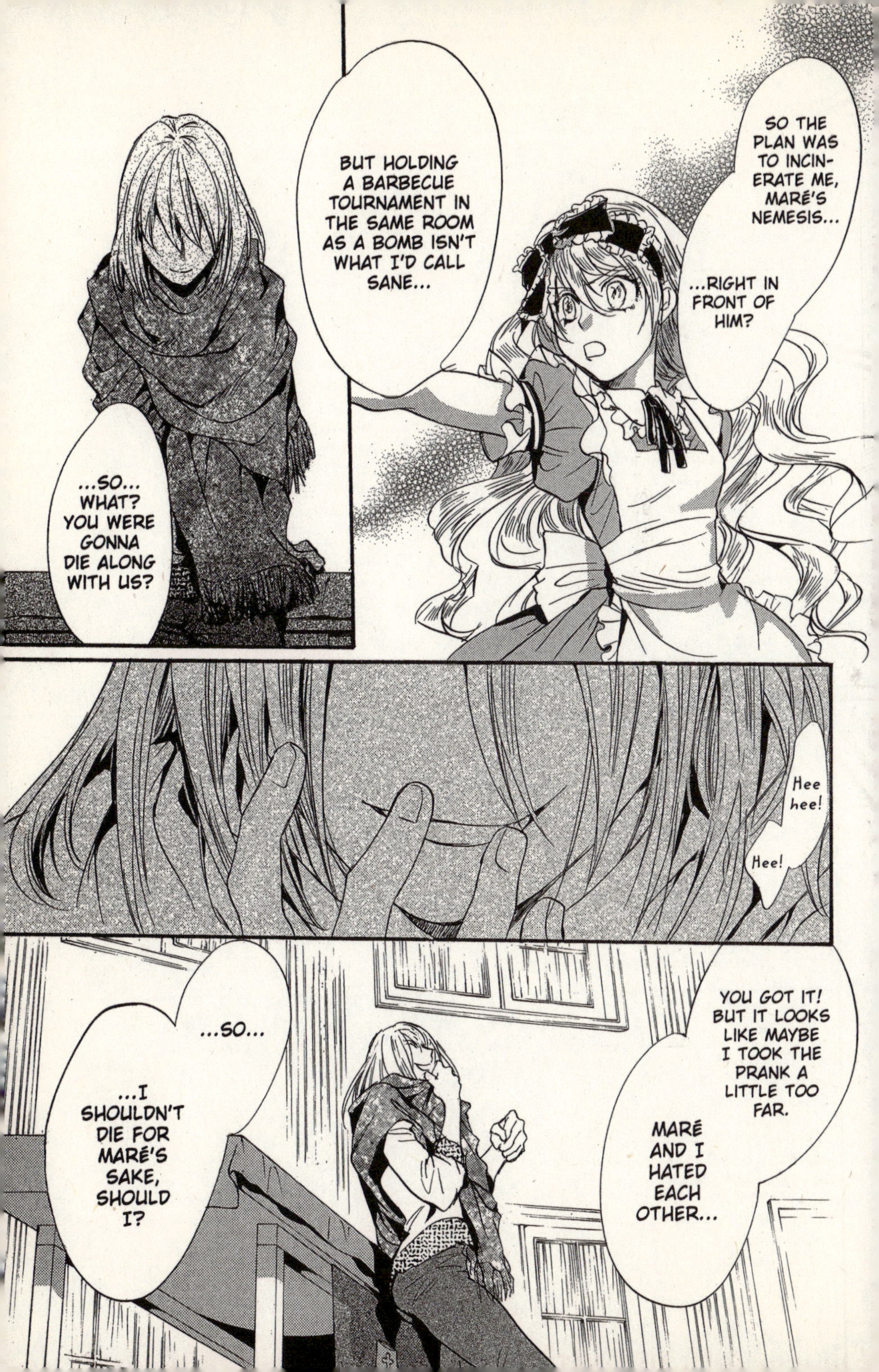
SO THE PLAN WAS TO INCIN-ERATE ME, MARÉ'S NEMESIS...
...RIGHT IN FRONT OF HIM?
BUT HOLDING A BARBECUE TOURNAMENT IN THE SAME ROOM AS A BOMB ISN'T WHAT I'D CALL SANE...
...SO... WHAT? YOU WERE GONNA DIE ALONG WITH US?
Hee hee!
Hee!
YOU GOT IT! BUT IT LOOKS LIKE MAYBE I TOOK THE PRANK A LITTLE TOO FAR.
MARÉ AND I HATED EACH OTHER...
...SO...
...I SHOULDN'T DIE FOR MARÉ'S SAKE, SHOULD I?

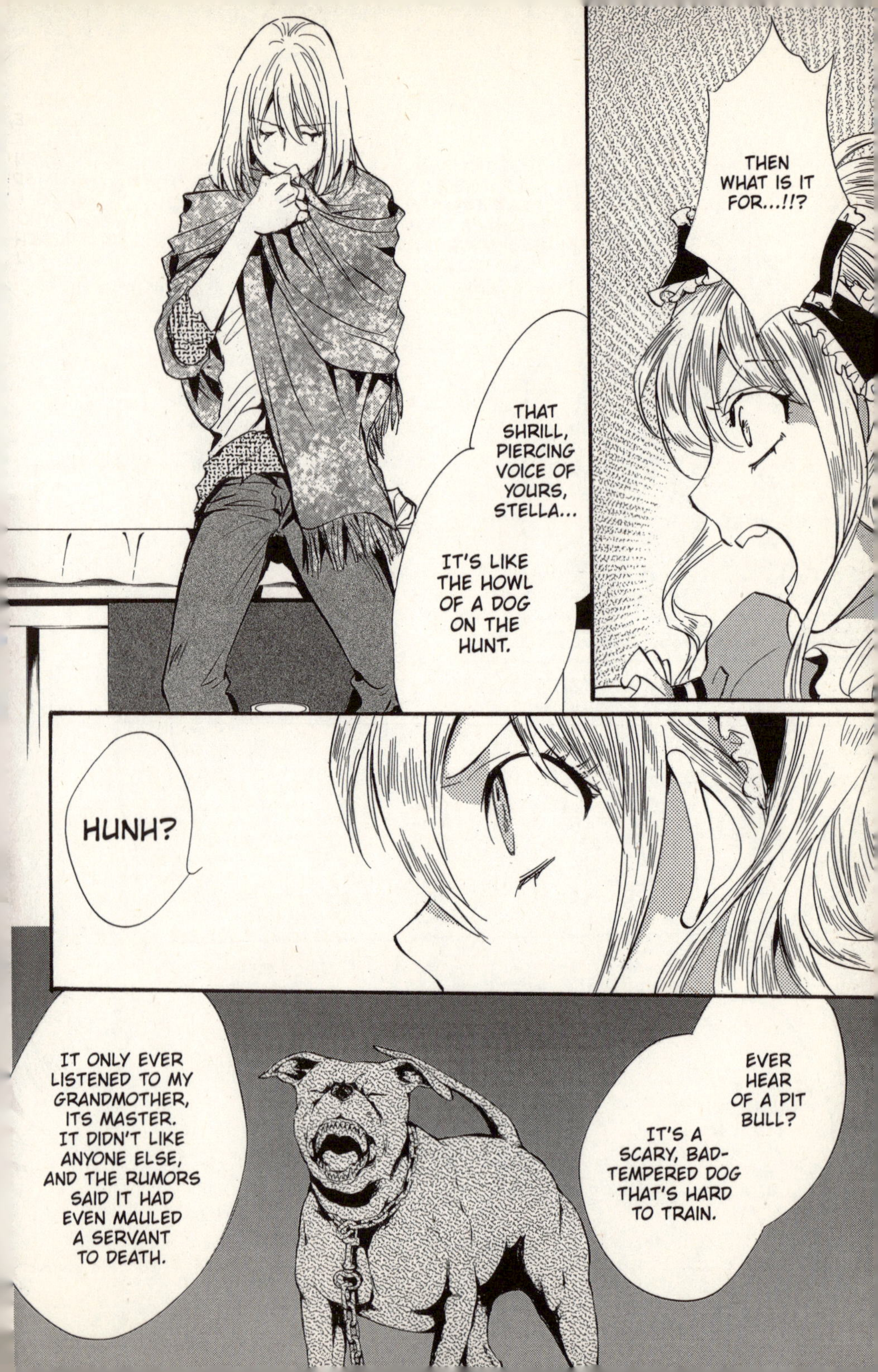
THEN WHAT IS IT FOR...!!?
THAT SHRILL, PIERCING VOICE OF YOURS, STELLA...
IT'S LIKE THE HOWL OF A DOG ON THE HUNT.
HUNH?
EVER HEAR OF A PIT BULL?
IT'S A SCARY, BAD-TEMPERED DOG THAT'S HARD TO TRAIN.
IT ONLY EVER LISTENED TO MY GRANDMOTHER, ITS MASTER. IT DIDN'T LIKE ANYONE ELSE, AND THE RUMORS SAID IT HAD EVEN MAULED A SERVANT TO DEATH.

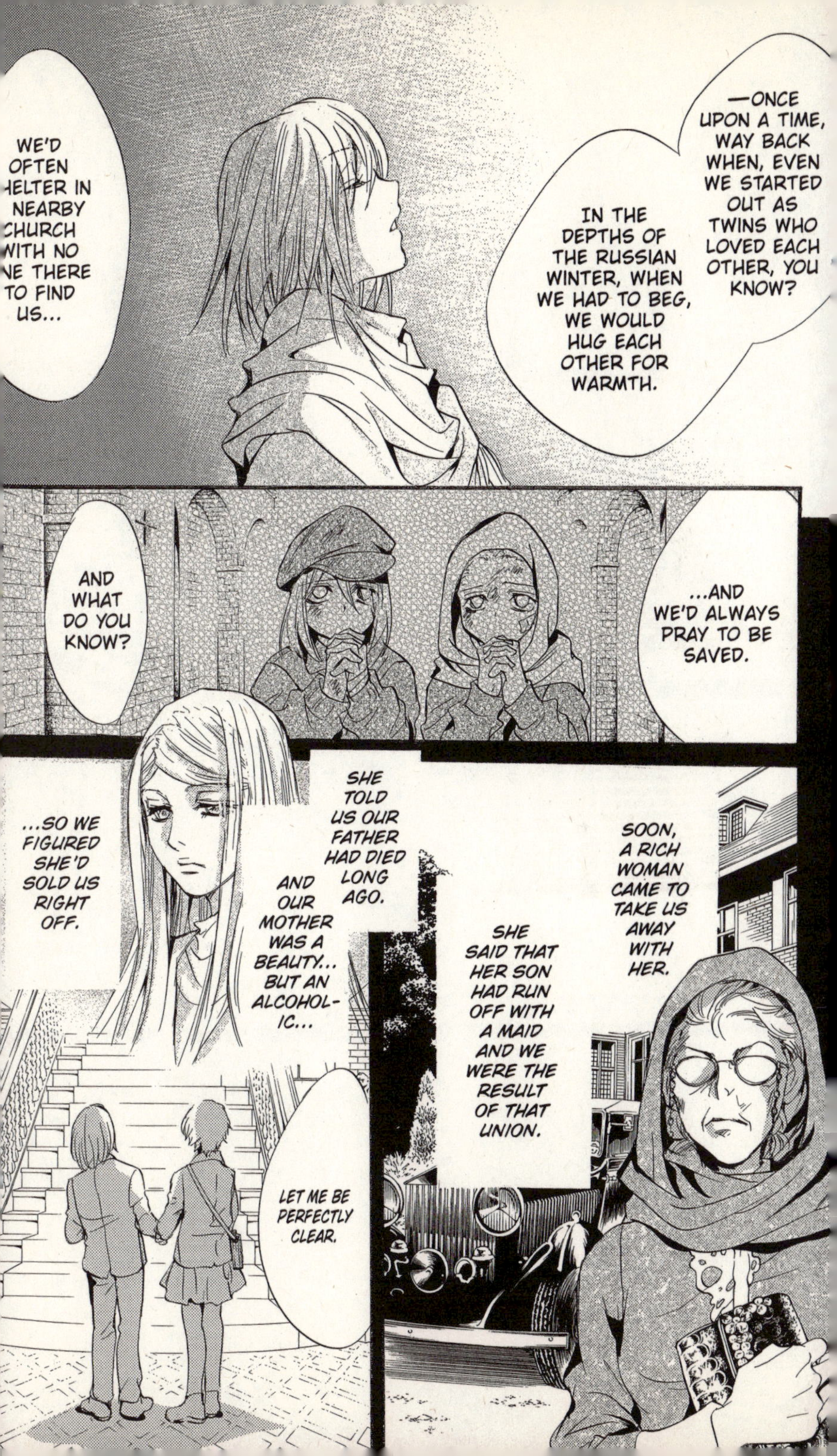
—ONCE UPON A TIME, WAY BACK WHEN, EVEN WE STARTED OUT AS TWINS WHO LOVED EACH OTHER, YOU KNOW?
IN THE DEPTHS OF THE RUSSIAN WINTER, WHEN WE HAD TO BEG, WE WOULD HUG EACH OTHER FOR WARMTH.
WE'D OFTEN HELTER IN NEARBY CHURCH WITH NO NE THERE TO FIND US...
...AND WE'D ALWAYS PRAY TO BE SAVED.
AND WHAT DO YOU KNOW?
SOON, A RICH WOMAN CAME TO TAKE US AWAY WITH HER.
SHE SAID THAT HER SON HAD RUN OFF WITH A MAID AND WE WERE THE RESULT OF THAT UNION.
SHE TOLD US OUR FATHER HAD DIED LONG AGO.
AND OUR MOTHER WAS A BEAUTY... BUT AN ALCOHOLIC...
...SO WE FIGURED SHE'D SOLD US RIGHT OFF.
LET ME BE PERFECTLY CLEAR.

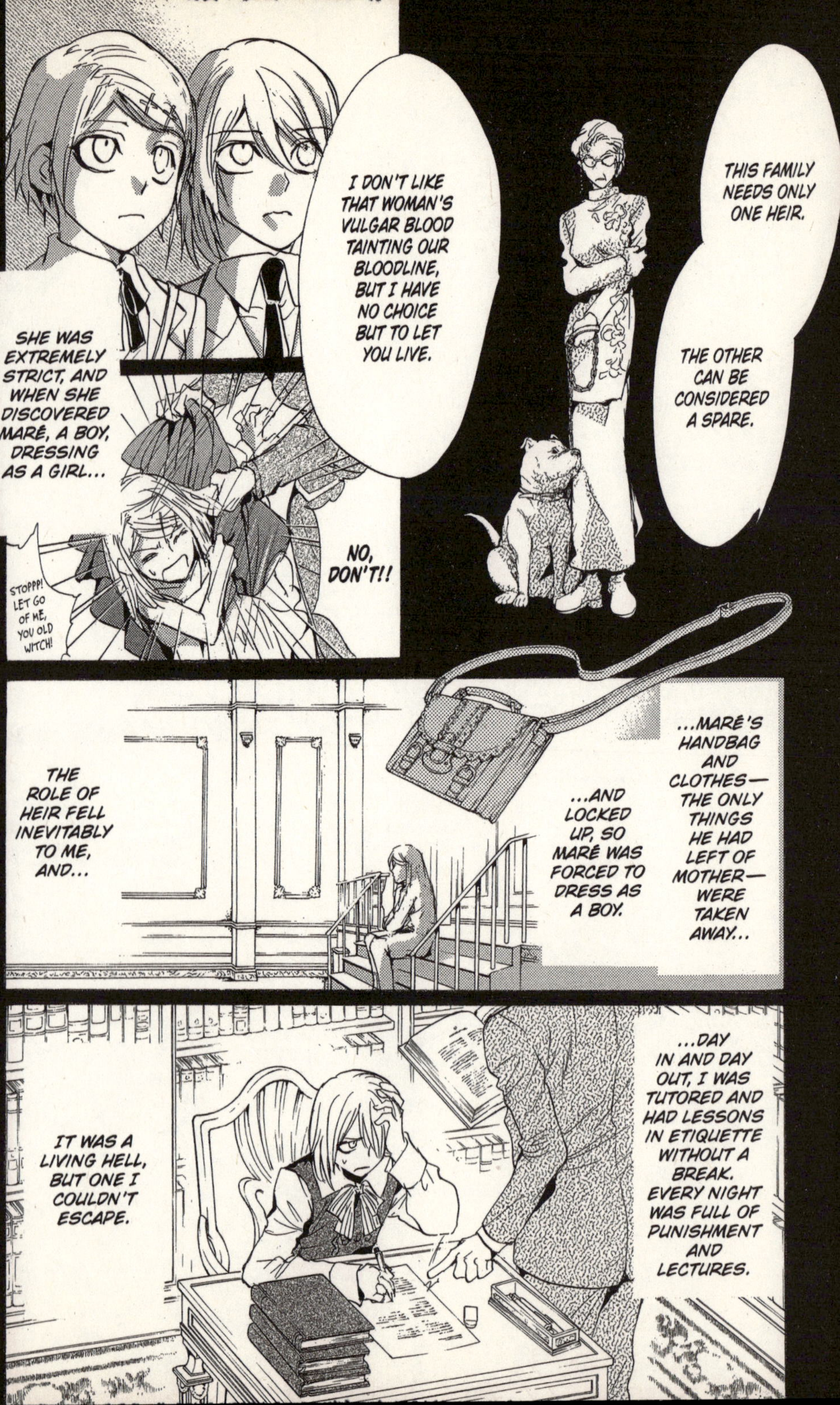
THIS FAMILY NEEDS ONLY ONE HEIR.
THE OTHER CAN BE CONSIDERED A SPARE.
I DON'T LIKE THAT WOMAN'S VULGAR BLOOD TAINTING OUR BLOODLINE, BUT I HAVE NO CHOICE BUT TO LET YOU LIVE.
SHE WAS EXTREMELY STRICT, AND WHEN SHE DISCOVERED MARÉ, A BOY, DRESSING AS A GIRL...
NO, DON'T!!
STOPPP! LET GO OF ME, YOU OLD WITCH!
...MARÉ'S HANDBAG AND CLOTHES—THE ONLY THINGS HE HAD LEFT OF MOTHER—WERE TAKEN AWAY...
...AND LOCKED UP, SO MARÉ WAS FORCED TO DRESS AS A BOY.
THE ROLE OF HEIR FELL INEVITABLY TO ME, AND...
...DAY IN AND DAY OUT, I WAS TUTORED AND HAD LESSONS IN ETIQUETTE WITHOUT A BREAK. EVERY NIGHT WAS FULL OF PUNISHMENT AND LECTURES.
IT WAS A LIVING HELL, BUT ONE I COULDN'T ESCAPE.

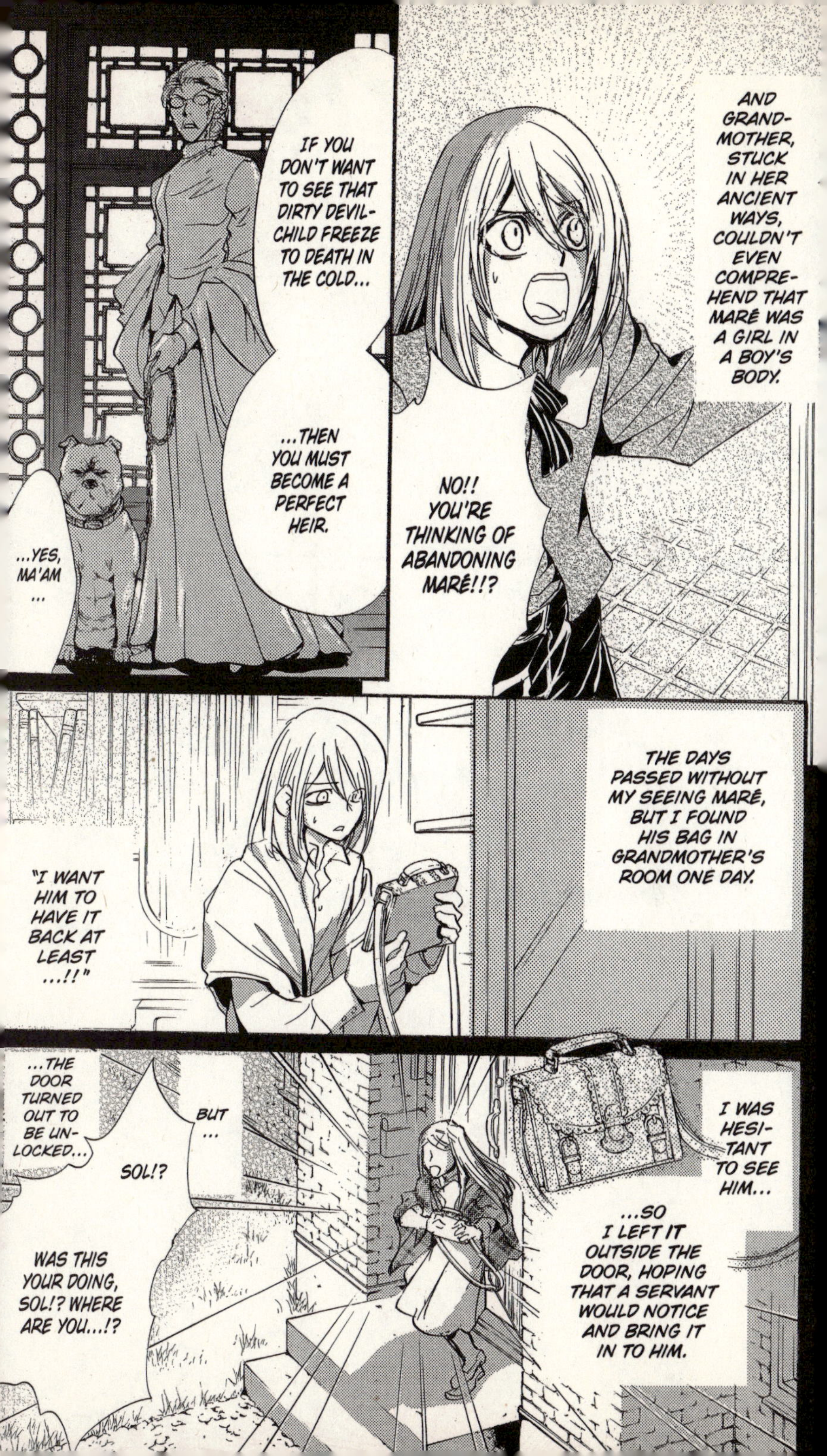
AND GRANDMOTHER, STUCK IN HER ANCIENT WAYS, COULDN'T EVEN COMPREHEND THAT MARÉ WAS A GIRL IN A BOY'S BODY.
NO!! YOU'RE THINKING OF ABANDONING MARÉ!!?
IF YOU DON'T WANT TO SEE THAT DIRTY DEVIL-CHILD FREEZE TO DEATH IN THE COLD...
...THEN YOU MUST BECOME A PERFECT HEIR.
...YES, MA'AM ...
THE DAYS PASSED WITHOUT MY SEEING MARÉ, BUT I FOUND HIS BAG IN GRANDMOTHER'S ROOM ONE DAY.
"I WANT HIM TO HAVE IT BACK AT LEAST ...!!"
I WAS HESITANT TO SEE HIM...
...SO I LEFT IT OUTSIDE THE DOOR, HOPING THAT A SERVANT WOULD NOTICE AND BRING IT IN TO HIM.
BUT ...
...THE DOOR TURNED OUT TO BE UNLOCKED...
SOL!?
WAS THIS YOUR DOING, SOL!? WHERE ARE YOU...!?

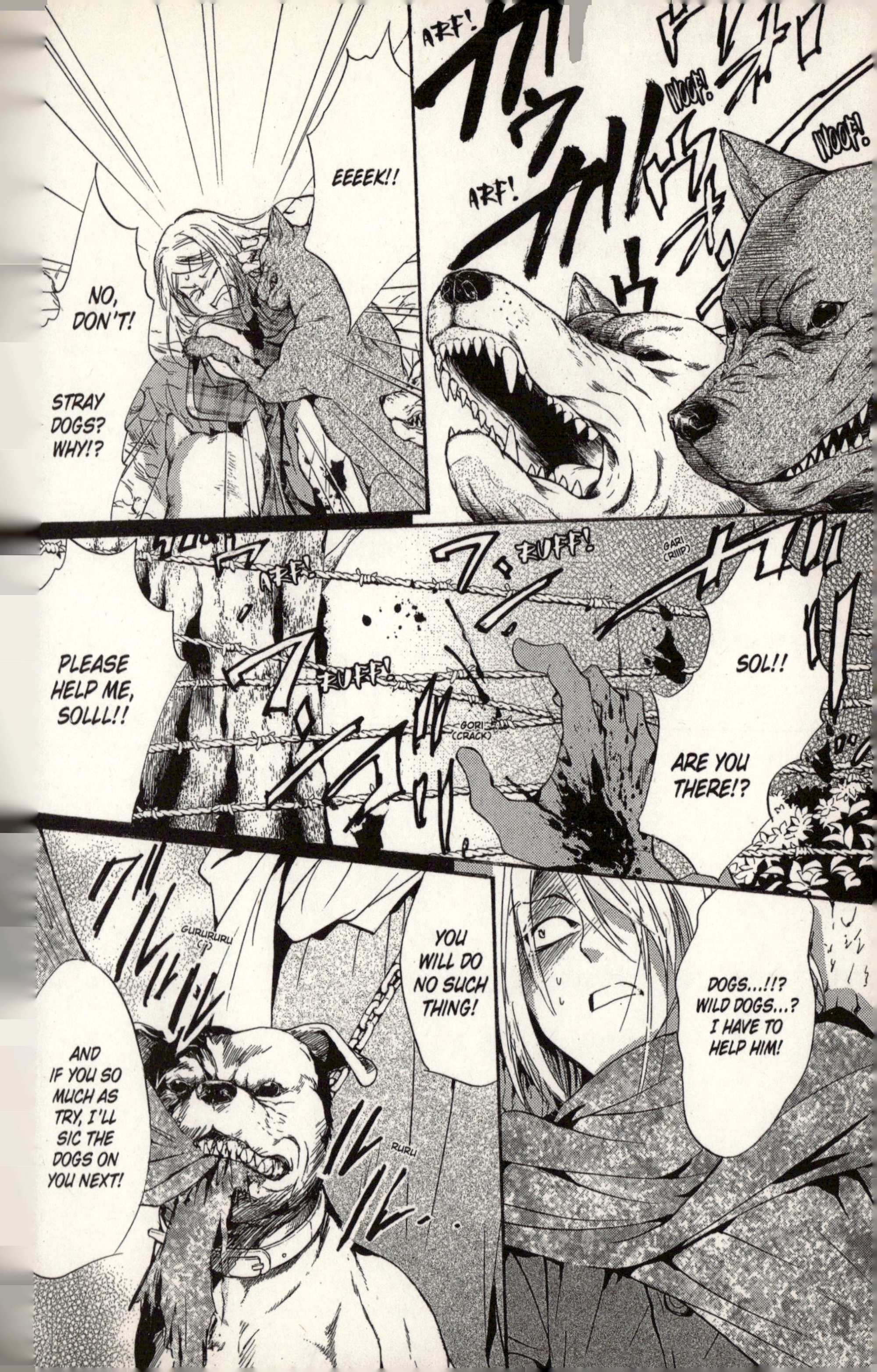
ARF!
WOOF!
WOOF!
ARF!
EEEEK!!
NO, DON'T!
STRAY DOGS? WHY!?
SOL!!
ARE YOU THERE!?
GARI (RIIIP)
RUFF!
GORI (CRACK)
RUFF!
ARF!
PLEASE HELP ME, SOLLL!!
DOGS...!!? WILD DOGS...? I HAVE TO HELP HIM!
YOU WILL DO NO SUCH THING!
GURURURU
AND IF YOU SO MUCH AS TRY, I'LL SIC THE DOGS ON YOU NEXT!
RURU

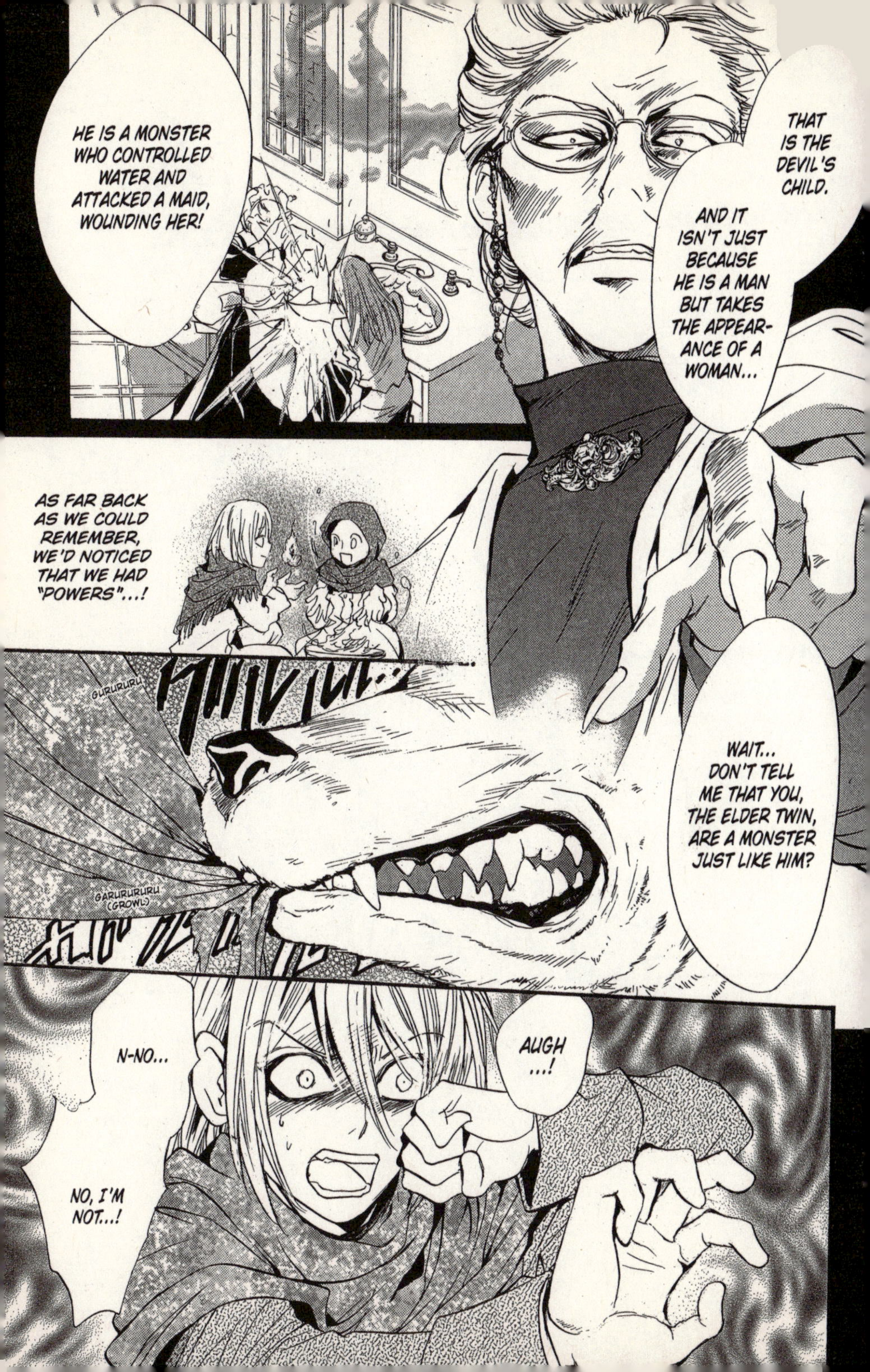

THAT IS THE DEVIL'S CHILD.
AND IT ISN'T JUST BECAUSE HE IS A MAN BUT TAKES THE APPEARANCE OF A WOMAN...
HE IS A MONSTER WHO CONTROLLED WATER AND ATTACKED A MAID, WOUNDING HER!
AS FAR BACK AS WE COULD REMEMBER, WE'D NOTICED THAT WE HAD "POWERS"...!
WAIT... DON'T TELL ME THAT YOU, THE ELDER TWIN, ARE A MONSTER JUST LIKE HIM?
GURURURU
GARURURURU (GROWL)
AUGH ...!
N-NO...
NO, I'M NOT...!

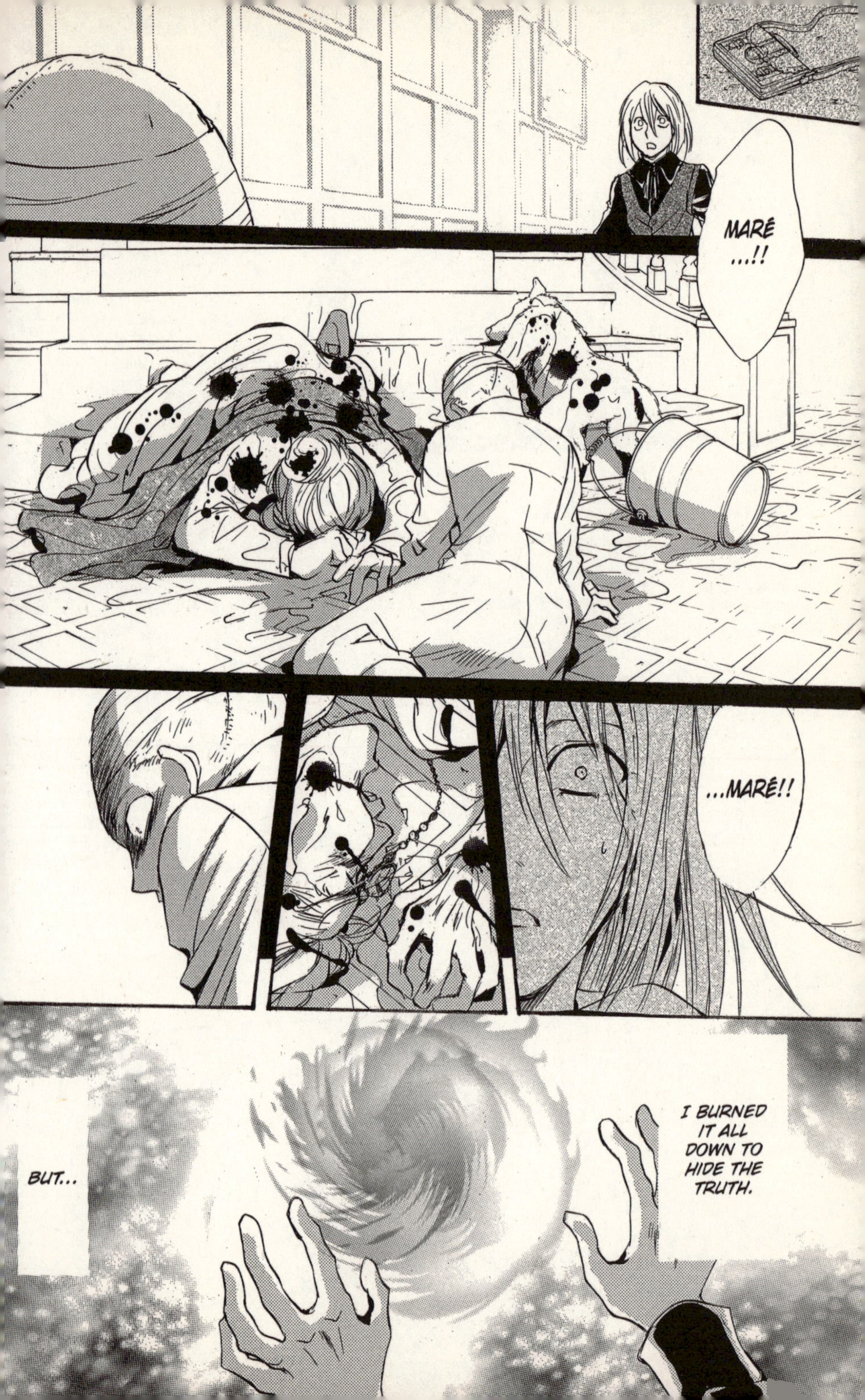
MARÉ ...!!
...MARÉ!!
I BURNED IT ALL DOWN TO HIDE THE TRUTH.
BUT...

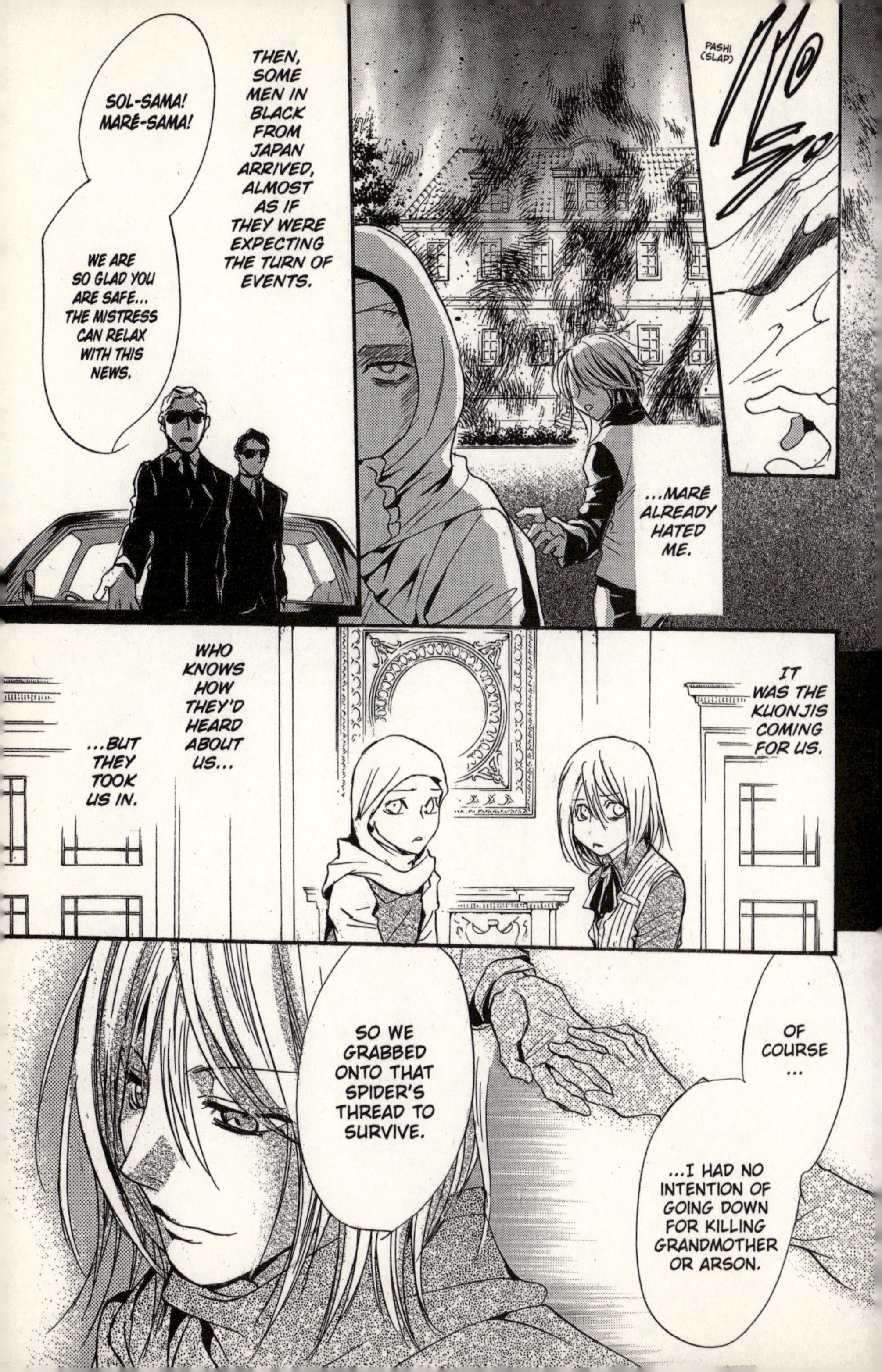
PASHI (SLAP)
...MARÉ ALREADY HATED ME.
THEN, SOME MEN IN BLACK FROM JAPAN ARRIVED, ALMOST AS IF THEY WERE EXPECTING THE TURN OF EVENTS.
SOL-SAMA! MARÉ-SAMA!
WE ARE SO GLAD YOU ARE SAFE... THE MISTRESS CAN RELAX WITH THIS NEWS.
IT WAS THE KUONJIS COMING FOR US.
WHO KNOWS HOW THEY'D HEARD ABOUT US...
...BUT THEY TOOK US IN.
OF COURSE...
...I HAD NO INTENTION OF GOING DOWN FOR KILLING GRANDMOTHER OR ARSON.
SO WE GRABBED ONTO THAT SPIDER'S THREAD TO SURVIVE.

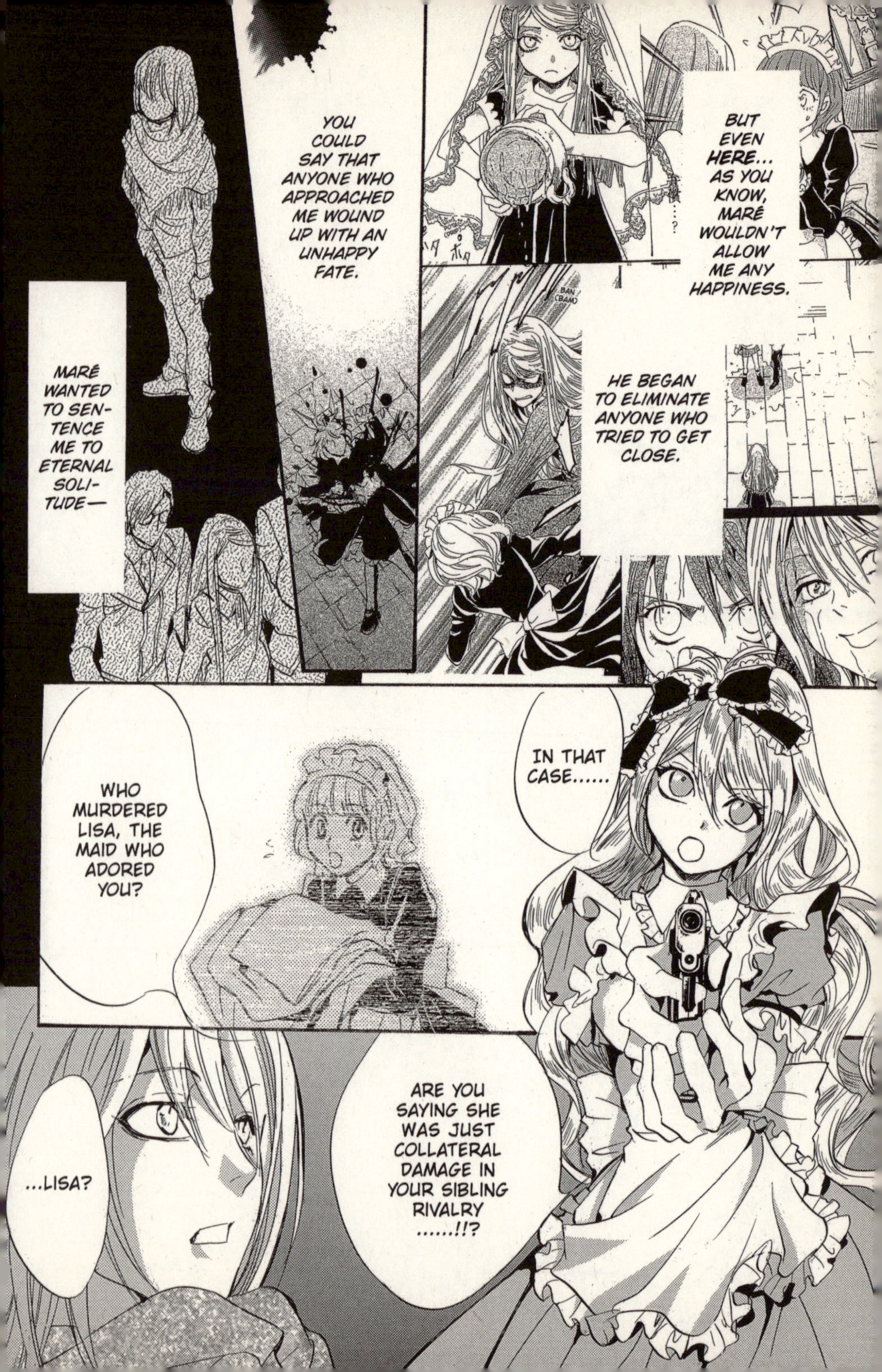
BUT EVEN HERE... AS YOU KNOW, MARÉ WOULDN'T ALLOW ME ANY HAPPINESS.
BAN (BAM)
HE BEGAN TO ELIMINATE ANYONE WHO TRIED TO GET CLOSE.
YOU COULD SAY THAT ANYONE WHO APPROACHED ME WOUND UP WITH AN UNHAPPY FATE.
MARÉ WANTED TO SEN-TENCE ME TO ETERNAL SOLI-TUDE—
IN THAT CASE......
WHO MURDERED LISA, THE MAID WHO ADORED YOU?
ARE YOU SAYING SHE WAS JUST COLLATERAL DAMAGE IN YOUR SIBLING RIVALRY ......!!?
...LISA?

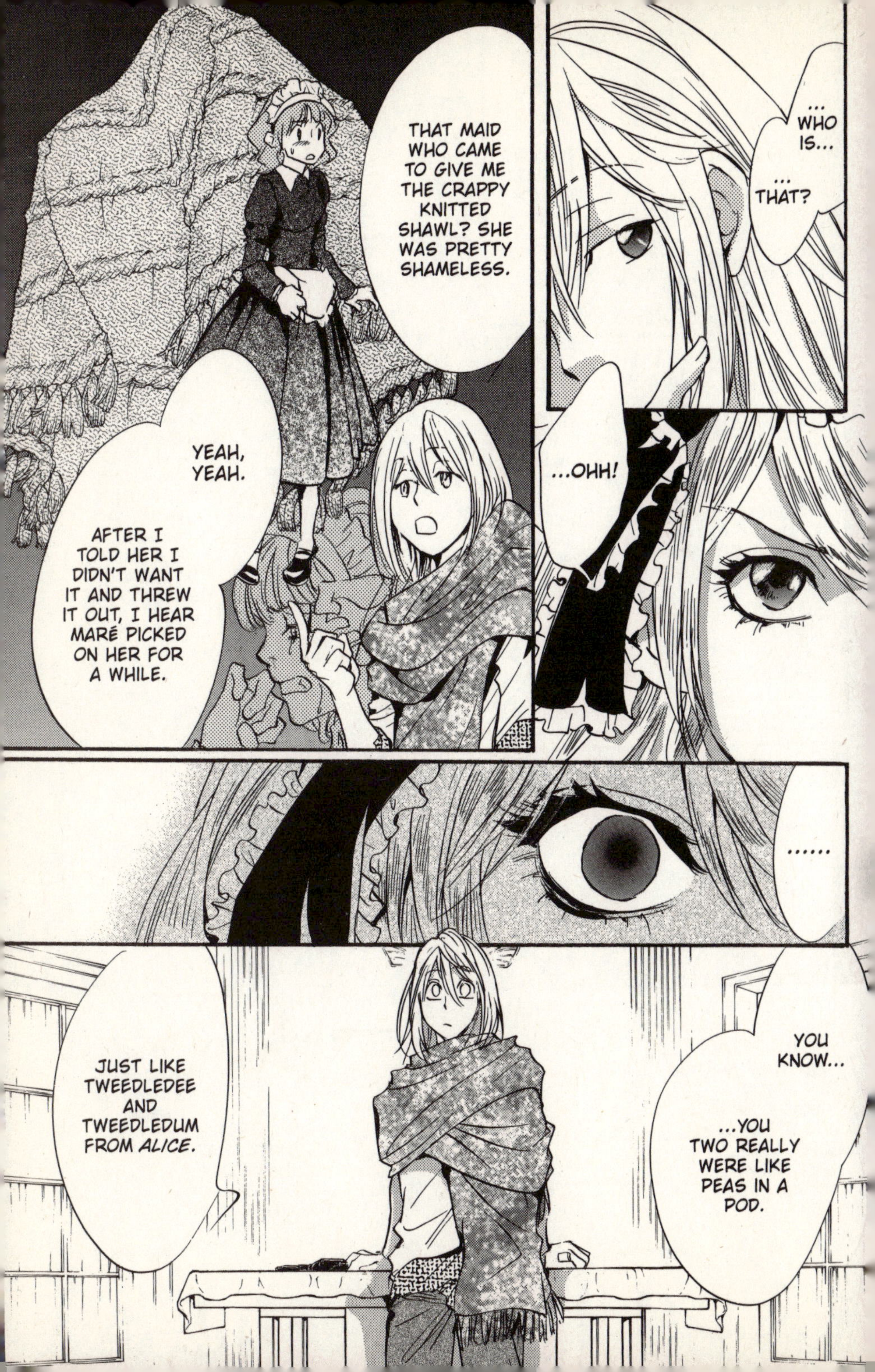
...WHO IS... ...THAT?
...OHH!
THAT MAID WHO CAME TO GIVE ME THE CRAPPY KNITTED SHAWL? SHE WAS PRETTY SHAMELESS.
YEAH, YEAH.
AFTER I TOLD HER I DIDN'T WANT IT AND THREW IT OUT, I HEAR MARÉ PICKED ON HER FOR A WHILE.
......
YOU KNOW...
...YOU TWO REALLY WERE LIKE PEAS IN A POD.
JUST LIKE TWEEDLEDEE AND TWEEDLEDUM FROM *ALICE*.

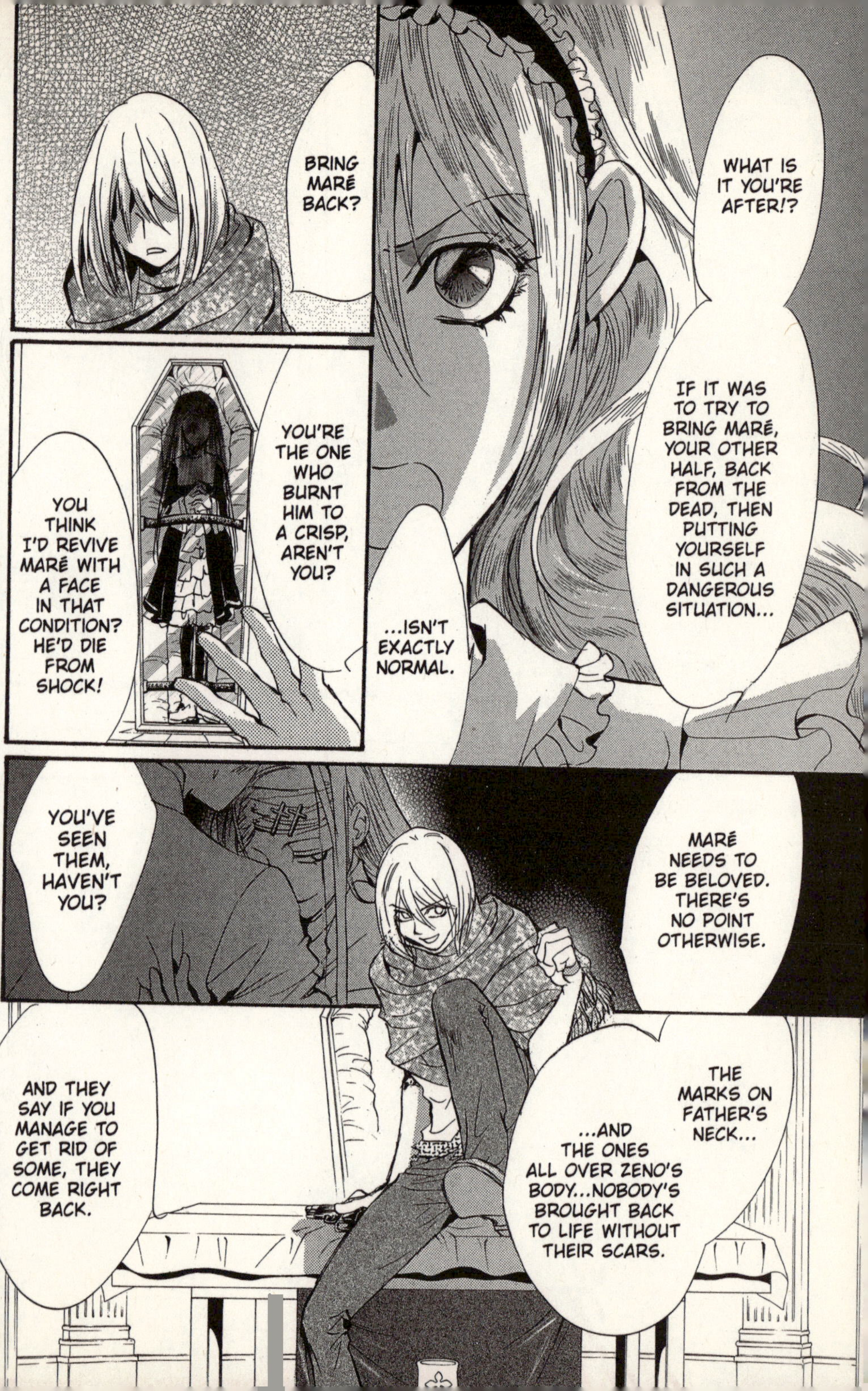
WHAT IS IT YOU'RE AFTER!?
IF IT WAS TO TRY TO BRING MARÉ, YOUR OTHER HALF, BACK FROM THE DEAD, THEN PUTTING YOURSELF IN SUCH A DANGEROUS SITUATION...
...ISN'T EXACTLY NORMAL.
BRING MARÉ BACK?
YOU'RE THE ONE WHO BURNT HIM TO A CRISP, AREN'T YOU?
YOU THINK I'D REVIVE MARÉ WITH A FACE IN THAT CONDITION? HE'D DIE FROM SHOCK!
MARÉ NEEDS TO BE BELOVED. THERE'S NO POINT OTHERWISE.
YOU'VE SEEN THEM, HAVEN'T YOU?
THE MARKS ON FATHER'S NECK...
...AND THE ONES ALL OVER ZENO'S BODY...NOBODY'S BROUGHT BACK TO LIFE WITHOUT THEIR SCARS.
AND THEY SAY IF YOU MANAGE TO GET RID OF SOME, THEY COME RIGHT BACK.

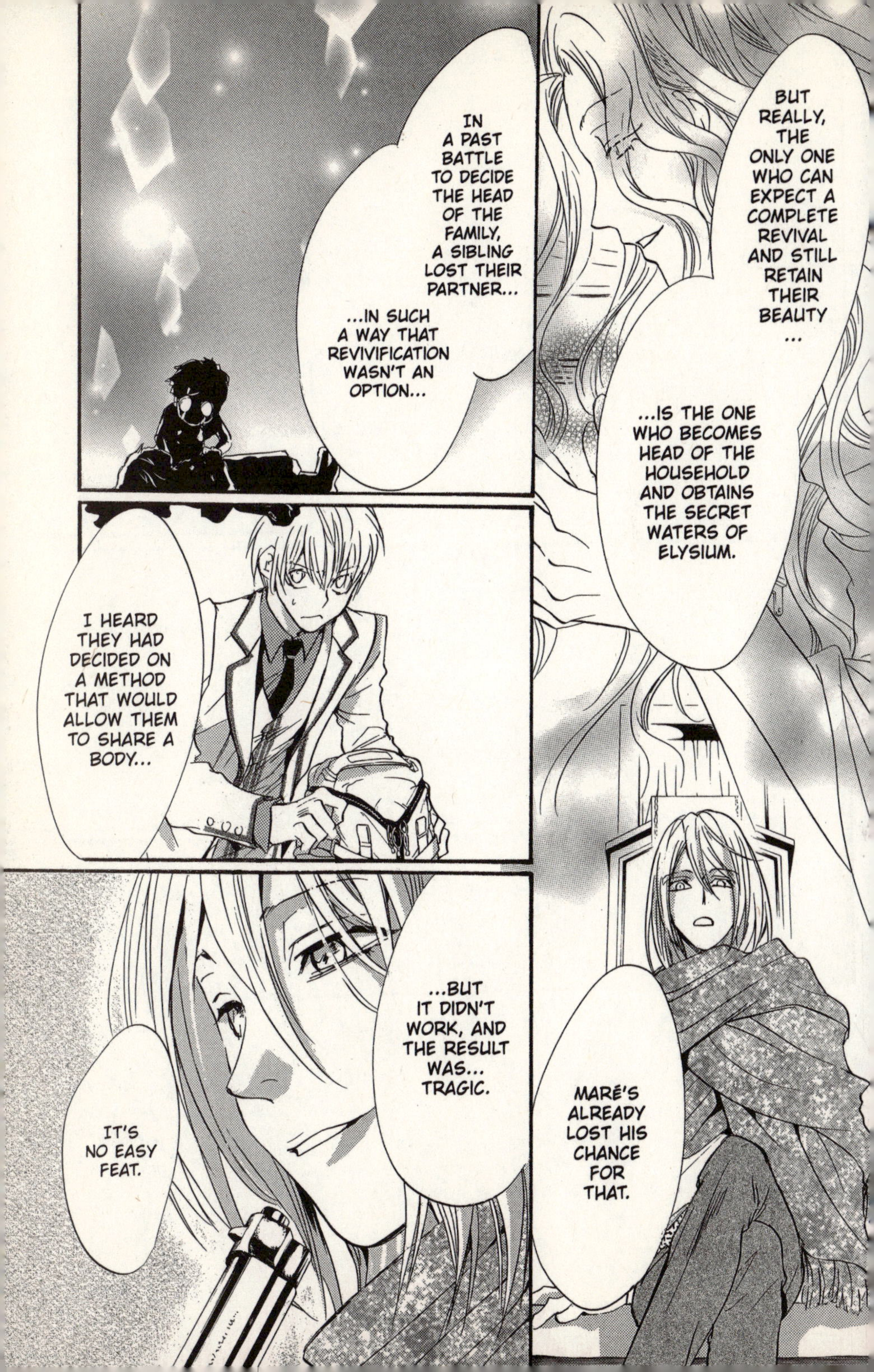
BUT REALLY, THE ONLY ONE WHO CAN EXPECT A COMPLETE REVIVAL AND STILL RETAIN THEIR BEAUTY...
...IS THE ONE WHO BECOMES HEAD OF THE HOUSEHOLD AND OBTAINS THE SECRET WATERS OF ELYSIUM.
MARÉ'S ALREADY LOST HIS CHANCE FOR THAT.
IN A PAST BATTLE TO DECIDE THE HEAD OF THE FAMILY, A SIBLING LOST THEIR PARTNER...
...IN SUCH A WAY THAT REVIVIFICATION WASN'T AN OPTION...
I HEARD THEY HAD DECIDED ON A METHOD THAT WOULD ALLOW THEM TO SHARE A BODY...
...BUT IT DIDN'T WORK, AND THE RESULT WAS... TRAGIC.
IT'S NO EASY FEAT.

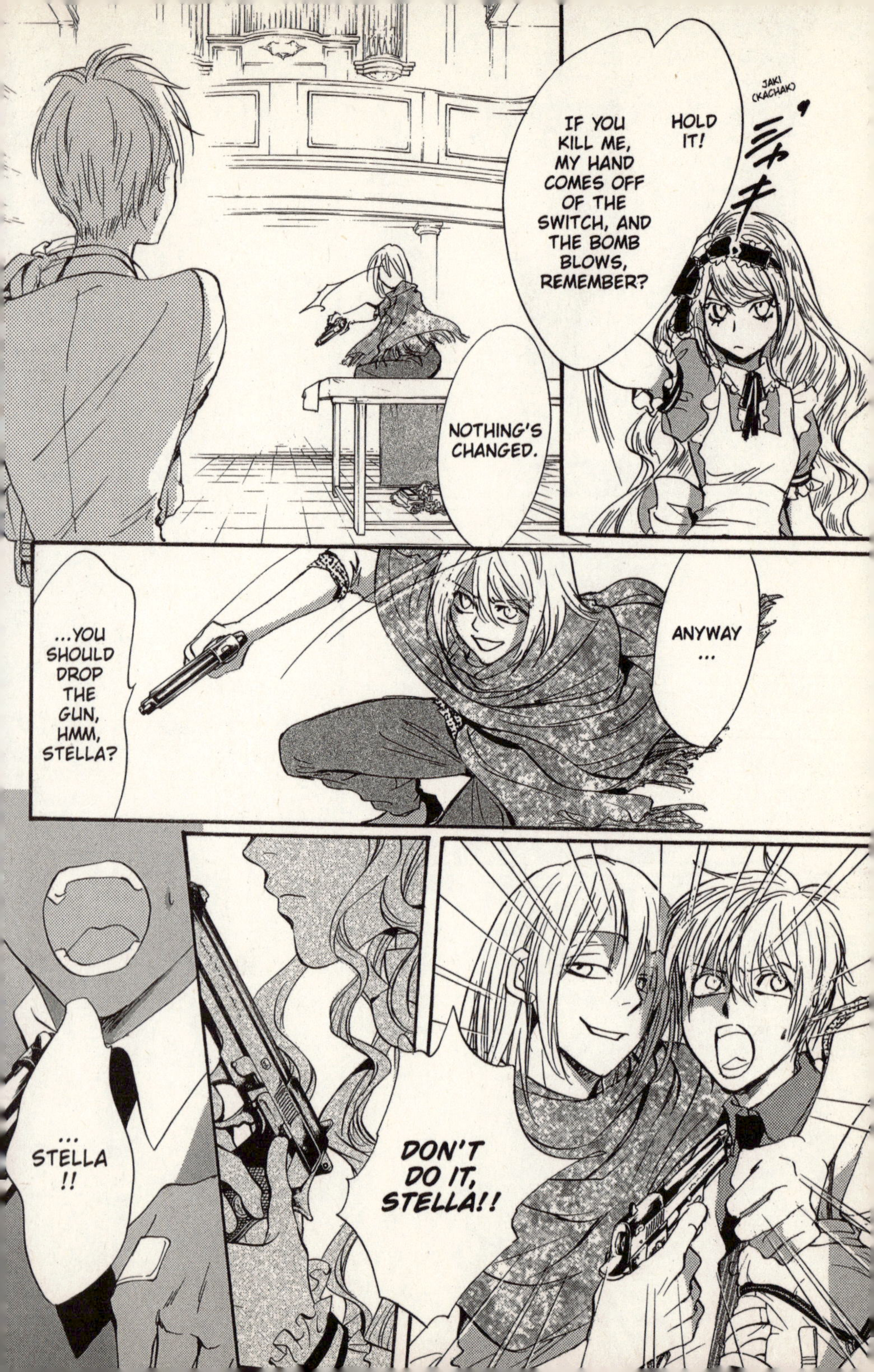
JAKI (KACHAK)
ジャキ
HOLD IT!
IF YOU KILL ME, MY HAND COMES OFF OF THE SWITCH, AND THE BOMB BLOWS, REMEMBER?
NOTHING'S CHANGED.
ANYWAY ...
...YOU SHOULD DROP THE GUN, HMM, STELLA?
DON'T DO IT, STELLA!!
... STELLA !!

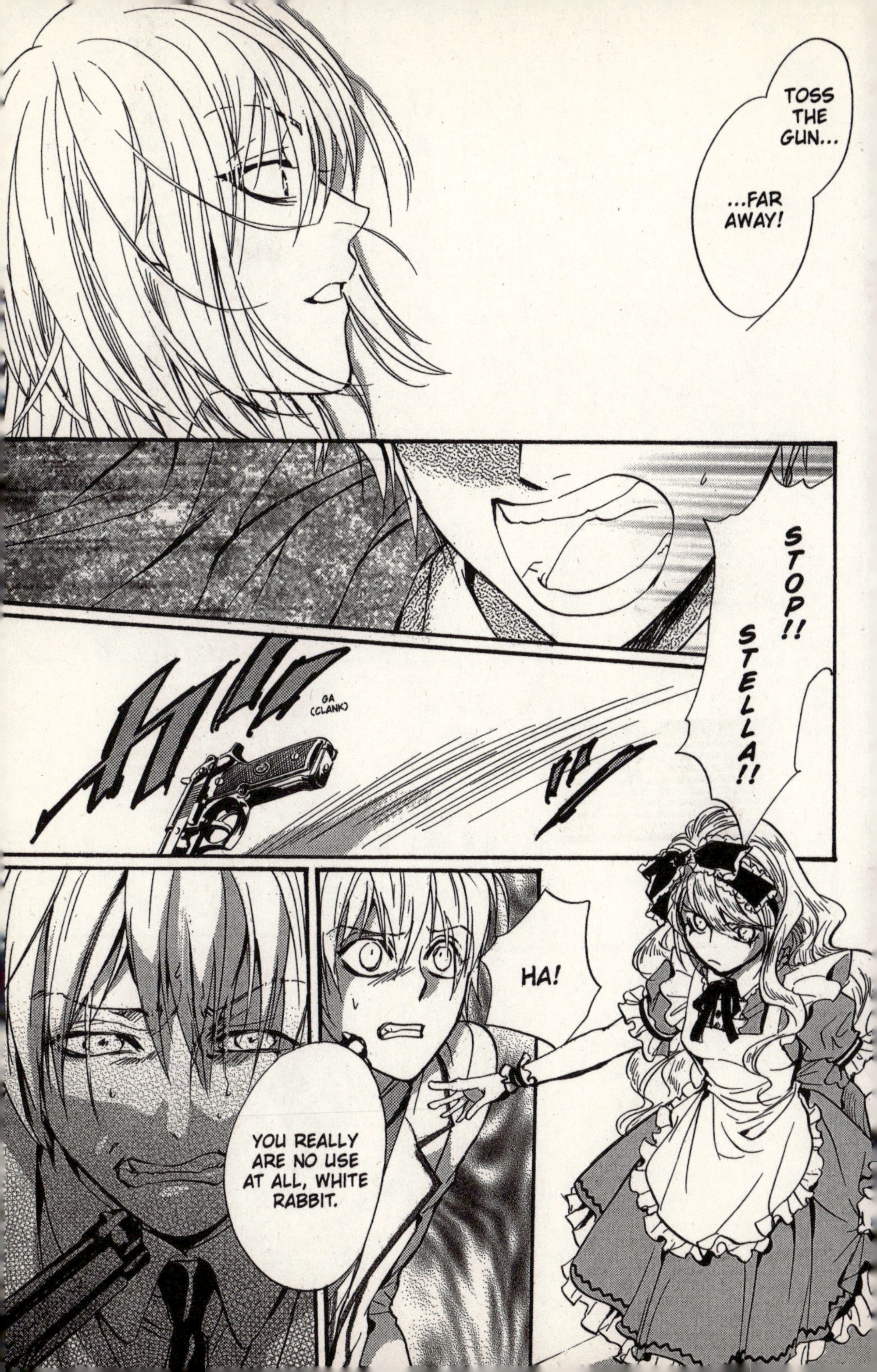
TOSS THE GUN...
...FAR AWAY!
STOP!! STELLA!!
GA (CLANK)
HA!
YOU REALLY ARE NO USE AT ALL, WHITE RABBIT.

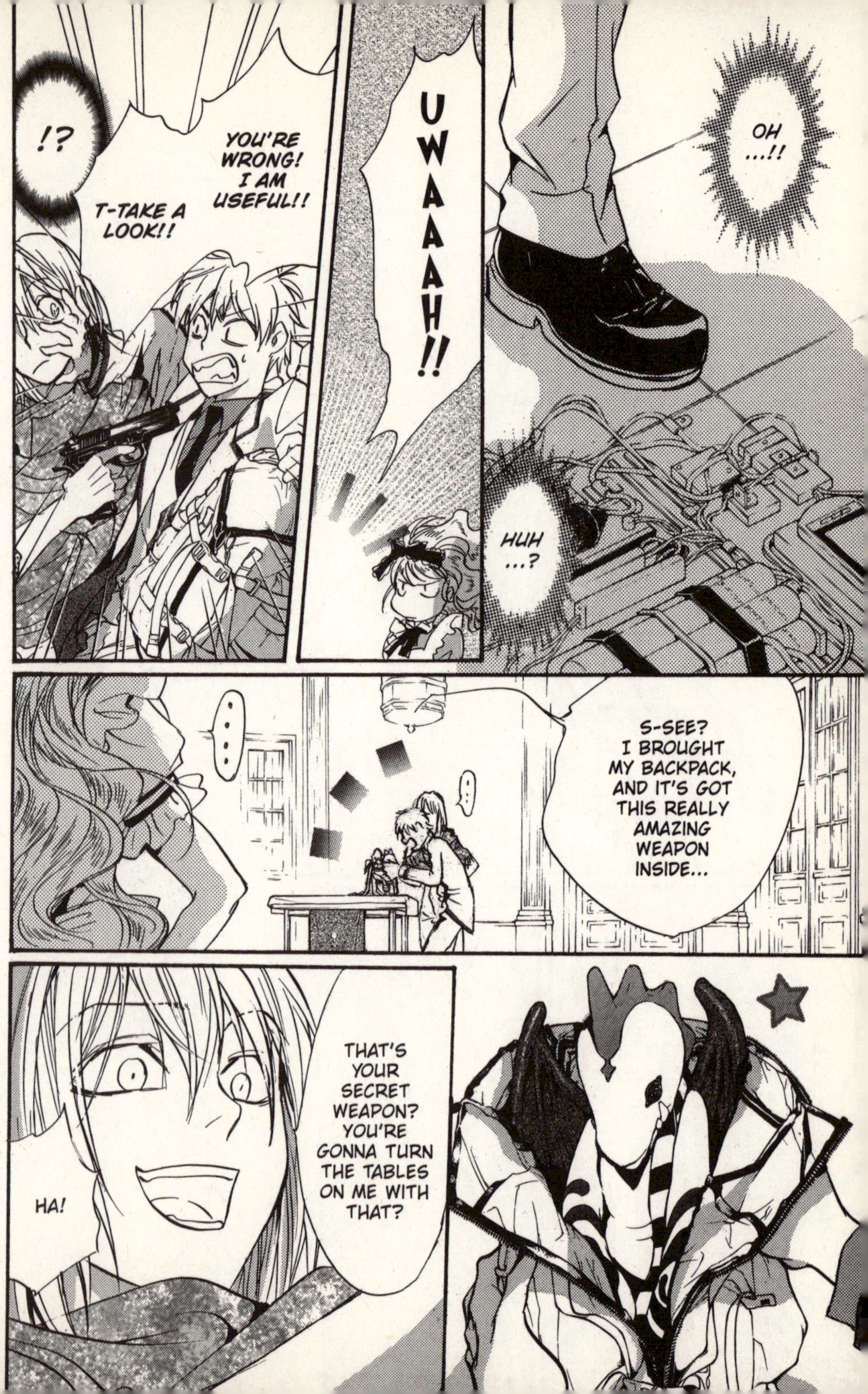
OH ...!!
HUH ...?
UWAAAAH!!
YOU'RE WRONG! I AM USEFUL!!
!?
T-TAKE A LOOK!!
S-SEE? I BROUGHT MY BACKPACK, AND IT'S GOT THIS REALLY AMAZING WEAPON INSIDE...
..
....
THAT'S YOUR SECRET WEAPON? YOU'RE GONNA TURN THE TABLES ON ME WITH THAT?
HA!

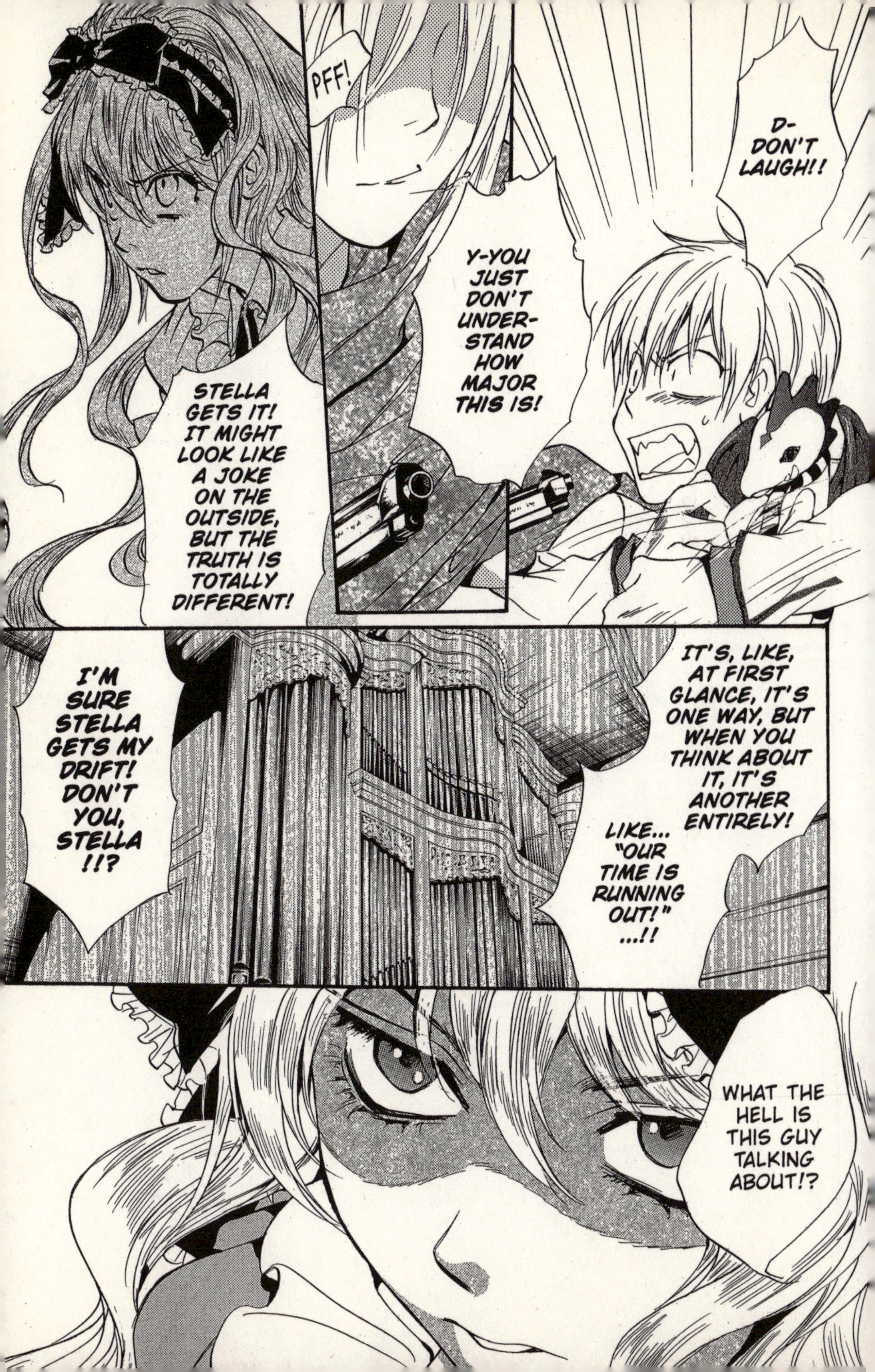
D-DON'T LAUGH!!
Y-YOU JUST DON'T UNDER-STAND HOW MAJOR THIS IS!
PFF!
STELLA GETS IT! IT MIGHT LOOK LIKE A JOKE ON THE OUTSIDE, BUT THE TRUTH IS TOTALLY DIFFERENT!
IT'S, LIKE, AT FIRST GLANCE, IT'S ONE WAY, BUT WHEN YOU THINK ABOUT IT, IT'S ANOTHER ENTIRELY!
LIKE... "OUR TIME IS RUNNING OUT!" ...!!
I'M SURE STELLA GETS MY DRIFT! DON'T YOU, STELLA!!?
WHAT THE HELL IS THIS GUY TALKING ABOUT!?

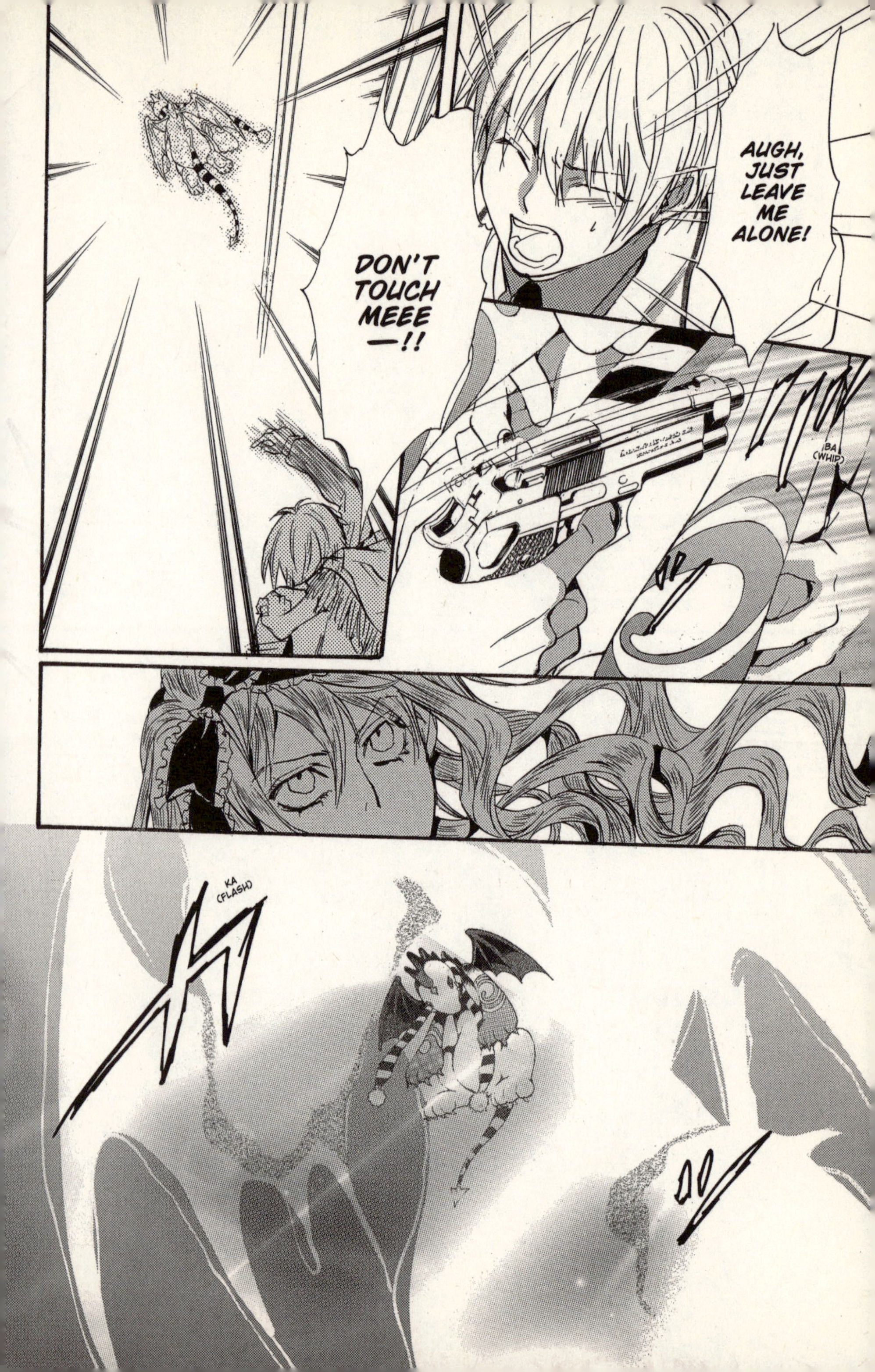
AUGH, JUST LEAVE ME ALONE!
DON'T TOUCH MEEE—!!
BA (WHIP)
KA (FLASH)

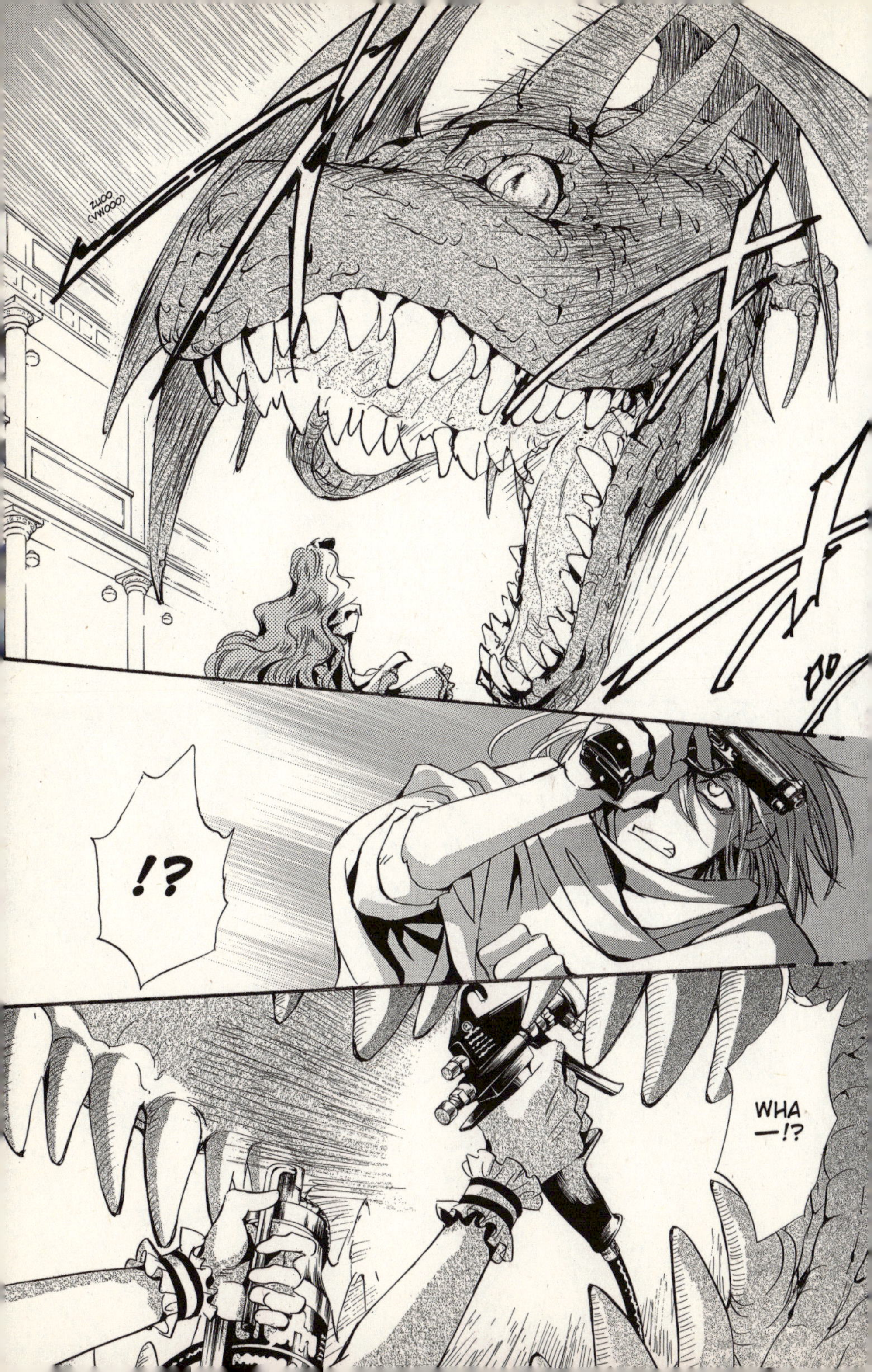
ZUOO
(VWOOO)
!?
WHA
—!?

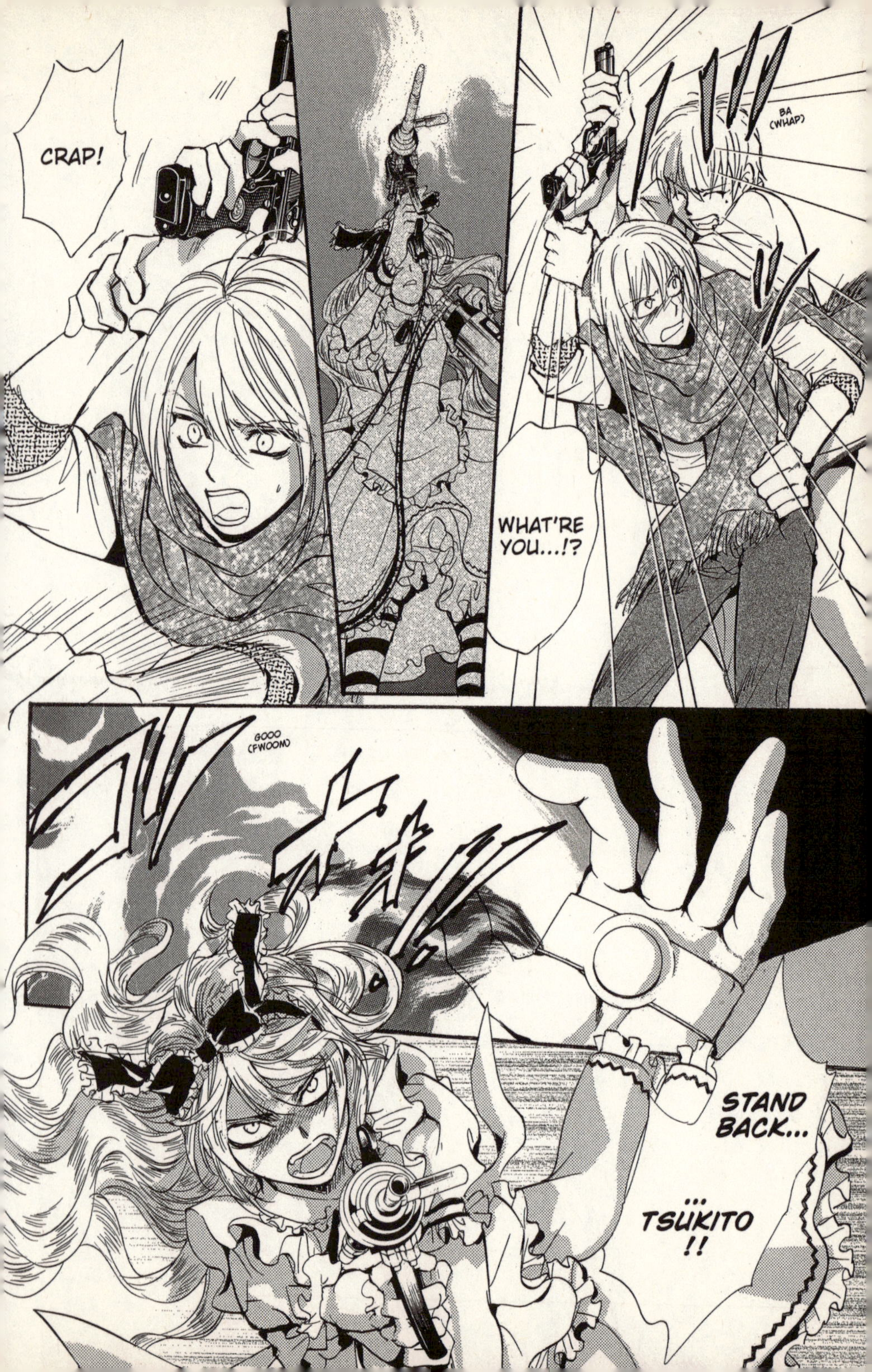
BA
(WHAP)
WHAT'RE YOU...!?
CRAP!
GOOO
(FWOOM)
STAND BACK...
... TSUKITO !!

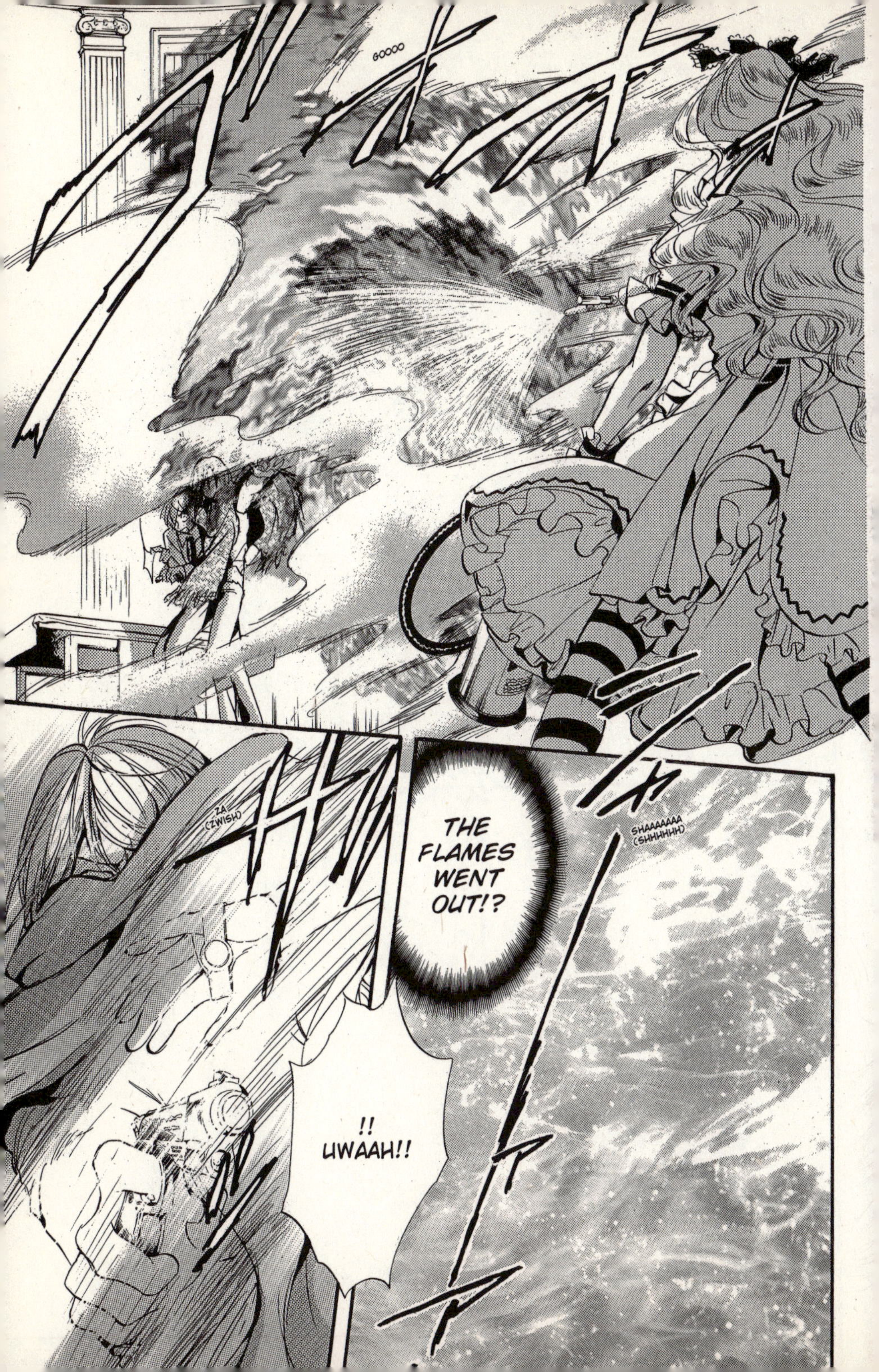
GOOOO
SHAAAAAAA (SHHHHHH)
THE FLAMES WENT OUT!?
ZA (ZWISH)
!! UWAAH!!

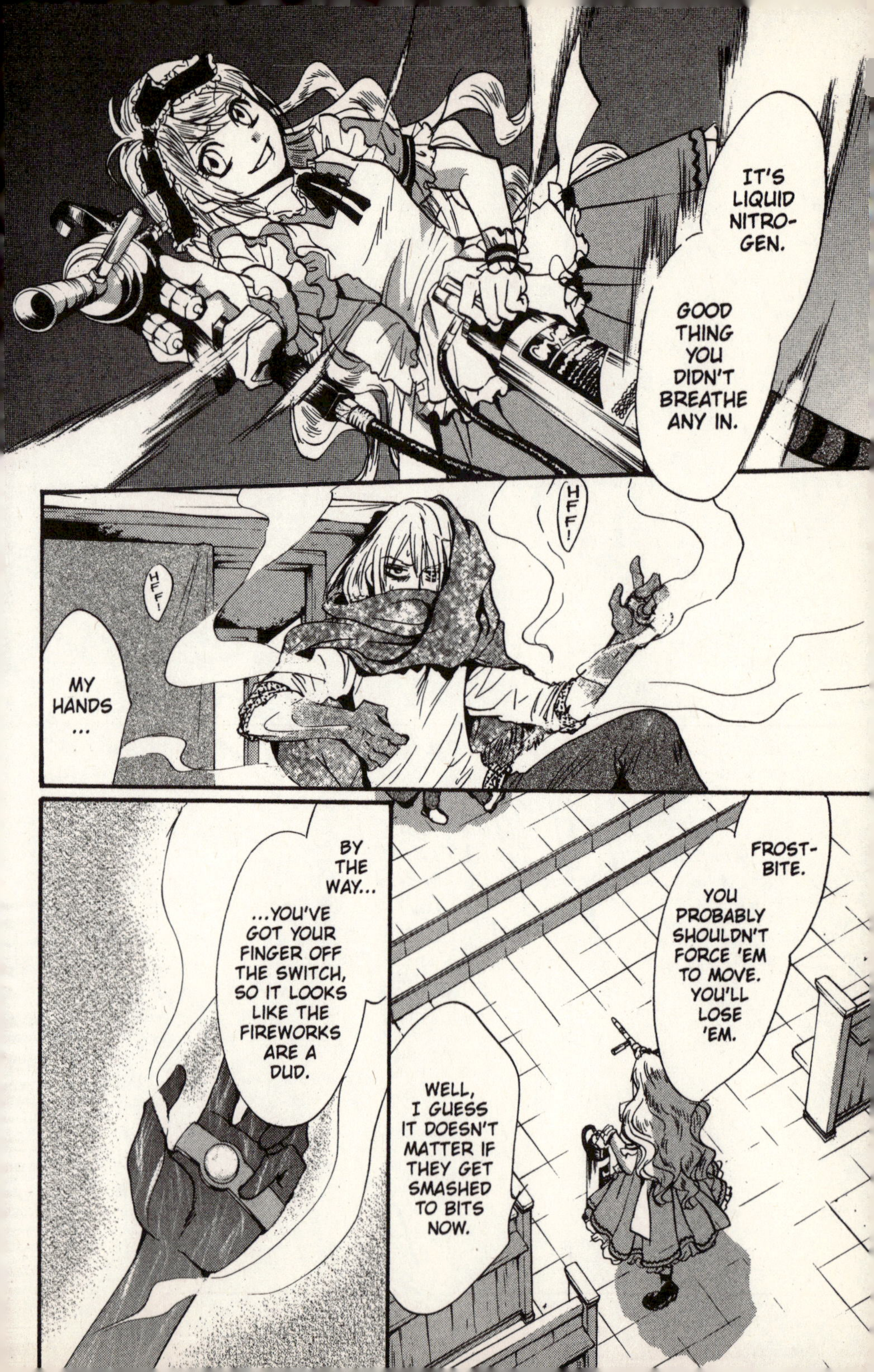
IT'S LIQUID NITRO-GEN.
GOOD THING YOU DIDN'T BREATHE ANY IN.
HFF!
HFF!
MY HANDS ...
FROST-BITE.
YOU PROBABLY SHOULDN'T FORCE 'EM TO MOVE. YOU'LL LOSE 'EM.
BY THE WAY...
...YOU'VE GOT YOUR FINGER OFF THE SWITCH, SO IT LOOKS LIKE THE FIREWORKS ARE A DUD.
WELL, I GUESS IT DOESN'T MATTER IF THEY GET SMASHED TO BITS NOW.

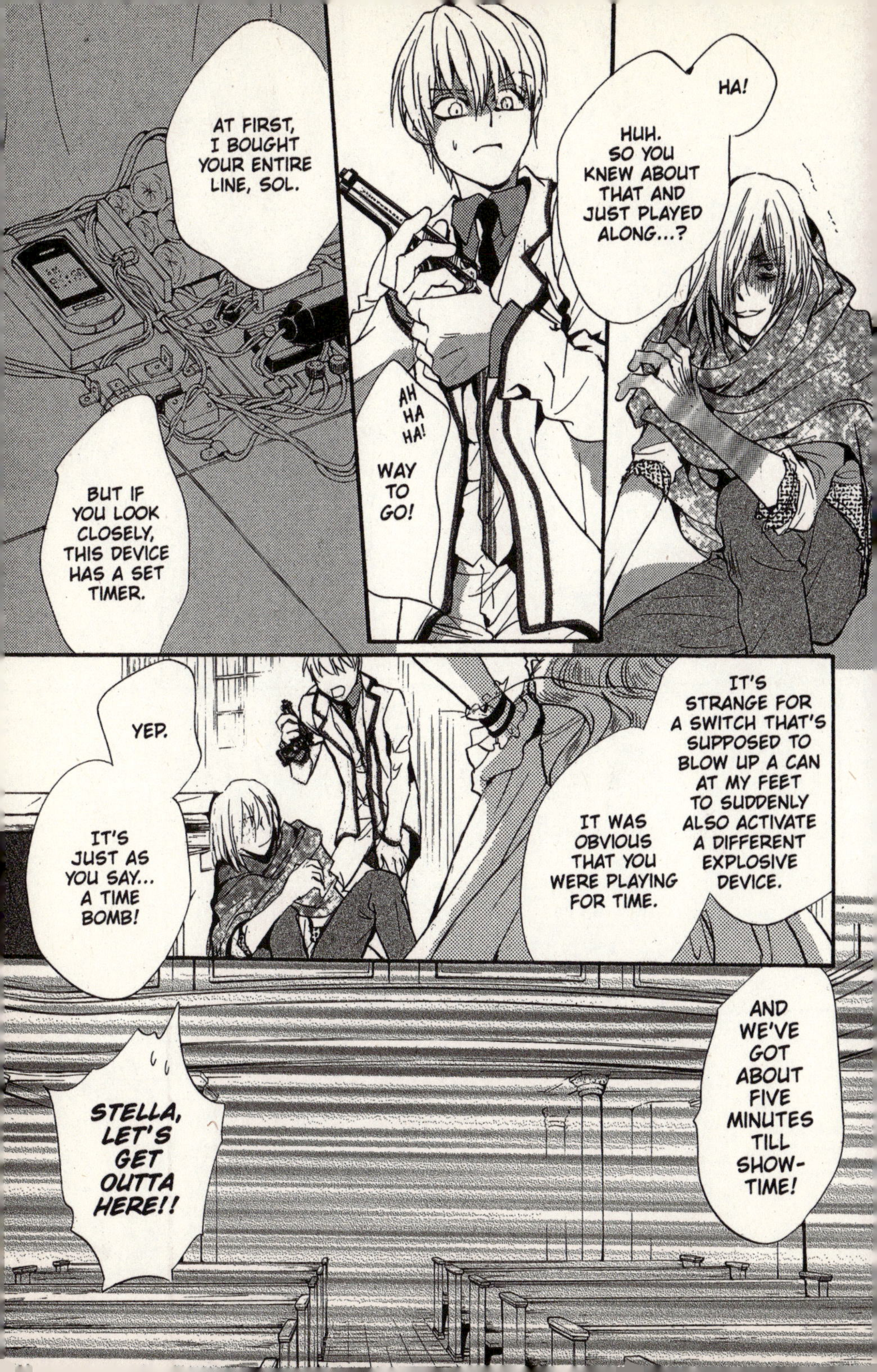
HA!
HUH. SO YOU KNEW ABOUT THAT AND JUST PLAYED ALONG...?
AH HA HA!
WAY TO GO!
AT FIRST, I BOUGHT YOUR ENTIRE LINE, SOL.
BUT IF YOU LOOK CLOSELY, THIS DEVICE HAS A SET TIMER.
IT'S STRANGE FOR A SWITCH THAT'S SUPPOSED TO BLOW UP A CAN AT MY FEET TO SUDDENLY ALSO ACTIVATE A DIFFERENT EXPLOSIVE DEVICE.
IT WAS OBVIOUS THAT YOU WERE PLAYING FOR TIME.
YEP.
IT'S JUST AS YOU SAY... A TIME BOMB!
AND WE'VE GOT ABOUT FIVE MINUTES TILL SHOW-TIME!
STELLA, LET'S GET OUTTA HERE!!

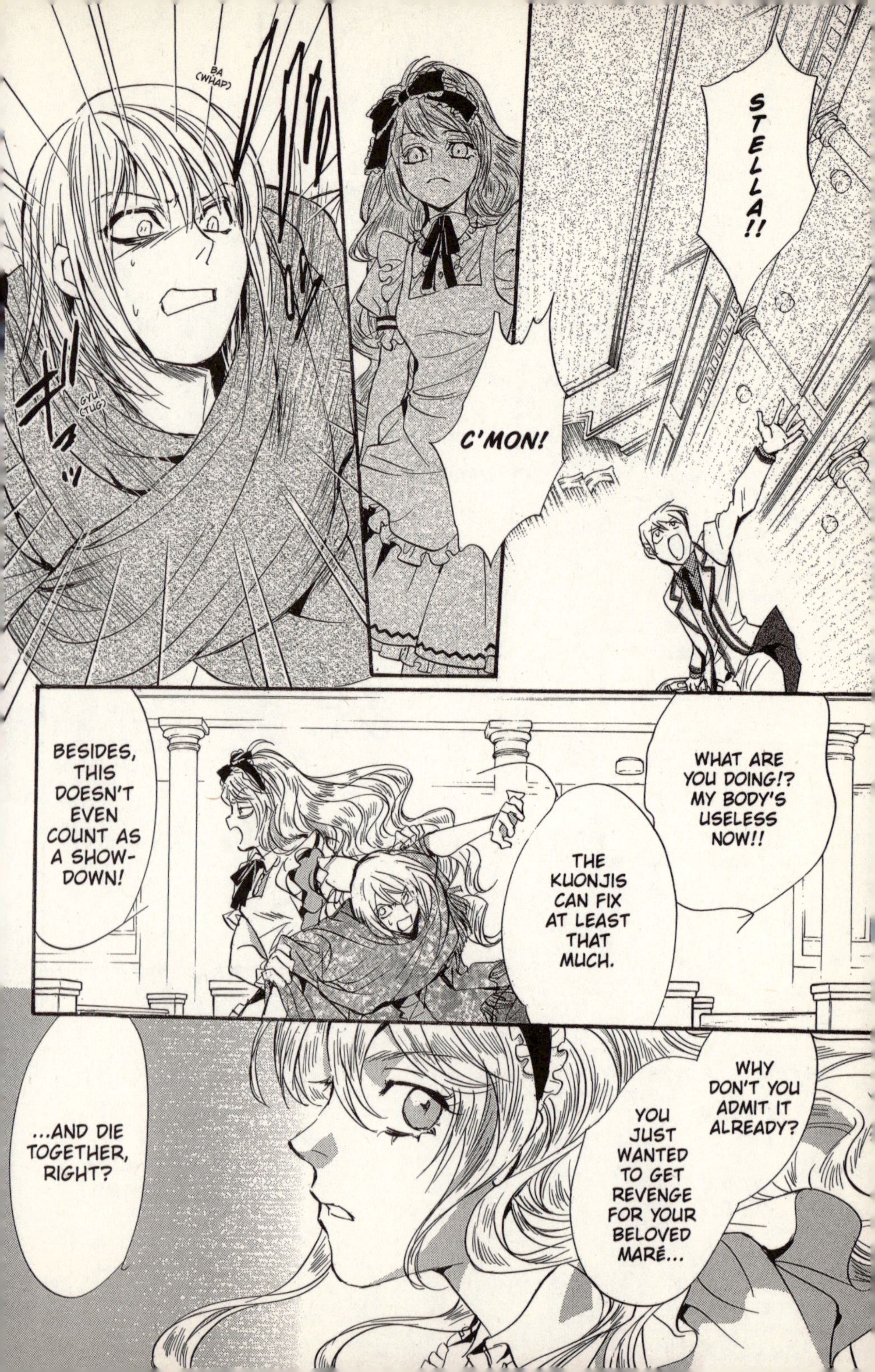
STELLA!!
C'MON!
BA (WHAP)
GYU (TUG)
WHAT ARE YOU DOING!? MY BODY'S USELESS NOW!!
THE KUONJIS CAN FIX AT LEAST THAT MUCH.
BESIDES, THIS DOESN'T EVEN COUNT AS A SHOW-DOWN!
WHY DON'T YOU ADMIT IT ALREADY?
YOU JUST WANTED TO GET REVENGE FOR YOUR BELOVED MARÉ...
...AND DIE TOGETHER, RIGHT?

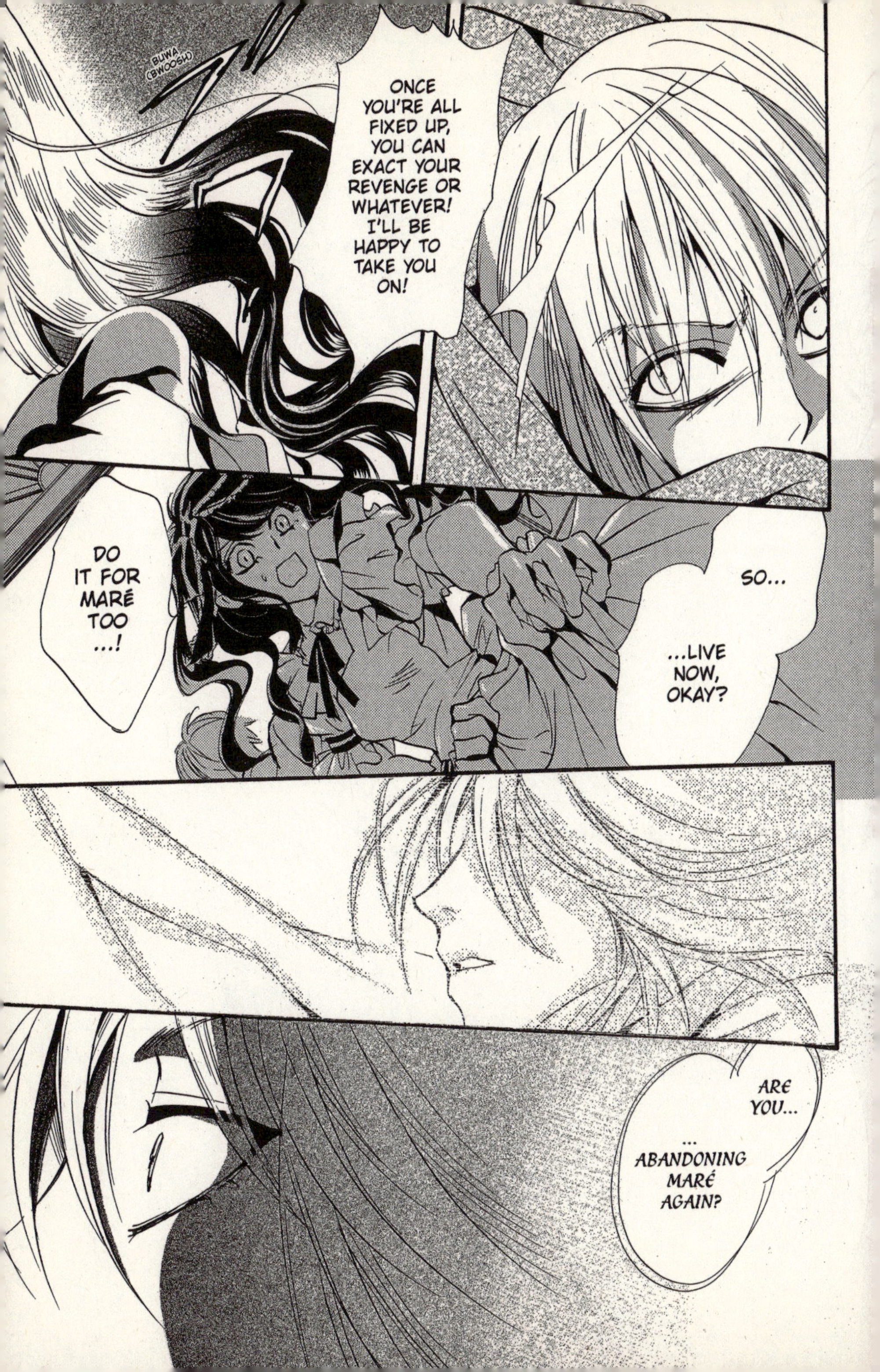
ONCE YOU'RE ALL FIXED UP, YOU CAN EXACT YOUR REVENGE OR WHATEVER! I'LL BE HAPPY TO TAKE YOU ON!
BUWA (BWOOSH)
SO...
...LIVE NOW, OKAY?
DO IT FOR MARÉ TOO ...!
ARE YOU...
...ABANDONING MARÉ AGAIN?

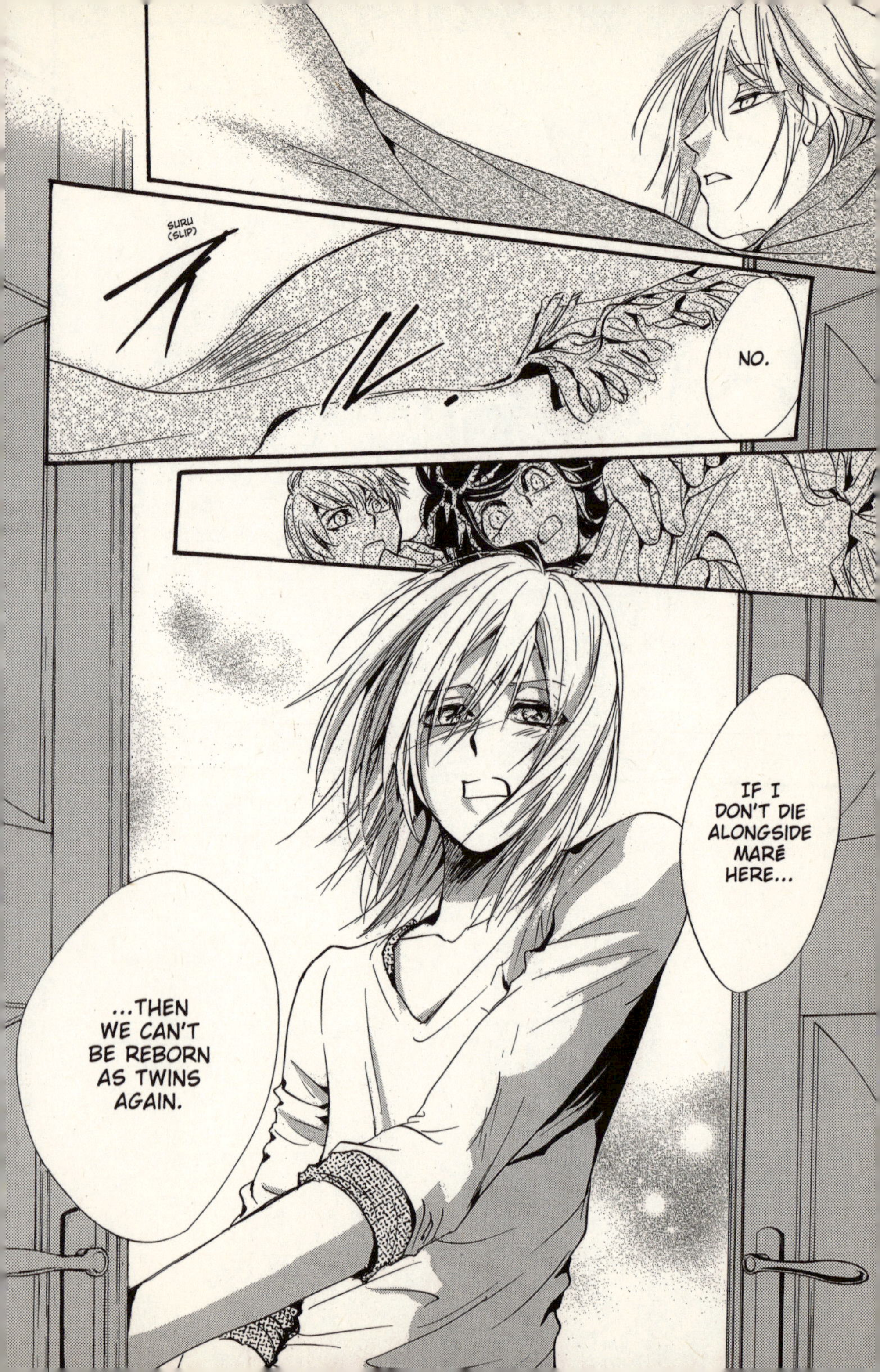
SURU (SLIP)
NO.
IF I DON'T DIE ALONGSIDE MARÉ HERE...
...THEN WE CAN'T BE REBORN AS TWINS AGAIN.

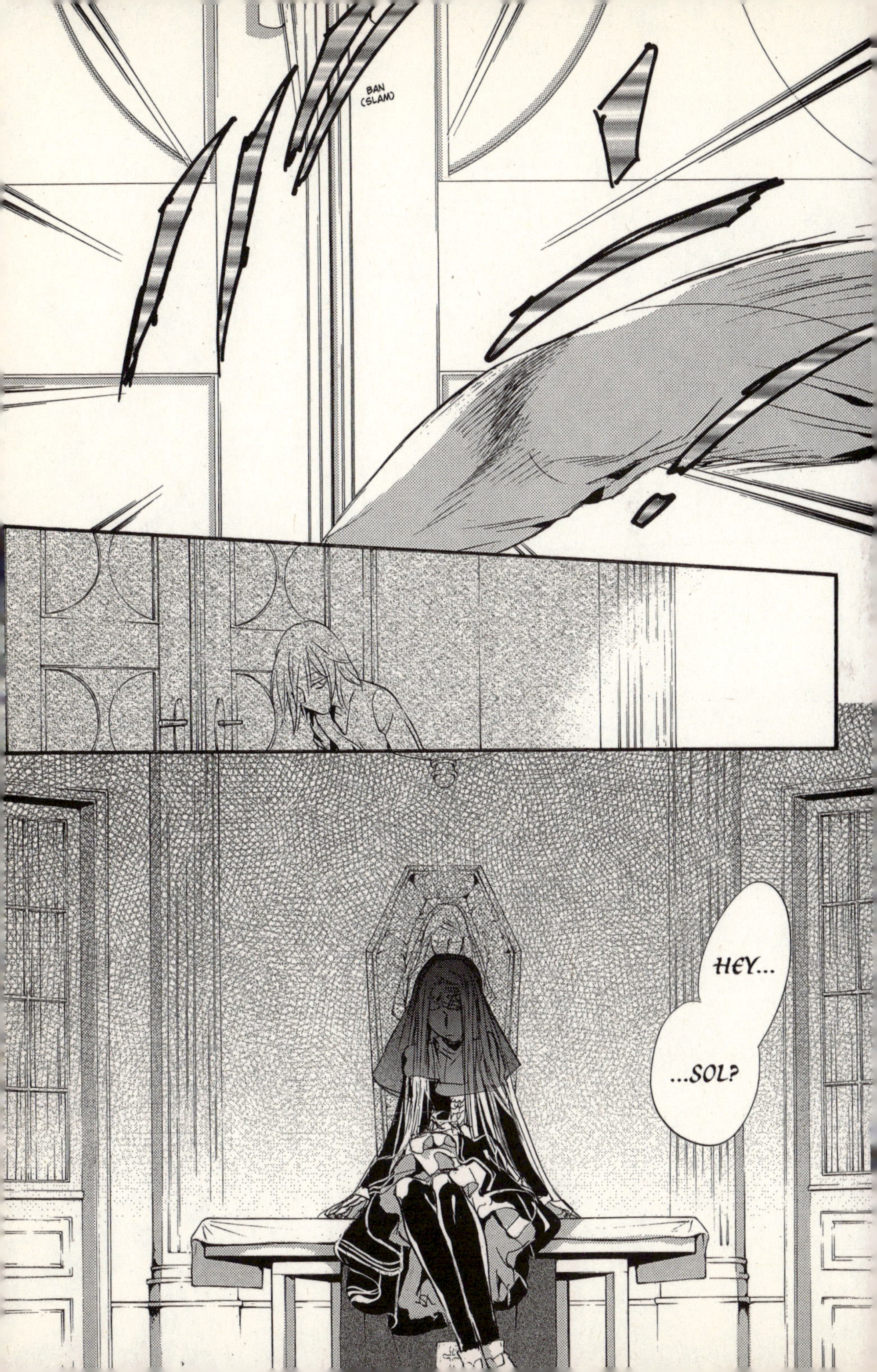
BAN (SLAM)
HEY...
...SOL?

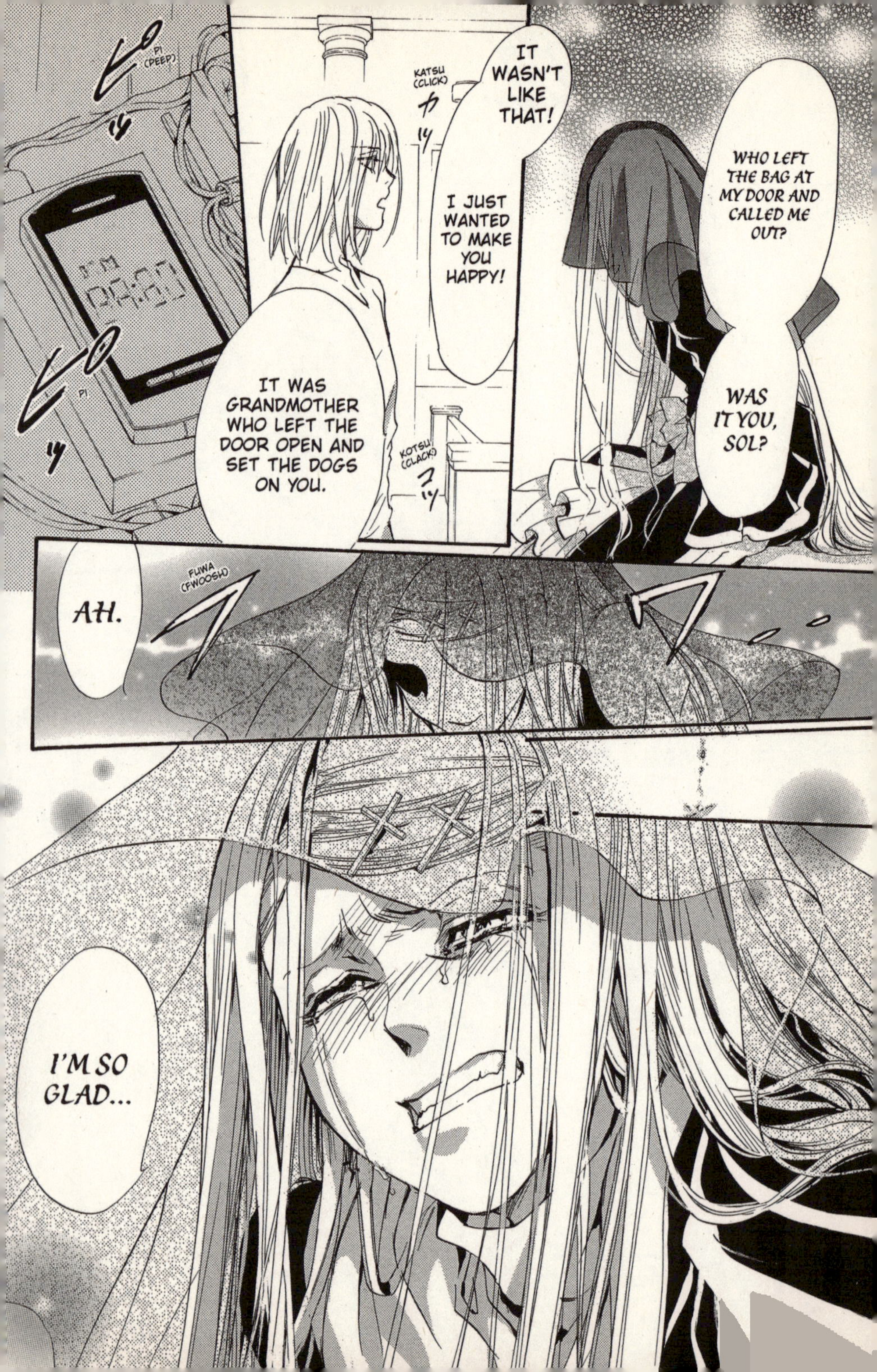
WHO LEFT THE BAG AT MY DOOR AND CALLED ME OUT?
WAS IT YOU, SOL?
IT WASN'T LIKE THAT!
KATSU (CLICK)
I JUST WANTED TO MAKE YOU HAPPY!
KOTSU (CLACK)
IT WAS GRANDMOTHER WHO LEFT THE DOOR OPEN AND SET THE DOGS ON YOU.
PI (PEEP)
PI
FUWA (FWOOSH)
AH.
I'M SO GLAD...

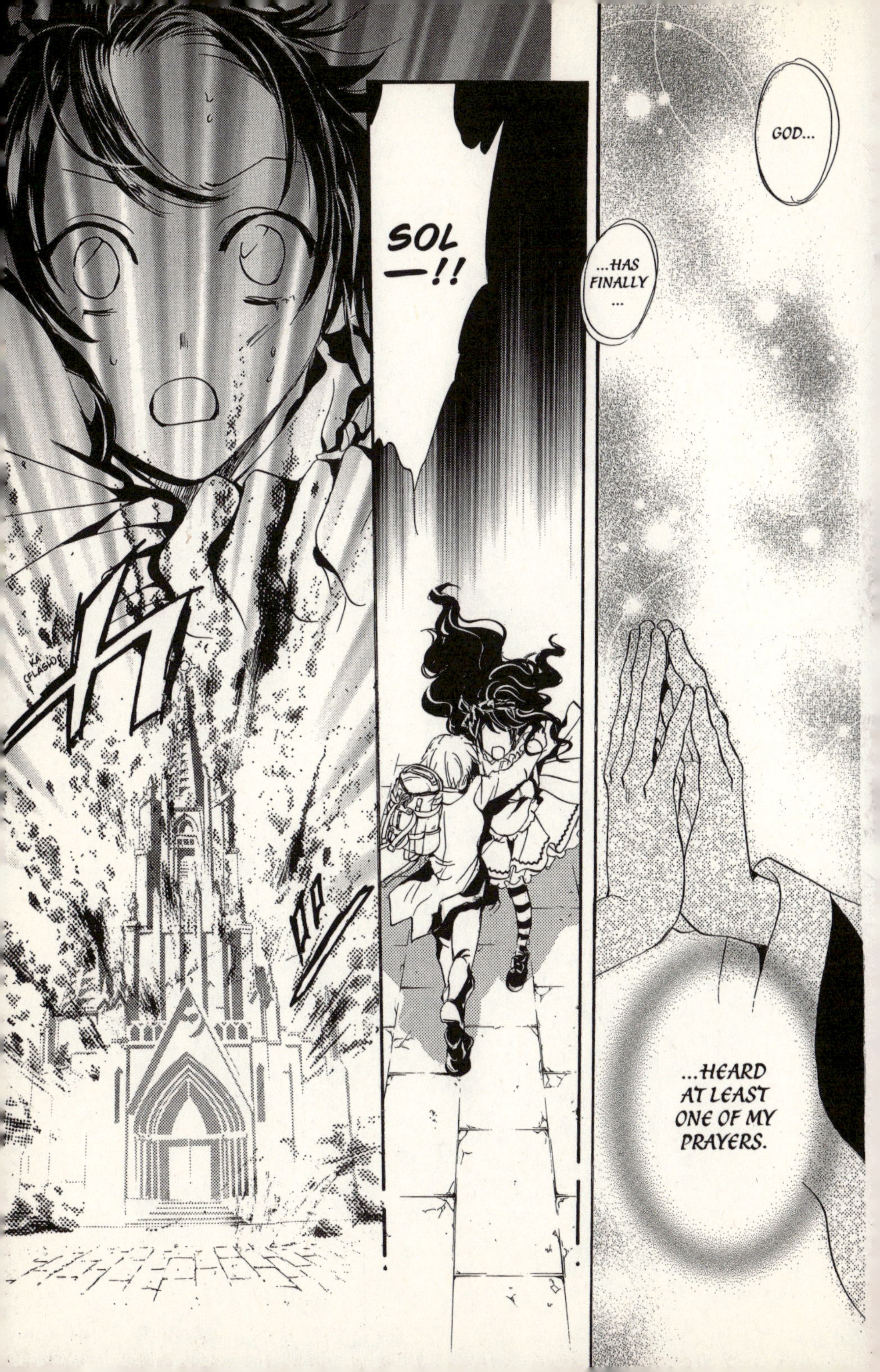
GOD...
...HAS FINALLY ...
...HEARD AT LEAST ONE OF MY PRAYERS.
SOL —!!
KA (FLASH)

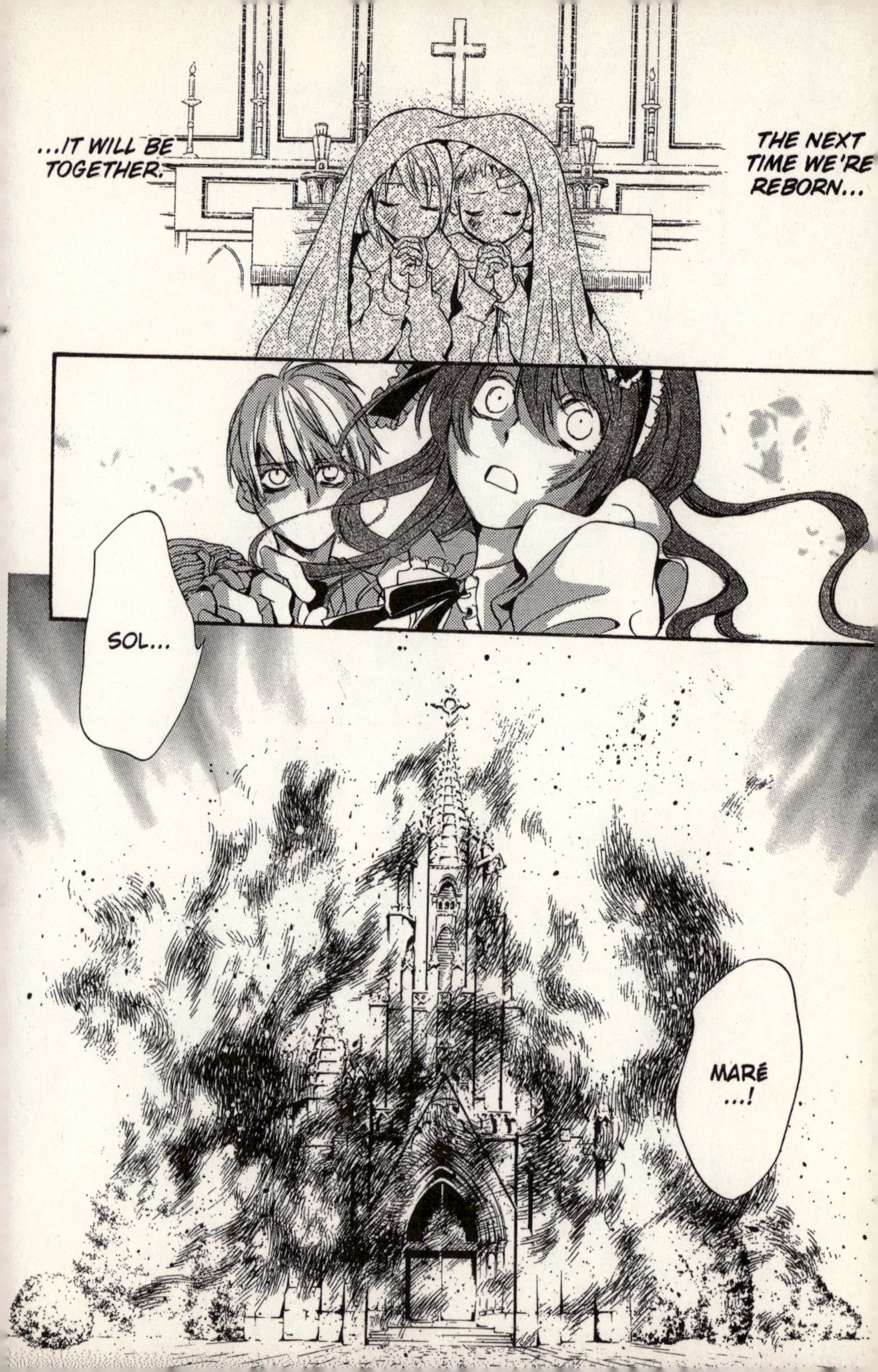
THE NEXT TIME WE'RE REBORN...
...IT WILL BE TOGETHER.
SOL...
MARÉ ...!

Alice in MURDERLAND

Alice in Murderland

Wonder 32

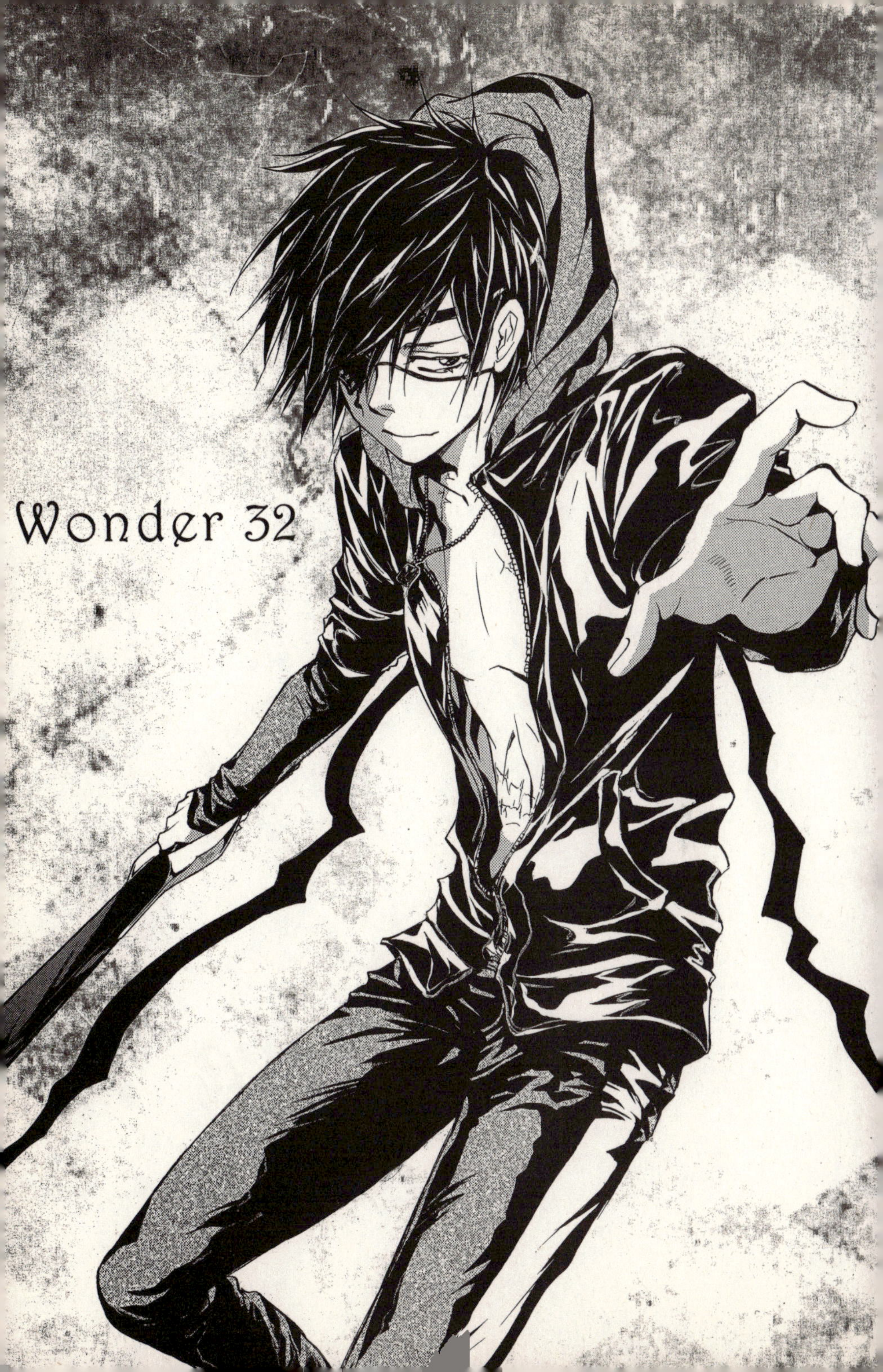

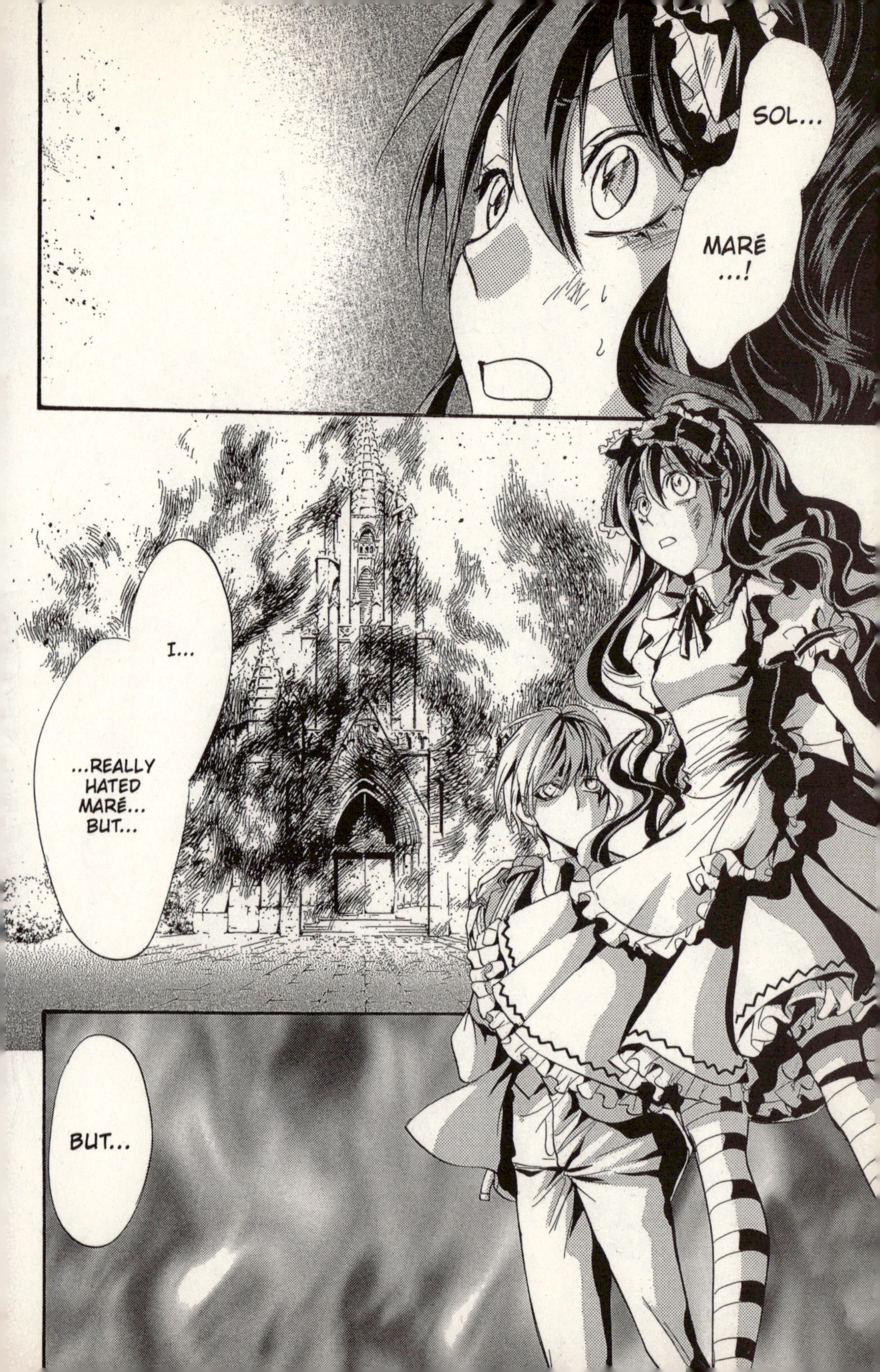
SOL...
MARÉ ...!
I...
...REALLY HATED MARÉ... BUT...
BUT...

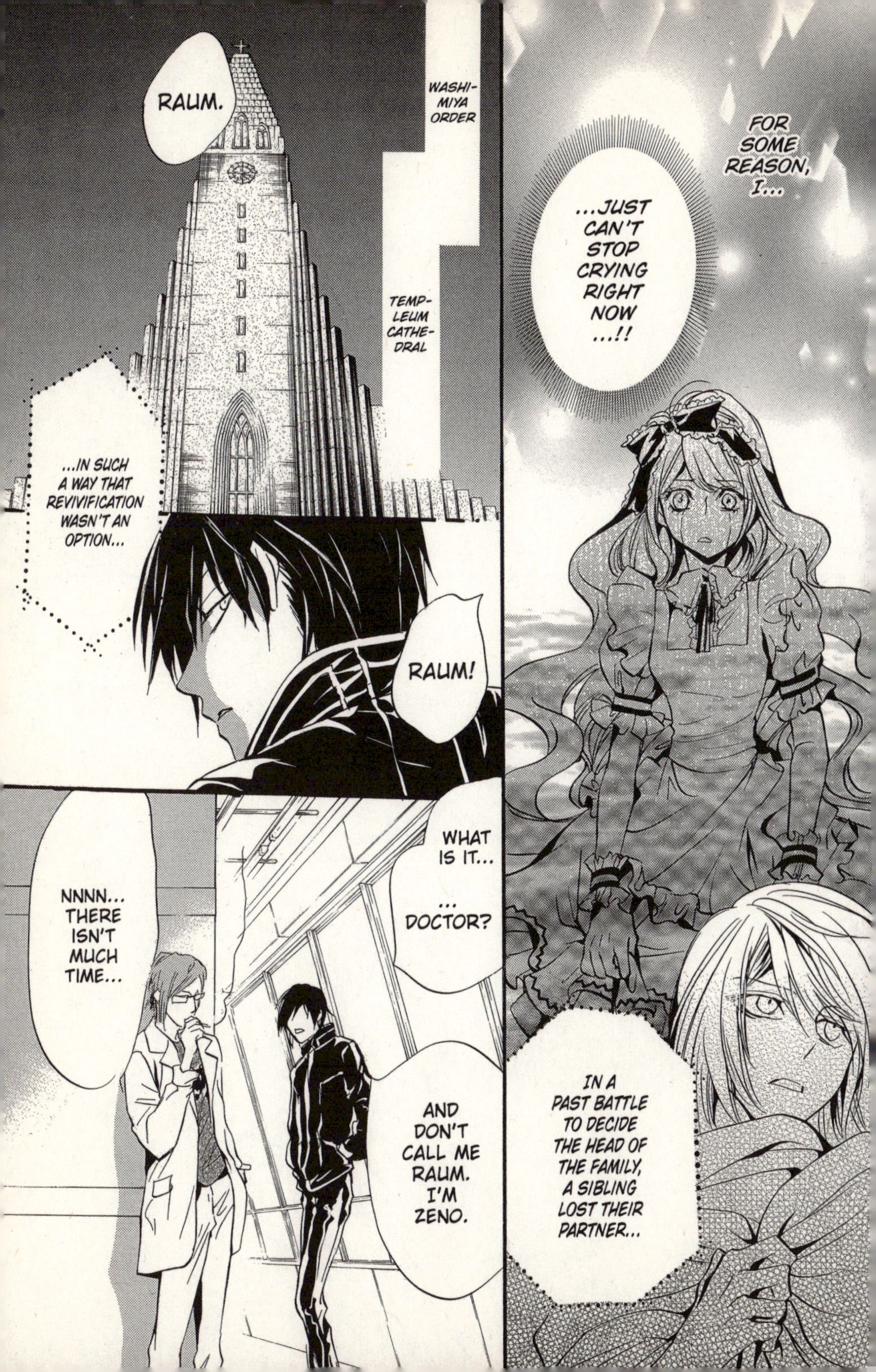
FOR SOME REASON, I...
...JUST CAN'T STOP CRYING RIGHT NOW ...!!
IN A PAST BATTLE TO DECIDE THE HEAD OF THE FAMILY, A SIBLING LOST THEIR PARTNER...
WASHI-MIYA ORDER
TEMP-LEUM CATHE-DRAL
RAUM.
...IN SUCH A WAY THAT REVIVIFICATION WASN'T AN OPTION...
RAUM!
WHAT IS IT... ...DOCTOR?
NNNN... THERE ISN'T MUCH TIME...
AND DON'T CALL ME RAUM. I'M ZENO.

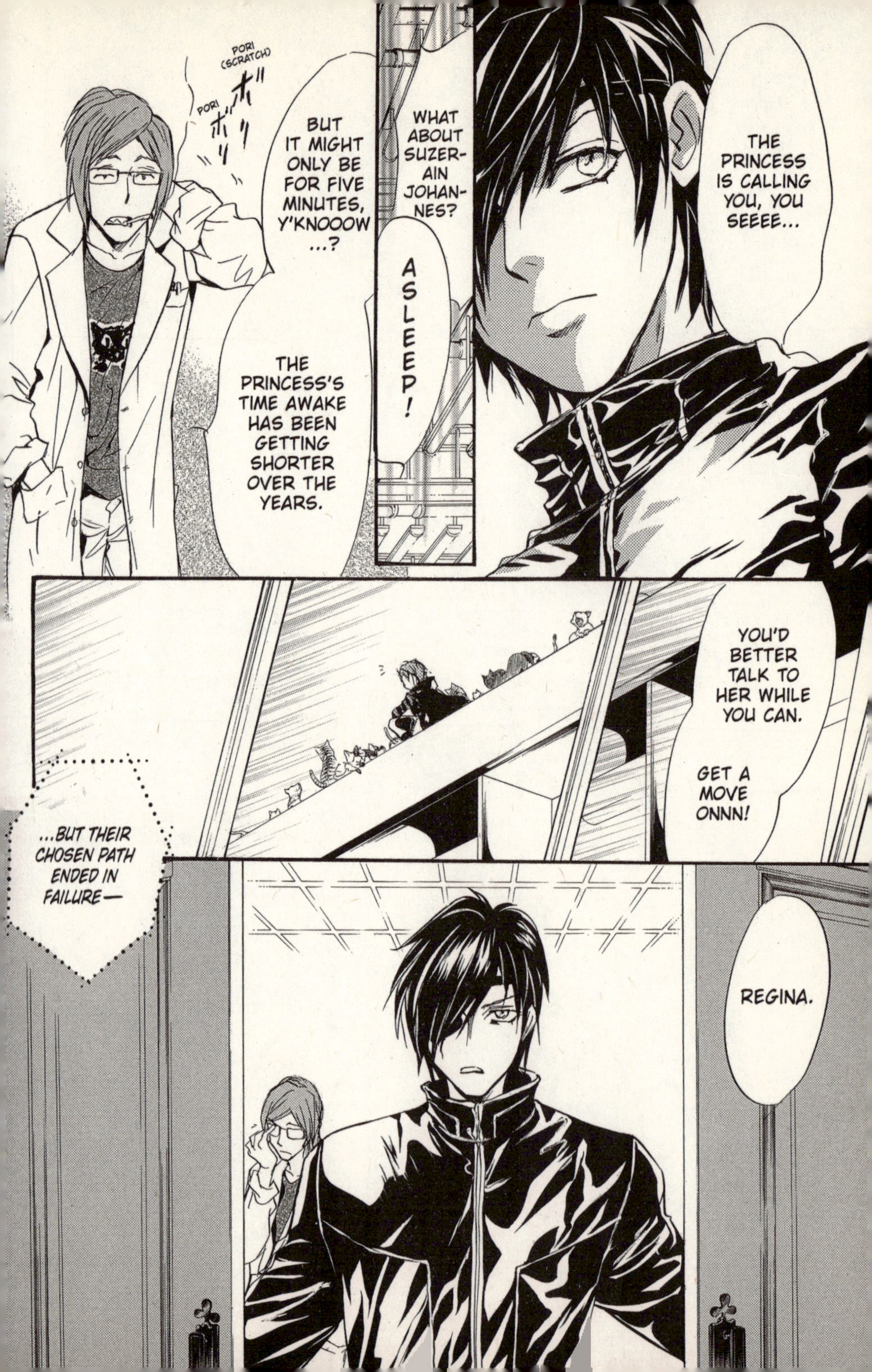
THE PRINCESS IS CALLING YOU, YOU SEEEE...
WHAT ABOUT SUZER-AIN JOHAN-NES?
ASLEEP!
PORI (SCRATCH)
PORI
BUT IT MIGHT ONLY BE FOR FIVE MINUTES, Y'KNOOOW ...?
THE PRINCESS'S TIME AWAKE HAS BEEN GETTING SHORTER OVER THE YEARS.
YOU'D BETTER TALK TO HER WHILE YOU CAN.
GET A MOVE ONNN!
REGINA.
...BUT THEIR CHOSEN PATH ENDED IN FAILURE—

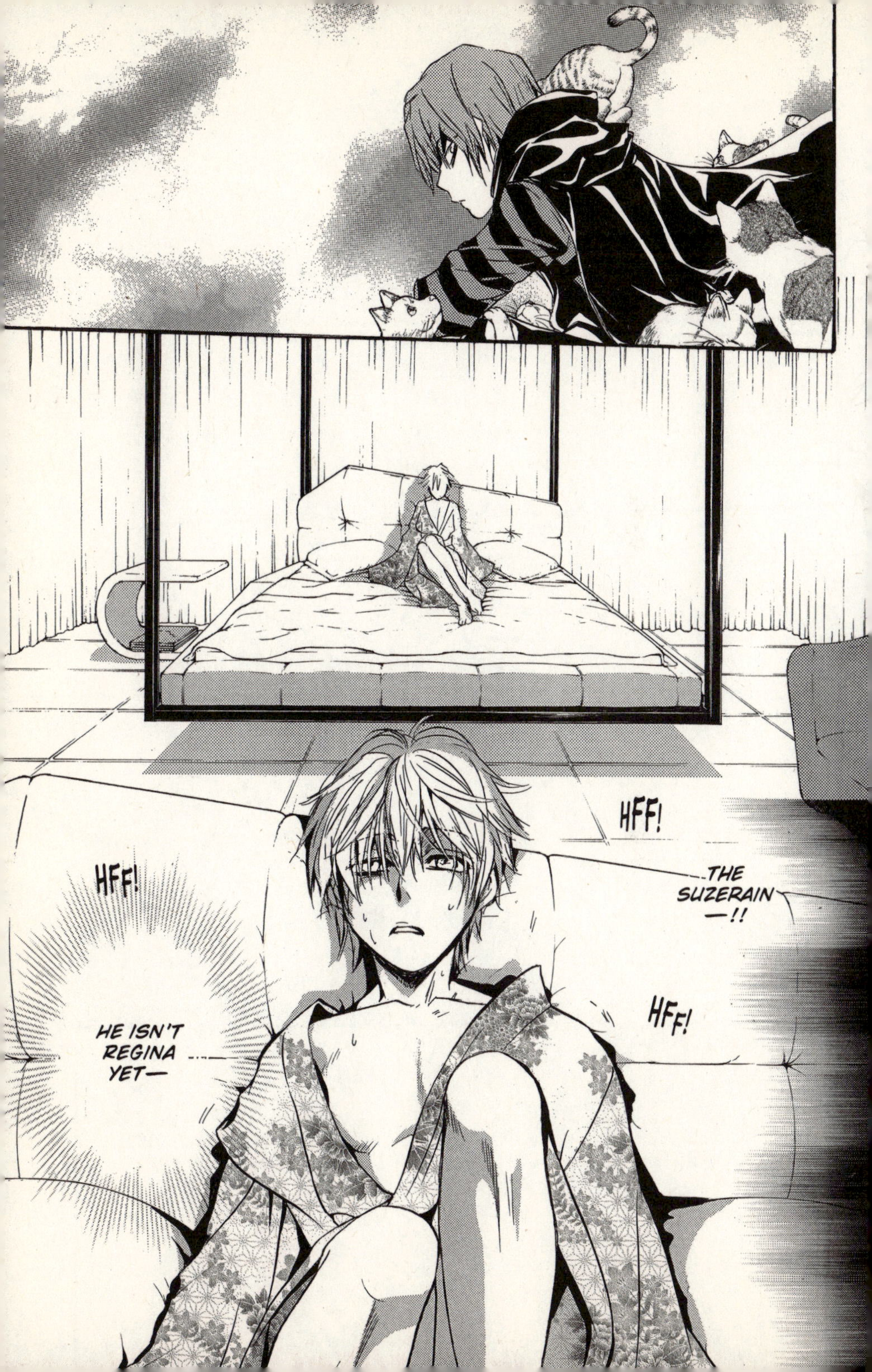
HFF!
...THE SUZERAIN—!!
HFF!
HFF!
HE ISN'T REGINA YET—

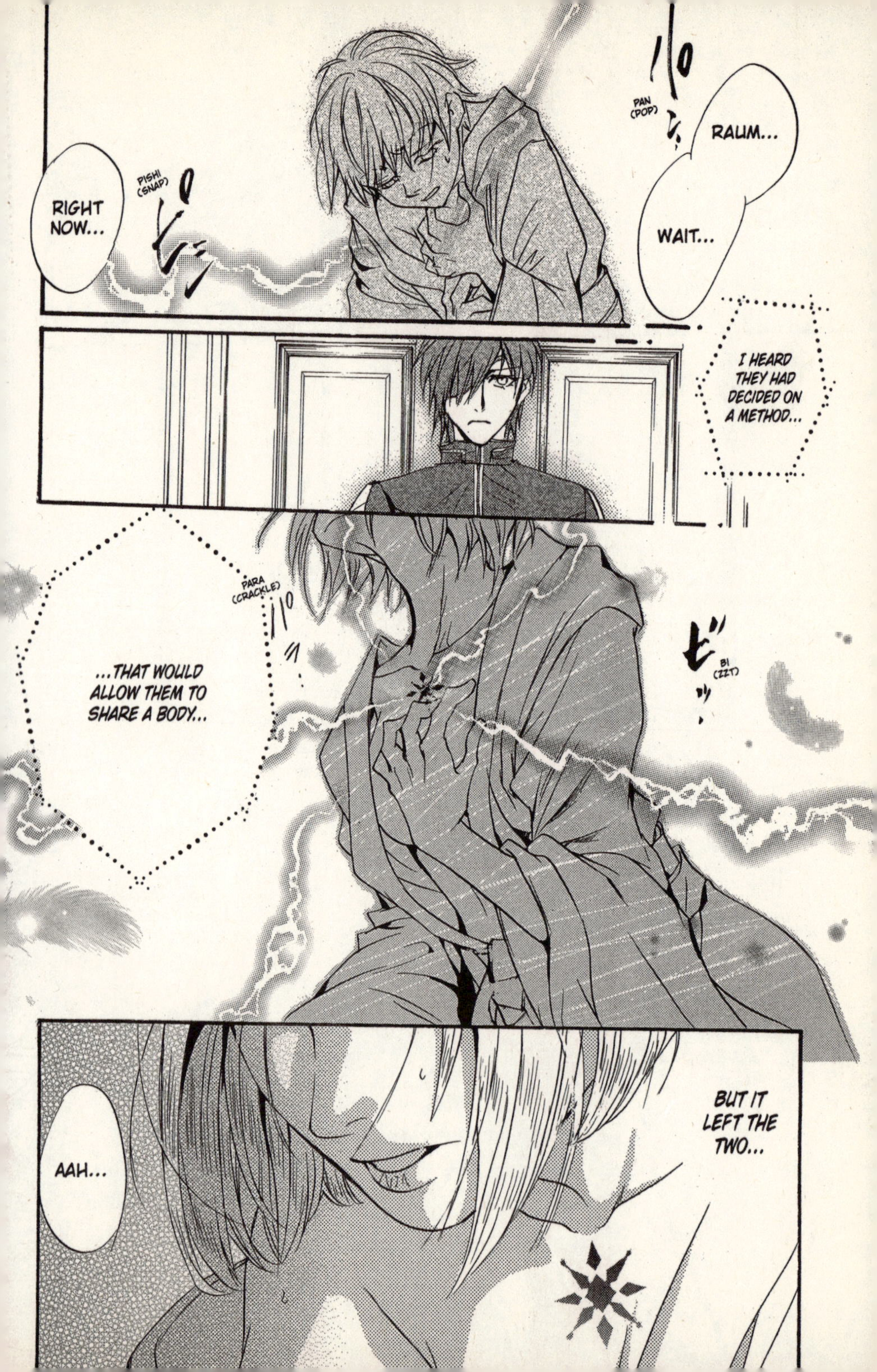
PAN (POP)
RAUM...
WAIT...
PISHI (SNAP)
RIGHT NOW...
I HEARD THEY HAD DECIDED ON A METHOD...
BI (ZZT)
PARA (CRACKLE)
...THAT WOULD ALLOW THEM TO SHARE A BODY...
BUT IT LEFT THE TWO...
AAH...

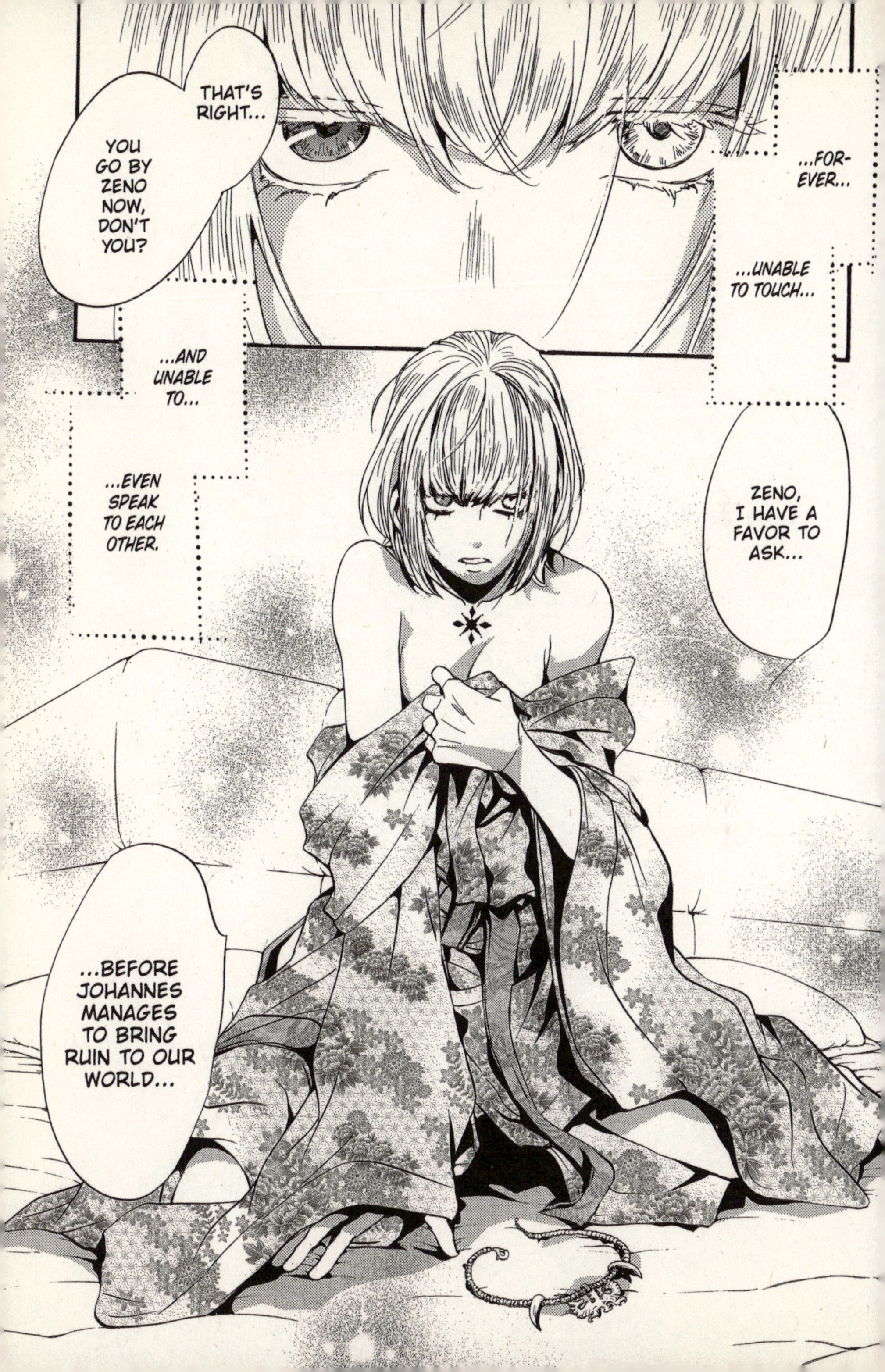
THAT'S RIGHT...
YOU GO BY ZENO NOW, DON'T YOU?
...FOR-EVER...
...UNABLE TO TOUCH...
...AND UNABLE TO...
...EVEN SPEAK TO EACH OTHER.
ZENO, I HAVE A FAVOR TO ASK...
...BEFORE JOHANNES MANAGES TO BRING RUIN TO OUR WORLD...

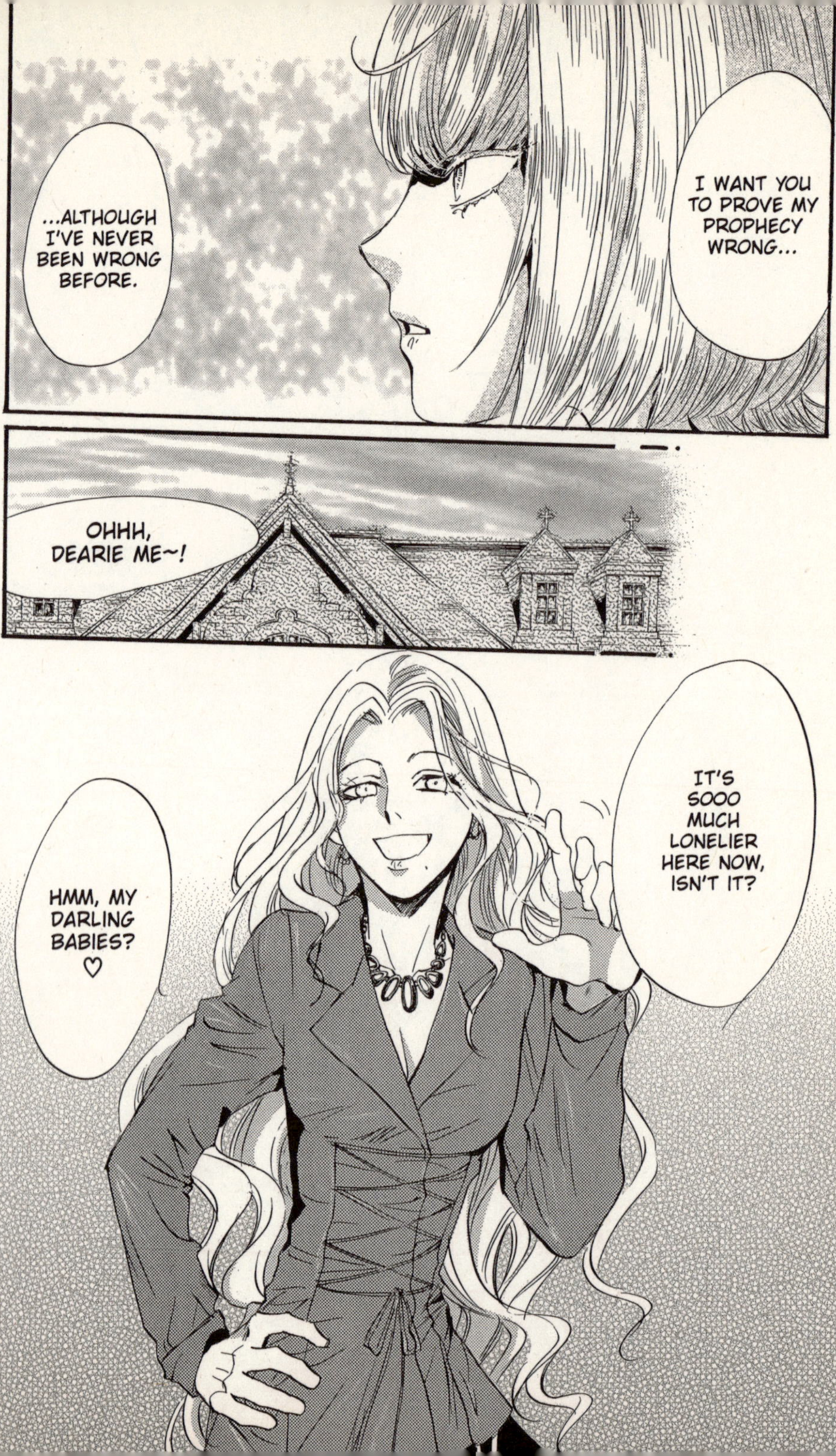
I WANT YOU TO PROVE MY PROPHECY WRONG...
...ALTHOUGH I'VE NEVER BEEN WRONG BEFORE.
OHHH, DEARIE ME~!
IT'S SOOO MUCH LONELIER HERE NOW, ISN'T IT?
HMM, MY DARLING BABIES? ♡

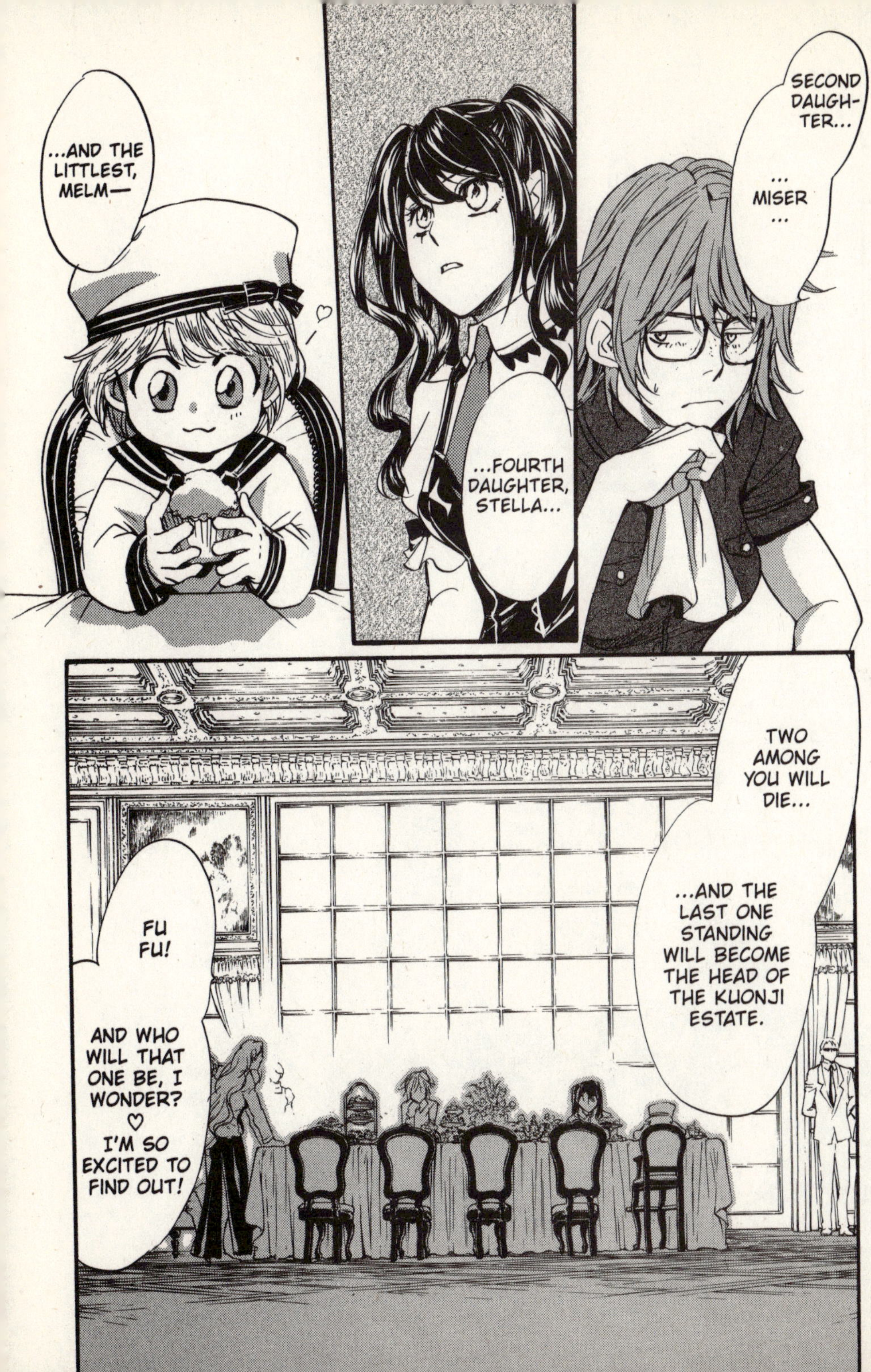
SECOND DAUGHTER... ... MISER ...
...FOURTH DAUGHTER, STELLA...
...AND THE LITTLEST, MELM—
TWO AMONG YOU WILL DIE...
...AND THE LAST ONE STANDING WILL BECOME THE HEAD OF THE KUONJI ESTATE.
FU FU!
AND WHO WILL THAT ONE BE, I WONDER? ♡ I'M SO EXCITED TO FIND OUT!

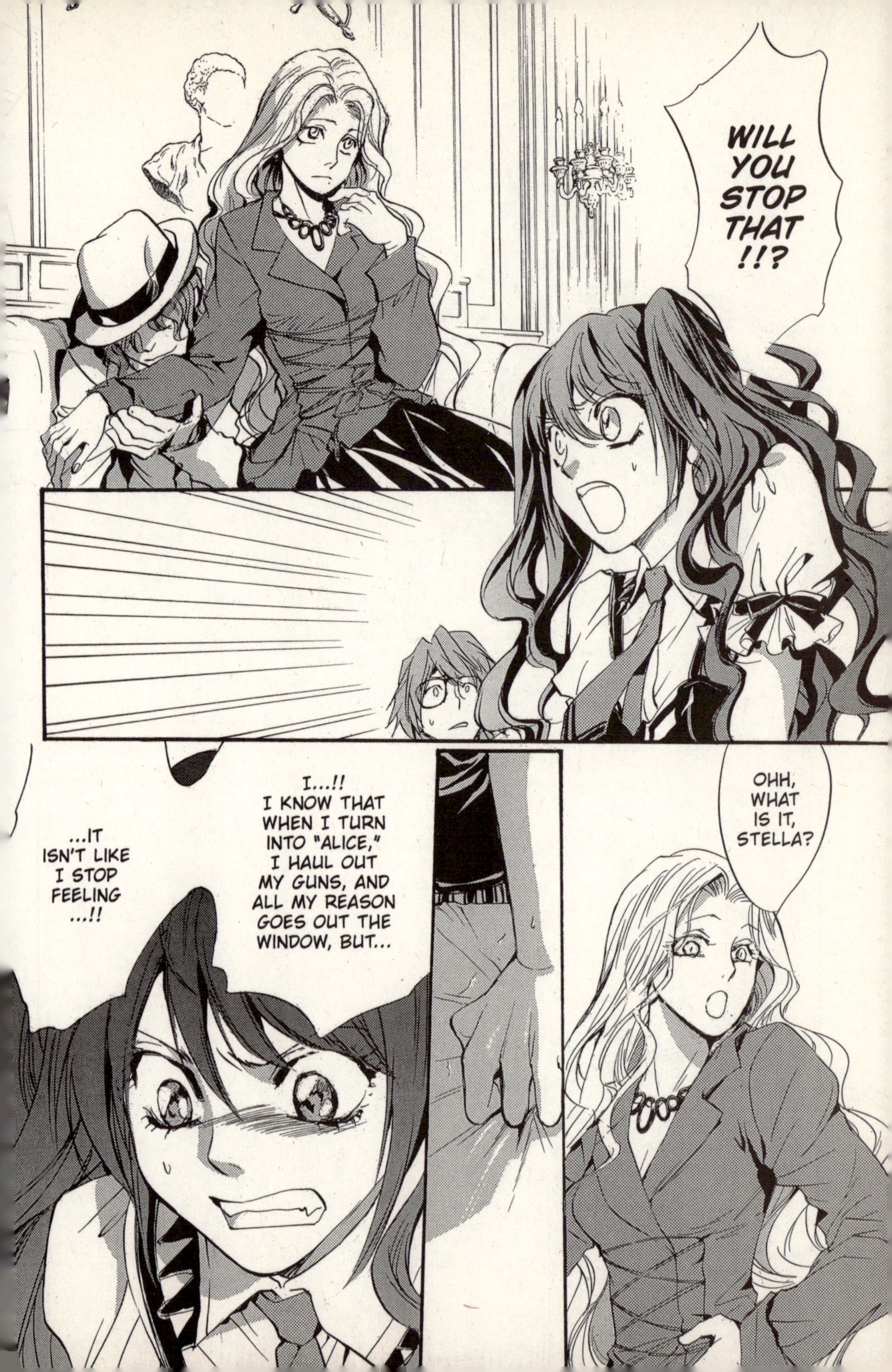
WILL YOU STOP THAT!!?
OHH, WHAT IS IT, STELLA?
I...!! I KNOW THAT WHEN I TURN INTO "ALICE," I HAUL OUT MY GUNS, AND ALL MY REASON GOES OUT THE WINDOW, BUT...
...IT ISN'T LIKE I STOP FEELING...!!

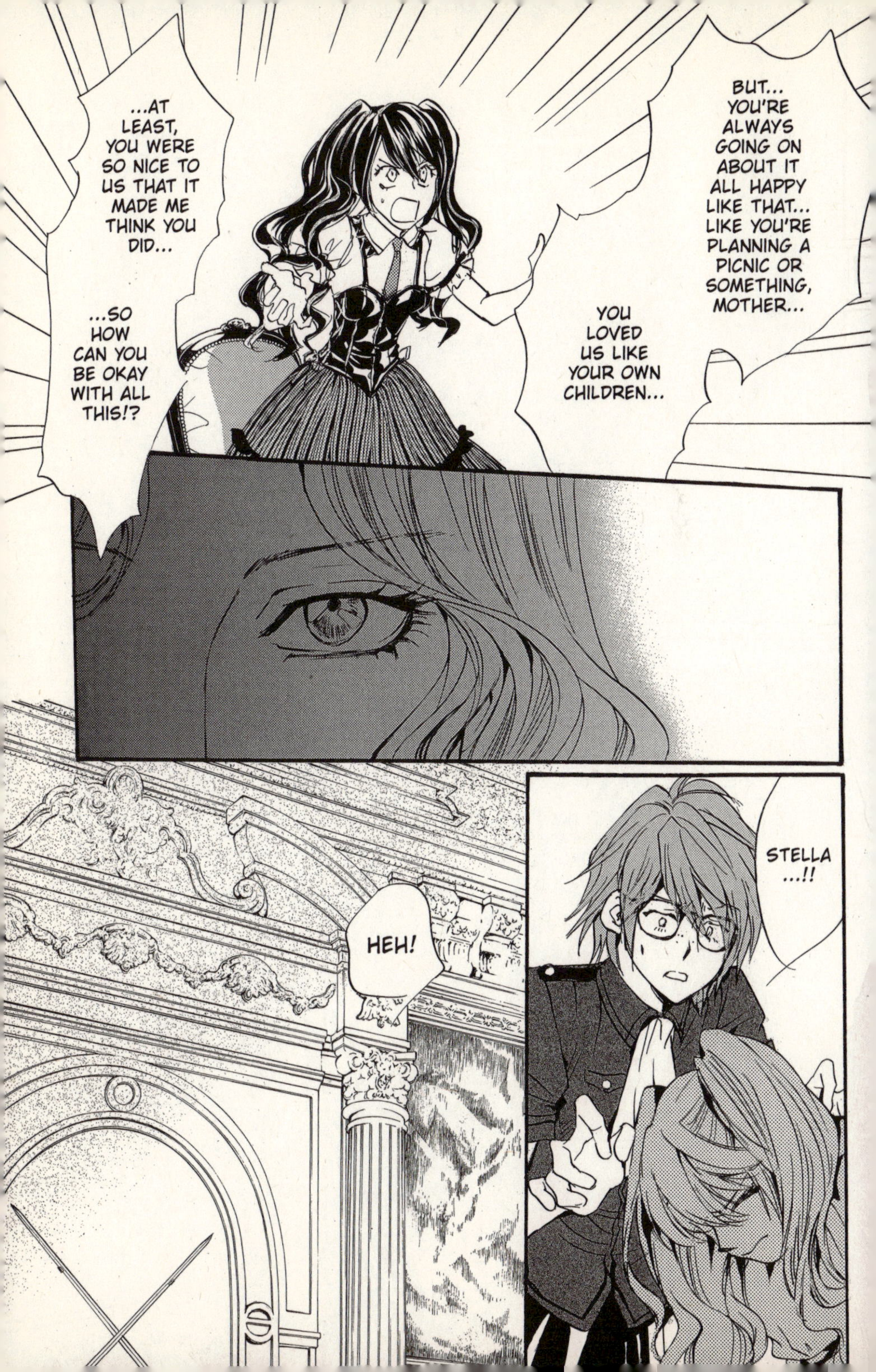
BUT... YOU'RE ALWAYS GOING ON ABOUT IT ALL HAPPY LIKE THAT... LIKE YOU'RE PLANNING A PICNIC OR SOMETHING, MOTHER...
YOU LOVED US LIKE YOUR OWN CHILDREN...
...AT LEAST, YOU WERE SO NICE TO US THAT IT MADE ME THINK YOU DID...
...SO HOW CAN YOU BE OKAY WITH ALL THIS!?
STELLA ...!!
HEH!

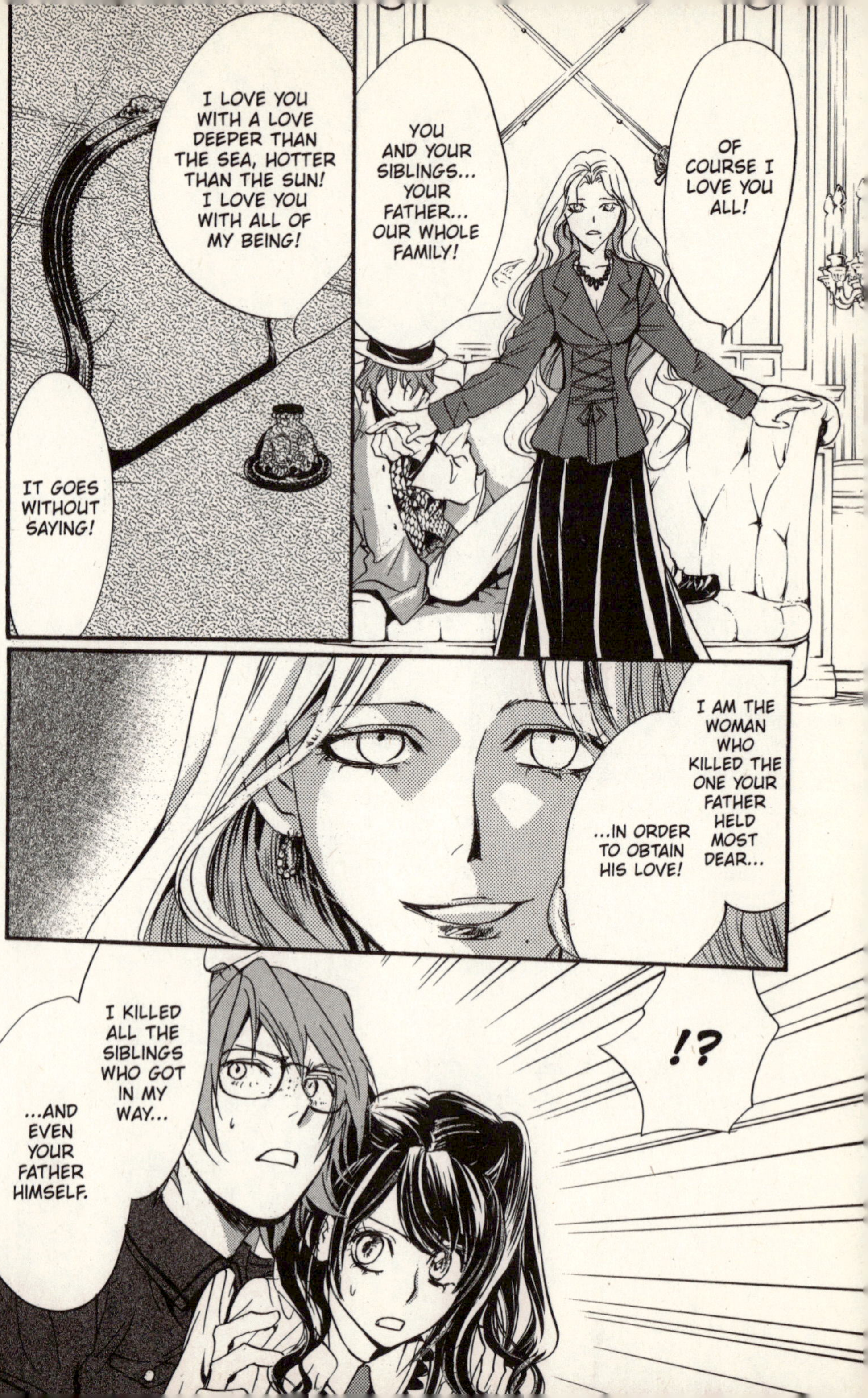
OF COURSE I LOVE YOU ALL!
YOU AND YOUR SIBLINGS... YOUR FATHER... OUR WHOLE FAMILY!
I LOVE YOU WITH A LOVE DEEPER THAN THE SEA, HOTTER THAN THE SUN! I LOVE YOU WITH ALL OF MY BEING!
IT GOES WITHOUT SAYING!
I AM THE WOMAN WHO KILLED THE ONE YOUR FATHER HELD MOST DEAR...
...IN ORDER TO OBTAIN HIS LOVE!
!?
I KILLED ALL THE SIBLINGS WHO GOT IN MY WAY...
...AND EVEN YOUR FATHER HIMSELF.

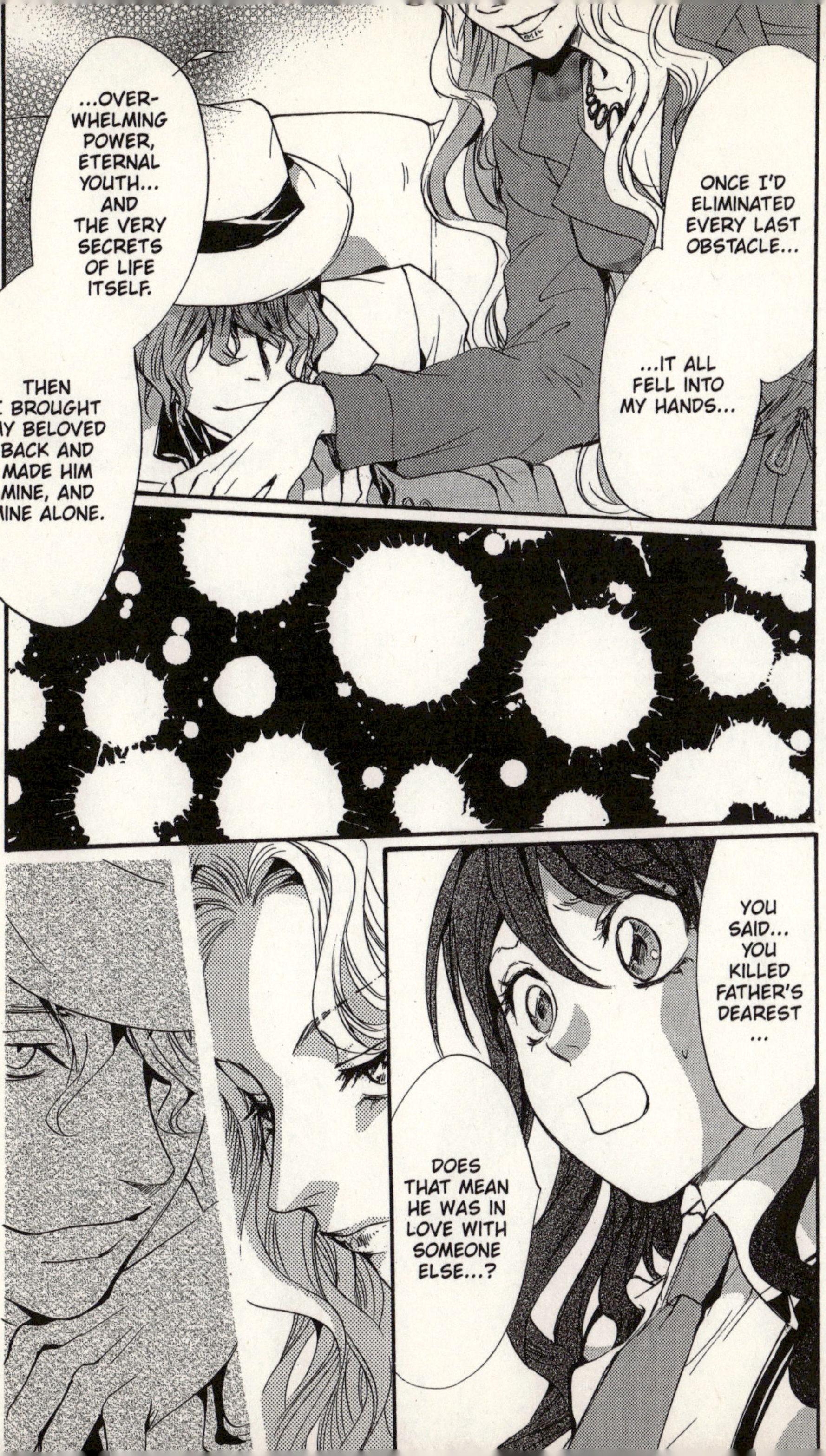
ONCE I'D ELIMINATED EVERY LAST OBSTACLE...
...IT ALL FELL INTO MY HANDS...
...OVER-WHELMING POWER, ETERNAL YOUTH... AND THE VERY SECRETS OF LIFE ITSELF.
THEN I BROUGHT MY BELOVED BACK AND MADE HIM MINE, AND MINE ALONE.
YOU SAID... YOU KILLED FATHER'S DEAREST ...
DOES THAT MEAN HE WAS IN LOVE WITH SOMEONE ELSE...?

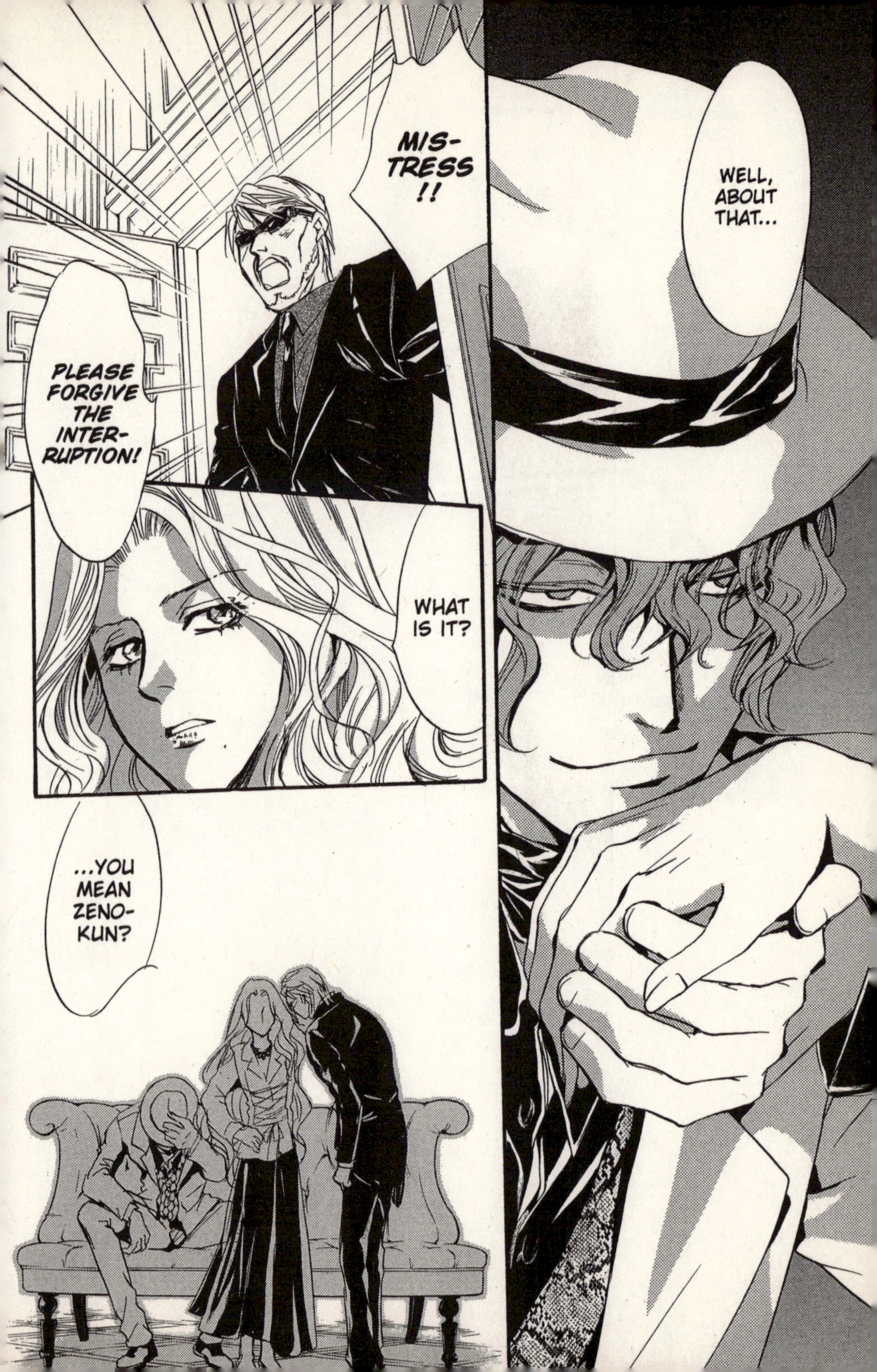
WELL, ABOUT THAT...
MIS-TRESS!!
PLEASE FORGIVE THE INTER-RUPTION!
WHAT IS IT?
...YOU MEAN ZENO-KUN?

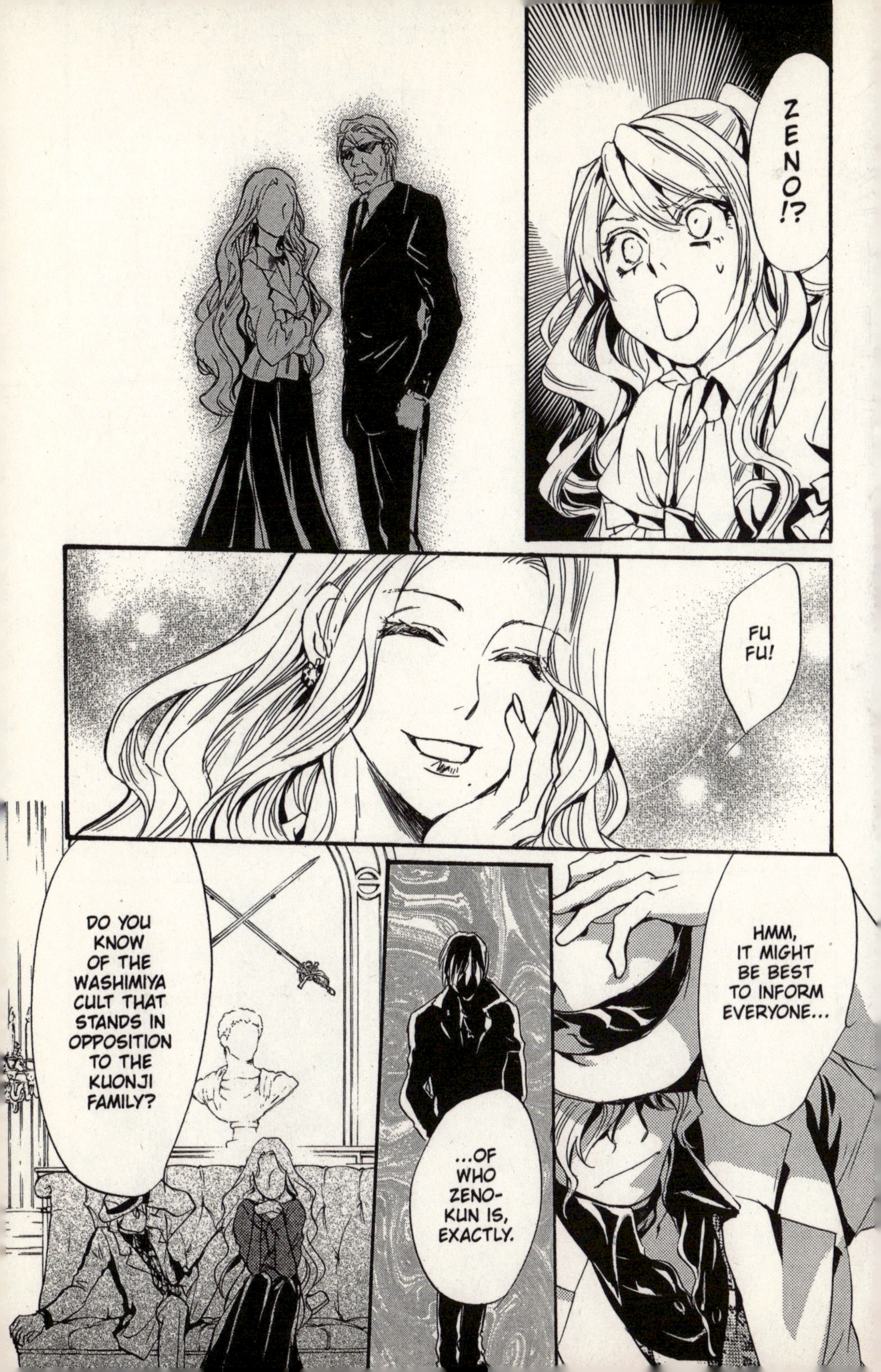
ZENO!?
FU FU!
HMM, IT MIGHT BE BEST TO INFORM EVERYONE...
...OF WHO ZENO-KUN IS, EXACTLY.
DO YOU KNOW OF THE WASHIMIYA CULT THAT STANDS IN OPPOSITION TO THE KUONJI FAMILY?

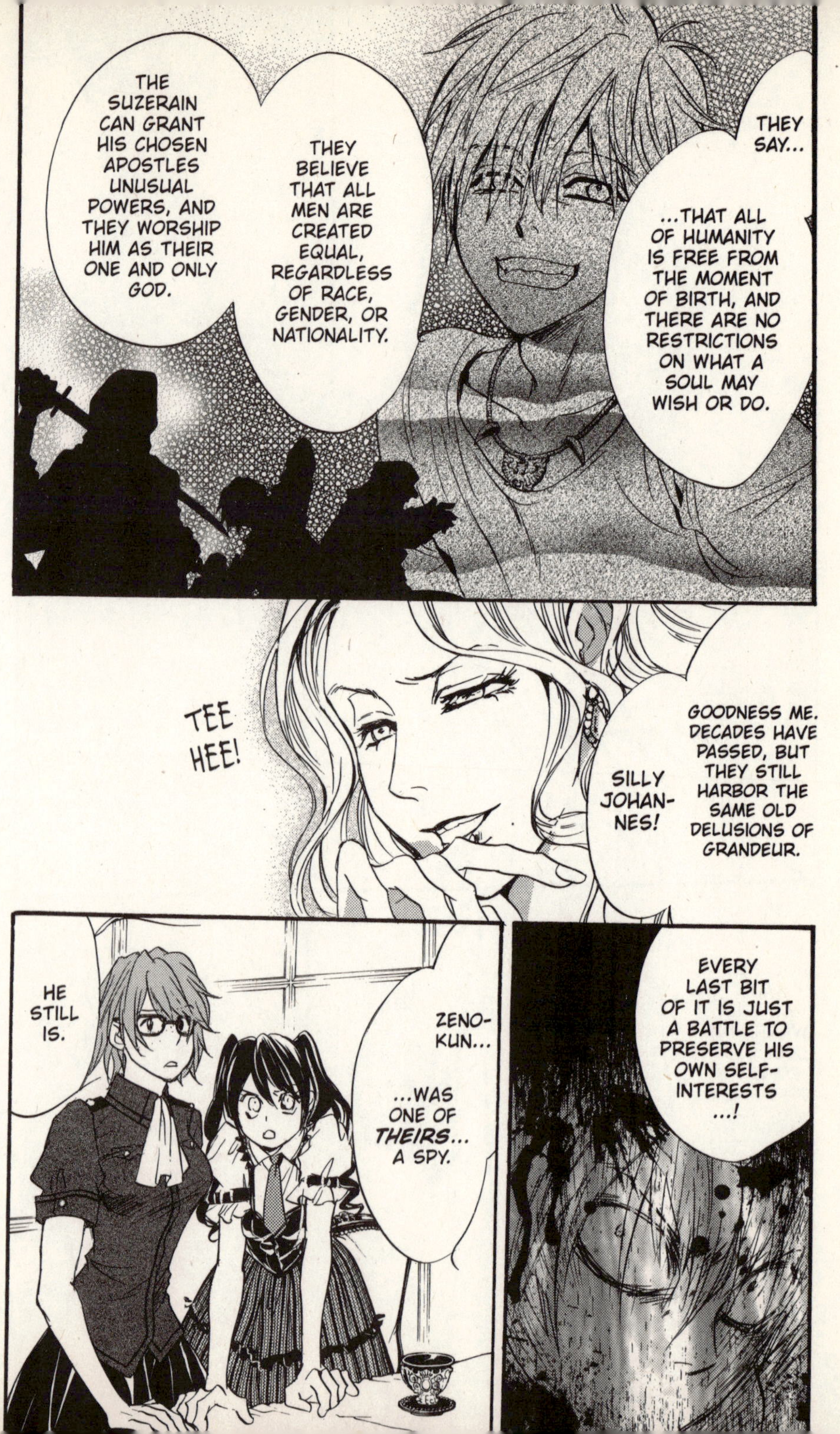
THEY SAY...
...THAT ALL OF HUMANITY IS FREE FROM THE MOMENT OF BIRTH, AND THERE ARE NO RESTRICTIONS ON WHAT A SOUL MAY WISH OR DO.
THEY BELIEVE THAT ALL MEN ARE CREATED EQUAL, REGARDLESS OF RACE, GENDER, OR NATIONALITY.
THE SUZERAIN CAN GRANT HIS CHOSEN APOSTLES UNUSUAL POWERS, AND THEY WORSHIP HIM AS THEIR ONE AND ONLY GOD.
GOODNESS ME. DECADES HAVE PASSED, BUT THEY STILL HARBOR THE SAME OLD DELUSIONS OF GRANDEUR.
SILLY JOHANNES!
TEE HEE!
EVERY LAST BIT OF IT IS JUST A BATTLE TO PRESERVE HIS OWN SELF-INTERESTS ...!
ZENO-KUN...
...WAS ONE OF *THEIRS*... A SPY.
HE STILL IS.

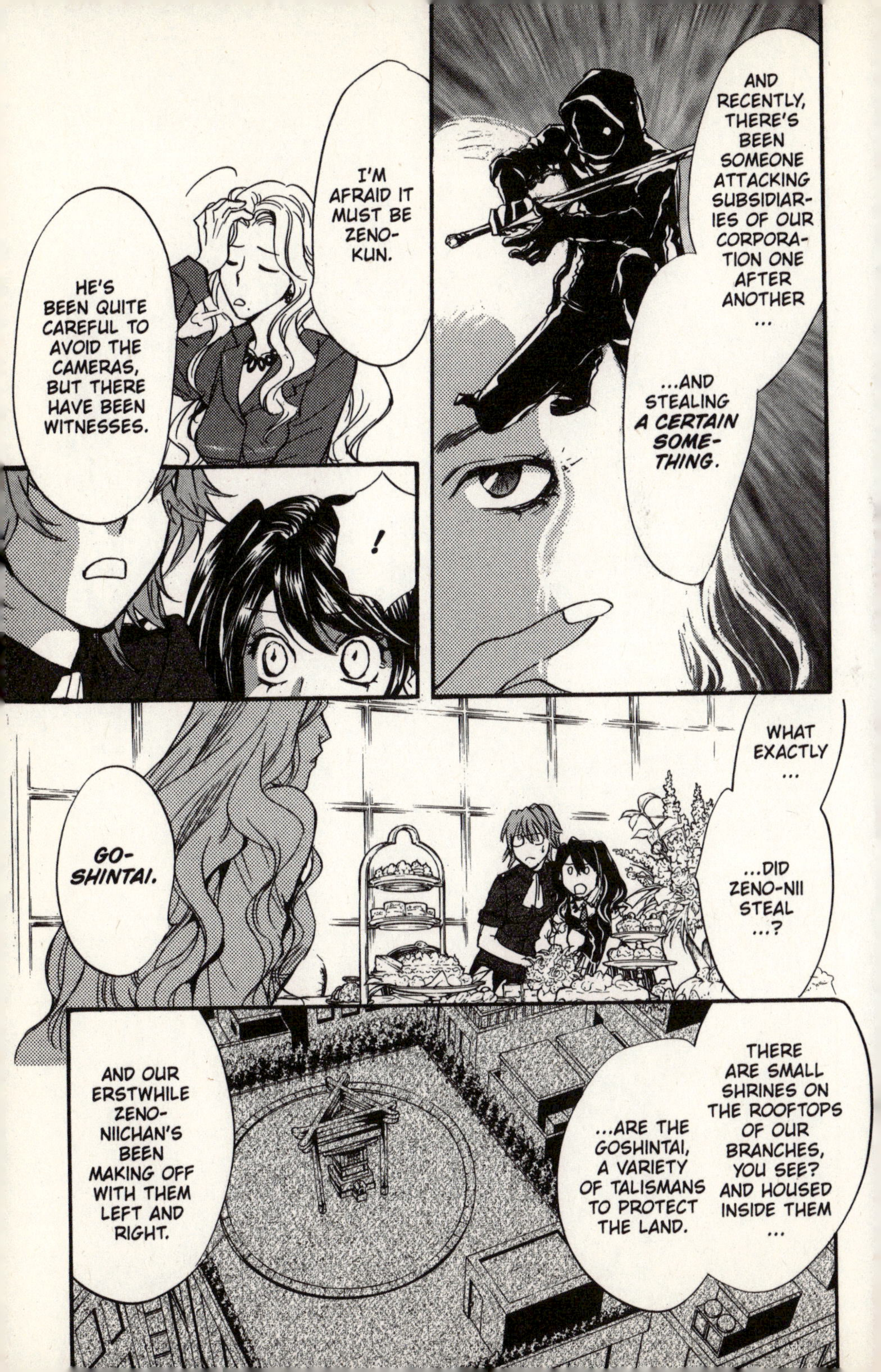
AND RECENTLY, THERE'S BEEN SOMEONE ATTACKING SUBSIDIARIES OF OUR CORPORATION ONE AFTER ANOTHER ...
...AND STEALING *A CERTAIN SOMETHING*.
I'M AFRAID IT MUST BE ZENO-KUN.
HE'S BEEN QUITE CAREFUL TO AVOID THE CAMERAS, BUT THERE HAVE BEEN WITNESSES.
!
WHAT EXACTLY ...
...DID ZENO-NII STEAL ...?
GO-SHINTAI.
THERE ARE SMALL SHRINES ON THE ROOFTOPS OF OUR BRANCHES, YOU SEE? AND HOUSED INSIDE THEM ...
...ARE THE GOSHINTAI, A VARIETY OF TALISMANS TO PROTECT THE LAND.
AND OUR ERSTWHILE ZENO-NIICHAN'S BEEN MAKING OFF WITH THEM LEFT AND RIGHT.

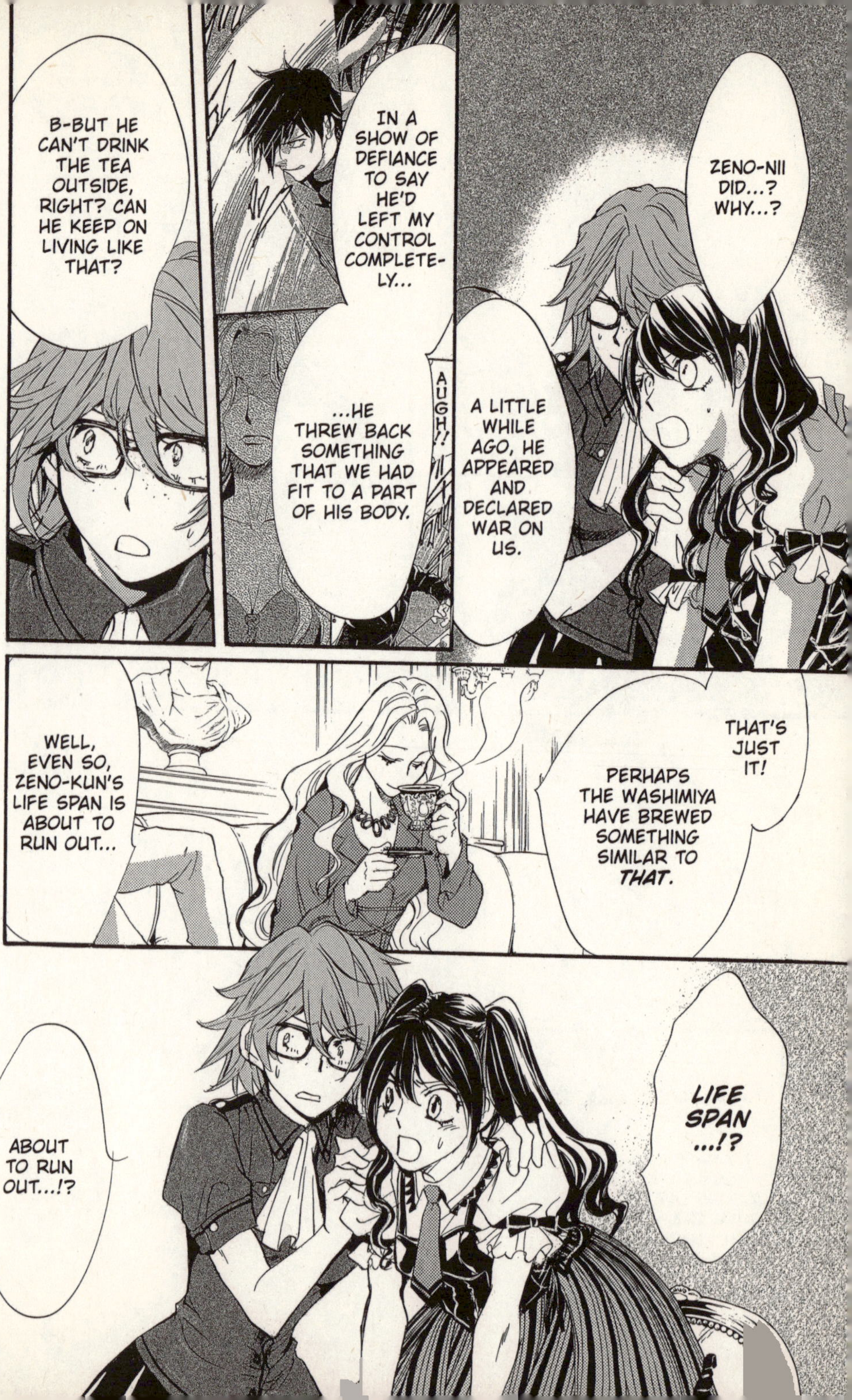
ZENO-NII DID...? WHY...?
A LITTLE WHILE AGO, HE APPEARED AND DECLARED WAR ON US.
IN A SHOW OF DEFIANCE TO SAY HE'D LEFT MY CONTROL COMPLETELY...
...HE THREW BACK SOMETHING THAT WE HAD FIT TO A PART OF HIS BODY.
AUGH!!
B-BUT HE CAN'T DRINK THE TEA OUTSIDE, RIGHT? CAN HE KEEP ON LIVING LIKE THAT?
THAT'S JUST IT!
PERHAPS THE WASHIMIYA HAVE BREWED SOMETHING SIMILAR TO *THAT*.
WELL, EVEN SO, ZENO-KUN'S LIFE SPAN IS ABOUT TO RUN OUT...
LIFE SPAN ...!?
ABOUT TO RUN OUT...!?

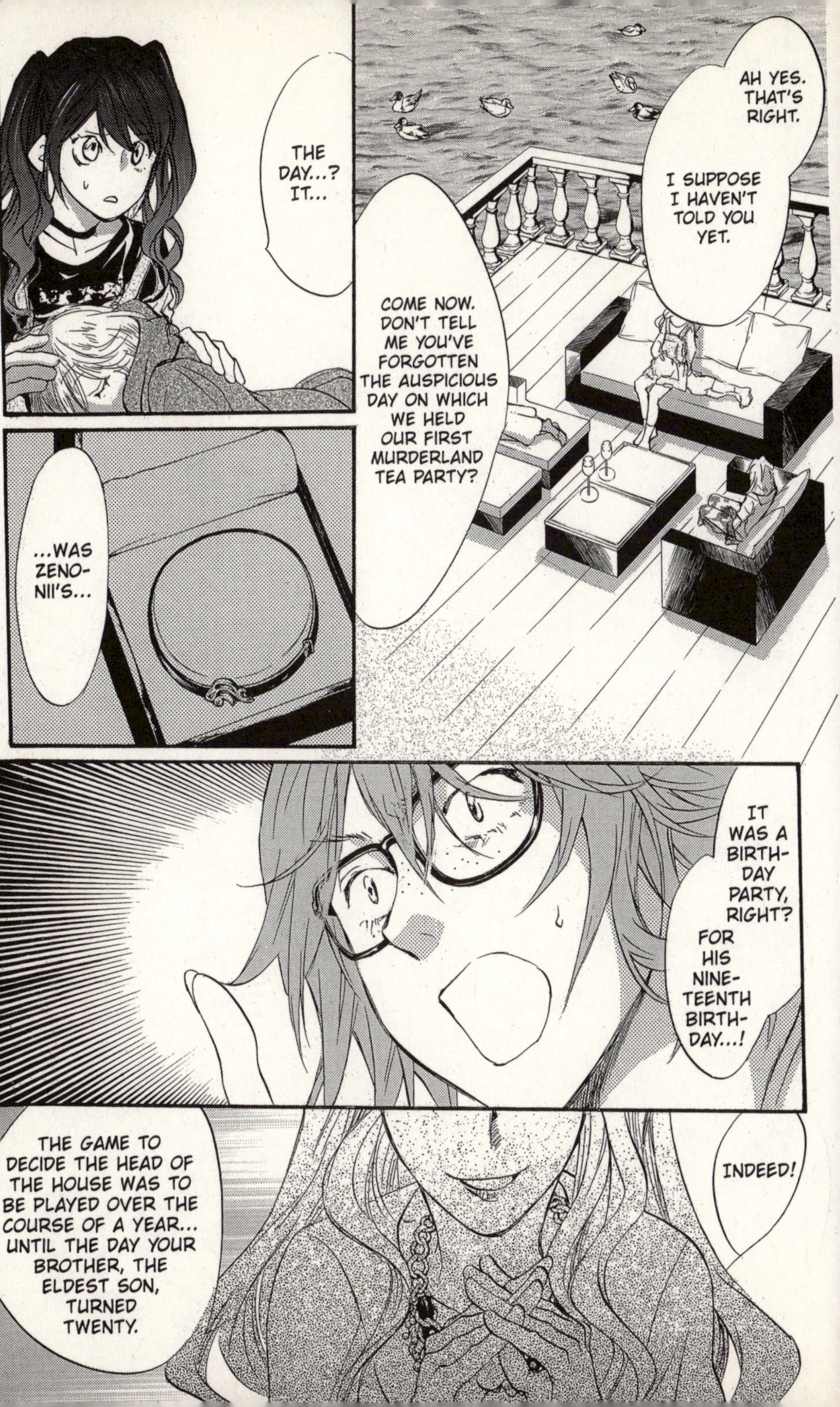
AH YES. THAT'S RIGHT.
I SUPPOSE I HAVEN'T TOLD YOU YET.
COME NOW. DON'T TELL ME YOU'VE FORGOTTEN THE AUSPICIOUS DAY ON WHICH WE HELD OUR FIRST MURDERLAND TEA PARTY?
THE DAY...? IT...
...WAS ZENO-NII'S...
IT WAS A BIRTH-DAY PARTY, RIGHT? FOR HIS NINE-TEENTH BIRTH-DAY...!
INDEED!
THE GAME TO DECIDE THE HEAD OF THE HOUSE WAS TO BE PLAYED OVER THE COURSE OF A YEAR... UNTIL THE DAY YOUR BROTHER, THE ELDEST SON, TURNED TWENTY.

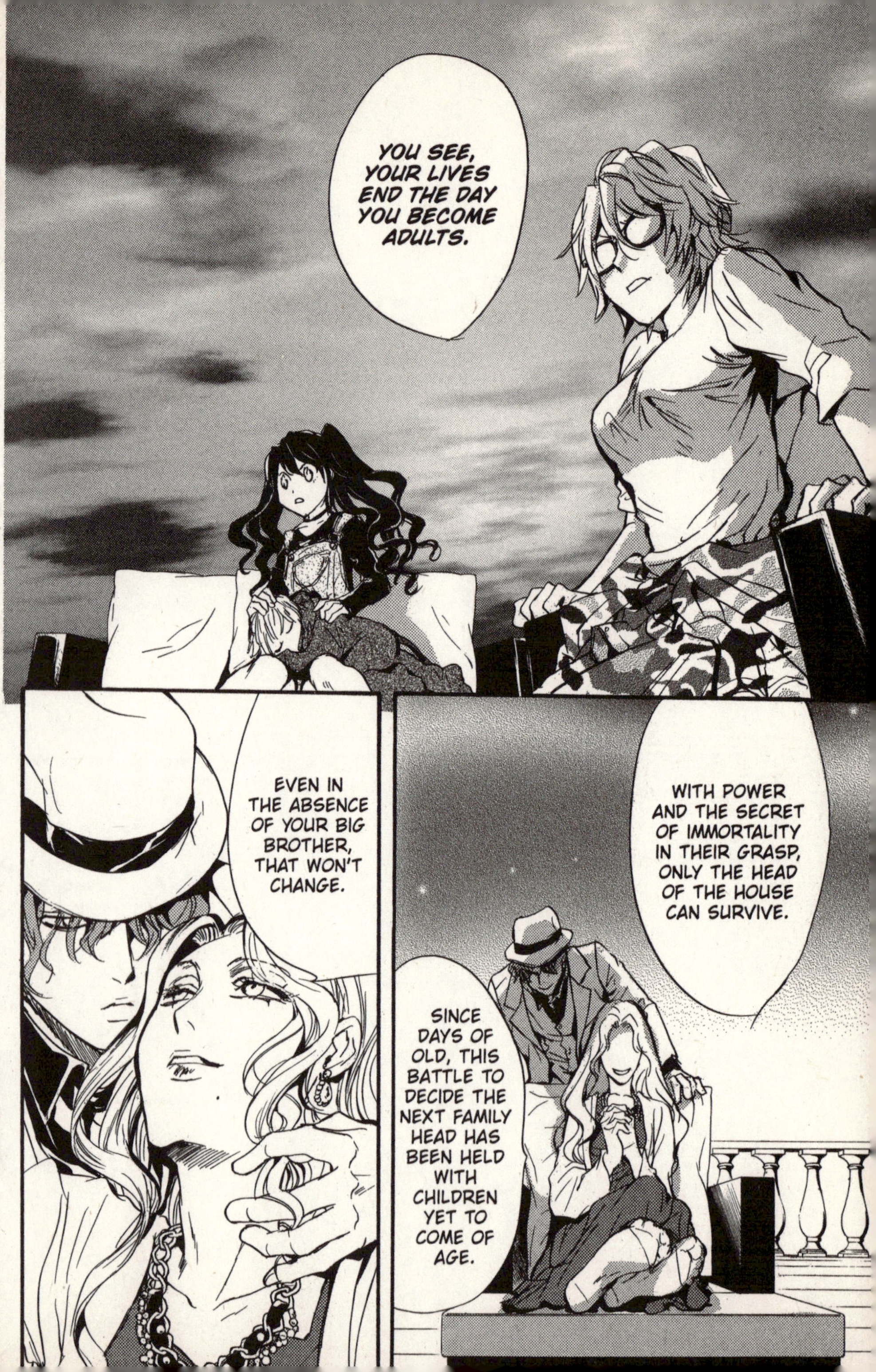
YOU SEE, YOUR LIVES END THE DAY YOU BECOME ADULTS.
WITH POWER AND THE SECRET OF IMMORTALITY IN THEIR GRASP, ONLY THE HEAD OF THE HOUSE CAN SURVIVE.
SINCE DAYS OF OLD, THIS BATTLE TO DECIDE THE NEXT FAMILY HEAD HAS BEEN HELD WITH CHILDREN YET TO COME OF AGE.
EVEN IN THE ABSENCE OF YOUR BIG BROTHER, THAT WON'T CHANGE.

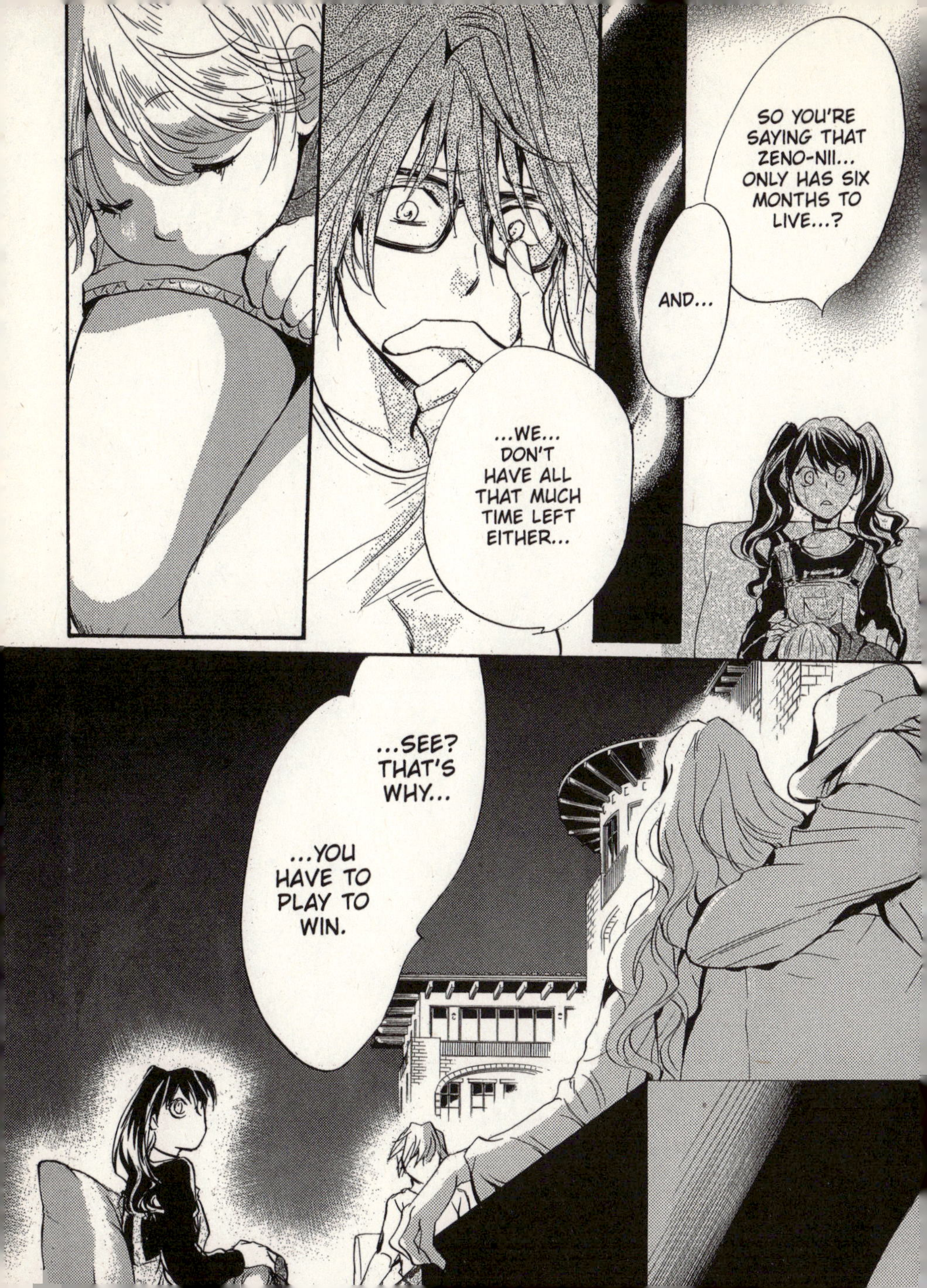
SO YOU'RE SAYING THAT ZENO-NII... ONLY HAS SIX MONTHS TO LIVE...?
AND...
...WE... DON'T HAVE ALL THAT MUCH TIME LEFT EITHER...
...SEE? THAT'S WHY...
...YOU HAVE TO PLAY TO WIN.

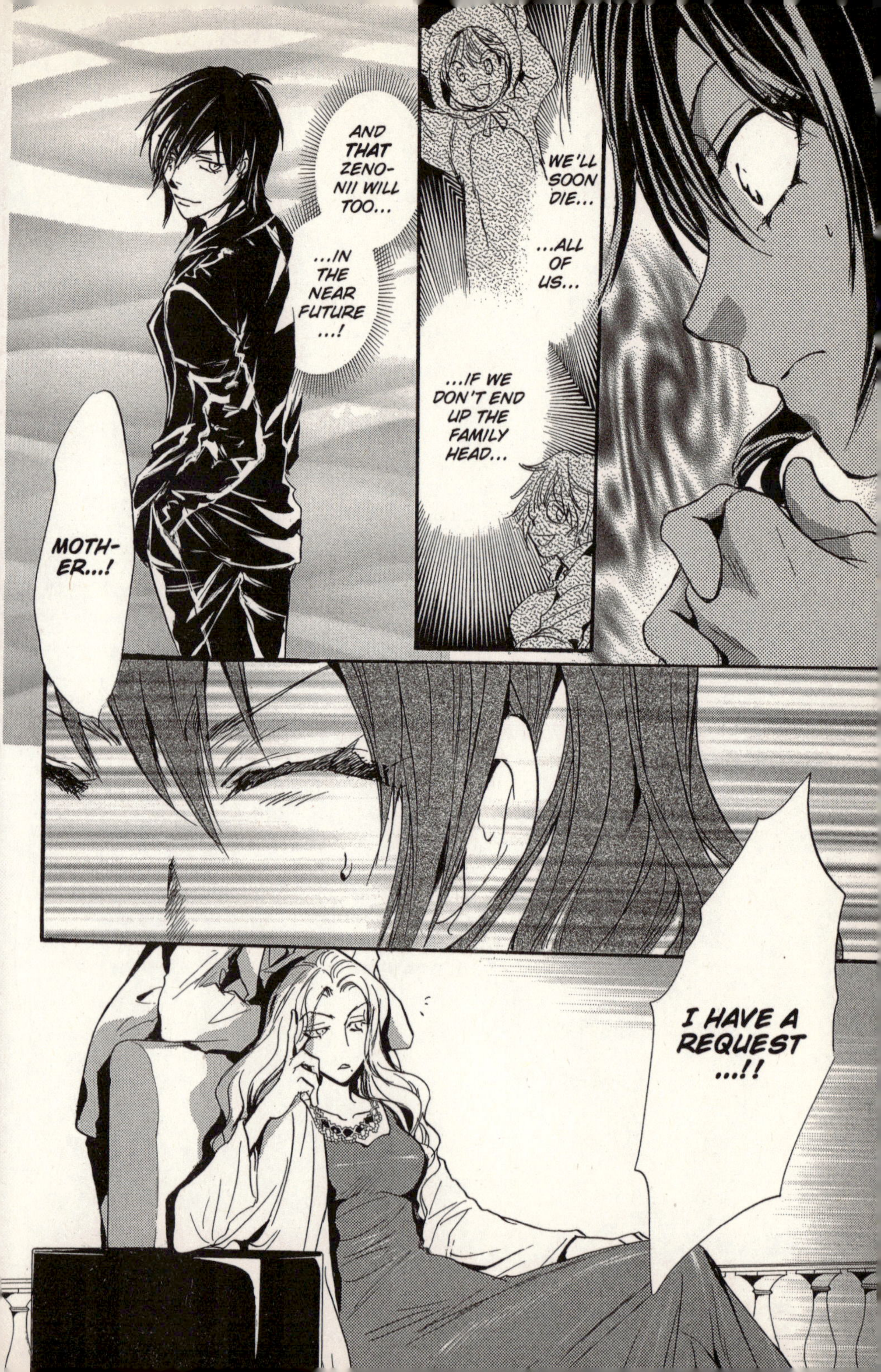
WE'LL SOON DIE...
...ALL OF US...
...IF WE DON'T END UP THE FAMILY HEAD...
AND THAT ZENO-NII WILL TOO...
...IN THE NEAR FUTURE...!
MOTHER...!
I HAVE A REQUEST...!!

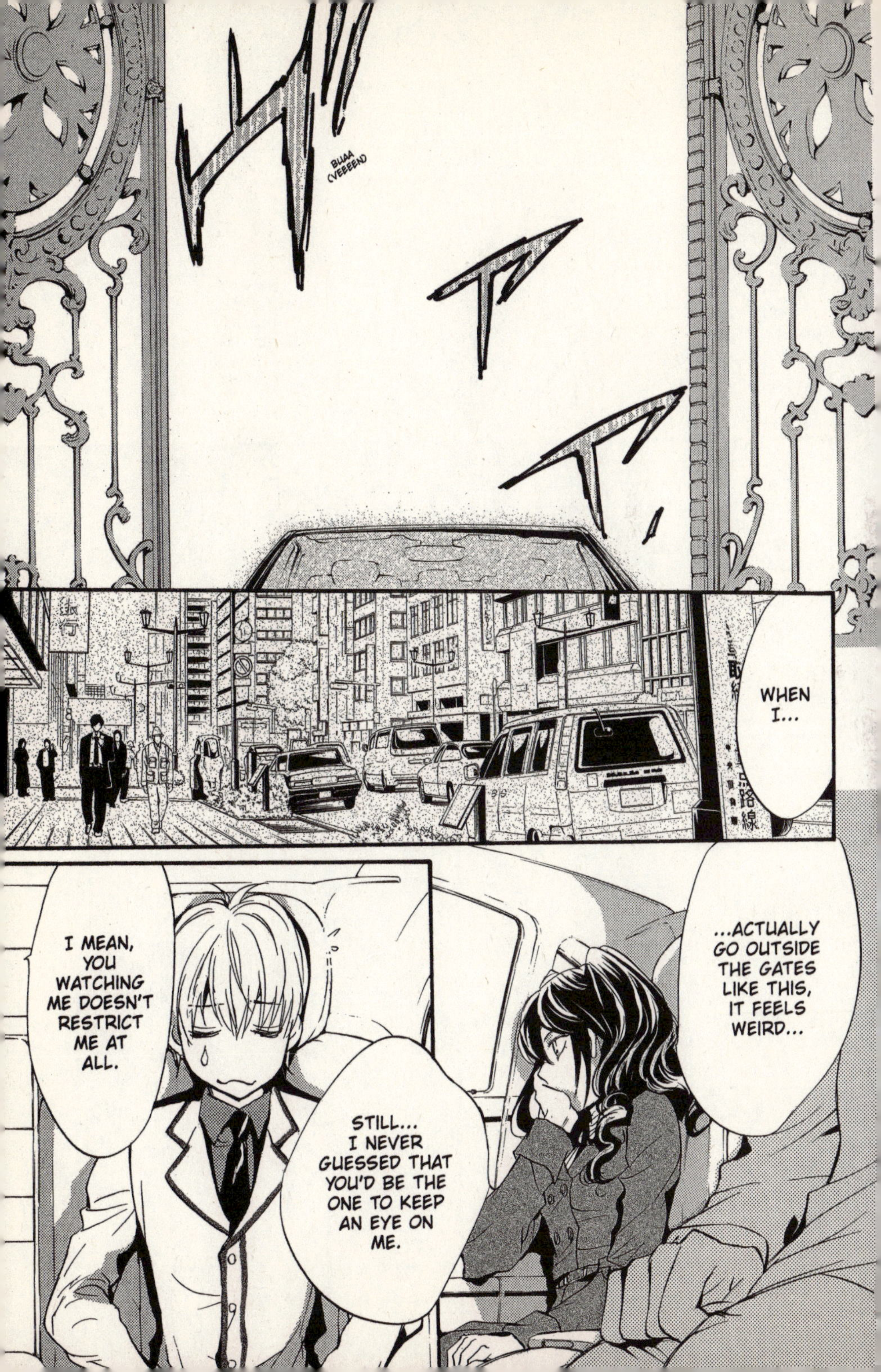
BUAA (VEEEEN)
WHEN I...
...ACTUALLY GO OUTSIDE THE GATES LIKE THIS, IT FEELS WEIRD...
I MEAN, YOU WATCHING ME DOESN'T RESTRICT ME AT ALL.
STILL... I NEVER GUESSED THAT YOU'D BE THE ONE TO KEEP AN EYE ON ME.

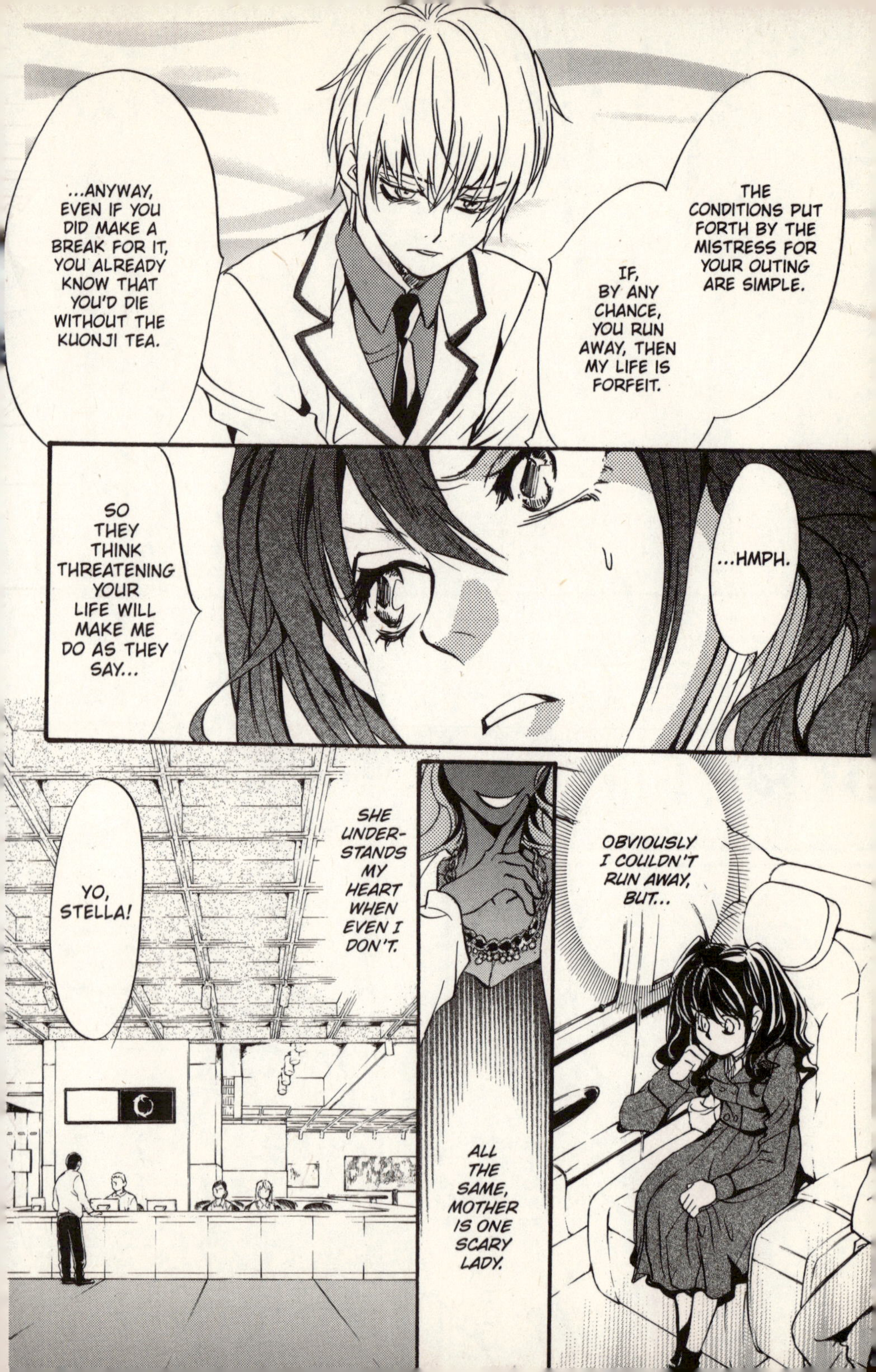
THE CONDITIONS PUT FORTH BY THE MISTRESS FOR YOUR OUTING ARE SIMPLE.
IF, BY ANY CHANCE, YOU RUN AWAY, THEN MY LIFE IS FORFEIT.
...ANYWAY, EVEN IF YOU DID MAKE A BREAK FOR IT, YOU ALREADY KNOW THAT YOU'D DIE WITHOUT THE KUONJI TEA.
...HMPH.
SO THEY THINK THREATENING YOUR LIFE WILL MAKE ME DO AS THEY SAY...
OBVIOUSLY I COULDN'T RUN AWAY, BUT...
ALL THE SAME, MOTHER IS ONE SCARY LADY.
SHE UNDER-STANDS MY HEART WHEN EVEN I DON'T.
YO, STELLA!

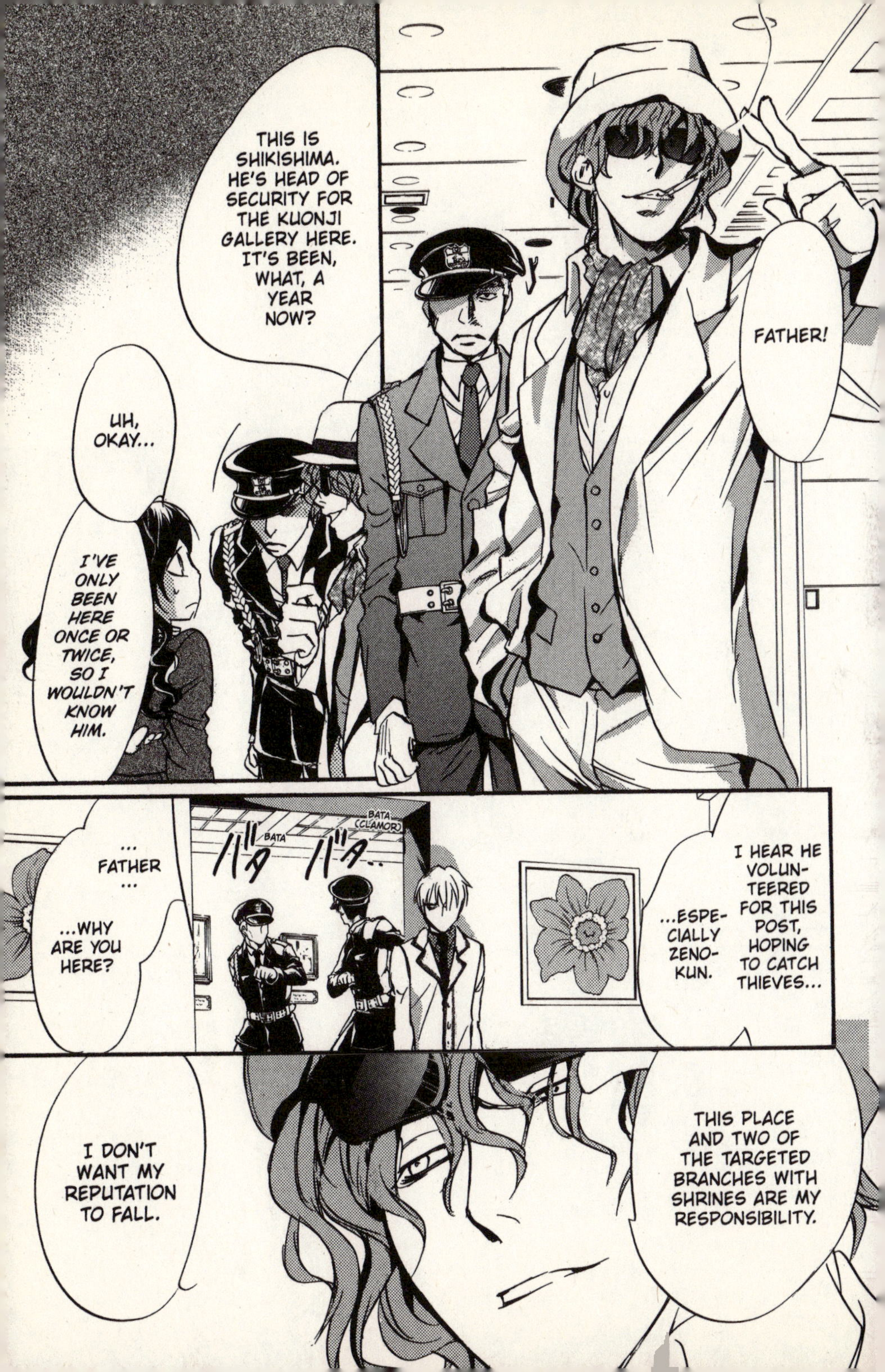
FATHER!
THIS IS SHIKISHIMA. HE'S HEAD OF SECURITY FOR THE KUONJI GALLERY HERE. IT'S BEEN, WHAT, A YEAR NOW?
UH, OKAY...
I'VE ONLY BEEN HERE ONCE OR TWICE, SO I WOULDN'T KNOW HIM.
I HEAR HE VOLUNTEERED FOR THIS POST, HOPING TO CATCH THIEVES...
...ESPECIALLY ZENO-KUN.
BATA (CLAMOR)
BATA
...FATHER...
...WHY ARE YOU HERE?
THIS PLACE AND TWO OF THE TARGETED BRANCHES WITH SHRINES ARE MY RESPONSIBILITY.
I DON'T WANT MY REPUTATION TO FALL.

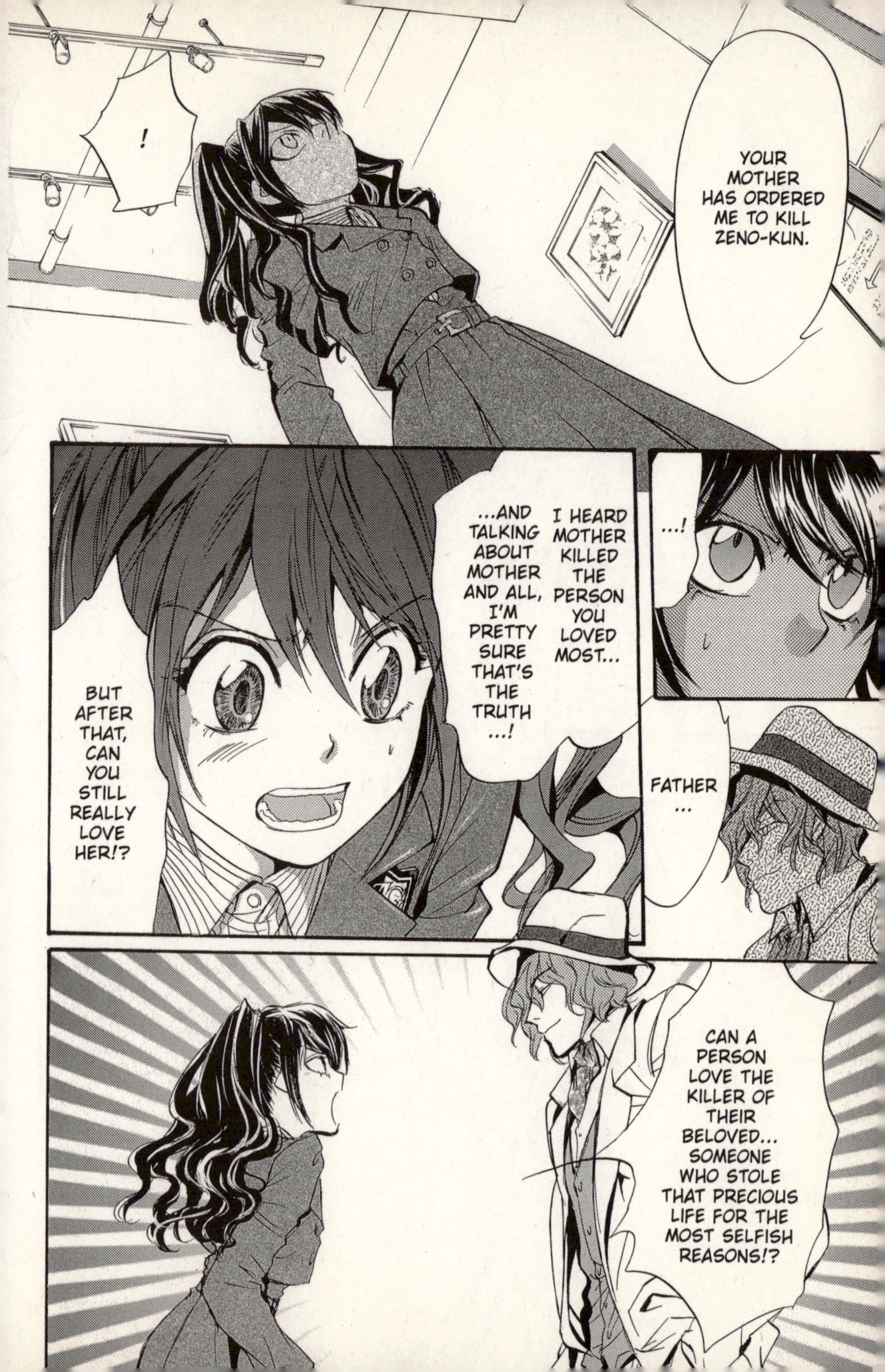
YOUR MOTHER HAS ORDERED ME TO KILL ZENO-KUN.
!
...!
FATHER ...
I HEARD MOTHER KILLED THE PERSON YOU LOVED MOST...
...AND TALKING ABOUT MOTHER AND ALL, I'M PRETTY SURE THAT'S THE TRUTH ...!
BUT AFTER THAT, CAN YOU STILL REALLY LOVE HER!?
CAN A PERSON LOVE THE KILLER OF THEIR BELOVED... SOMEONE WHO STOLE THAT PRECIOUS LIFE FOR THE MOST SELFISH REASONS!?

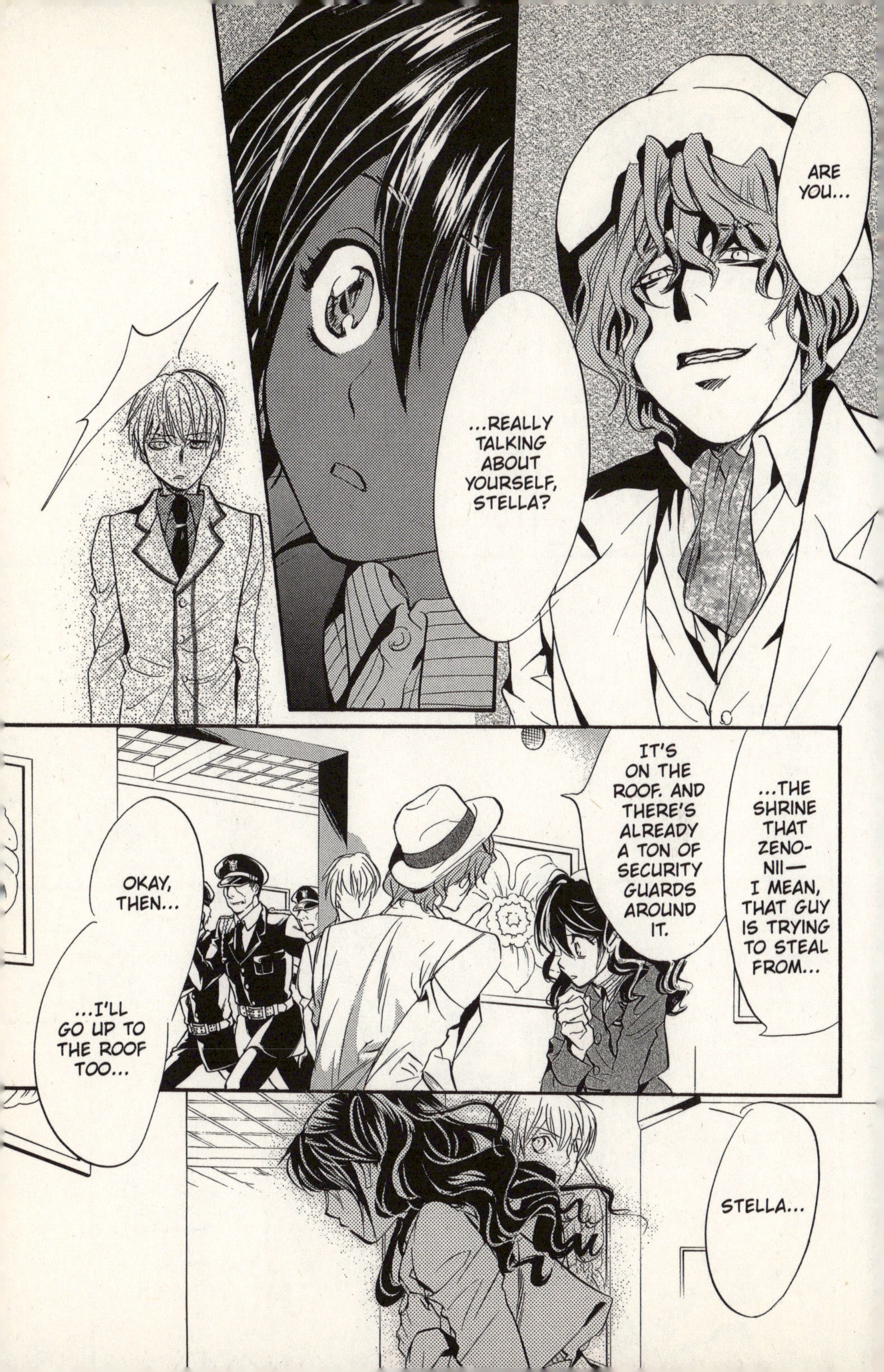
ARE YOU...
...REALLY TALKING ABOUT YOURSELF, STELLA?
...THE SHRINE THAT ZENO-NII— I MEAN, THAT GUY IS TRYING TO STEAL FROM...
IT'S ON THE ROOF. AND THERE'S ALREADY A TON OF SECURITY GUARDS AROUND IT.
OKAY, THEN...
...I'LL GO UP TO THE ROOF TOO...
STELLA...

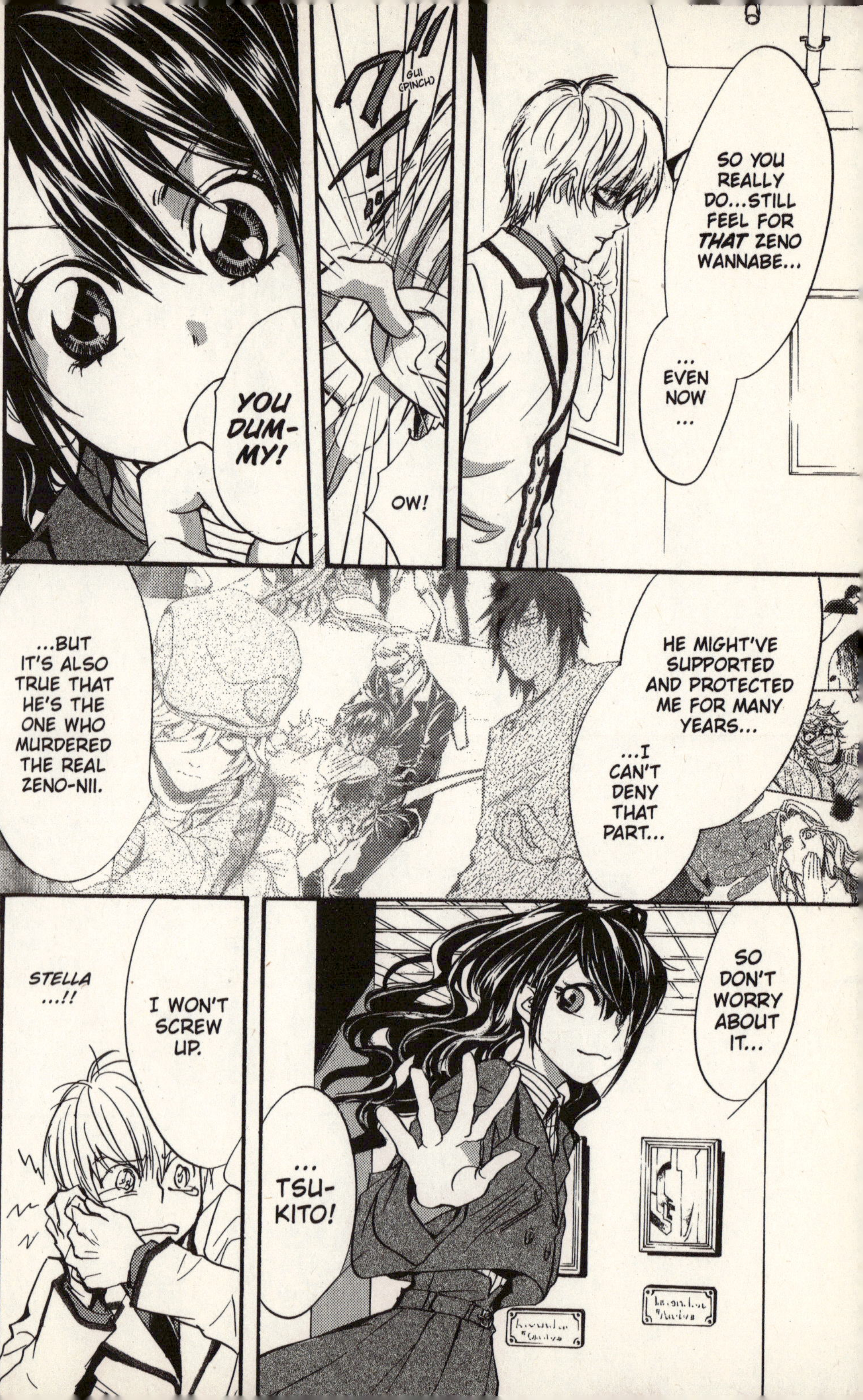
SO YOU REALLY DO...STILL FEEL FOR THAT ZENO WANNABE...
...EVEN NOW...
GUI (PINCH)
OW!
YOU DUM-MY!
HE MIGHT'VE SUPPORTED AND PROTECTED ME FOR MANY YEARS...
...I CAN'T DENY THAT PART...
...BUT IT'S ALSO TRUE THAT HE'S THE ONE WHO MURDERED THE REAL ZENO-NII.
SO DON'T WORRY ABOUT IT...
...TSU-KITO!
I WON'T SCREW UP.
STELLA ...!!

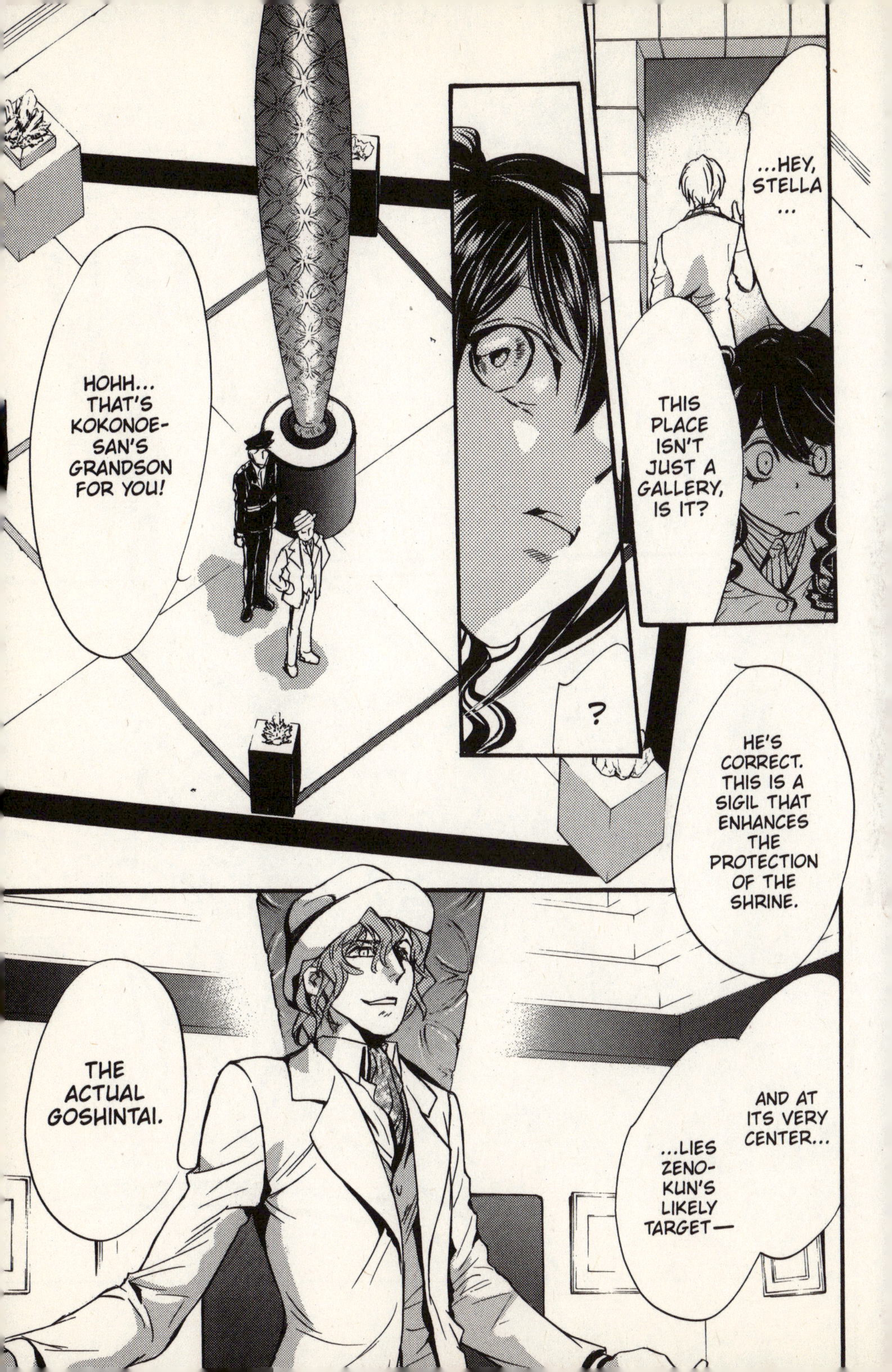
...HEY, STELLA ...
THIS PLACE ISN'T JUST A GALLERY, IS IT?
?
HOHH... THAT'S KOKONOE-SAN'S GRANDSON FOR YOU!
HE'S CORRECT. THIS IS A SIGIL THAT ENHANCES THE PROTECTION OF THE SHRINE.
AND AT ITS VERY CENTER...
...LIES ZENO-KUN'S LIKELY TARGET—
THE ACTUAL GOSHINTAI.

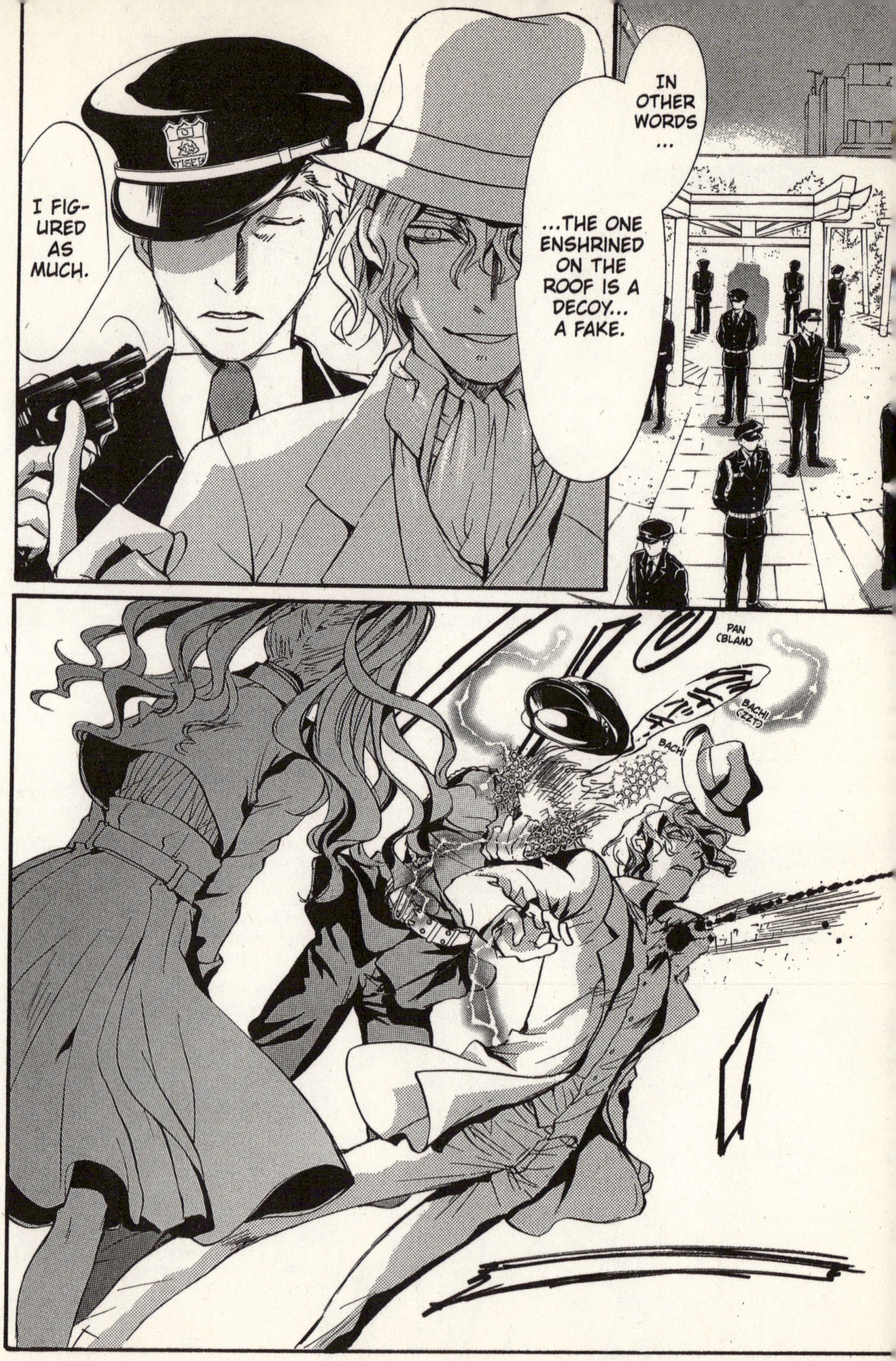
IN OTHER WORDS ...
...THE ONE ENSHRINED ON THE ROOF IS A DECOY... A FAKE.
I FIGURED AS MUCH.
PAN (BLAM)
BACHI (ZZZT)
BACHI

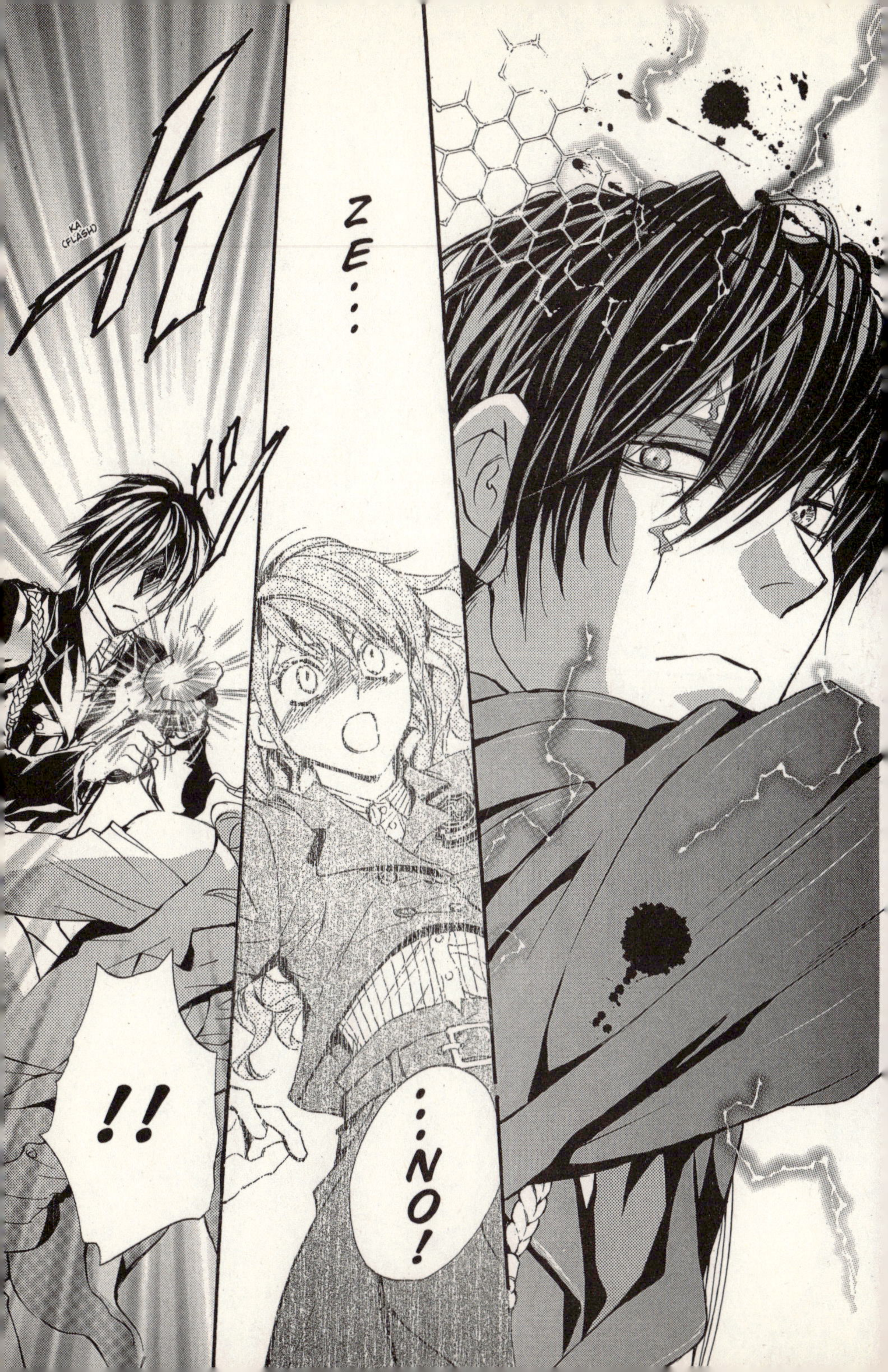
ZE...
...NO!
KA (FLASH)
!!

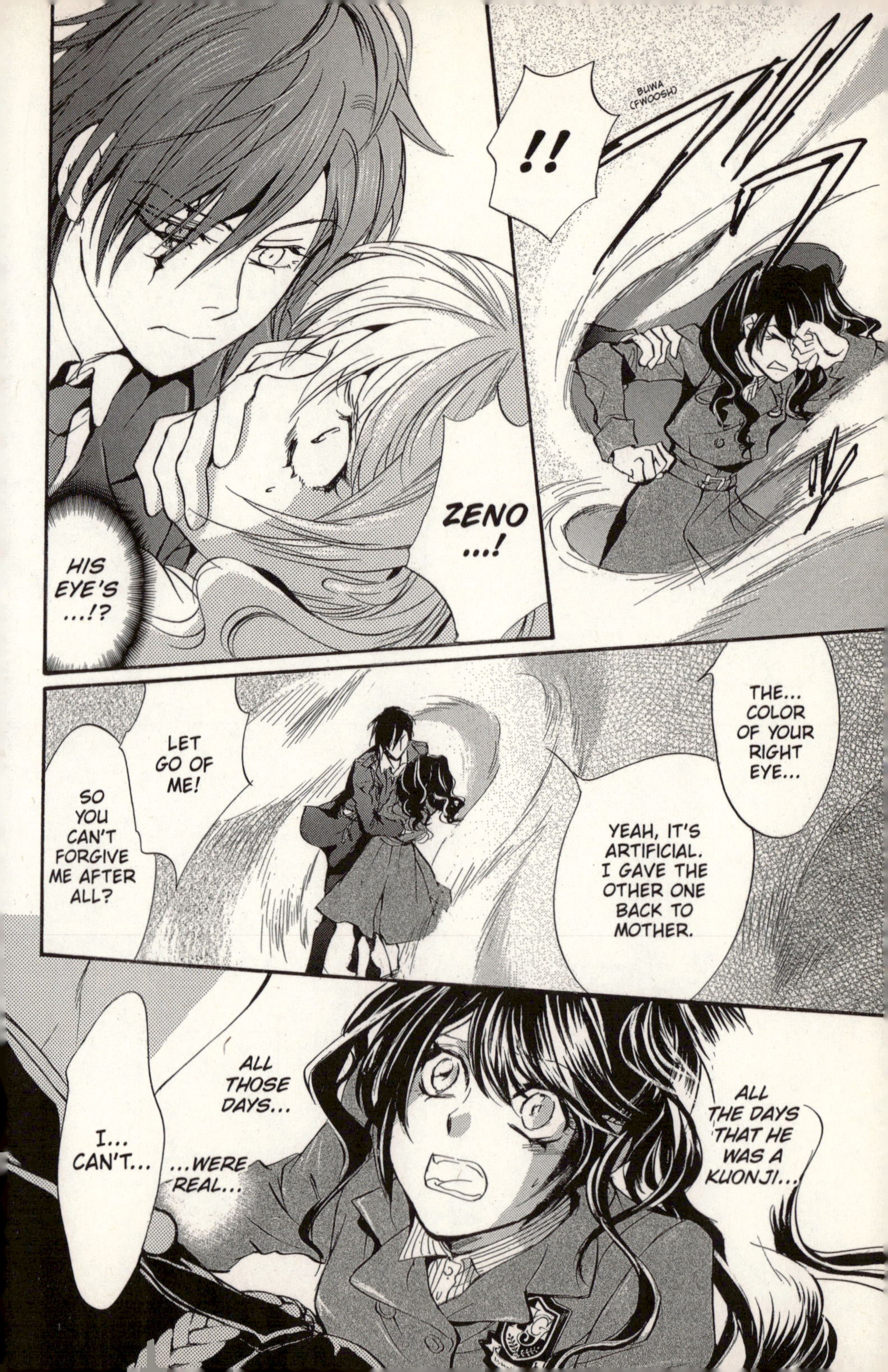
BUWA (FWOOSH)
!!
ZENO ...!
HIS EYE'S ...!?
THE... COLOR OF YOUR RIGHT EYE...
YEAH, IT'S ARTIFICIAL. I GAVE THE OTHER ONE BACK TO MOTHER.
LET GO OF ME!
SO YOU CAN'T FORGIVE ME AFTER ALL?
ALL THE DAYS THAT HE WAS A KUONJI...
ALL THOSE DAYS...
...WERE REAL...
I... CAN'T...

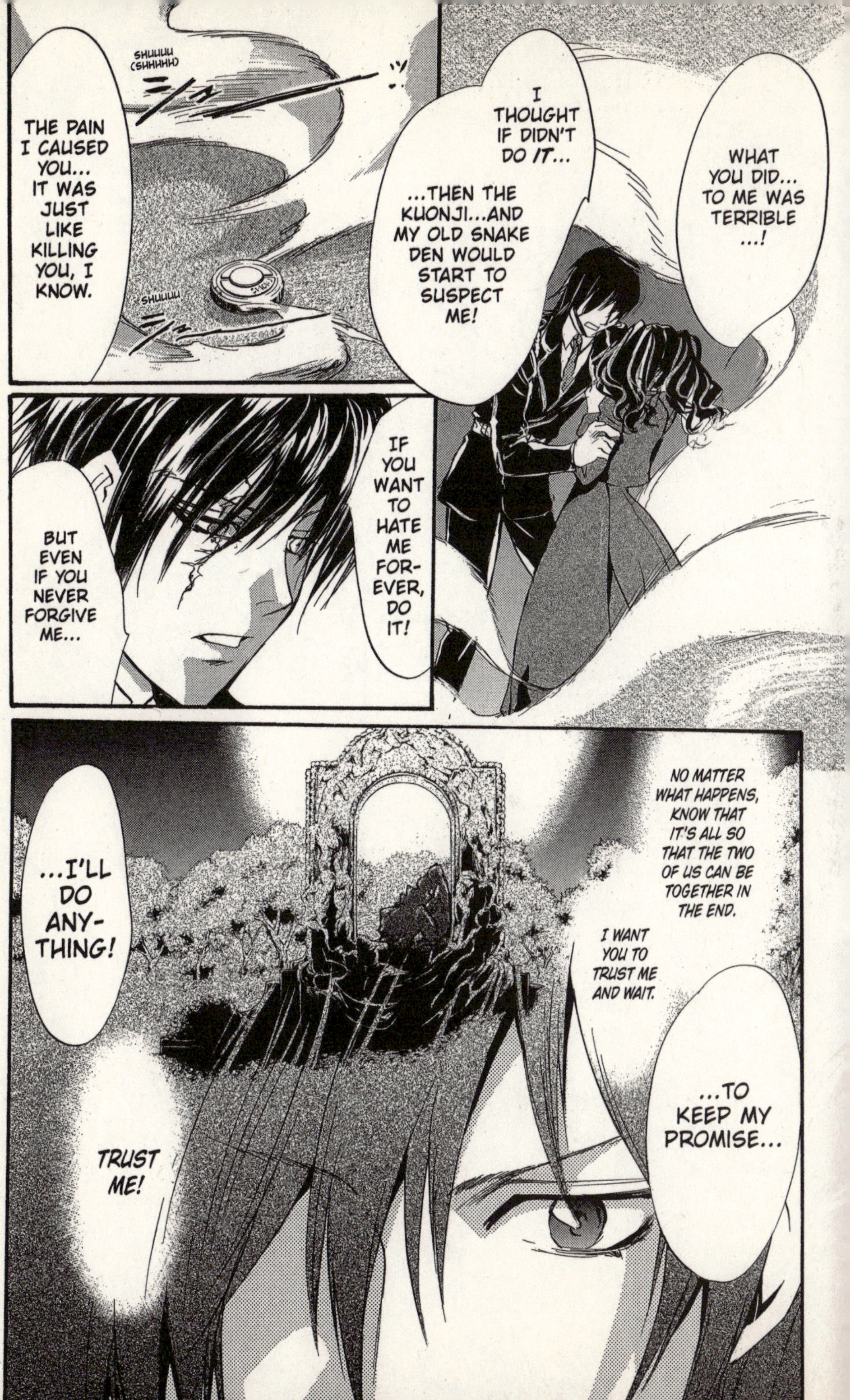
WHAT YOU DID... TO ME WAS TERRIBLE ...!
I THOUGHT IF DIDN'T DO *IT*...
...THEN THE KUONJI...AND MY OLD SNAKE DEN WOULD START TO SUSPECT ME!
SHUUUU (SHHHHH)
THE PAIN I CAUSED YOU... IT WAS JUST LIKE KILLING YOU, I KNOW.
SHUUUU
IF YOU WANT TO HATE ME FOR-EVER, DO IT!
BUT EVEN IF YOU NEVER FORGIVE ME...
NO MATTER WHAT HAPPENS, KNOW THAT IT'S ALL SO THAT THE TWO OF US CAN BE TOGETHER IN THE END.
I WANT YOU TO TRUST ME AND WAIT.
...TO KEEP MY PROMISE...
...I'LL DO ANY-THING!
TRUST ME!

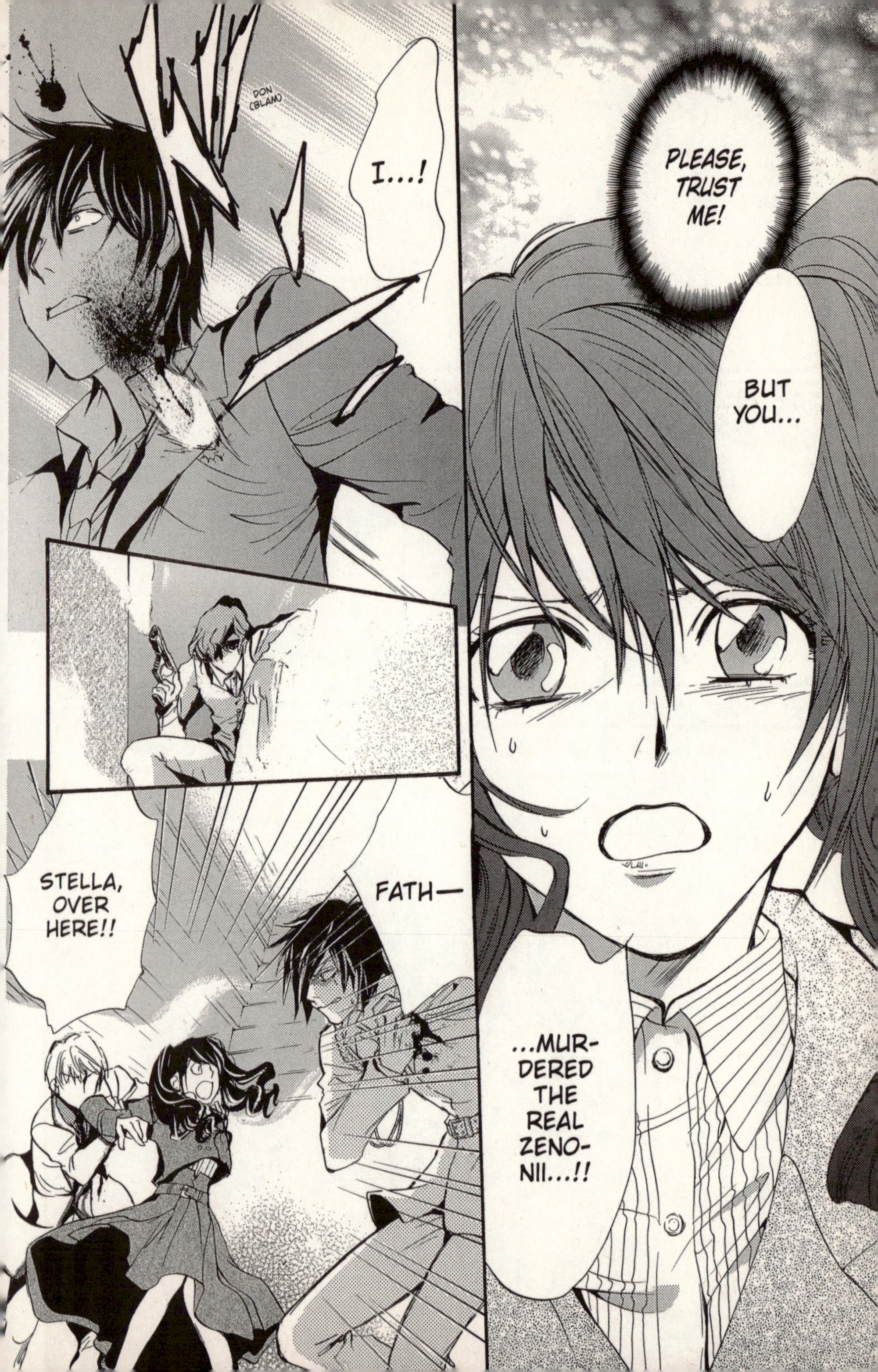
PLEASE, TRUST ME!
BUT YOU...
...MURDERED THE REAL ZENO-NII...!!
DON (BLAM)
I...!
FATH—
STELLA, OVER HERE!!

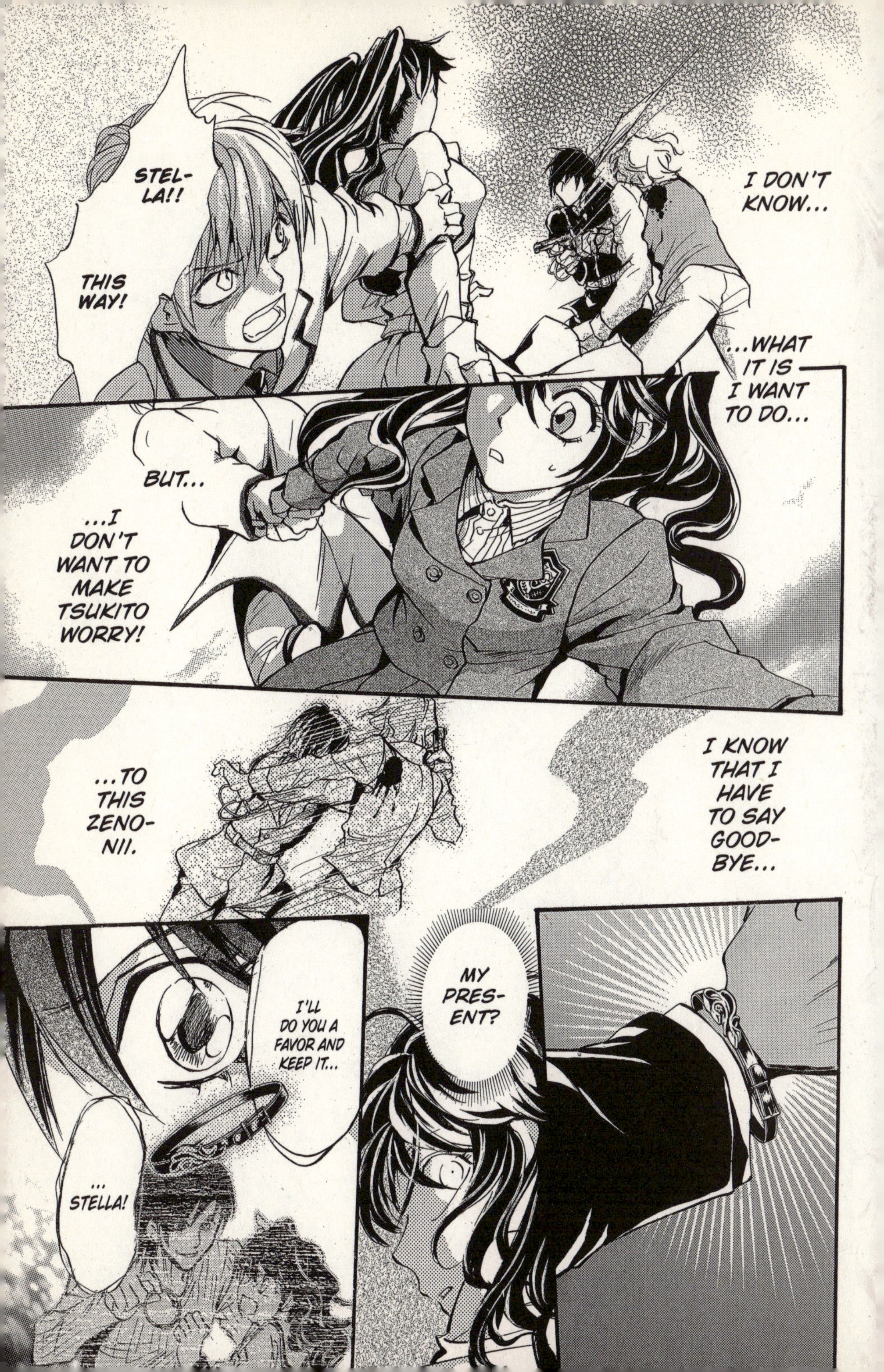
I DON'T KNOW...
STEL-LA!!
THIS WAY!
...WHAT IT IS I WANT TO DO...
BUT...
...I DON'T WANT TO MAKE TSUKITO WORRY!
I KNOW THAT I HAVE TO SAY GOOD-BYE...
...TO THIS ZENO-NII.
MY PRES-ENT?
I'LL DO YOU A FAVOR AND KEEP IT...
...STELLA!

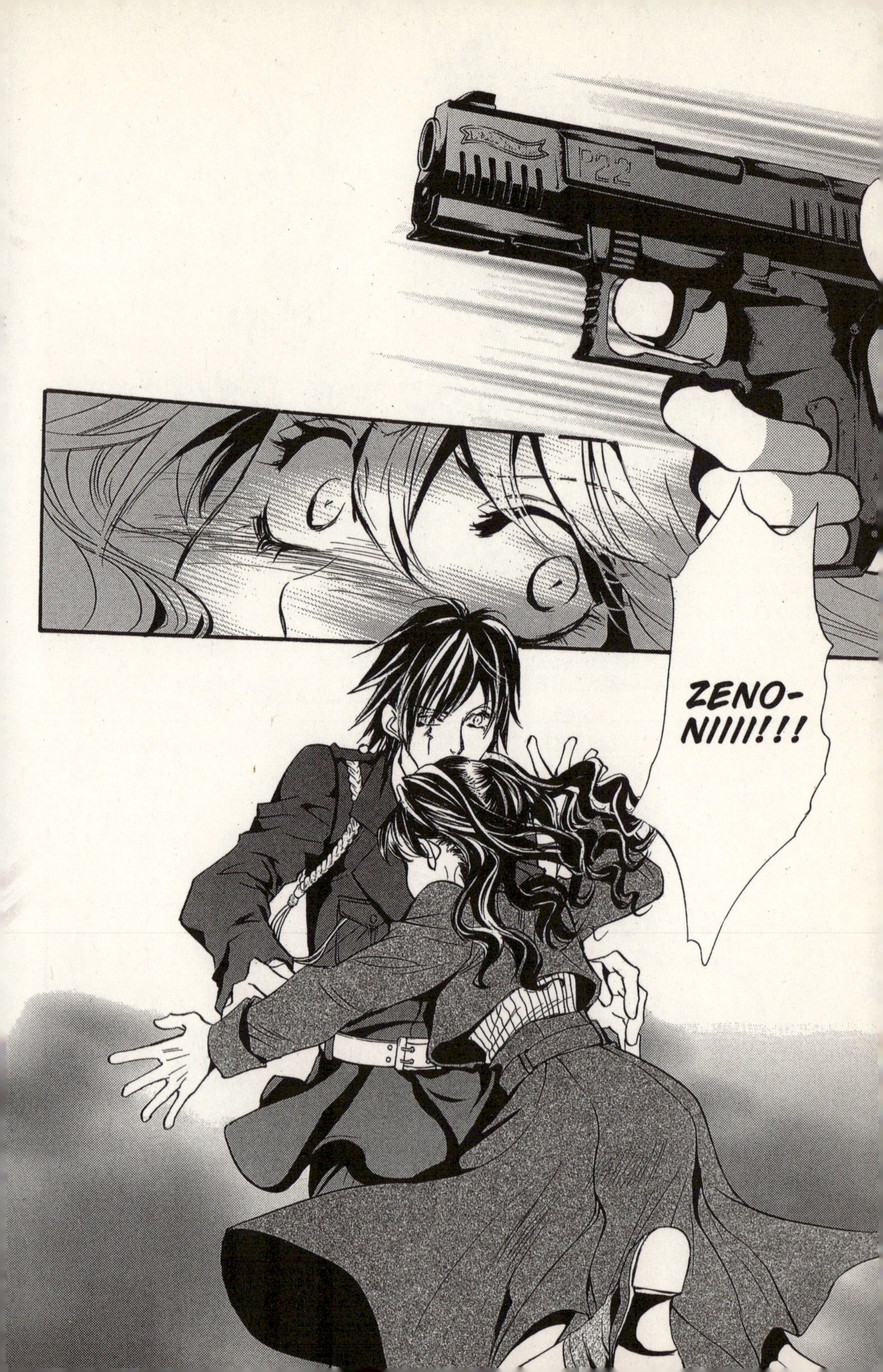
ZENO-
NIIII!!!

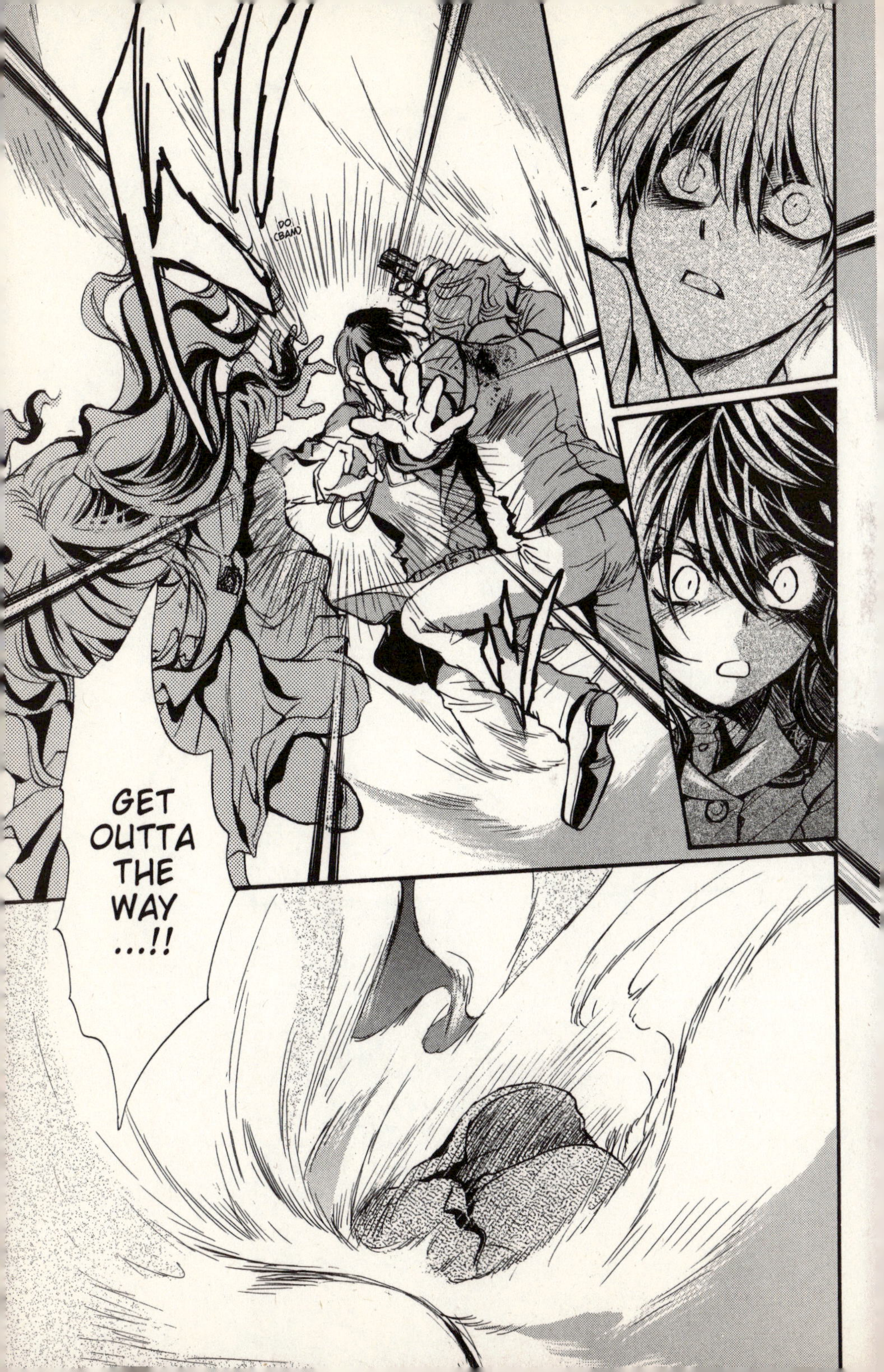
DO (BAM)
GET OUTTA THE WAY ...!!

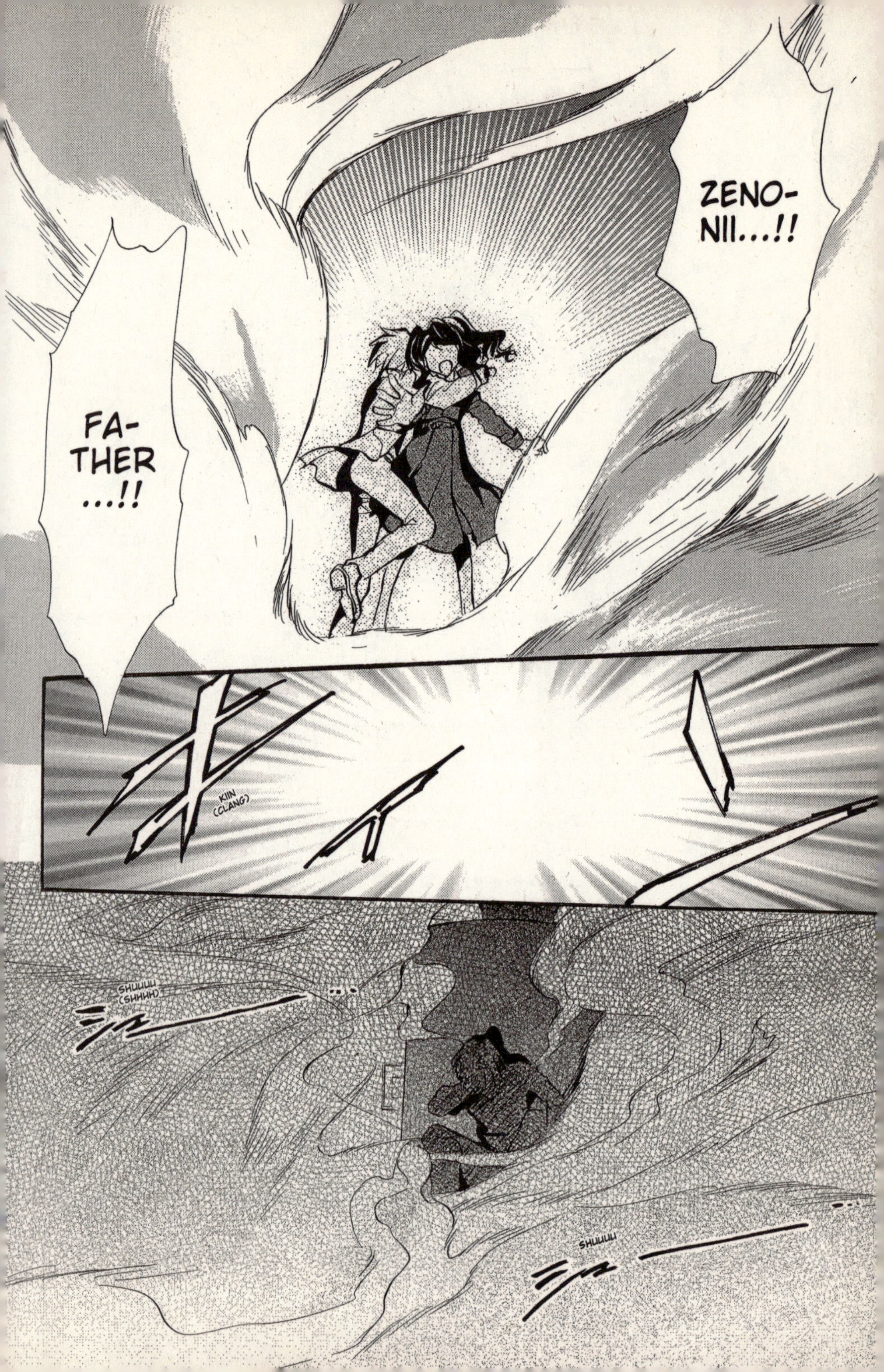
ZENO-NII...!!
FA-THER...!!
KIIN (CLANG)
SHUUUU (SHHHH)
SHUUUU

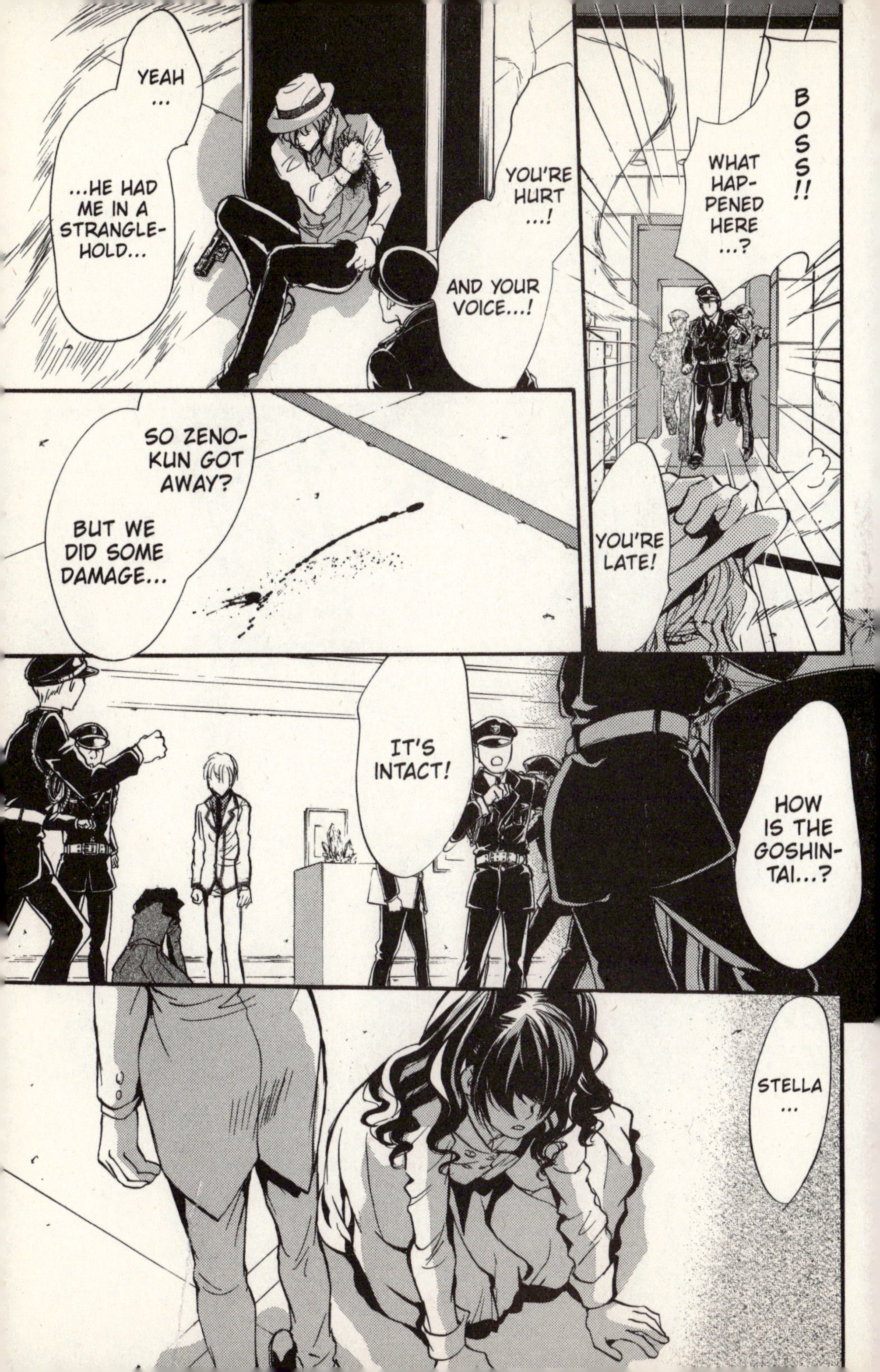
BOSS!!
WHAT HAP-PENED HERE ...?
YOU'RE LATE!
YOU'RE HURT ...!
AND YOUR VOICE...!
YEAH ...
...HE HAD ME IN A STRANGLE-HOLD...
SO ZENO-KUN GOT AWAY?
BUT WE DID SOME DAMAGE...
HOW IS THE GOSHIN-TAI...?
IT'S INTACT!
STELLA ...

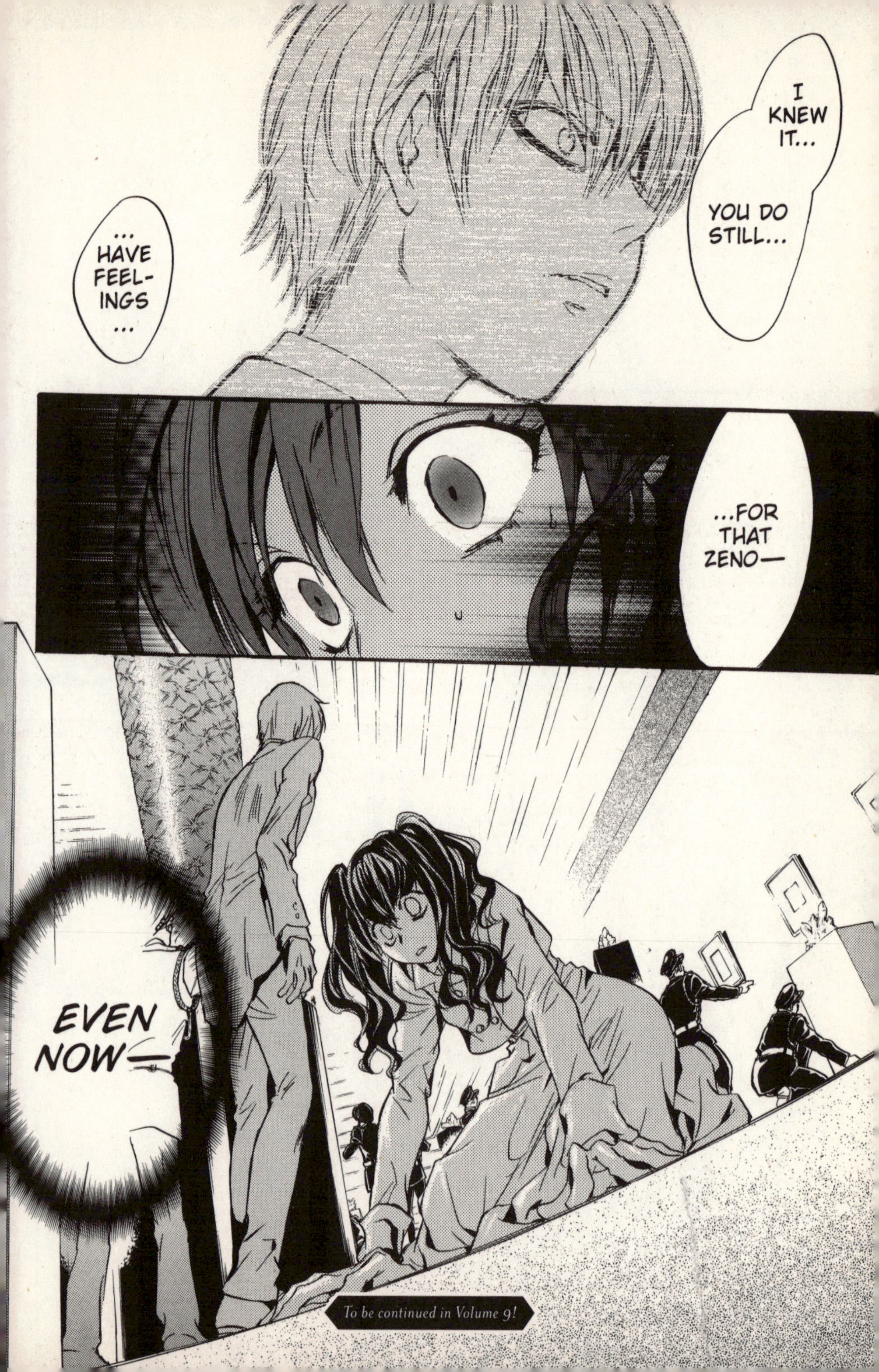
I KNEW IT...
YOU DO STILL...
...HAVE FEEL-INGS...
...FOR THAT ZENO—
EVEN NOW—
To be continued in Volume 9!

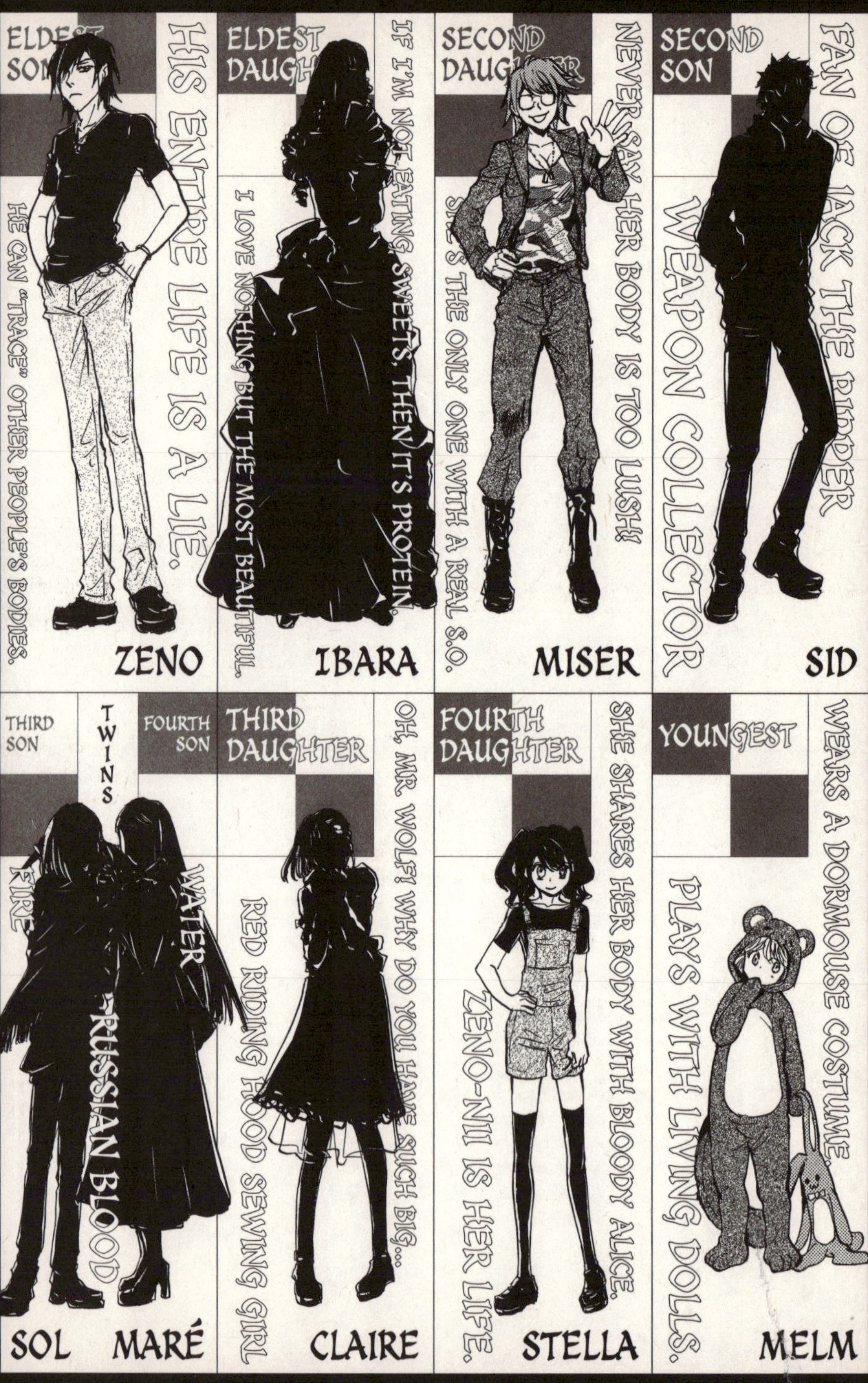
SECOND SON
FAN OF JACK THE RIPPER
WEAPON COLLECTOR
SID
SECOND DAUGHTER
NEVER SAY HER BODY IS TOO LUSH!
SHE'S THE ONLY ONE WITH A REAL S.O.
MISER
ELDEST DAUGHTER
IF I'M NOT EATING SWEETS, THEN IT'S PROTEIN.
I LOVE NOTHING BUT THE MOST BEAUTIFUL.
IBARA
ELDEST SON
HIS ENTIRE LIFE IS A LIE.
HE CAN "TRACE" OTHER PEOPLE'S BODIES.
ZENO
YOUNGEST
WEARS A DORMOUSE COSTUME.
PLAYS WITH LIVING DOLLS.
MELM
FOURTH DAUGHTER
SHE SHARES HER BODY WITH BLOODY ALICE.
ZENO-NII IS HER LIFE.
STELLA
THIRD DAUGHTER
OH, MR. WOLF! WHY DO YOU HAVE SUCH BIG...
RED RIDING HOOD SEWING GIRL
CLAIRE
FOURTH SON
TWINS
THIRD SON
WATER
FIRE
RUSSIAN BLOOD
MARÉ
SOL

I used a motif from *Alice in Wonderland* and *Through the Looking-Glass.*
Tweedledee and Tweedledum are a pair of male twins.
That's why Maré is set as a boy who goes around looking like a girl.
And now that we've come this far, the cast is getting a little lonely.
I know it's tough on the readers seeing their favorite characters fall,
but I'm trying my best in drawing this story to keep you from
being disappointed.
I have the feeling that all those maids in the chapel died in the fire.
The people employed by the Kuonji estate include living human civilians
and two types of "people" brought back to life...
When Stella becomes Alice, she kills maids and Black Rabbits alike,
but they aren't human.
Nor are Alice's brothers and sisters; they're "Bandersnatches."
So my way of thinking is that they aren't killing people
when they battle each other.
I still feel sorry for them though.

Twitter (Japanese): @angelaid
Kaori Yuki

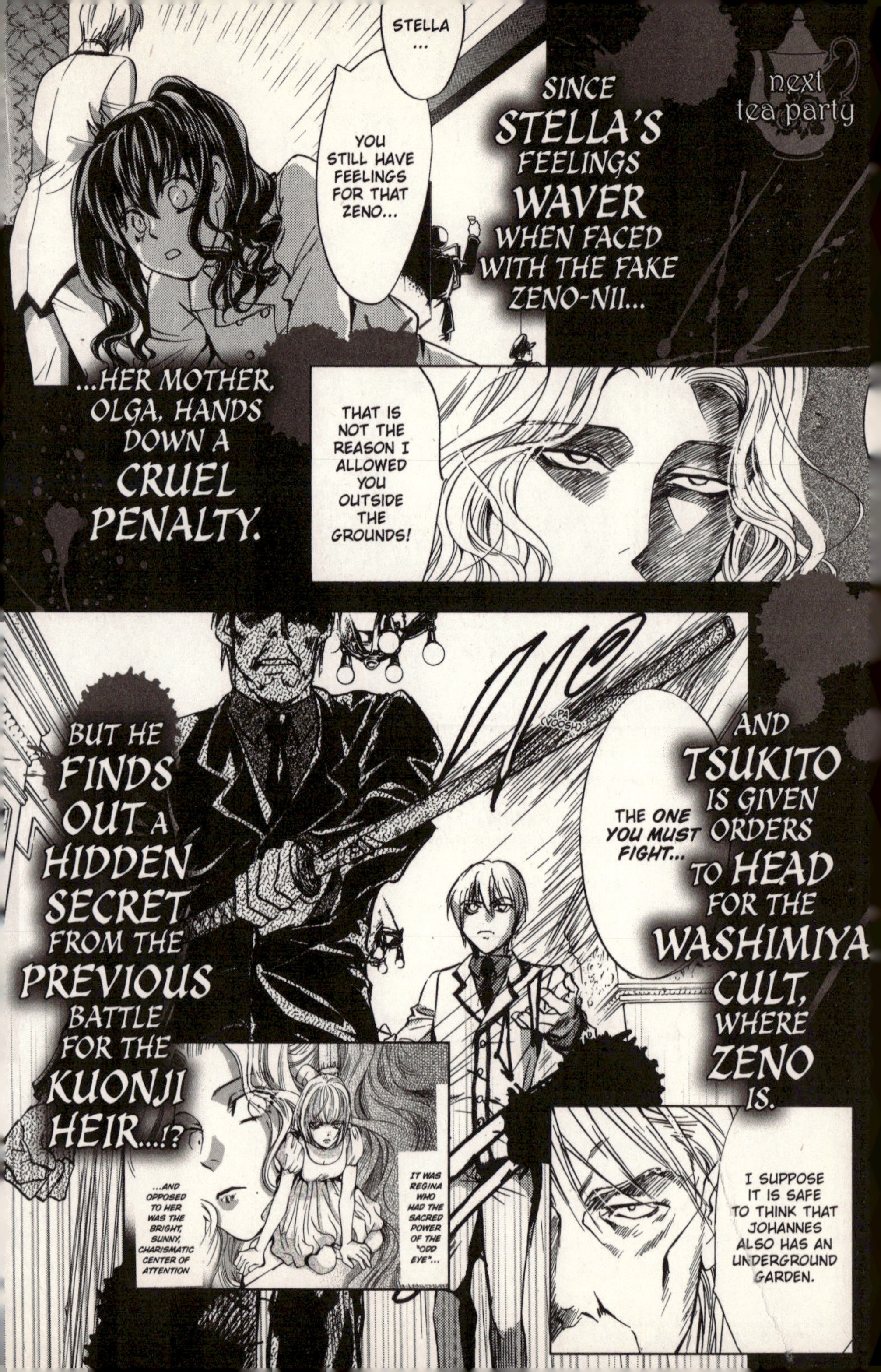

next tea party
SINCE STELLA'S FEELINGS WAVER WHEN FACED WITH THE FAKE ZENO-NII...
STELLA ...
YOU STILL HAVE FEELINGS FOR THAT ZENO...
...HER MOTHER, OLGA, HANDS DOWN A CRUEL PENALTY.
THAT IS NOT THE REASON I ALLOWED YOU OUTSIDE THE GROUNDS!
AND TSUKITO IS GIVEN ORDERS TO HEAD FOR THE WASHIMIYA CULT, WHERE ZENO IS.
THE ONE YOU MUST FIGHT...
PA (VOOSH)
BUT HE FINDS OUT A HIDDEN SECRET FROM THE PREVIOUS BATTLE FOR THE KUONJI HEIR...!?
I SUPPOSE IT IS SAFE TO THINK THAT JOHANNES ALSO HAS AN UNDERGROUND GARDEN.
IT WAS REGINA WHO HAD THE SACRED POWER OF THE "ODD EYE"...
...AND OPPOSED TO HER WAS THE BRIGHT, SUNNY, CHARISMATIC CENTER OF ATTENTION

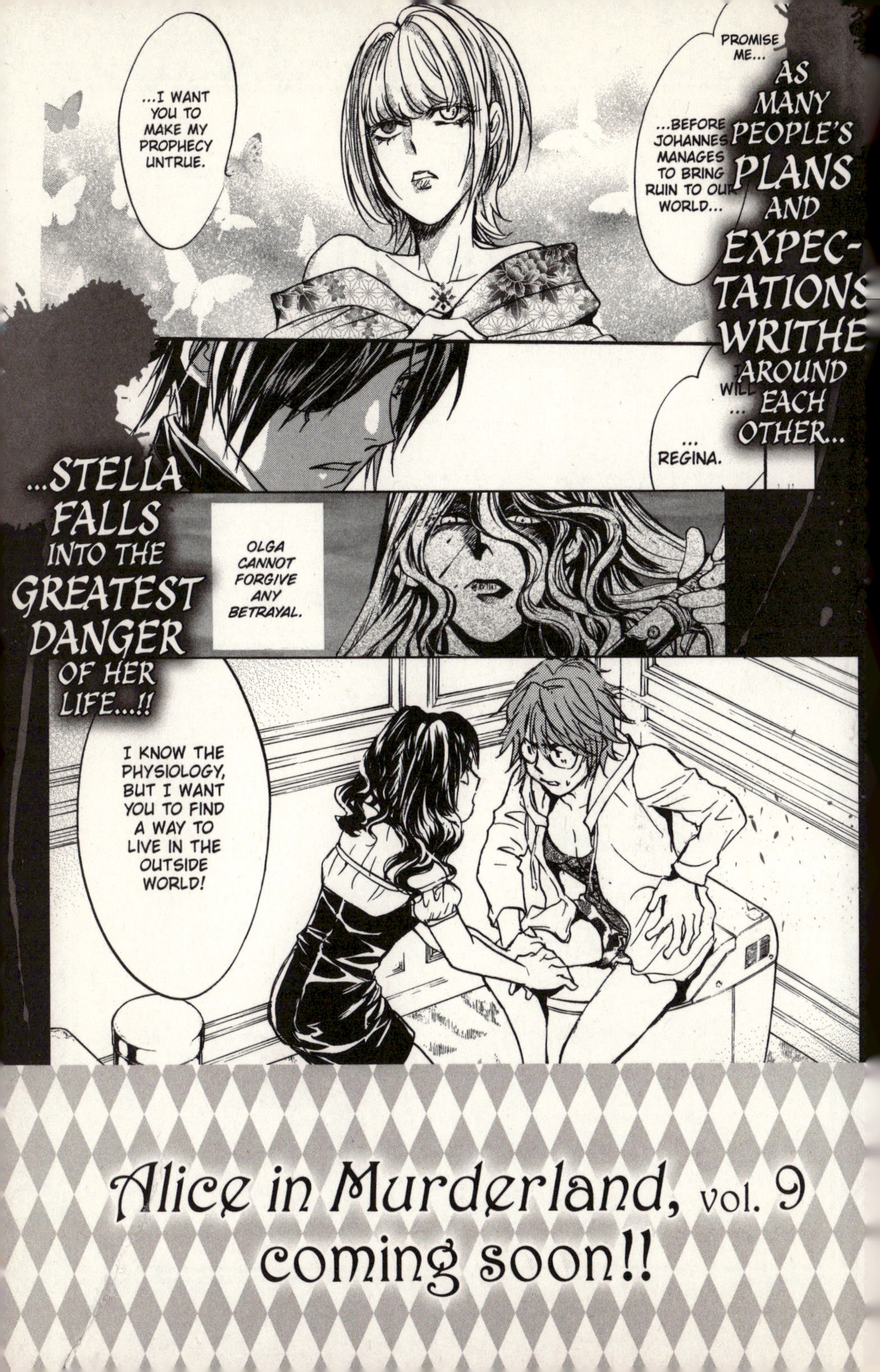
PROMISE ME...
...BEFORE JOHANNES MANAGES TO BRING RUIN TO OUR WORLD...
...I WANT YOU TO MAKE MY PROPHECY UNTRUE.
AS MANY PEOPLE'S PLANS AND EXPECTATIONS WRITHE AROUND EACH OTHER...
I WILL...
...REGINA.
OLGA CANNOT FORGIVE ANY BETRAYAL.
...STELLA FALLS INTO THE GREATEST DANGER OF HER LIFE...!!
I KNOW THE PHYSIOLOGY, BUT I WANT YOU TO FIND A WAY TO LIVE IN THE OUTSIDE WORLD!

Alice in Murderland, vol. 9 coming soon!!

Alice in MURDERLAND 8

Kaori Yuki

Translation: William Flanagan   Lettering: Lys Blakeslee

KAKEI NO ALICE
© 2017 Kaori Yuki. All rights reserved.
First published in Japan in 2017 by Kodansha Ltd., Tokyo. Publication rights for this English language edition arranged through Kodansha Ltd., Tokyo.

English translation © 2018 by Yen Press, LLC

Yen Press
1290 Avenue of the Americas
New York, NY 10104

Visit us at yenpress.com
facebook.com/yenpress
twitter.com/yenpress
yenpress.tumblr.com
instagram.com/yenpress

First Yen Press Edition: February 2018

Yen Press is an imprint of Yen Press, LLC.
The Yen Press name and logo are trademarks of Yen Press, LLC.

Library of Congress Control Number: 2014504636

ISBN: 978-0-316-41597-2

10 9 8 7 6 5 4 3 2 1

BVG

Printed in the United States of America